2017

To My Talented,
Thespian
Performer

All My Love this
Christmas & Always
Mum
/x

THE SHAKESPEARE BOOK

DK LONDON

PROJECT ART EDITORS
Katie Cavanagh, Saffron Stocker

SENIOR EDITOR
Georgina Palffy

EDITOR
Satu Fox

MANAGING ART EDITOR
Lee Griffiths

MANAGING EDITOR
Stephanie Farrow

PUBLISHING DIRECTOR
Jonathan Metcalf

ART DIRECTOR
Phil Ormerod

PUBLISHER
Liz Wheeler

JACKET EDITOR
Claire Gell

JACKET DESIGNER
Laura Brim

JACKET DESIGN
DEVELOPMENT MANAGER
Sophia MTT

PRE-PRODUCTION PRODUCER
Luca Frassinetti

PRODUCER
Mandy Inness

ILLUSTRATIONS
James Graham, Ben Ruocco

produced for DK by
TALLTREE LTD

EDITORS
Rob Colson, Scarlett O'Hara,
David John

DESIGN AND ART DIRECTION
Ben Ruocco

DK DELHI

EDITORIAL TEAM
Priyanka Kharbanda, Rupa Rao

ART EDITOR
Heena Sharma

DTP DESIGNER
Bimlesh Tiwari

MANAGING EDITOR
Kingshuk Ghoshal

MANAGING ART EDITOR
Govind Mittal

PRE-PRODUCTION MANAGER
Balwant Singh

MANAGING JACKETS EDITOR
Saloni Talwar

JACKET DESIGNERS
Suhita Dharamjit, Dhirendra Singh

original styling by
STUDIO 8

First published in Great Britain in
2015 by Dorling Kindersley Limited,
80 Strand, London, WC2R 0RL

Copyright © 2015
Dorling Kindersley Limited

A Penguin Random House Company

8 10 9 7
018 - 258603 - Mar/2015

A CIP catalogue record for this
book is available from
the British Library.

ISBN: 978-0-2411-8261-1

Printed and bound in China
by Leo Paper Products Ltd

Discover more at
www.dk.com

CONTRIBUTORS

STANLEY WELLS, CONSULTANT EDITOR

Stanley Wells, CBE, FRSL, Honorary President of
The Shakespeare Birthplace Trust, is Professor Emeritus
of Shakespeare Studies of the University of Birmingham,
Honorary Governor Emeritus of the Royal Shakespeare
Company, and an Honorary Fellow of Balliol College Oxford.
He is general editor of the Oxford and Penguin editions
of Shakespeare and co-editor of *The Oxford Companion to
Shakespeare*. His books include *Shakespeare for All Time*,
Shakespeare, Sex, and Love, and *Great Shakespeare Actors*.

ANJNA CHOUHAN

Anjna Chouhan is Lecturer in Shakespeare Studies at the
Shakespeare Birthplace Trust. She has published articles on
Victorian theatre, farce, and religious stage props, and edited
a sourcebook on the Victorian actor-manager Henry Irving.
She spoke on the BBC programme *Great British Rail Journeys*
about Shakespeare in the 19th century. She contributes to
the Cambridge School Shakespeare digital resource.

GILLIAN DAY

Dr Gillian Day lectures at the Shakespeare Birthplace
Trust and York University. She has taught English and
Drama in Britain, North America, and Scandinavia, and
held visiting lectureships at the universities of Helsinki
and Düsseldorf. Her publications include *King Richard III*
in the Arden *Shakespeare at Stratford* series (as editor),
and the introduction to *Henry VI Part III* and
the performance history of *Richard III* in editions
of the plays for Penguin Shakespeare.

JOHN FARNDON

John Farndon is a Royal Literary Fellow at Anglia Ruskin
University in Cambridge and an author, playwright,
composer, and poet. He has written many international
bestsellers such as *Do You Think You're Clever?* and
translated into English verse the plays of Lope de Vega
and the poetry of Alexander Pushkin. He taught the history
of drama at the Actor's Studio, studied playwriting at
Central School of Speech and Drama, and is now Assessor
for new plays for London's OffWestEnd Theatre Awards.

JANE KINGSLEY-SMITH

Jane Kingsley-Smith is a Reader at Roehampton University,
London. She has written two monographs – *Shakespeare's
Drama of Exile* and *Cupid in Early Modern Literature and
Culture* – and most recently edited for Penguin John
Webster's *The Duchess of Malfi* and *The White Devil*, and
John Ford's *The Broken Heart* and *'Tis Pity She's a Whore*.
She is a regular lecturer at Shakespeare's Globe, London.

NICK WALTON

Nick Walton is Shakespeare Courses Development Manager
at the Shakespeare Birthplace Trust in Stratford-upon-Avon,
and serves as Executive Secretary to the International
Shakespeare Association. He has written introductory
material for the Penguin editions of *Timon of Athens* and
Love's Labour's Lost, and is co-author of *The Shakespeare
Wallbook*. He has worked closely with professional theatre
companies at home and abroad, and has been a guest
speaker at the British Museum and the National Theatre.

CONTENTS

10 INTRODUCTION

THE FREELANCE WRITER
1589–1594

24 In love, who respects friend?
The Two Gentlemen of Verona

30 I know now how to tame a shrew
The Taming of the Shrew

36 The commons, like an angry hive of bees that want their leader, scatter up and down
Henry VI Part 2

40 I can smile, and murder whiles I smile
Henry VI Part 3

44 This brawl today... shall send, between the red rose and the white, a thousand souls to death and deadly night
Henry VI Part 1

48 Why, there they are, both bakèd in this pie
Titus Andronicus

54 Made glorious summer by this son of York
Richard III

62 To die is all as common as to live
Edward III

68 What error drives our eyes and ears amiss?
The Comedy of Errors

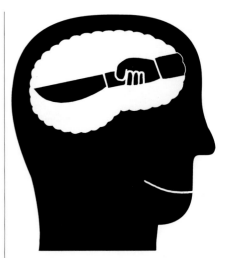

74 Hunting he loved, but love he laughed to scorn
Venus and Adonis

78 Who buys a minute's mirth to wail a week
The Rape of Lucrece

THE LORD CHAMBERLAIN'S MAN
1594–1603

86 Who can sever love
from charity
Love's Labour's Lost

92 Down, down I come,
like glist'ring Phaethon
Richard II

100 A pair of star-crossed
lovers
Romeo and Juliet

110 The course of true love
never did run smooth
A Midsummer Night's Dream

118 There is no sure
foundation set on blood
The Life and Death
of King John

124 If you prick us, do we
not bleed?
The Merchant of Venice

132 Honour is a mere
scutcheon
Henry IV Part 1

140 Wives may be merry,
and yet honest, too
The Merry Wives of Windsor

146 We have heard
the chimes at midnight
Henry IV Part 2

154 Out on thee, seeming!
I will write against it
Much Ado About
Nothing

162 Once more unto the
breach, dear friends,
once more
Henry V

170 There is a tide in the
affairs of men which,
taken at the flood,
leads on to fortune
Julius Caesar

THE KING'S MAN
1603–1613

232 Man, proud man, dressed
in a little brief authority
Measure for Measure

240 Beware, my lord, of
jealousy. It is the
green-ey'd monster
Othello

250 A man more sinned
against than sinning
King Lear

260 The middle of humanity
thou never knew'st,
but the extremity of
both ends
Timon of Athens

178 All the world's a stage, and
all the men and women
merely players
As You Like It

188 The slings and arrows
of outrageous fortune
Hamlet

198 Youth's a stuff will
not endure
Twelfth Night

206 War and lechery
confound all
Troilus and Cressida

214 I scorn to change my
state with kings'
Shakespeare's Sonnets

224 That false fire which
in his cheek so glowed
A Lover's Complaint

225 Truth and beauty
buried be
The Phoenix and Turtle

226 With selfsame hand,
self reasons, and self
right, would shark on you
Sir Thomas More

308 Thou metst with things dying, I with things new-born
The Winter's Tale

316 Hang there like fruit, my soul, till the tree die
Cymbeline

324 We are such stuff as dreams are made on
The Tempest

332 Farewell, a long farewell, to all my greatness!
Henry VIII

338 Is there record of any two that loved better than we do, Arcite?
The Two Noble Kinsmen

266 Blood will have blood
Macbeth

276 Age cannot wither her, nor custom stale her infinite variety
Antony and Cleopatra

286 The web of our life is of a mingled yarn, good and ill together
All's Well That Ends Well

294 This world to me is but a ceaseless storm whirring me from my friends
Pericles, Prince of Tyre

300 What is the city but the people?
Coriolanus

344 INDEX

352 ACKNOWLEDGMENTS

INTRODU

CTION

Born more than four and a half centuries ago, William Shakespeare (1564–1616) is generally acknowledged to be the greatest imaginative writer in the English language. He was a major poet, writing two narrative poems, 154 sonnets, and other verses. But above all, he was a poetic dramatist, the author or part-author of almost 40 plays, which range from the most delicate of romantic comedies, such as *A Midsummer Night's Dream*, *As You Like It*, and *Twelfth Night*, through a series of plays about English and Roman history, to the most profound tragedies, including *Hamlet*, *Macbeth*, and *King Lear*.

Far from dwindling with the passage of time, Shakespeare's reputation and influence have grown from year to year. His works, in their original texts, in translation into most of the world's languages, and in an enormous range of adaptations, are read, taught, and performed all over the globe. They have influenced countless other works of art, and nobody with a claim to a liberal education can afford to be ignorant of them. This book offers a comprehensive guide to his plays and poems, concentrating on their content and form, while also considering their reception and influence.

Shakespeare and Stratford

William Shakespeare was baptized in Holy Trinity Church in the town of Stratford-upon-Avon, England, on Wednesday 26 April 1564. His exact date of birth is not known, but since the 18th century his birthday has been celebrated on 23 April.

Shakespeare's father, John, came from farming stock and worked in Stratford as a "whitawer" – a tanner of white leather – and glover (glove maker). John's wife, Mary, whose maiden name was Arden, came from a more prosperous background. They lived in the house in Henley Street, Stratford, now known as Shakespeare's Birthplace, a place of pilgrimage for hundreds of thousands of visitors from all parts of the world every year. They had two daughters who died in infancy before William came along, and went on to have two more daughters and three more sons. The youngest, Edmund, was 16 years younger than William. Like his older brother, Edmund became an actor in London. Very little is

All the world's a stage,
And all the men and women merely players.
They have their exits and their entrances,
And one man in his time plays many parts
Jaques
As You Like It

Shall I compare thee to a summer's day?
Thou art more lovely and more temperate.
Rough winds do shake the darling buds of May,
And summer's lease hath all too short a date.
Sonnet 18

known about him except that he died, aged only 27, a few months after the death in infancy of his illegitimate son.

John Shakespeare was a businessman who played a major part in civic life, becoming an alderman and rising to the rank of bailiff or mayor in 1568. At this time, churchgoing was required by law. Both at church and at home, Shakespeare would have gained the familiarity with the Bible, the Book of Common Prayer, and the Books of Homilies (sermons) that is apparent from his writings.

Stratford was a market town with a splendid church, a well-established grammar school where education for boys (only) was free, fine houses, and townsmen who were educated and wealthy. The records for the school are lost, but Shakespeare's writings show that he had a typical grammar-school education of the period. Such schools provided a rigorous training in oratory, rhetoric, and classical literature comparable to that of university graduates studying Classics today. From an early age, the boys were required to write and speak in Latin. In a scene (4.1) in *The Merry Wives of Windsor,* a boy called William is put through his paces in Latin grammar, and

quotes from a textbook prescribed for use in every such school. It is surely the most autobiographical scene in all Shakespeare's plays.

Marriage and children

As a boy, Shakespeare would have been able to attend and act in plays in Stratford. Touring professional companies regularly visited the town during his boyhood and youth, playing in the guildhall, while local amateurs put on entertainments, especially at Whitsuntide.

Shakespeare probably left school when he was about 15. We don't know what he did for a living at first, but he may have helped in

Articles are borrowed of the pronoun, and be thus declined. *Singulariter nominativo: 'hic, haec, hoc'.*
William
The Merry Wives of Windsor

his father's workshop. When he was only 18, towards the end of 1582, he married Anne Hathaway. She was 26. A daughter, Susanna, was baptized six months later. Twins, Hamnet and Judith, followed in late January or early February 1585. Hamnet died and was buried in Stratford on 11 August 1596. The location of his grave is unknown.

William and Anne had no more children. Except for a passing mention in a law case of 1587, there is a gap in the record of Shakespeare's life from the birth of the twins to 1592 (when he is first credited as a writer). The best guess is that at some point he joined a theatre company – perhaps even one of those that visited Stratford – as actor or writer or both. His wife and children appear to have stayed in Stratford.

In 1596, the College of Heralds granted Shakespeare a coat of arms, bestowing on him and his descendants the status of gentleman and the right to be termed "Master". His father died in 1601, presumably at more than 70 years old, and was buried in Stratford. In 1602, Shakespeare spent the great sum of £320 for the purchase of 107 acres of land in Old Stratford. In 1605, he was » wealthy enough to pay £440 for an interest in the Stratford tithes, entitling him to a share in the area's farming income, which would have brought him an annual income of around £40. In London, he lived only in modest lodgings. His daughter Susanna married the physician John Hall in 1607; their only child, Elizabeth, was born nine months later. Judith married a vintner named Thomas Quiney, with whom she had three children, all of whom died young. Elizabeth Hall died in 1670, and was Shakespeare's last descendant.

Shakespeare's first texts

The first reference to Shakespeare as a writer comes from 1592, by which time he was well established on the London theatrical scene. In 1593, his name appears in print for the first time, not as a dramatist but as the author of the narrative poem *Venus and Adonis*. His second narrative poem, *The Rape of Lucrece*, appeared in the following year. These poems were exceptionally successful, and were reprinted more frequently than any of Shakespeare's plays. In part, this is because plays were written primarily to be acted, so many never reached print. In 1594, *Titus Andronicus* was the first of

Shakespeare's plays to be printed, but it seems certain that he must have written a number of other plays before then.

In 1595, he is named along with two actors – Richard Burbage and Will Kemp – as having been paid for performances during the previous Christmas season at the court of Queen Elizabeth I by a company of players formed late the previous year under the patronage of the Lord Chamberlain, Lord Hunsdon. From now on, he was the resident playwright of the most important theatre company in the land. No other playwright of the period had so long and stable a relationship with a single company. Shakespeare was also an actor and a "sharer" – a

What win I if I gain the thing I seek? A dream, a breath, a froth of fleeting joy.
The Rape of Lucrece

businessman with a financial interest in the company's success. Plays were normally the property of the acting company for which they were written, rather than of their author. There was, however, a reading public for dramatic texts, and about half of Shakespeare's plays were printed in his lifetime. These, along with the missing texts, were assembled by his colleagues after he died and published as the *First Folio* in 1623.

The theatrical scene

Shakespeare grew up during a period of increasing stability and prosperity in England. Queen Elizabeth I was unifying the nation, and patriotic sentiment was growing. The arts of music, painting, architecture, and literature were flourishing. Great works of classical and continental, especially Italian, literature were appearing in translation and finding a wide readership. Many of these were to provide Shakespeare with inspiration and with plot material for his plays.

Both English dramatic literature and the theatrical profession developed greatly during the early years of Shakespeare's working life. A major development came in 1576 with the construction of the first successful professional playhouse, called simply the Theatre, in London. A new generation of dramatic writers emerged, including playwrights such as John Lyly and George Peele, with whom Shakespeare was to collaborate on *Titus Andronicus*. Figures from the later 1580s, such as Thomas Kyd, Robert Greene, and above all Christopher Marlowe, author of plays including the two-part drama *Tamburlaine*, *Dr Faustus*, *The Jew of Malta*, and *Edward II*, were all to influence Shakespeare. Growth in the size of acting companies and in the popularity of theatrical entertainment encouraged the writing of longer and more ambitious plays, interweaving plot with subplot, tragedy with comedy, and diversifying with songs, dances, masques, and spectacular effects made possible by the increasing sophistication of theatrical design.

Theatrical performances

Theatres of the time were three-storeyed buildings with open roofs and uncurtained platform stages that thrust forwards into the auditorium. Performances were given during daylight hours. At the back of the stage were doors from which the actors entered, and behind them the tiring house, or dressing room. There was an upper acting level that could represent a balcony or the walls of a city. A canopy over the stage held machinery to allow the descent of gods. There was no scenery. Musicians had their own space. The audience stood at ground level, or occupied the tiers of seating built into the walls. In London today, at Shakespeare's Globe on Bankside, there is a reconstruction of the Globe Theatre, originally built in 1599, for which many of Shakespeare's plays were written.

In 1609, the company started to use a more exclusive indoor theatre, the Blackfriars, which had more elaborate stage machinery. These new possibilities are reflected in the stage effects required by, for instance, *Cymbeline* and *The Tempest*. Indoor theatres were lit by candles, and as the candles required frequent trimming to keep them alight, playwrights began to divide their plays more clearly into five acts. The Sam Wanamaker Playhouse at Shakespeare's Globe is an indoor stage that gives an impression of this kind of theatre. »

Hell hath no limits,
nor is circumscribed
In one self place,
for where we are is hell,
And where hell is must
we ever be.
Mephistopheles
Christopher Marlowe's
Dr Faustus

Can this cock-pit hold
The vasty fields of France?
Or may we cram
Within this wooden O
the very casques
That did affright the air
at Agincourt?
Chorus
Henry V

The actors who first performed Shakespeare's plays were skilled professionals, required by law to be organized into companies under the patronage of a high-ranking person – such as a nobleman, or even the Queen herself. A typical company was made up of 12 or 14 men, who could be supplemented by extras, known as hired men. Some of Shakespeare's plays require no more than the standard number of actors, but in others the same actor would have had to play two or even three roles in the same performance. All female roles were played by boys – no professional female actors appeared on the English stage before 1660. This explains the relatively small number of female parts in each play: for instance, only two in *Julius Caesar* – Portia and Calpurnia – and the same number in *Hamlet* – Ophelia and Gertrude.

Music and special effects

Music played an important part in performances, as is evident from the number of songs and dances in the plays. Actors would sometimes have accompanied their songs on lutes, and a band of playhouse musicians supplied incidental music. Ceremonial entries of royal persons and great warriors would be heralded by fanfares and drum rolls. Thunder could be imitated by the use of a thunder run – cannon balls rolled down a wooden trough – and it was even possible to imitate lightning by the use of special stage effects.

Theatres were closed during the 40-day religious observance of Lent, and companies frequently went on tour in the English provinces. As there were no custom-built playhouses outside London, they had to play in improvised settings such as inn yards, the halls of great houses, guildhalls, and even occasionally in churches. Facilities would be limited, so play texts were adapted to suit the constraints of the new venues.

A wealth of plays

Shakespeare was an extremely versatile playwright, constantly experimenting with new styles of drama and developing his range of subject matter and the depth of understanding of character throughout his career. His first plays include the light comedies *The Two Gentlemen of Verona* and *The Taming of the Shrew*, the bloody tragedy of *Titus Andronicus*, and four plays, also more or less tragic in form, based on English

> But it is certain I am loved of all ladies, only you excepted. And I would I could find in my heart that I had not a hard heart, for truly I love none.
> **Benedick**
> **Much Ado About Nothing**

> Life's but a walking shadow, a poor player That struts and frets his hour upon the stage, And then is heard no more.
> **Macbeth**
> **Macbeth**

history – three on the reign of Henry VI and a follow-up about Richard III. All these were written before the founding of the Lord Chamberlain's Men, in 1594. The end of that year saw a performance of his brilliantly plotted *Comedy of Errors*, in which he interweaves a tale of mistaken identity derived from Roman comedy with the romantic tale of a family parted but eventually reunited.

A successful playwright

As a shareholder in the Lord Chamberlain's Men from 1594, and no longer needing to work in collaboration with other playwrights, Shakespeare had more independence to write what he wanted, but clearly felt he had to provide his colleagues with plays written in a variety of styles, keeping up an average of roughly two a year.

During the next five years or so, he wrote a dazzling series of romantic comedies – *Love's Labour's Lost, A Midsummer Night's Dream, The Merchant of Venice, Much Ado About Nothing,* and *As You Like It,* along with more plays about English history – *Richard II* and *King John*, both in tragic form, the two parts of *Henry IV*, which feature his

greatest comic character, Sir John Falstaff, and their triumphant sequel *Henry V*, as well as the romantic tragedy of *Romeo and Juliet*, the somewhat unromantic comedy *The Merry Wives of Windsor*, which also has Falstaff at its centre, and the Roman tragedy *Julius Caesar*.

His company acquired a new theatre, the Globe, in 1599. For this playhouse, he wrote the last two of his romantic comedies, *As You Like It* and *Twelfth Night*. This is the period, too, of his greatest success to date, the tragedy of *Hamlet*. After this, his plays become darker in tone. They include the highly original, bitter

My lips, two blushing pilgrims, ready stand
To smooth that rough touch with a tender kiss.
Romeo
Romeo and Juliet

tragicomedy *Troilus and Cressida*, and two other plays – *Measure for Measure* and *All's Well that Ends Well* – which, though comic in form raise serious moral concerns. In this period, he also wrote the profound tragedies *Othello, Macbeth,* and *King Lear*. On the death of the Queen, in 1603, his company became the King's Men.

Collaborators and rivals

Around 1606, for reasons unknown, Shakespeare returned to his former practice of collaborating with other playwrights. Thomas Middleton who, along with Ben Jonson, had emerged as his most serious rival, worked with him on *Timon of Athens*, but the only text of this play that has come down to us is incomplete. A new departure in dramatic style comes with *Pericles*, written with the minor playwright George Wilkins, a tragicomic narrative that foreshadows the later, singly authored *Cymbeline, The Winter's Tale*, and *The Tempest*.

During this phase of his career, he wrote two highly contrasting tragedies of ancient Rome, the austere *Coriolanus* and the flamboyant *Antony and Cleopatra*, and, with John Fletcher, some fifteen years his junior, a now lost play, *Cardenio, The Two Noble* »

Kinsmen, and the play known in its time as *All is True* but printed in the First Folio as *Henry VIII*. During an early performance of *All is True* in 1613, the firing of a stage cannon set the thatch of the Globe playhouse on fire, burning it to the ground. Shakespeare's career as a playwright ended with the destruction of the playhouse that had seen some of his greatest successes.

In the last three years of his life, Shakespeare wrote little or nothing. He died in April 1616, leaving most of his property to Susanna, and £150 to his younger daughter Judith. Among other bequests he left 26s and 8d each to three colleagues in his acting company, the King's Men – Richard Burbage, Henry Condell, and John Heminges – to buy mourning rings, a common practice of the time.

What makes him great?

Why is it that Shakespeare, a long-dead author of plays conceived for playhouses very different from those of the present day, written in an increasingly archaic language, employing unrealistic dramatic conventions, and telling stories that are often remote from the daily experience of his audiences, should be celebrated both in English-speaking countries and elsewhere as an author of enduring significance?

Part of the answer is that he was a master of both prose and verse. He could construct powerful pieces of rhetoric, such as Mark Antony's speech to the Roman citizens in the Forum in *Julius Caesar,* and the king's address to his troops before the battle of Agincourt in *Henry V*. He could write beautiful passages of lyrical verse, such as the love scenes of *Romeo and Juliet* and the exquisite speeches of Oberon and Titania in

This is the excellent foppery of the world: that, when we are sick in fortune – often the surfeits of own behaviour – we make guilty of our disasters the sun, the moon, and the stars
Edmond
King Lear

A Midsummer Night's Dream. He could write speeches that are both witty and comic, such as those that Lance addresses to his dog Crab, in *The Two Gentlemen of Verona*, or those of Bottom and his colleagues in *A Midsummer Night's Dream*.

He could write with powerful simplicity, piercing our hearts with simple statements such as Leontes's "O, she's warm!" in *The Winter's Tale*, or Prospero's "Tis new to thee" in response to Miranda's "O brave new world, / That has such people in it" in *The Tempest*, or the largely monosyllabic reunion of King Lear and Cordelia.

Memorable characters

Shakespeare could also tell gripping stories. The overall design of the plays drives the plots forwards – and sometimes there are complex stories with more than one plot, as in *Hamlet* or *King Lear*. He builds tension in individual scenes, such as the trial scene in *The Merchant of Venice* and the banquet scene in *Macbeth*, with great dramatic effectiveness.

He gives us a strong sense of individual character, making us believe in the reality of the people in his plays, often by making them speak in individual ways –

such as the Nurse in *Romeo and Juliet*, or Shylock in *The Merchant of Venice* – sometimes by making them behave in a manner that is at once unexpected but credible.

Crucially, he is not judgmental or moralistic. Even the characters who behave badly, such as Paroles in *All's Well That Ends Well*, (perhaps above all) Falstaff in the *Henry IV* plays, or a villainous murderer such as Macbeth, can make us feel what they feel rather than pass judgment on their sins.

His plays provide a wealth of complex and theatrically effective roles, which offer rich and demanding opportunities to actors. Tragic roles such as Hamlet and King Lear, Lady Macbeth and Cleopatra, heroic ones such as Henry V and Coriolanus, wittily comic roles such as Benedict and Beatrice in *Much Ado About Nothing*, and broadly comic ones such as Bottom in *A Midsummer Night's Dream*, all provide actors with exceptional opportunities to demonstrate their skills.

Stories for all times
Many of the stories that he tells, such as in *King Lear* or *The Tempest*, have a quality of myth or legend that enables people of later ages to relate to them easily. Some plays, such as the history plays and *Julius Caesar*, also have a political dimension that can easily seem relevant to issues of modern times.

To speak of Shakespeare as the world's greatest dramatist is inadequate. It would be closer to the mark to speak of him as a philosopher, a psychologist, or a poet possessed of the artistry that enables him to express his perceptions in dramatic form, and in so doing render them with unique subtlety and communicative power.

Structure of this book
This book offers a section on each of Shakespeare's plays, giving information about their major themes, a concise description of their principal characters, a breakdown of the action arranged by act and scene, and a full synopsis of their plots. This is followed by information about each play's reputation and impact over the ages. There are also informative sections on Shakespeare's narrative poems, *Venus and Adonis* and *The Rape of Lucrece*, on his sonnets, and on his other two poems, *A Lover's Complaint* and *The Phoenix and the Turtle*.

The exact order in which Shakespeare wrote his works is uncertain. In this book, we follow both the text and the chronology of the *Complete Oxford Shakespeare*, General Editors Stanley Wells and Gary Taylor, first published in 1986. It was reissued in 2005 with the addition of *Edward III*, which by that time was generally agreed to have been written at least partly by Shakespeare, and the full text of *Sir Thomas More*, a play that survives only in manuscript, and to which Shakespeare appears to have contributed at least one fine scene. ∎

Come, you spirits
That tend on mortal thoughts,
Unsex me here,
And fill me from the crown
to the toe top-full
Of direst cruelty.
Lady Macbeth
Macbeth

THE FRE
WRITER
1589–1594

ELANCE

Shakespeare **arrives in London**, and writes his first play, *The Two Gentlemen of Verona*.

1589

Christopher Marlowe writes *The Jew of Malta*. The play influences Shakespeare's *Merchant of Venice*.

1589

Fifteen-year-old **Anne of Denmark** is crowned Queen of Scotland. Upon the **union** of the crowns **in 1604**, she becomes **Queen of England**.

1590

Shakespeare writes the **history plays** *Henry VI Part 3*, *Henry VI Part 1*, and the **tragedy** *Titus Andronicus*.

1591

1589

Henry III of France is **murdered**, and the Protestant Huguenot Henry of Navarre becomes Henry IV, but is not recognized by Catholics.

1590

A **comedy** and a **history play** by Shakespeare appear, *The Taming of the Shrew* and *Henry VI Part 2*.

1590

Urban VII is **pope for just 12 days** before he dies. Christopher Marlowe writes *Tamburlaine*.

1591

Engish actor **James Burbage** moves his company, the **Admiral's Men**, to the **Rose Theatre**.

The young William Shakespeare probably arrived in London in the late 1580s. We do not know exactly when, however. After the birth of his twins in early 1585, no more is heard of him for seven years.

Some believe he spent these years as a school teacher; others that he travelled to Italy, although there is no real evidence for this. One theory is that he lived with a Catholic family in Lancashire, where he developed Catholic sympathies that he had to keep secret ever after to avoid running foul of England's Protestant regime.

Provincial upstart
All we can really be sure of is that he was living in London and writing plays by 1590 or so. We know this because he was clearly

ruffling feathers among the university-educated literary dramatists used to ruling the roost in the capital until he came along. One of these dramatists was Robert Greene (1558–92), who, in 1592, as he lay dying in poverty, wrote bitterly in a pamphlet: "for there is an upstart Crow, beautified with our feathers, that with his Tyger's hart wrapt in a Players hyde, supposes he is as well able to bombast out a blanke verse as the best of you: and…is in his owne conceit the onely Shake-scene in a countery." The phrase "Tyger's hart wrapt in a Player's hyde" is a parody of a line from *Henry VI Part 3*. So it would seem that by this point Shakespeare was already well known, yet still sufficiently new on the scene for Greene to call him an "upstart".

Exciting times
London in the late 1580s was an exciting time to be a playwright. It was the fastest-growing city in Europe, a bustling metropolis rivalled in size only by Paris and Naples. It was a young city – most of the population was under the age of 30 – and the theatre scene was booming. Beyond the city walls, in the lively, squalid city fringes, new theatres were beginning to attract large audiences. James Burbage had opened the Theatre in Shoreditch in 1576, and his rival Philip Henslowe had opened the Curtain Theatre nearby in 1577.

It is speculated that Shakespeare may have started his career with one of these companies as an actor, and he may have started writing plays soon after. His earliest surviving works, *The Two*

The Earl of Essex leads **English troops** to **help Henry of Navarre at Rouen**. The Rialto Bridge in Venice is completed.

The **Marquess of Huntly sets fire to Donibristle Castle** in Scotland, **murdering the Earl of Moray** in a vendetta.

An arrest warrant is issued on the playwright **Christopher Marlowe**, who is accused of heresy.

Henry IV, converted to Catholicism, is **crowned King of France**.

1591   **1592**   **1593**   **1594**

1592   **1593**   **1594**   **1594**

Richard III and *Edward III* are staged. In June, an outbreak of **bubonic plague** closes the theatres.

The poem *Venus and Adonis* is published. Protestant suppression of Catholics is tightened with the **Act Against Papists**.

In Ireland, the earls Hugh O'Neill and Hugh O'Donnell **unite to fight English rule**.

Shakespeare completes his poem *The Rape of Lucrece*, another **commercial success**.

Gentleman of Verona and *The Taming of the Shrew*, date from about 1590. He may even have written for several companies at the same time.

The Armada effect

These were dangerous times, too. The wounds caused by Henry VIII's break from Catholic Church were still raw, and Catholic sympathizers everywhere were constantly watched by government spies.

In 1587, the long-imprisoned Catholic Mary Queen of Scots was executed after being implicated in a plot to kill her cousin, Queen Elizabeth I. In response, Philip II of Spain sent the 140-ship Armada, the "greatest fleet that ever swam upon the sea". Philip, who had been married to Elizabeth's Catholic sister, Mary I, aimed to invade

England, depose the "heretic" Elizabeth, and restore the Catholic faith. Remarkably, the smaller, more manoeuvrable English fleet, with the aid of tides and storms, routed the vast Armada. And though this was a crushing blow for Catholic hopes, there was probably hardly anyone in England, Protestant or Catholic, who did not feel a glow of pride at this unlikely triumph. It secured Elizabeth's reign and sent a wave of patriotic feeling through the country, which Shakespeare rode, writing so successfully about England's history over the following years with his raft of history plays.

He made his mark quickly, and by 1592 already had half a dozen popular successes, including his first series of plays about the Wars of the Roses: the *Henry VI* plays and *Richard III*, and *Titus Andronicus*.

Plague and poetry

Then, disaster struck. A major outbreak of plague ravaged London. To impede the spread of the epidemic, the theatres were closed from June 1592 to May 1594, and theatre companies banished from the city. Some went on tour, but it is not known what Shakespeare did. He probably used this time to turn his hand to poetry: in April 1593, his great poem *Venus and Adonis* was published. It proved to be the biggest literary success of his life, far outselling any of his plays and going through many reprints. A second poem, *The Rape of Lucrece*, came out the following year. He may also have been writing plays. Perhaps anticipating a hunger for entertainment with the reopening of the theatres, his next two works were comedies. ∎

IN LOVE WHO RESPECTS FRIEND?

THE TWO GENTLEMEN OF VERONA (1589–1591)

DRAMATIS PERSONAE

Proteus A young Veronese gentleman.

Valentine Also a gentleman of Verona. Friend to Proteus.

Julia Proteus's first love, later disguised as the page Sebastian.

Lucetta Julia's maid, who makes the breeches and codpiece for Julia's disguise as a boy.

Silvia Daughter of the Duke of Milan, and Valentine's beloved.

Speed Valentine's servant, who is far cleverer than his dim-witted master.

Lance Proteus's servant, and a clownish fellow.

Crab Lance's dog, to which Lance addresses impassioned monologues.

Duke of Milan Silvia's father.

Thurio The Duke's preferred suitor for his daughter. He is not taken seriously by his rivals.

Antonio Proteus's father, who insists that Proteus should follow Valentine to Milan.

Panthino Antonio's servant.

Eglamour A knight who has taken a vow of chastity after the death of his love.

Outlaws Living in the forest outside Milan.

Host Keeper of the inn where Julia lodges.

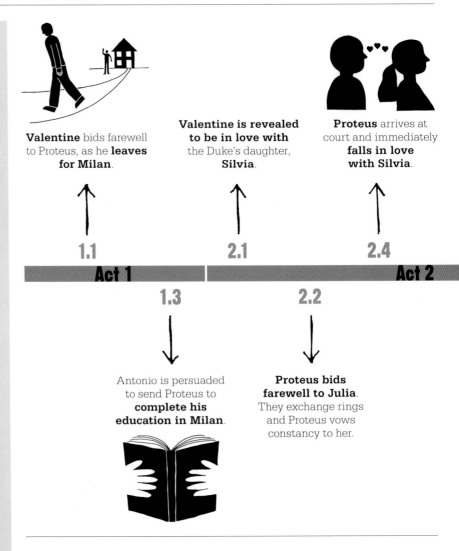

1.1 **Valentine** bids farewell to Proteus, as he **leaves for Milan**.

2.1 **Valentine is revealed to be in love with** the Duke's daughter, **Silvia**.

2.4 **Proteus** arrives at court and immediately **falls in love with Silvia**.

Act 1

Act 2

1.3 Antonio is persuaded to send Proteus to **complete his education in Milan**.

2.2 **Proteus bids farewell to Julia**. They exchange rings and Proteus vows constancy to her.

Valentine prepares to leave for the Duke of Milan's court to complete his education as a gentleman. Proteus refuses to go with him because of his love for Julia. Valentine deplores the effects of love upon his friend.

Julia discusses her suitors with her maid, Lucetta. Lucetta singles out Proteus for admiration, but Julia observes that he has made no suit to her. When Speed delivers a letter from Proteus, Julia pretends that she doesn't want to read it, and tears it up. In private, she pieces the letter together and admits her love.

Proteus is celebrating Julia's confession of love in a further letter, when his father announces that he must join Valentine. Proteus says goodbye to Julia. They exchange rings, and he vows to be faithful to her. Lance gives a comic account of his leave-taking in which only the dog, Crab, remained dry-eyed.

At the court of Milan, Valentine has changed his attitude to love, having become infatuated with Silvia, the Duke's daughter, who is intended for the wealthy Thurio. Proteus arrives at court and is instantly enamoured of Silvia, too.

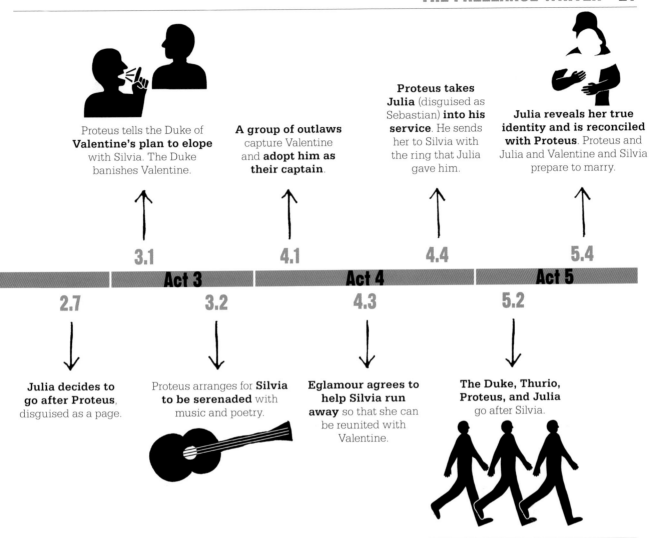

Proteus tells the Duke of **Valentine's plan to elope** with Silvia. The Duke banishes Valentine.

A group of outlaws capture Valentine and **adopt him as their captain**.

Proteus takes Julia (disguised as Sebastian) **into his service**. He sends her to Silvia with the ring that Julia gave him.

Julia reveals her true identity and is reconciled with Proteus. Proteus and Julia and Valentine and Silvia prepare to marry.

3.1

4.1

4.4

5.4

Act 3   Act 4   Act 5

2.7

3.2

4.3

5.2

Julia decides to go after Proteus, disguised as a page.

Proteus arranges for **Silvia to be serenaded** with music and poetry.

Eglamour agrees to help Silvia run away so that she can be reunited with Valentine.

The Duke, Thurio, Proteus, and Julia go after Silvia.

Valentine reveals he and Silvia are betrothed and plan to elope. Proteus betrays this plot to Silvia's father, who tricks Valentine into revealing the rope ladder and letter, hidden in his cloak. The Duke banishes Valentine from Milan.

Proteus offers to help Thurio by praising him in front of Silvia and slandering Valentine. As he sings beneath her window, he is overheard by Julia, who has come in search of her lover, disguised as the page boy Sebastian. Proteus takes her into his employment and sends her to woo Silvia, giving her

a letter and a ring (the one Julia gave him). Silvia sends Proteus a portrait of herself, but refuses to read his letter and tears it up. Julia's account of Proteus's betrayal of his first love makes Silvia cry.

Silvia enlists the help of Eglamour, a knight who has taken a vow of chastity after his true love died. They meet at Friar Patrick's cell after confession and make their way towards Mantua, where Silvia believes Valentine to be living.

In the forest, Proteus rescues Silvia from the outlaws who have captured her. Silvia still refuses

Proteus's love, and he is about to rape her, but Valentine intervenes. Proteus is immediately contrite. Valentine pities him and renounces all his affection for Silvia. Julia returns to Proteus the ring she had forgotten to deliver. Proteus recognizes it as one he gave Julia and becomes suspicious. Julia reveals who she is, and Proteus remembers his love for her. Thurio relinquishes his claim to Silvia and the Duke agrees that Valentine shall marry her. The outlaws are repealed from exile and the couples prepare for a double wedding. »

IN CONTEXT

THEMES
Friendship, love, lust, ambition, change, betrayal, sacrifice

SETTING
Verona, the court of Milan, a forest near Mantua

SOURCES
1531 The Proteus–Valentine plot echoes the story of *Titus and Gisippus* from Boccaccio's *Decameron*. Shakespeare may have read this in Sir Thomas Elyot's *The Governor* (1531).

1542 Jorge de Montemayor's prose romance *Diana* (1542, translated into English in 1598) may have provided the plot for Julia in male disguise sent to woo her lover's new mistress. (This could also have come from a lost play *Felix and Felismena* (1585).)

LEGACY
1931 *Yi Jian Mei* (directed by Bu Wancang) – a black-and-white silent film – sets the play in 20th-century China.

1971 *The Two Gentlemen of Verona*, a musical adaptation (libretto by John Guare and Mel Shapiro) is originally performed at Joe Papp's Public Theatre, but transfers to Broadway where it wins a Tony award for Best Musical.

2014 The Royal Shakespeare Company stages its first full production of the play in its main house. The performance is filmed and played live in cinemas across the country.

For a romantic comedy, *The Two Gentlemen of Verona* is surprisingly negative about the experience of love. Passion is seen to inhibit the development of young men, who should be fighting in wars, studying at university, or travelling abroad. Not only does it stall their intellectual development, it is imagined as being physically destructive: "As the most forward bud / Is eaten by the canker ere it blow, / Even so by love the young and tender wit / Is turned to folly, blasting in the bud" (1.1.45–48).

Valentine may well be reliant on "writers" for this opinion – having never experienced love himself – but when he does fall for Silvia, his behaviour only reinforces the point. His wit is so enfeebled that he does not realize that Silvia is declaring her affections for him when she asks him to write love poetry on her behalf.

Throughout the play, characters describe themselves as being "metamorphosed" by love. Julia puts on male attire and makes a dangerous journey to follow her beloved Proteus. Valentine changes his clothing and behaviour for those

To leave my Julia shall
I be forsworn;
To love fair Silvia shall
I be forsworn;
To wrong my friend I shall
be much forsworn.
Proteus
Act 2, Scene 6

What should it be that
he respects in her
But I can make respective
in myself,
If this fond love were
not a blinded god?
Julia
Act 4, Scene 4

of the stereotypical lover. Although Speed's account of this is largely comic, his acknowledgement that "when I look on you I can hardly think you my master" (2.1.29–30) reflects the deeper anxieties that surrounded male erotic desire in Shakespeare's time, where to love was to be rendered effeminate. But Proteus's transformation is the most serious. In classical mythology, Proteus was a sea god who could change his shape at will. However, Shakespeare's character has little control over his shape-shifting, which causes him to betray his vows to Julia, and destroy his friendship with Valentine.

Friendship versus love
Shakespeare's times placed great value on male-male friendship, imagining it a pure and ennobling love, without the turbulence of lust. It was thought to enable friends to perfect themselves through the mirror they provided to one another: "true friends should be two in body, but one in minde, / As it were one transformed into another", said Richard Edwardes in his 1564 play *Damon and Pythias*.

Given that friends were meant to share the same judgment, taste, and appetite, and to hold all things in common, it is no surprise that Proteus should desire Valentine's beloved. One theory that *The Two Gentlemen of Verona* has been used to illustrate is that we are taught what to admire by other people – encouraged to see with their eyes. It is what Proteus does next that is a breach against the friendship code, when he betrays Valentine in order to steal his mistress, insisting that "I to myself am dearer than a friend" (2.6.23).

Furthermore, in Shakespeare's most notorious addition to the drama, Proteus threatens to rape Silvia. His immediate confession and penitence when interrupted by Valentine can hardly atone for the crime he was about to perpetrate, or the betrayals that have brought him to this point. And yet, Valentine immediately forgives him and, renouncing all ties to Silvia, offers her to Proteus. Proteus seems invigorated by lust, and his betrayal of their friendship might imply that he has escaped the confines of the friendship narrative, even if Valentine has not.

The place of women

Shakespeare's rape threat has also proven controversial because of the way in which it undermines the

> It is the lesser blot,
> modesty finds,
> Women to change their shapes
> than men their minds.
> **Julia**
> **Act 5, Scene 4**

play's women. The male characters insist that women say "no" when they mean yes; their characters are soft, as if moulded out of wax. Yet it is the men who are fickle, while Julia and Silvia remain attached to their first loves. As Proteus asserts: "O heaven, were man / But constant, he were perfect" (5.4.109–110). Silvia's fate is finally decided by Valentine, Thurio, and her father, without her uttering a word, and the likelihood of Julia's happiness with the ever-changing, would-be rapist Proteus is not meant to trouble us. The friendship theme gains the upper hand, with Valentine's anticipation of "One feast, one house, one mutual happiness" (5.4.171) invoking less the terms of the marriage service (man and wife becoming "one flesh") than the image of male friends as "one in mind".

While Shakespeare would return to many of the themes and motifs of this play, he would never again risk subordinating romantic love to friendship in this way. ∎

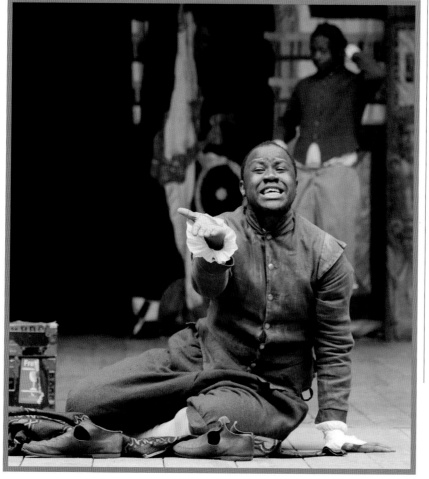

A 2012 Shona production related the play's themes of exile and deception to life in contemporary Zimbabwe. All 15 characters were played by one pair of actors.

I KNOW NOW HOW TO TAME A SHREW

THE TAMING OF THE SHREW (1590–1594)

DRAMATIS PERSONAE

Christopher Sly A drunken tinker.

Baptista The father of Katherine and Bianca, who negotiates with their suitors.

Katherine A strong, opinionated woman with a reputation that precedes her.

Bianca Katherine's younger sister, who is the object of affection for several suitors.

Petruccio A gentleman of Verona who travels to Padua to marry into a wealthy family.

Grumio Petruccio's servant, who taunts Katherine with food when his master has forbidden her to eat.

Gremio An old wealthy man who is in love with Bianca.

Hortensio Bianca's suitor, who disguises himself as the teacher Licio in order to gain access to her.

Lucentio A young man from Pisa who disguises himself as the teacher Cambio in order to woo Bianca.

Vincentio Lucentio's father who travels to Padua and is shocked to discover that another man has assumed his identity.

Tranio Lucentio's servant who pretends to be his master while his master plays the part of Cambio.

Biondello Another servant to Lucentio.

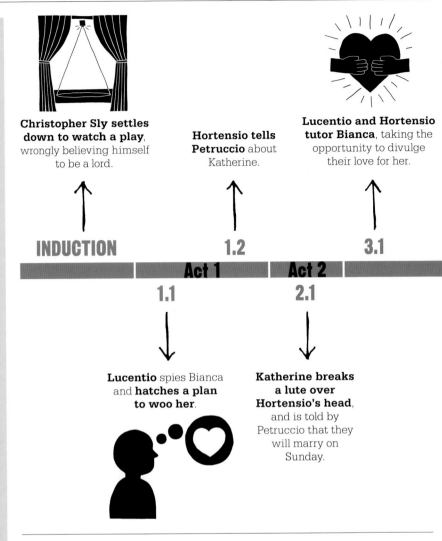

Christopher Sly settles down to watch a play, wrongly believing himself to be a lord.

Hortensio tells Petruccio about Katherine.

Lucentio and Hortensio tutor Bianca, taking the opportunity to divulge their love for her.

INDUCTION **1.2** **3.1**

Act 1 **1.1** **Act 2** **2.1**

Lucentio spies Bianca and **hatches a plan to woo her**.

Katherine breaks a lute over Hortensio's head, and is told by Petruccio that they will marry on Sunday.

A drunken tinker called Christopher Sly argues with the hostess of an alehouse and is thrown out. A passing Lord and his servants trick him into believing that he is a lord, and invite him to watch a play. The play is set in Italy and begins with Lucentio and his servant Tranio arriving in Padua. They overhear Baptista Minola explaining to Hortensio and Gremio, suitors to his daughter Bianca, that they cannot marry her until a husband is found for Katherine, his eldest daughter. Lucentio also falls in love

with Bianca, and plans to beat the other suitors for her hand in marriage. He decides to don a disguise and offer his services as her tutor, and instructs his servant, Tranio, to impersonate him.

Hortensio's friend Petruccio arrives in Padua and declares his intention to marry a woman with a large dowry. Hortensio suggests Katherine Minola and Petruccio determines to woo, win, and wed her, despite her shrewish reputation.

Petruccio comes to woo Katherine and presents Licio (Hortensio in disguise) as a music

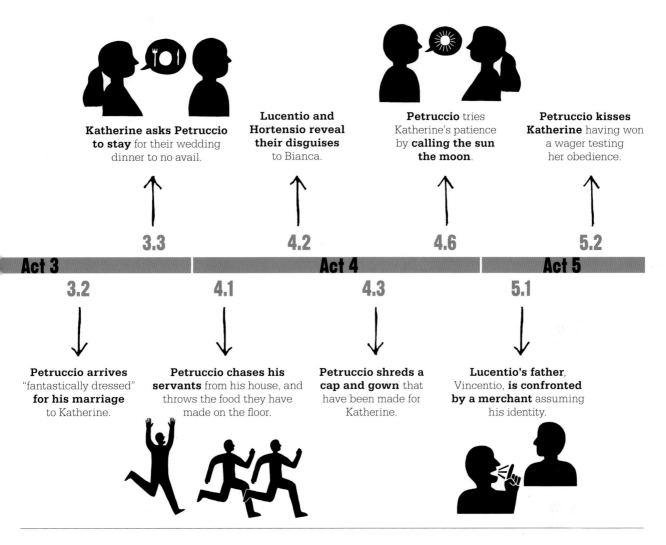

Katherine asks Petruccio to stay for their wedding dinner to no avail.

Lucentio and Hortensio reveal their disguises to Bianca.

Petruccio tries Katherine's patience by **calling the sun the moon**.

Petruccio kisses Katherine having won a wager testing her obedience.

3.3

4.2

4.6

5.2

Act 3   Act 4   Act 5

3.2

4.1

4.3

5.1

Petruccio arrives "fantastically dressed" **for his marriage** to Katherine.

Petruccio chases his servants from his house, and throws the food they have made on the floor.

Petruccio shreds a cap and gown that have been made for Katherine.

Lucentio's father, Vincentio, **is confronted by a merchant** assuming his identity.

master for the sisters; Hortensio will attempt to woo Bianca, while Petruccio secures his marriage to her sister. Gremio enlists Lucentio (disguised as Cambio) to woo on his behalf, while Tranio, already disguised as Lucentio, continues to woo Bianca for his master.

After a lively exchange of words with Katherine, Petruccio confirms his intention to marry her, and a date is set for the wedding. The wedding party is kept waiting due to Petruccio's late arrival, but when he appears, his clothing does not befit the occasion. Petruccio then

declares that he and his wife will not attend the wedding dinner, but return to his home immediately. Petruccio denies his wife food and sleep in an attempt to tame her shrewish behaviour.

Having revealed his true identity, Lucentio wins Bianca's heart, leaving Hortensio to marry a widow. Lacking funds, Lucentio and Tranio convince a merchant to imitate Lucentio's father, Vincentio. All is well until Lucentio's real father arrives, and is bemused to meet the impostor. The confusion is explained by Lucentio. As

Katherine and Petruccio return to Padua for a banquet, Katherine obeys Petruccio's commands.

Petruccio wagers that his wife will prove more obedient than both Lucentio and Hortensio's wives. When the men call for their wives to attend them, only Katherine appears; Petruccio wins the wager. Katherine speaks forcefully to the other women about what is expected of a good wife, and about the nature of the relationship between husband and wife. The guests are left surprised by Katherine's transformation. »

IN CONTEXT

THEMES
Love, marriage, power, fathers, daughters, money, status, men, women

SETTING
Warwickshire, England, Padua, Italy

SOURCES
10th century Christopher Sly's story shares similarities with a tale from *The Arabian Nights*, while the tale of the shrewish woman takes its inspiration from ballads and folk stories of the period.

1566 The plot involving Bianca, Lucentio, Hortensio, and Gremio is based on George Gascoigne's comedy *Supposes*.

LEGACY
1611 John Fletcher writes *The Woman's Prize* or *The Tamer Tamed* as a response to Shakespeare's play.

1874 Hermann Goetz writes an opera based on the play called *Der Widerspänstigen Zähmung.*

1929 First Shakespeare "talkie" directed by Sam Taylor, with Hollywood stars Mary Pickford and Douglas Fairbanks.

1948 Cole Porter's musical adaptation titled *Kiss Me Kate* is first performed.

1967 Franco Zeffirelli's film, starring Richard Burton and Elizabeth Taylor, is released.

1999 US teen-movie *10 Things I Hate About You*, based on the play, is set in a Seattle High School.

Some critics may wish that Shakespeare had never written *The Taming of the Shrew*. There are actresses today who would not want to be cast as Katherine, and theatre reviewers who would prefer to see the play disappear from the stage. Others, however, would include the play in their list of favourite Shakespearean comedies, and identify Katherine as one of the playwright's most memorable early creations.

In his presentation of the "taming" of a "shrew" Shakespeare gave voice to a variety of attitudes towards women and marriage that were common to his times. Such attitudes are more likely to offend than entertain contemporary audiences, but they reflect the playwright's engagement with the period in which he was living. At this time a woman could be described as "shrewish" if she openly disagreed with a man or seemed bad tempered. The very title of Shakespeare's play promised drama and extreme behaviour. It also promised a battle of the sexes.

The property of men

Women are often spoken about in this play as commodities, owned by men. Katherine's first utterance is one of disgust at hearing the way in which her father speaks of her to Gremio and Hortensio, underlining her father's financial interest in her marital status. Financial gain is the first thing that occurs to Petruccio when he accepts the challenge of wooing Katherine: "I come to wive it wealthily in Padua; / If wealthily, then happily in Padua." (1.2.74–75). Love does not enter his thoughts, though he clearly has sex in mind: "For I will board her though she

Sexual tension or brutal bullying? Productions have reflected the sexual politics of their time. Franco Zeffirelli's film of 1967 starred husband and wife Elizabeth Taylor and Richard Burton.

Have I not in my time heard
lions roar?
Petruccio
Act 1, Scene 2

chide as loud / As thunder when the clouds in autumn crack." (1.2.94–95). It is clear that Katherine, who is thought of by the men as a "fiend of hell" (1.1.88) will be turned into a "gentler, milder mould" (1.1.60). The question remains whether the transformation will be consensual.

Taming tactics

Shakespeare has Petruccio rehearse his "taming" strategy through soliloquy before meeting Katherine: "Say that she rail, why then I'll tell her plain / She sings as sweetly as a nightingale. / Say that she frown, I'll say she looks as clear / As morning roses newly washed with dew. / Say she be mute and will not speak a word, / Then I'll commend her volubility, / And say she uttereth piercing eloquence." (2.1.170–176). Without recourse to this soliloquy, Petruccio's behaviour would seem eccentric and insensitive. While this soliloquy does not excuse his conduct (including withholding food and denying sleep), it serves to emphasize that he is donning a role to achieve a desired result.

As the couple make their way to the banquet at the close, Petruccio's "reign" (4.1.174) over Katherine is apparent. He has essentially talked her (or in some productions, beaten her) into submission. He

treats her, in his own words, like a falcon (4.1.176), shaping her appetites to suit his will. Petruccio's treatment of Katherine is ruthless. It contrasts strongly with the farcical romantic sub-plot in which Bianca is besieged by starry-eyed suitors. Petruccio does not seem interested in having the love as well as the obedience of his wife. Katherine is bewildered by his behaviour and angered that "He does it under name of perfect love" (4.3.12).

At the close of the play Katherine performs the role of Petruccio's "perfect wife", appearing at his command and echoing his words in her final speech to the women at the banquet: "Thy husband is thy lord, thy life, thy keeper, / Thy head, thy sovereign, one that cares for thee, / And for thy maintenance commits his body / To painful labour both by sea and land, / … / And craves no other tribute at thy hands / But love, fair looks, and true obedience, / Too little payment for so great a debt." (5.2.151–159).

Whether or not the play ends in joy is open to interpretation. There have been productions where Kates and Petruccios have left the stage arm in arm into a happy future together; but there have also been those left staring at one another in stony silence. ∎

Why there's a wench!
Come on, and kiss me, Kate.
Petruccio
Act 5, Scene 2

Shrewish women

In the 16th century a woman had to do little more than challenge a man's opinion to be termed a "shrew". She might be labelled "shrewish" if she spoke too much, or appeared mean spirited or sexually promiscuous.

There were many ballads and folk tales about unruly wives that Shakespeare could have based his presentation of Katherine around. Here is a verse of a ballad called *The Cruel Shrew*: "She never lins her brawling, / Her tongue it is so loud; / But always she'll be railing, / And will not be controlled. / For she the breeches still will wear, / Although it breeds my strife. / If I were now a bachelor, / I'd never have a wife."

Punishments in the 16th century for being thought "shrewish" were brutal. Women could be forced to wear a horrific metal device called a scold's bridle. This fit over the woman's head and pushed a metal plate into her mouth to hold down her tongue. Having silenced his wife, a husband could tie a rope around her neck and parade her in front of his neighbours.

THE COMMONS, LIKE AN ANGRY HIVE OF BEES THAT WANT THEIR LEADER, SCATTER UP AND DOWN

HENRY VI PART 2 (1590–1591)

DRAMATIS PERSONAE

THE KING'S PARTY
King Henry VI
Queen Margaret
William de la Pole, Marquis, later **Duke, of Suffolk**
Duke of Gloucester
Dame Eleanor Cobham
Cardinal Beaufort
Duke of Buckingham
Duke of Somerset
Lord Clifford

DUKE OF YORK'S PARTY
Richard, Duke of York
Edward
Earl of Salisbury
Earl of Warwick

OTHERS
Jack Cade
Sir Humphrey Stafford

Young King Henry VI is overjoyed as Suffolk hands the beautiful Margaret of Anjou to him to be his queen. Lord Protector Gloucester, and Warwick, are appalled at the political cost – the return of Anjou and Maine to France. York reveals that he aims to take the crown himself. Gloucester's wife Eleanor dreams that he should be king. Margaret and her lover Suffolk determine to bring down Gloucester by setting a trap for his wife. Eleanor is seen consulting with witches who prophesy the king's overthrow. She is arrested.

While he is out hawking with the queen at St Albans, Henry receives news of the arrest of

Henry VI marries Margaret. Richard of York bides his time. **Eleanor of Gloucester dreams of making her husband king.**

York **gains the support of Salisbury and Warwick** for his claim to the throne.

York ordered to Ireland. **Suffolk is blamed** for the murder of Gloucester and **banished**.

Cade's rebellion is dispersed and Cade is killed. **York has landed** from Ireland **demanding Somerset's arrest.**

1.1–2   **2.2**   **3.1–2**   **4.7–9**

Act 1 | **Act 2** | **Act 3** | **Act 4** | **Act 5**

1.3   **3.1**   **4.1–3**   **5.1–4**

Margaret and her lover Suffolk seek to bring down Gloucester and **set a trap for Gloucester's wife**.

News that **all England's territories in France are lost** goes almost unnoticed amid the infighting.

Suffolk is beheaded. Jack Cade's rebellion gains momentum and heads to London.

York learns that Somerset is free and **determines to dethrone Henry**. York kills Clifford, Richard kills Somerset, and **Henry and Margaret flee.**

Gloucester's wife. Gloucester resigns as Protector. York reveals his claim to the throne to Salisbury and his son Warwick who pledge allegiance. Gloucester is distressed when Eleanor is banished.

In Parliament, Margaret and Suffolk denounce Gloucester, but Henry defends him feebly. England's territories in France have been lost, while York and Suffolk order the arrest of Gloucester. Henry is upset, but Margaret, York, and the Cardinal agree that Suffolk should have Gloucester murdered. York is sent to Ireland to quell a rebellion and, given

an army, he sees his chance. When Henry hears of Gloucester's death, he is distraught and turns against Suffolk. Warwick shows Gloucester's body to prove he was murdered and accuses Suffolk. Despite Margaret's pleas, Henry banishes Suffolk. Margaret and Suffolk part sadly.

After a sea battle, Suffolk is beheaded and his head sent to Margaret. Jack Cade, encouraged by York, begins a peasant's rebellion, killing Stafford and others. The rebels head to London, where Margaret cradles Suffolk's head. The rebels are persuaded to

disperse. Cade hides but is killed. York has landed in England in force, demanding the arrest of Somerset.

York reaches London intent on claiming the throne. Buckingham and the King assure him that Somerset is in the Tower, but Margaret arrives with Somerset. York explodes and tells Henry that his rule is over. As Salisbury and Warwick switch allegiance to York, war begins. At St Albans, York kills Clifford and his son Richard kills Somerset. Margaret drags Henry away to London. The Yorkists march on London to proclaim their victory. **»**

IN CONTEXT

THEMES
Ambition, weakness, social order, kingship

SETTING
London, Kent, Blackheath, St Albans

SOURCES
1548 One source for the play is Edward Hall's *The Union of the Two Noble and Illustre Families of Lancaster and York*.

1587 As for many of his History plays, Shakespeare also drew on Raphael Holinshed's *Chronicles of England, Scotland, and Ireland*.

LEGACY
1591 Evidence suggests that *Henry VI Part 2* was first staged in 1591 or 1592.

1864 Performance to celebrate Shakespeare's tercentenary at the Surrey Theatre in London.

1963 John Barton and Peter Hall at the RSC combine the three *Henry VI* plays and *Richard III* into the two-part *The Wars of the Roses*.

1987 An English Shakespeare Company production directed by Michael Bogdanov, stresses the play's political issues. It tours Japan, Italy, and Australia.

2001 A production combines the *Henry VI/Richard III* tetralogy into one at the Colorado Shakespeare Festival.

2012 The National Theatre of Albania performs the play as part of the Globe to Globe Festival, at the Globe, London.

Henry VI Part 2 is often considered the strongest of Shakespeare's three plays about Henry VI, who, historically, was the king of England from the age of nine months in 1422 until 1461 and again from 1470 until 1471. The play focuses on the dark period in English history leading up to a Yorkist challenge to the Lancastrian monarchy that spiralled into the civil and dynastic war known as the Wars of the Roses.

This first of Shakespeare's great plays about English history – written before *Henry VI Part 1* – may have first been performed in 1591. It was printed as early as 1594 in a quarto version under an extraordinarily lengthy title, which was presumably the publisher's publicity blurb rather than Shakespeare's own title. Most people refer to it as *The Second Part of Henry VI* (as it is entitled in the 1623 Folio edition) or *Henry VI Part 2*.

Making history
Although the rawness of the verse shows the young Shakespeare still developing his craft, its attraction lies in the way it brings a panoply of shadowy historical figures and

Henry VI (depicted with his wife Margaret of Anjou in this 15th-century manuscript) gave away territories to Margaret's father. Shakespeare portrays Henry as easily influenced by his wife.

events vividly to life and shapes them into a gripping narrative. Characters from history, from the brutally ambitious Richard of York to the strong-willed Margaret of Anjou, attain such intensity each time the play is performed that it is difficult for historians to escape Shakespeare's re-creation of them.

Using the poetic style and stage techniques of his contemporaries, Shakespeare creates a heightened, emotionally charged drama, and he reshapes the material in his historical sources to create a pattern to the events, drawing out themes of kingship and ambition.

Recasting Cade
One of the most vivid characters in the play is Jack Cade, the lively rabble-rouser who, egged on by York, stirs up the common-folk of Kent to rebellion and leads them on a terrifying assault on London. But the Cade in *Henry VI Part 2* is not

> It is great sin to swear
> unto a sin,
> But greater sin to keep
> a sinful oath.
> **Salisbury**
> Act 5, Scene 1

the well-educated young man described in Holinshed's *Chronicles*; he is a conflation of the historical Jack Cade who led a rebellion in 1450, and an earlier rebel, Wat Tyler, who led the Peasant's Revolt of 1381.

In the play, Cade instructs the rebels to hang a clerk because he can write, and Dick the Butcher calls, "let's kill all the lawyers" (4.2.78). But it was Tyler's rebellion, according to Holinshed, that condemned literacy and lawyers for being socially divisive, not Cade's. Shakespeare mixes the two, emphasizing the chaos that ensues when proper social and political relationships are cast aside: "like an angry hive of bees / That want their leader" (3.2.125–126). However, Cade is no egalitarian – change will happen when Cade is king himself, "as king I will be" (4.2.71–72), an echo of York's claims to kingship. However, it would be wrong to assume that Shakespeare is out of sympathy with the plight of the poor, whose suffering in such unhinged times is made very clear.

The empty centre
At the heart of this breakdown in relationships is King Henry himself. He wants to be a peacemaker. But York and Queen Margaret condemn his "church-like humours" (1.1.247) as unfit for the crown, and describe his obsession with prayer as unmanly. Ultimately, his piety becomes simply vacillation, and his indecision makes him increasingly irrelevant. "What are you made of?" Margaret cries desperately when they are caught in the Battle of St Albans at the end, "You'll nor fight nor fly" (5.4.3).

The emptiness at the centre creates a power vacuum that sucks in and destroys all but the strongest – from Eleanor, the "good" Duke of Gloucester's wife, who is caught conspiring with witches, to the queen's unfortunate lover, Suffolk, who is beheaded at sea. Suffolk's departure is one of the most touching scenes in the play. He is a brutal schemer, responsible for entrapping Eleanor and arranging the murder of Gloucester. Yet their parting is poignant: "To France, sweet Suffolk. Let me hear from thee. / For wheresoe'er thou art in this world's Globe, / I'll have an Iris that shall find thee out." (3.2.409–412). When Margaret cradles Suffolk's decapitated head in her lap, it is a moment of true anguish.

Henry's weakness has unleashed the demons, and at the end of the play, the ruthless ambition of York and his sons chillingly takes control. ∎

> Can we outrun the heavens?
> **King Henry**
> Act 5, Scene 4

Performance history
Despite the weakness of the character of King Henry, who vacillates and hesitates, the powerful parts of Richard of York and Queen Margaret provide challenging roles that dominate and drive the play.

Many directors have presented the *Henry VI* trilogy along with *Richard III*, creating a tetralogy on the Wars of the Roses. Often the same actor plays the same character across the plays, as Chuck Iwuji (pictured) did in 2008, playing Henry VI for the RSC.

Well-regarded theatrical performances include the 1963 John Barton and Peter Hall adaptation at the RSC titled *The Wars of the Roses* with Peggy Ashcroft as Margaret and Donald Sinden as York. These productions highlighted the political and social unrest prevalent in the plays, which reflected the civil upheaval of the 1960s – a period of momentous events such as the erection of the Berlin Wall and the assassination of John F Kennedy.

Acclaimed television productions include a 1981 BBC version of all four plays directed by Jane Howell, which stayed very close to the play.

I CAN SMILE, AND MURDER WHILES I SMILE

HENRY VI PART 3 (1591)

DRAMATIS PERSONAE

THE KING'S PARTY
King Henry VI
Queen Margaret
Prince Edward
Lord Clifford

HOUSE OF NEVILLE
Earl of Warwick

DUKE OF YORK'S PARTY
Richard, Duke of York
Edward Later King Edward IV.
Lady Gray
George Plantagenet Later Duke of Clarence.
Richard Plantagenet Later Duke of Gloucester, York's son.
Earl of Rutland York's son.

THE FRENCH
King Louis
Lady Bona

After the Yorkists' victory at St Albans, Henry VI is forced to make a pledge: he will remain king, but Richard of York will become king after his death. York agrees to this, but his son Richard Plantagenet persuades him to break the oath. War breaks out and Clifford murders York's son Rutland. After the Battle of Wakefield, York is cornered and Queen Margaret and Clifford taunt him with Rutland's blood before killing him.

York's sons Edward, Richard, and George plan their revenge and are joined, crucially, by Warwick. Margaret and Clifford, confronted by the rampant York brothers, try

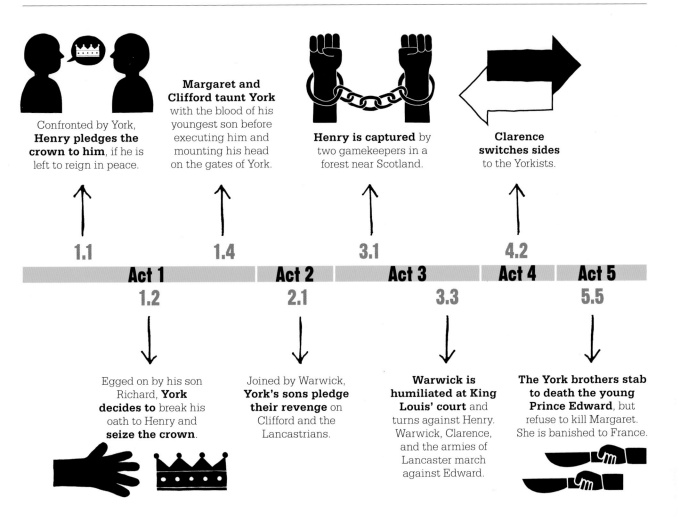

Confronted by York, **Henry pledges the crown to him**, if he is left to reign in peace.

Margaret and Clifford taunt York with the blood of his youngest son before executing him and mounting his head on the gates of York.

Henry is captured by two gamekeepers in a forest near Scotland.

Clarence switches sides to the Yorkists.

1.1   **1.4**   **3.1**   **4.2**

Act 1   **Act 2**   **Act 3**   **Act 4**   **Act 5**

1.2   **2.1**   **3.3**   **5.5**

Egged on by his son Richard, **York decides to** break his oath to Henry and **seize the crown**.

Joined by Warwick, **York's sons pledge their revenge** on Clifford and the Lancastrians.

Warwick is humiliated at King Louis' court and turns against Henry. Warwick, Clarence, and the armies of Lancaster march against Edward.

The York brothers stab to death the young Prince Edward, but refuse to kill Margaret. She is banished to France.

to rouse Henry to fight. In the Battle of Towton, Warwick saves Richard from Clifford. Henry laments the tragedy of civil war. Clifford is killed, the Yorkists are victorious, and Edward is crowned King Edward IV.

Henry is captured. In London, Edward IV blackmails Lady Gray into a marriage. Richard (now Duke of Gloucester), railing against his deformities, reveals his ambition to be king. Meanwhile, Henry has been sent to the Tower of London. Margaret appeals for help to the French king Louis and learns that Warwick is arranging a wedding between Edward and Louis' sister, Lady Bona. Just as Louis agrees to the wedding, news arrives of Edward's marriage to Lady Gray. Warwick disavows Edward and joins with Margaret.

In England, Edward learns that his brother George, now Duke of Clarence, has joined Warwick and the Lancastrian forces. Warwick raids Edward's camp, takes the crown from Edward, and makes him a prisoner. Henry VI, restored to power, makes Warwick and Clarence his Protectors. But Edward, with the help of Gloucester, escapes. At the head of his foreign army, Edward is victorious and reclaims the throne, imprisoning Henry in the Tower.

The Yorkists capture Coventry, and Clarence rejoins his brothers. Warwick flees but is killed. Queen Margaret leads an army against the Yorkists but is defeated and taken prisoner. Edward IV, Gloucester, and Clarence kill her young son, Edward, but refuse to kill Margaret. In the Tower, Henry taunts the deformed Gloucester, who kills him and vows to kill his brothers. Edward IV and his queen have a new baby, but Gloucester is already plotting. »

IN CONTEXT

THEMES
Kingship, revenge, betrayal, civil war, battles

SETTING
London, Yorkshire, Warwickshire, and various towns around England

SOURCES
1513 Thomas More's *History of King Richard III.*

1545 Edward Halle's *Union of the Two Noble and Illustrious Families of Lancaster and York*, a biased, Tudor-friendly account of the events covered in the play.

1587 Raphael Holinshed's *Chronicles of England, Scotland, and Ireland.*

LEGACY
1592 Playwright Robert Greene makes reference to the play to express his contempt for Shakespeare. This indicates that the play had been performed, although no records survive.

1595 The play is first published with the title *The True Tragedy of Richard Duke of York and the Death of King Henry the Sixth, with the Whole Contention of the two Houses Lancaster and York.*

1680 John Crowne writes an adaptation of the play called *The Misery of Civil War.*

1977 At the Swan Theatre in Stratford-upon-Avon, Helen Mirren plays an acclaimed Margaret as the play receives a rare almost-uncut treatment.

enry VI Part 3 is the last of Shakespeare's three plays about the reign of Henry VI (1422–61 and 1470–71). It covers the bloodiest period of the Wars of the Roses, in which the Yorkist faction gained ascendancy over Henry's Lancastrians in the battle for the throne, and the eldest of the Duke of York's sons snatched the crown from Henry to become Edward IV. It ends with the murder of Henry in the Tower of London in 1471 by another son of York, Richard of Gloucester, later Richard III.

Henry VI Part 3 was performed first in about 1591. England was wracked by the violent aftermath of Henry VIII's break from Rome and Elizabeth I's hold on the throne was still under threat. The depiction of leaders cynically playing for power would have struck a chord with audiences. The Yorkists Edward and Richard are portrayed in a very poor light, while the Earl of Richmond, later Henry VII, and Elizabeth's grandfather, is praised.

A molehill for a kingdom

In this vicious world, the weak but well-intentioned Henry is entirely lost. When he is banned from the Battle of Towton, he meekly agrees,

My Crown is in my heart, not on my head;
Not decked with diamonds and Indian stones
Henry VI
Act 3, Scene 1

Why, what is pomp, rule, reign, but earth and dust?
And, live we how we can, yet die we must.
Earl of Warwick
Act 5, Scene 2

admitting with unwitting irony: "They prosper best of all when I am thence" (2.5.18). But his abdication of responsibility turns him, like the audience, into an appalled spectator watching the tragedy unfold. As he sits away from the battle on the molehill to which his kingdom has shrunk, he witnesses the real horror of civil war in the affecting tableau of a soldier who has killed his son and another who has killed his father. He laments, "And let our hearts and eyes, like civil war, / Be blind with tears, and break, o'ercharged with grief" (2.5.77–78). But there is self-indulgence too when he sighs, "Here sits a king more woeful than you are" (2.5.124).

Henry's absence allows two characters to dominate the action – Richard, Duke of Gloucester, and Queen Margaret. Both are seen as "monstrous", freaks of nature that have thrived in the absence of normal moral values – Richard physically deformed at birth with his "crookback" and shrivelled arm, and Margaret unnaturally manly.

A tiger's heart

As Margaret stands exultant over Richard of York, handing him a handkerchief soaked in his son's

Henry VI meditates on the brutality of civil war, watching son kill father and father kill son, in this amalgam of Shakespeare's works titled *Forests*, by Catalan director Calixto Bieito.

the battle, although she could also be seen as a strong woman who is protecting a childlike man.

The shape-shifter

Richard, Duke of Gloucester, will have his own play in *Richard III*, but his personality emerges here. In a soliloquy in Act 3, Scene 2, he explains that his character has been shaped by his physical deformity. Deprived from birth of normal love by his misshapen body, he has turned himself into a Machiavel, a political player who sets himself apart from common humanity. He is interested only in the tactics that bring the highest prize, the crown, and becomes the consummate actor: "Why, I can smile, and murder whiles I smile" (3.2.182).

By means of this soliloquy and other asides, Shakespeare allowed audiences to join the characters on their psychological journeys. This was a new form of stage drama. ∎

blood, he describes her famously as the "She-wolf of France" (1.4.112) – a "tiger's heart wrapped in a woman's hide" (1.4.138). She is an "amazon" who does not behave as women should – "soft, mild, pitiful, and flexible" (1.4.142). In Shakespeare's play, she seems to represent a world turned upside down. While enemies describe Margaret in disparaging terms, her strength inspires great loyalty among her supporters.

However, when her own son is killed, she responds with tender, motherly outrage: "O Ned, sweet Ned – speak to thy mother, boy. / … No, no, my heart will burst an if I speak; / And I will speak that so my heart may burst…You have no children, butchers; if you had, / The thought of them would have stirred up remorse." (5.5.50, 58–59, 62–63). In her exasperation at her husband's weakness, Margaret bans him from

Revenge in the play

Revenge drives much of the action in this energetic piece – which features no fewer than four battles (Wakefield, Towton, Barnet, and Tewkesbury), more than any other of Shakespeare's plays. Both the Lancastrians and the Yorkists are hungry to wreak vengeance on the other side to right various wrongs that have been committed. Clifford, in particular, is eaten up with the desire to revenge the death of his father. Margaret exults in the murder of Rutland (Richard's son) by Clifford, only to have to suffer in retaliation the murder of her son before her eyes.

Richard's sons, Edward, Gloucester, and Clarence seek to avenge his death, along with the previously loyal Warwick, who after suffering a humiliation at the French court, turns against Henry and joins his enemies.

Even Gloucester's ambitions for the crown appear to be an urge to even the score for the unkind treatment he received as a boy. Near the end of the play, when he kisses King Edward's baby, he whispers the ominous "so Judas kissed his master" (5.7.33), promising more betrayal and vengeance to come.

THIS BRAWL TODAY... SHALL SEND, BETWEEN THE RED ROSE AND THE WHITE, A THOUSAND SOULS TO DEATH AND DEADLY NIGHT

HENRY VI PART 1 (1591)

DRAMATIS PERSONAE

Henry VI King of England.

Duke of Gloucester Henry's uncle and Protector of England.

Duke of Bedford Henry's uncle and Regent of France.

Bishop of Winchester Later Cardinal, Henry's great-uncle.

Duke of Somerset The Duke of Exeter's nephew.

Richard Plantagenet Later Third Duke of York.

Earls of Warwick, Salisbury, and Suffolk

Lord Talbot Commander of English forces in France.

Charles Dauphin of France.

Margaret French noble betrothed to Henry.

Duke of Burgundy Henry's uncle.

Joan la Pucelle (Joan of Arc)

A t the funeral of Henry V, a row breaks out between the young King Henry VI's uncles, Gloucester and Winchester. Messengers arrive from France. Town after town has fallen to the French, and England's hero Talbot has been captured. Outside besieged Orléans, the Dauphin Charles meets the maid Joan la Pucelle, whose visions promise victory for France. Talbot is freed in a prisoner exchange. The French triumph over the English. Joan beats Talbot in a duel but spares his life. Talbot retakes Orléans.

In the garden of the Temple in London's lawyers' quarter, a quarrel between Richard Plantagenet and

As rivalries emerge at the funeral of Henry V, **news comes of English defeats in France**.

Talbot captures Orléans by stealth. The Dauphin Charles blames Joan for her false prophecy.

Henry pleads with his quarrelling uncles Winchester and Gloucester **to make peace**, as their rival factions are causing havoc in London.

The captured **Joan pleads for her life**, saying she should be spared because of her chastity, but **she is burned**. France sends peace overtures to the English.

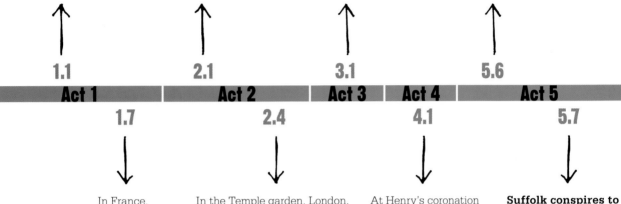

1.1

2.1

3.1

5.6

| Act 1 | Act 2 | Act 3 | Act 4 | Act 5 |

1.7

2.4

4.1

5.7

In France, Lord Talbot is astonished to see his **troops being defeated under the leadership of a woman**, Joan la Pucelle.

In the Temple garden, London, Richard Plantagenet and Suffolk pick roses of a different colour to mark their rivalry, and **the feud between the houses of Lancaster and York begins**.

At Henry's coronation in Paris, he learns of his uncle Burgundy's defection, and **vicious quarrelling breaks out between Lancastrians and Yorkists**.

Suffolk conspires to control Henry by telling him that he should marry Margaret for love.

Somerset ends in them plucking red and white roses to signify their opposing loyalties. Richard's uncle Mortimer tells him how the king's grandfather, Henry IV, deposed the rightful Richard II, and says that Richard has a claim to the throne.

In Parliament, a fight breaks out between the men of Gloucester and Winchester. As King Henry tries to calm them, he agrees to make Richard Duke of York. In France, Joan takes Rouen from the English, but Talbot retakes it. Joan persuades Henry's uncle Burgundy to switch sides. Talbot travels to Paris where Henry is to be crowned. There, Henry learns of Burgundy's treachery. He urges York and Somerset to put aside their quarrel but unwittingly insults York by donning a red rose. To repair the damage, Henry makes York Regent of France and orders Somerset to back him. Meanwhile, outside Bordeaux, Talbot and his son are fatally wounded in a battle; Talbot dies with his son's body in his arms.

Gloucester tells the king that the French Earl of Armagnac wishes to arrange a peace. Henry agrees, and is persuaded to marry Armagnac's daughter to seal the deal. The people of Paris revolt and Charles and Joan march on Paris. Joan conjures spirits to help her cause, but the English triumph and Joan is captured. Suffolk is bewitched by the beauty of Margaret of Anjou, and promises to make her Henry's wife. York condemns Joan to burn as a witch, and rails against the "effeminate" peace Henry is making with France. Suffolk excites Henry with his account of Margaret's beauty and he agrees to marry her. »

IN CONTEXT

THEMES
Battle, kingship, family ties, civil war

SETTING
London, Paris, Orleans, Auvergne, and Angiers

SOURCES
1516 Some scenes were inspired by Robert Fabyan's *New Chronicle of England and France.*

1545 Edward Halle's *Union of the Two Noble and Illustrious Families of Lancaster and York.*

1577 Raphael Holinshed's *Chronicles of England, Scotland, and Ireland.*

LEGACY
1592 The play is a huge success when it is first staged at the Rose Theatre.

1738 The first recorded performance following Shakespeare's death takes place at Covent Garden, London. Several dance sequences are added.

1873 *Henry VI Part 1* is performed in Vienna.

1906 British director Frank Benson stages all three *Henry VI*s without changing any of them, the first time this has been done since the 1590s.

1990 Director Michael Bogdanov releases a film of all three *Henry VI* plays, recorded on consecutive nights at the Grand Theatre, Swansea.

Evidence suggests that *Henry VI Part 1* was written after the second two parts of the *Henry VI* trilogy, and staged, to great acclaim, for the first time in 1592. So it is essentially a prequel, setting the events of the later two plays in context. It is grand in scale, encompassing England and France with sweeping battle scenes and thrilling hand-to-hand duels, while the other two parts are more narrowly focused.

The death of the heroic Henry V leaves English rule in France in chaos, as the new king, Henry VI, still little more than a child, finds himself unable to quell the quarrels at home. At first, the strife is between his uncles Gloucester and Winchester over who should be his protector. But conflict soon erupts between the supporters of the Lancastrian faction led by Somerset and the Yorkists led by Richard Plantagenet (who secretly believes the throne is rightfully his). Each faction chooses a rose for its emblem: white for York; red for Lancaster. The play presents this choice in a scene in the Inner Temple garden in London, in which Richard Plantagenet asks the assembled lords to pluck a rose. The lawyer

After defeating him in hand-to-hand combat, Joan la Pucelle (Katy Stephens) spares the life of Lord Talbot (Keith Bartlett) in a 2006 production at the Courtyard Theatre, London.

picks a white rose, suggesting that he thinks Richard's case is strong in law. Challenged to make his case, Somerset replies that his argument is his sword. The scene is set for the Wars of the Roses.

Against this civil conflict, the maid of Orléans, Joan la Pucelle, known today as Joan of Arc, emerges to lead the French with her divine visions. She is pitted against a worthy English hero in Talbot, who at the end is failed by his quarrelling countrymen.

Dubious authorship
Because of the variable quality of the verse, critics have long questioned the play's authorship. The poet Samuel Taylor Coleridge was certain Shakespeare could not have written it, or at least not all of it. Many critics now think it was a collaborative work with writers such as Thomas Nashe, who perhaps wrote Act 1. Computer

Break thou in pieces, and consume to ashes, Thou foul accursèd minister of hell.
Richard, Duke of York
Act 5, Scene 6

analysis of language patterns suggest that, while Shakespeare probably wrote *Henry VI Part 2* and most of *Part 3*, he was the author of only some of *Part 1* – the Temple garden scene, and the scene in Act 4 between Talbot and his son.

Early commentators, such as the English playwright Ben Jonson, criticized *Henry VI Part 1* for its crowd-pleasing battle scenes. Jonson insisted that, in a proper literary play, such battles would have been created in the imagination with skilful use of words, not crude stage techniques. However, over the last half century, critics have rediscovered in the play some of the excitement and political sharpness that would have engaged audiences in 1592.

Family crisis

At the heart of the play lies the importance of family as the glue that binds society together. After all, claims to be the rightful king – claims that foment the terrible strife to come between the Yorkists and Lancastrians – hinge on proper family relationships. But it goes further than that. Familial bonds, such as the deep bond between Talbot and his son, are fundamental – and when these are lost, society is set adrift. Legitimacy is crucial. Gloucester emphasizes that Winchester is the "bastard of my grandfather", while Talbot inveighs against the "bastard Orléans" who killed his trueborn son. The play omits Talbot's real-life illegitimate son, Henry, who also died in the same battle. Political crisis emerges from a crisis in the family. Some critics argue that this is why the women in *Henry VI* are so negatively portrayed – Joan la Pucelle, Margaret, and the Countess of Auvergne are all presented as dangerous women

> How say you, madam? Are you now persuaded That Talbot is but a shadow of himself?
> **Talbot**
> Act 2, Scene 3

who cause chaos by their effect on men and on proper relationships. In the first four acts, Joan is mostly portrayed as a holy visionary, but in Act 5, she morphs into the witch, conjuring up demons. She engages with York to beg for her life with hysterical ferocity and wild curses (understandable, perhaps, when she is about to be burned alive).

Some directors have noticed that the very moment one *femme fatale*, Joan, leaves the centre of the action, another, Margaret of Anjou,

makes her entrance. When the *Henry VI* plays are performed together, the same actress sometimes plays both Joan and Margaret to underscore the point that they are part of the same danger, although Margaret, Henry's future queen, is very different. While Joan dresses as a man to win her battles, Margaret remains womanly on the outside and her power comes from her sexual allure. Suffolk, the earl who enticed Henry with Margaret's charms, closes the play with the promise that: "Margaret shall now be queen and rule the King; / But I will rule both her, the King, and realm" (5.7.107–108).

But Suffolk is deluded. He likens himself to Paris, who elopes with the beautiful Helen to Troy. But it is a telling choice. Like Helen, Margaret will only bring strife, and Suffolk is banished and gruesomely beheaded. ∎

An illustration from a 15th-century French manuscript shows Joan of Arc leading the siege of Paris in 1429. It suited the play's anti-French politics to portray Joan as a demon-invoking witch.

WHY, THERE THEY ARE, BOTH BAKED IN THIS PIE

TITUS ANDRONICUS (1591–1592)

DRAMATIS PERSONAE

Titus Andronicus
Celebrated military hero
of Rome, conqueror of the
Goths, father of 25 sons
and one daughter.

Tamora Queen of the Goths,
later married to Saturninus;
mother of Alarbus, Chiron,
and Demetrius.

Saturninus Emperor of Rome
and husband of Tamora.

Aaron A Moor in Tamora's
service; also Tamora's lover
and a self-professed villain.

Demetrius and Chiron
Malevolent sons of Tamora.

Lavinia Titus's only daughter,
betrothed to Bassianus.

Bassianus Saturninus's
younger brother and the
husband of Lavinia.

Marcus Andronicus
Titus's brother.

Lucius One of Titus's sons,
later banished from Rome.

Martius and Quintus
Titus's sons, later framed
for Bassianus's murder.

Mutius One of Titus's sons,
accidentally killed by Titus.

Young Lucius Lucius's son.

Publius Son of
Marcus Andronicus.

**Sempronius, Caius, and
Valentine** Relatives of the
Andronicus family.

Aemilius A Roman noble,
who acts as a herald and
a messenger.

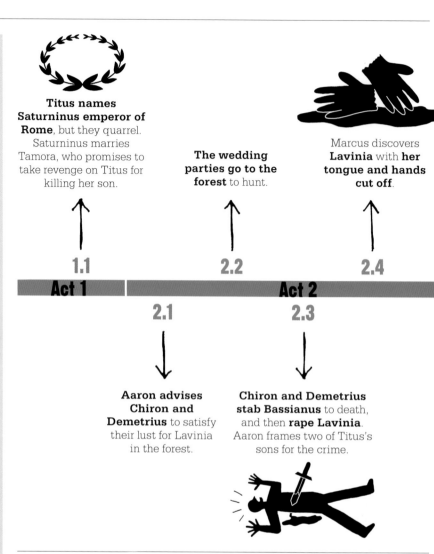

**Titus names
Saturninus emperor of
Rome**, but they quarrel.
Saturninus marries
Tamora, who promises to
take revenge on Titus for
killing her son.

1.1

**The wedding
parties go to the
forest** to hunt.

2.2

Marcus discovers
Lavinia with **her
tongue and hands
cut off**.

2.4

Act 1

Act 2

2.1

Aaron advises
**Chiron and
Demetrius** to satisfy
their lust for Lavinia
in the forest.

2.3

**Chiron and Demetrius
stab Bassianus** to death,
and then **rape Lavinia**.
Aaron frames two of Titus's
sons for the crime.

Saturninus and Bassianus
quarrel over who should
become Emperor of Rome.
Marcus tells them that the hero,
Titus Andronicus, is also a
candidate, but Titus uses his
influence with the people to name
Saturninus emperor. Saturninus
offers to marry Titus's daughter
Lavinia as a reward, but Bassianus
insists that he is betrothed to her.
Saturninus is angry and decides to
marry Tamora instead. She makes
peace between the new emperor
and Titus, but secretly vows to take
revenge upon the whole family.

The weddings of Saturninus and
Tamora and Lavinia and Bassianus
are celebrated with a hunt. Aaron
finds Chiron and Demetrius
arguing over their love for Lavinia,
and tells them to use the occasion
of the hunt to rape Lavinia and
murder Bassianus. He plots to pin
the crime on Titus's sons, Martius
and Quintus. Chiron and Demetrius
kill Bassianus and throw his body
into a pit. They rape Lavinia. Aaron
leads Martius and Quintus to the
pit, into which they fall. Saturninus
discovers his brother's body and
has Quintus and Martius arrested.

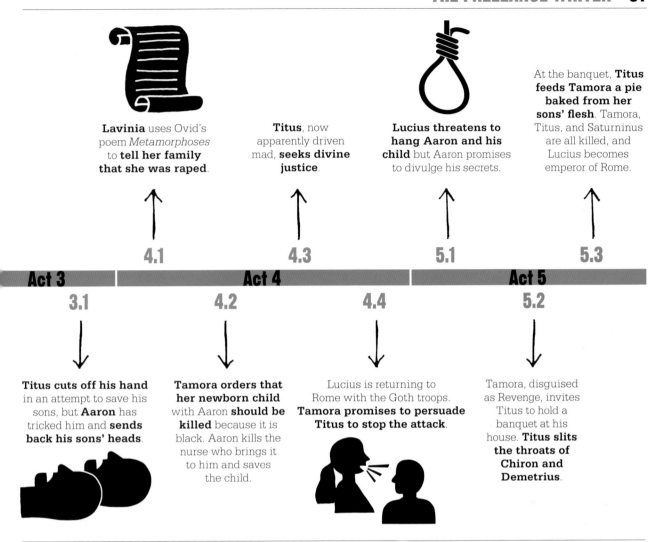

Lavinia uses Ovid's poem *Metamorphoses* to **tell her family that she was raped**.

Titus, now apparently driven mad, **seeks divine justice**.

Lucius threatens to hang Aaron and his child but Aaron promises to divulge his secrets.

At the banquet, **Titus feeds Tamora a pie baked from her sons' flesh**. Tamora, Titus, and Saturninus are all killed, and Lucius becomes emperor of Rome.

4.1

4.3

5.1

5.3

Act 3   Act 4   Act 5

3.1

4.2

4.4

5.2

Titus cuts off his hand in an attempt to save his sons, but **Aaron** has tricked him and **sends back his sons' heads**.

Tamora orders that her newborn child with Aaron **should be killed** because it is black. Aaron kills the nurse who brings it to him and saves the child.

Lucius is returning to Rome with the Goth troops. **Tamora promises to persuade Titus to stop the attack**.

Tamora, disguised as Revenge, invites Titus to hold a banquet at his house. **Titus slits the throats of Chiron and Demetrius**.

Titus's son Lucius reveals that he has been banished, and sees the mutilated Lavinia. Aaron tells Titus that if he, Marcus, or Lucius will cut off his hand and send it to the emperor, his sons' lives will be spared. Titus sends his own hand, which is returned to him, with the heads of Martius and Quintus.

Lavinia writes the names of her attackers in the sand. Marcus, Titus, Young Lucius, and Lavinia swear an oath of vengeance.

The Nurse brings to Aaron an infant – his child with Tamora – and tells him that because the child is black, Tamora wishes it killed. Aaron plots to swap it for a white infant, and to have the latter's parents bring up his child.

When news arrives that Lucius is returning with Goth troops, Tamora promises to persuade Titus to call off the attack. In disguise as Revenge, with Demetrius and Chiron as Murder and Rape, she visits Titus whom she thinks does not recognize them. She asks him to invite Lucius to a banquet, where she will bring Saturninus and the Empress. Tamora leaves her sons with Titus, who kills them.

Titus, dressed as a cook, presides over the banquet at his house. He kills Lavinia in front of his guests, saying that she had been raped by Chiron and Demetrius, both of whom have been baked in the pie the guests have been eating. He stabs Tamora, and Saturninus kills Titus. Lucius then kills Saturninus. Marcus and Lucius tell the Roman people what has happened and Lucius is named emperor. Aaron is sentenced to death. Saturninus, Titus, and Lavinia are interred in their family tombs, but Tamora is denied any funeral rites. »

IN CONTEXT

THEMES
Revenge, fatherhood, motherhood, lust, madness

SETTING
Late Imperial Rome

SOURCES
No direct sources are known, but Shakespeare may have drawn on the following:
8 CE Ovid's *Metamorphoses*. A copy of the poem is used on stage in the play.

1st century CE *Thyestes*, a gory revenge story by Roman playwright Seneca.

13th century *Gesta Romanorum*, an anonymous collection of fictionalized Roman legends and myths.

LEGACY
1594 The first recorded performance is in January, at the Rose Theatre, London. The play appears in print in February of that year.

1850s American actor Ira Aldridge plays Aaron in a heavily adapted version. It is the only 19th-century revival.

1923 The unexpurgated version of the play is staged at the Old Vic, London, for the first time in 250 years.

1987 Deborah Warner's uncut production for the RSC, with Brian Cox as Titus, brings out the full horror of the play.

1999 American director Julie Taymor casts Anthony Hopkins as Titus in a film adaptation of the play.

Titus Andronicus is perhaps best known for its extreme violence. It features at least five stabbings, two throat slittings, and one hand amputation – and this is only the violence that happens onstage. It does not include the rape and mutilation of Lavinia.

The play was probably written in collaboration with George Peele, who is thought to be responsible mainly for the first act. It was undoubtedly influenced by theatrical fashion, and may have recalled Peele's *The Battle of Alcazar* (*c.*1591), in which severed heads appear in a banquet, or the hand-chopping scene in *Selimus* (*c.*1592), by Robert Greene and Thomas Lodge. The play's violence has been called gratuitous – to the extent that critics used to deny that Shakespeare could have written it. However, the violence has deeper political and cultural meanings.

Demetrius and Chiron are soon to be baked into pie in this 2006 production of *Titus Andronicus* at the Globe Theatre, London, with Douglas Hodge in the lead role.

Escalating violence

Perhaps most horrifying is the moment when Tamora realizes that she has consumed the flesh of her own children, but cannibalism is an idea that resonates throughout the play. One of the challenges of revenge tragedy is how to exceed the initial crime. Titus's main act of revenge against Tamora for destroying his family will be murder. Why should he also require that she devour her sons?

One explanation is his need to punish her sexual appetite by turning it into a kind of monstrous feeding, "bid[ding] that strumpet, your unhallowed dam, / Like to the earth swallow her own increase" (5.2.190–191). But the play is also pervaded by a kind of maternal dread, where the mother is an all-consuming figure, against whom the male child must struggle to define himself. This fear emerges in some unlikely places. For example, the pit into which Martius and Quintus fall (with dead Bassianus at the bottom) is hailed: "What subtle hole is this, / Whose mouth is covered with rude-growing briers / Upon whose

> A nobler man, a braver warrior,
> Lives not this day within
> the city walls.
> **Marcus Andronicus**
> **Act 1, Scene 1**

leaves are drops of new-shed blood / …A very fatal place it seems to me" (2.3.198–200, 202). In this way, the play anticipates the literal feeding that the female mouth will perform at the end.

Roman values

A mother figure is absent among the Andronici clan. The mother of Titus's 26 children is dead, and there is no mention of a wife for Lucius. Nevertheless, disturbing parallels emerge between father and mother, Roman and Goth, which complicate the roles of both Titus and Tamora. Titus has buried 20 sons before the play begins, all killed in wars, and his first action in the play is to place a coffin in the family tomb. In the original staging, the trapdoor would probably have been used to signify the tomb, and also the pit in Act 2 – thereby creating a sinister likeness between these spaces. At the start of the play we discover that Titus is "surnamèd *Pius*" (1.1.23). This was a title associated with Aeneas, one of the founders of Rome. It signified the best Roman values of honour, piety, and familial loyalty.

By contrast, Tamora is described as all that is un-Roman: promiscuous, treacherous, and bestial. And yet,

Titus himself shapes what Tamora becomes by making her first-born son, Alarbus, a sacrifice. Tamora's accusation, "O cruel, irreligious piety!" (1.1.130), is hard to argue with. Titus and Tamora are both driven to violence through their sense of shame: Titus kills his son, Mutius, in a rage at being defied in front of the Emperor; Tamora vows revenge against Andronicus for making a queen kneel to him. Both characters represent a challenge to the core Roman values Titus is supposed to embody, implying that there are dangerous tensions between them, not least between personal honour and family loyalty.

Rome itself fulfils its reputation for ingratitude when it banishes one of Titus's sons and condemns two others to death, ignoring his pleas for mercy. By making Tamora devour her sons, Titus could be seen as forcing her to act like the ungrateful city. But although Tamora's body may be cast beyond the walls at the end, the anxieties and tensions she represents will remain at the very heart of Rome. ∎

> Hark, villains, I will grind
> your bones to dust,
> And with your blood and
> it I'll make a paste,
> And of the paste a coffin
> I will rear,
> And make two pasties of
> your shameful heads,
> **Titus Andronicus**
> **Act 5, Scene 2**

Aaron

Aaron is an early villain in Shakespeare, the forefather of Don John in *Much Ado About Nothing* (pp.154–61), and Iago in *Othello* (pp.240–49).

The monstrous glee he shows at his own villainy links him to the comic Vice of the medieval morality play, but he has become a much more troubling figure in modern times because of the connection that he makes between his evil and his ethnicity. In particular, his wish to "have his soul black like his face" (3.1.204) might seem to justify long-held associations of blackness with devil-worship, treachery, and lust. The ease with which Aaron assimilates himself into Rome suggests that he can convincingly assume Roman values – he can read Latin texts better than Chiron and Demetrius, and he is more paternal than Titus. But he remains a difficult figure for modern productions. Julie Taymor's 1999 film *Titus* was accused by critics of simply updating its racial stereotypes by identifying Aaron with the contemporary "supercool hipster", "sexual athlete", and "nihilistic gangster".

MADE GLORIOUS SUMMER BY THIS SON OF YORK

RICHARD III (1592)

DRAMATIS PERSONAE

Richard, Duke of Gloucester Later Richard III.

King Edward IV and George, Duke of Clarence Richard's brothers.

Duchess of York Their mother.

Queen Elizabeth Wife of Edward IV and mother of Edward, Prince of Wales, Richard, Duke of York, and Princess Elizabeth.

Edward, Prince of Wales and Richard, Duke of York Young sons of Edward IV and Queen Elizabeth.

Duke of Buckingham Trusted confidant who assists Richard to the throne.

Lord Hastings Lord Chamberlain to Edward IV.

Lord Stanley Earl of Derby and stepfather to Richmond.

Rivers, Grey, and Dorset Queen Elizabeth's brother, and her sons by her first marriage.

Queen Margaret Widow of Henry VI, the last of the Lancastrians, who prophesies against the House of York.

Lady Anne Widow of Henry VI's son, Edward.

Henry, Earl of Richmond Stepson to Stanley, and later Henry VII.

Tyrrel An assassin employed by Richard.

Richard describes the transition from war-torn past to Edward's present sunny reign, and **confides to us his destructive plans**.

1.1

At court, **Richard angers Queen Elizabeth** and her family by accusing them of ambitious plotting.

1.3

Although **Clarence** believes that his brother Richard loves him, he **is murdered in prison** by Richard's assassins.

1.4

Act 1

1.2

1.3

Richard woos Lady Anne across the coffin of her father-in-law, Henry VI.

Old **Queen Margaret curses the whole court**, predicting that Richard will bring each of them down.

The long and bloody civil war between the houses of York and Lancaster has ended with the murder, in prison, of the Lancastrian King Henry VI. Edward IV of York now reigns, and England can rejoice in peace. This is what Edward's brother Richard tells us at the opening of the play. He then invites us to watch as, with devious skill, he takes the throne for himself.

Initially, we are intrigued by Richard's daring. He woos and wins Lady Anne as she escorts the funeral cortège of her father-in-law, Henry VI. Then Richard plots against family and friends. He engineers the imprisonment and death of his brother Clarence, news of which sends his eldest brother, King Edward IV, to an early grave.

Helped by the Duke of Buckingham, Richard sends Edward's sons – the young Edward V and Richard, Duke of York – to the Tower of London. When their mother's family objects, he has her male relatives executed. All of this is predicted by Henry VI's widow, old Queen Margaret

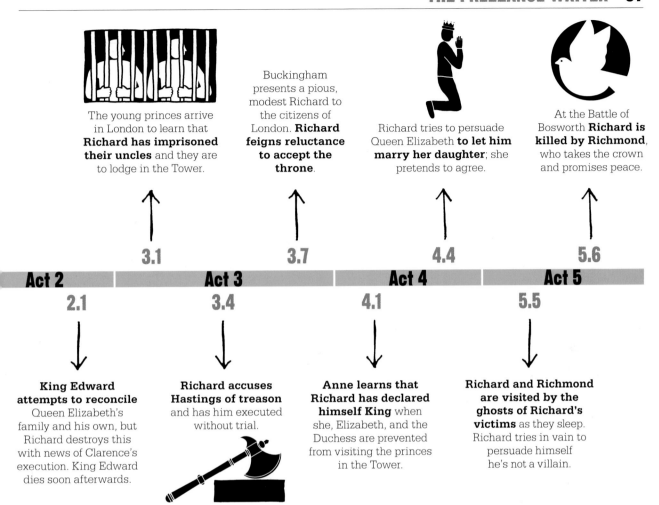

The young princes arrive in London to learn that **Richard has imprisoned their uncles** and they are to lodge in the Tower.

Buckingham presents a pious, modest Richard to the citizens of London. **Richard feigns reluctance to accept the throne**.

Richard tries to persuade Queen Elizabeth **to let him marry her daughter**; she pretends to agree.

At the Battle of Bosworth **Richard is killed by Richmond**, who takes the crown and promises peace.

3.1　　**3.7**　　**4.4**　　**5.6**

Act 2　　**Act 3**　　**Act 4**　　**Act 5**

2.1　　**3.4**　　**4.1**　　**5.5**

King Edward attempts to reconcile Queen Elizabeth's family and his own, but Richard destroys this with news of Clarence's execution. King Edward dies soon afterwards.

Richard accuses Hastings of treason and has him executed without trial.

Anne learns that Richard has declared himself King when she, Elizabeth, and the Duchess are prevented from visiting the princes in the Tower.

Richard and Richmond are visited by the ghosts of Richard's victims as they sleep. Richard tries in vain to persuade himself he's not a villain.

who, filled with grief, haunts the palace and in vain warns everyone against Richard.

Richard now seeks the support of London's citizens in making himself king. Their silence shows public unease at Richard's ambition but Buckingham stage-manages this into approval and Richard takes the crown. Denied access to her sons, Queen Elizabeth fears the worst. Once he's on the throne, Richard tells Buckingham he wants his nephews dead. When Buckingham hesitates, Richard orders Tyrrel to kill them.

Clouds gather for Richard as his surviving friends and enemies join forces. Buckingham deserts him to assist an invasion force from France led by the Earl of Richmond. As Richard moves from London to challenge Richmond, his progress is interrupted by his mother, the Duchess of York, and Queen Elizabeth who condemn him. He tries to turn this to his advantage by persuading the Queen to let him marry Princess Elizabeth, now that Anne, too, is dead. Their encounter is a powerful one and Richard believes he has won. But the

Queen won't change sides. On the eve of the Battle of Bosworth, both Richard and Richmond dream of the ghosts of Richard's victims, who promise Richmond fortune and curse Richard as a traitor, murderer, and villain. Richard wakes sweating and tries to dismiss their words. But the voice of his conscience declares him guilty. When they meet in battle Richmond kills the unhorsed Richard. Finally, Richmond promises that he and Elizabeth will bring England the peace and prosperity that Richard described at the start. »

IN CONTEXT

THEMES
Murderous villainy, ambition, loss, retribution

SETTING
15th-century London and Leicestershire

SOURCES
1st century The tragedies of Roman playwright Seneca.

14th–15th centuries The figure of Vice in morality plays; the cyclical pattern and biblical parallels of the mystery plays.

c.1520 Thomas More's *History of King Richard III*.

LEGACY
1590s Date of the first performance is unknown, but five reprints of the text by 1623 suggest the play was popular.

1700 Colley Cibber's adaptation dominates the stage until the late 1800s.

1955 Laurence Olivier's Old Vic production is, for some, the definitive *Richard III*.

1963–64 Peter Hall and John Barton's RSC adaptation makes Richard, portrayed by a boyish Ian Holm, the dysfunctional product of a bloody feud.

1985 Antony Sher's spider-like Richard uses his crutches to dominate this RSC production.

1991 Richard Eyre's National Theatre production set the play in 1930s England where a fascist Richard, played by Ian McKellen, is a vengeful, mutilated war veteran.

ichard's opening speech sets the stage by moving us from the wintry horrors of the battlefield to the summer holiday that peace has brought, "Now is the winter of our discontent / Made glorious summer by this son of York" (1.1.1–2). Only Richard's discontent remains. Mocking the idle courtly life in a tone that is increasingly ironic, he resolves to let his dissatisfaction darken Edward IV's sun-filled reign.

Politics and the past

Richard is a more subtle operator in this fourth play of Shakespeare's Henry VI tetralogy than he was in part 3. Where once he would have used violence, now he manipulates court in-fighting and the self-interest of ambitious men. Shakespeare gives him the cunning of a Machiavel, and reinforces this by moving most of the bloodletting off-stage – although not every modern director keeps it there.

Queen Elizabeth was a widow who married Edward IV after refusing to be his mistress, much to his family's disgust. Richard plays on class consciousness, setting up her brother and two young sons by her former marriage as social

I am determinèd to
prove a villain
And hate the idle pleasures
of these days.
Richard
Act 1, Scene 1

Are you drawn forth among
a world of men
To slay the innocent?
Clarence
Act 1, Scene 4

climbers – "silken, sly, insinuating jacks" (1.3.53). He then blames them for his plots – the imprisonment of his brother Clarence and Lord Hastings – and accuses them of having ambitious designs on the new young king. This allows him to play the kindly uncle and lodge the two boys in the Tower of London. Shortly afterwards he has Rivers, Dorset, and Gray executed.

Such a swift rise to power relies on the collusion of others. Buckingham, Catesby, Hastings, the Bishop of Ely, even Richmond's stepfather, Stanley, may not be duped by Richard but they all stay silent about what they know.

Settling history's account

To a degree, Richard's plotting brings down those figures who were disloyal to the House of York during the civil war. Most of this is predicted by old Queen Margaret, the widow of Henry VI, who appears anachronistically at court to call down vengeance on those who for so long set brother against brother. She conveniently forgets her own role in the fighting, as Richard observes, but she sets out a pattern of retributive vengeance that echoes history's script; one that we watch Richard go on to fulfil.

Apart from Margaret, no one at court speaks out against Richard's acts. But in the London streets the citizens do. The first half of the play is confined to a London that Richard clearly regards as his domain. But the commoners represent a wider audience whose judgement Richard's clever performance can't control. Another part of this audience comprises the women – Anne, Queen Margaret, the Duchess of York, and Queen Elizabeth. They watch and remember. As Richard's mother points out, women are often the sole surviving keepers of accounts.

The landscape widens
Dreams, nightmares, curses, prophecies, and premonitions present a metaphysical dynamic in the play beyond Richard's control. As soon as he murders the innocent princes in the Tower his fortunes begin to fail. He becomes prey to doubts and fears, and Anne reveals that he's long had "timorous dreams" (4.1.84). With his first careful words as king he tries to share responsibility for the coup with Buckingham: "Thus high by thy advice / And thy assistance is King Richard seated" (4.2.4–5). But Buckingham grows suspicious

Would you enforce me to a world of cares? Call them again. I am not made of stone…
Richard
Act 3, Scene 7

English actor Laurence Olivier played Richard as an alluring, Satanic jester in the 1955 film adaptation. He was often shot in close-up, malevolently confiding to camera.

and this puts their double-act under strain. Just when Richard needs help from his self-interested friends, confined as he now is at the centre of the action, he finds himself increasingly isolated and dependent on strangers such as Tyrrel to complete his plots.

Buckingham's departure from the court heralds the waning of Richard's sole command of the action. It also prompts Richmond's arrival on the scene. We learn of his planned invasion from France, secretly supported by Lord Stanley and Queen Elizabeth. Now the action of the play opens up and moves from London's square mile to rural Leicestershire, the heart of England, and to Bosworth Field. »

As the seasons turn from Richard's busy sunshine to his autumnal fall, Margaret returns. In a counterpart to Richard's prologue she ushers in the inevitable conclusion: "So now prosperity begins to mellow / And drop into the rotten mouth of death" (4.4.1–2).

The shape of villainy

Richard's physical shape is a gift to any dramatist and Shakespeare makes much of it. Many in the audience would have enjoyed the hugely successful Henry VI plays and also known the crookback figure as he is portrayed in Tudor history – a monstrous creature of bloody civil war and a future demon king.

Shakespeare capitalizes on Richard's physical non-conformity by making it his motivating force. In the preceding play, he severs all links to family and faction and sets himself against the principle of blood bond that took York and Lancaster to war. Given his deformity he feels that family bonds and natural inheritance have let him down. He decides, therefore, to be self-sufficient – "I am myself alone" – and, like an actor, turn his shape to advantage by playing his way to the throne. This is the performance he introduces us to at the opening of the play. There he lets us in on his plots and simplifies history into fiction with its heroes, lovers, and villains.

The disruptive force of Richard's villainous nonconformity is clear in his first five appearances in the play. Upsetting the smooth running of Edward IV's new state, he interrupts a series of courtly ceremonies and meetings and redirects them all. Some productions show him appearing through a different entrance from that used by the other characters as if, like the morality play figure Vice, he comes to create chaos from quite another place.

Wit and wordplay

Richard shows us he's the master of improvised duplicity, especially with language, and is equally at home in street speech and witty repartee. His versatility takes him from mock anger to mock modesty. The wit and smooth rhetoric that let him catch his opponents off-guard often take us in the same way.

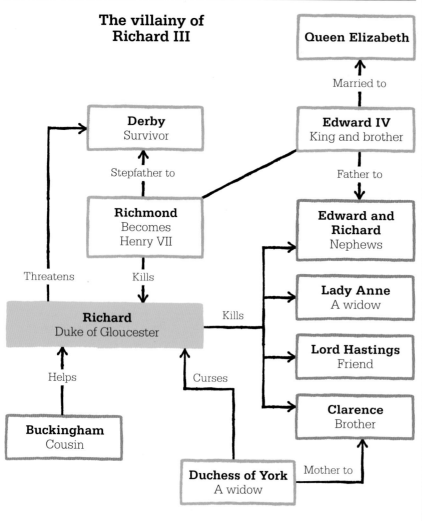

The villainy of Richard III

- Queen Elizabeth
- Derby — Survivor
- Edward IV — King and brother
- Richmond — Becomes Henry VII
- Edward and Richard — Nephews
- Richard — Duke of Gloucester
- Lady Anne — A widow
- Lord Hastings — Friend
- Buckingham — Cousin
- Clarence — Brother
- Duchess of York — A widow

Married to · Stepfather to · Father to · Threatens · Kills · Helps · Curses · Kills · Mother to

Comes back as a ghost

If something thou wouldst swear to be believed, Swear then by something that thou hast not wronged.
Queen Elizabeth
Act 4, Scene 4

American actor Kevin Spacey played Richard as a self-hating, power-crazed despot, who revolted the play's women, in Sam Mendes's acclaimed 2011 production at the Old Vic, London.

His verbal skills are to the fore when he persuades Lady Anne to be his wife (1.2), and Queen Elizabeth to let him marry her daughter (4.4). Strategically placed at each end of the play, these parallel scenes chart the rise and fall of Richard's fortunes. He approaches Queen Elizabeth with the same bravado but she turns his tactics back on him. This time the woman leads the debate. Her put-downs are delivered with such feeling that they stifle Richard's efforts to defend his evil actions.

At the end, Richard stops the performance and no longer draws us into his confidence. When he tries not to despair on the night before Bosworth his soliloquy addresses a fresh audience: his conscience. The debate is a judicial examination, devoid of witty self-deceptions, with Richard both the prosecution and defence. Finally his conscience tells him that he is the villain he promised to be: "My conscience hath a thousand several tongues... / And every tale condemns me for a villain" (5.5.147, 149).

From sun to shade

Now we watch as Richard is disturbed by prophesies and curses. He can't sleep before his final battle and the sun fails to shine the day he dies. Ultimately he's defeated both by history in the form of Richmond, and by himself – "Myself, myself confound" (4.4.330). He admits that he has no pity even for himself. In performance, it's the strength of Richard's prowess in the battle that often determines our feelings about him at the end. Perhaps his cry "A horse! A horse! My kingdom for a horse!" (5.7.7) reminds us that he was always happiest in a fight. Richmond ends the play, but the final focus rests also on Richard. Behind Richmond's perfect picture of "smiling plenty, and fair prosperous days" (5.7.34) there lingers a shadow of Richard's sun-filled opening words. ■

Tudor propaganda?

John Rous, a historian writing during the reign of Richard III, described his king as a "good lord" with a "great heart" who enacted just laws. But by the reign of the first Tudor king, Henry VII, Rous had reversed his opinion. Richard, he wrote, was a freak: stunted and physically weak, he was responsible for killing Henry VI and for poisoning his own wife. Other historians, among them Sir Thomas More, joined in the vilification of Richard, citing his "crook-backed" deformity as evidence of inward corruption. It may be that More and others were seeking to legitimize Tudor rule with anti-Yorkist propaganda. But it is from their accounts that Shakespeare drew his material. More described Richard as being devious and flattering while he plotted, but also clever and courageous. Shakespeare retained all these features, and gave the king added depth by encumbering him with a formidable conscience. The character is so enduring that the historical Richard has been obliterated. Indeed, there is no surviving account by anyone who knew him in person.

TO DIE

IS ALL AS COMMON AS

TO LIVE

EDWARD III (1592–1593)

DRAMATIS PERSONAE

Edward III King of England.

Queen Philippa Wife of Edward III.

Edward, the Black Prince Son of Edward III and Queen Philippa.

Earl of Salisbury

Countess of Salisbury Salisbury's wife.

Earl of Warwick The Countess's father.

Sir William de Montague Salisbury's nephew.

Earl of Derby

Sir James Audley

Henry, Lord Percy

John Copland Esquire, later Sir John Copland.

Lodowick King Edward's secretary.

Robert, Comte d'Artois

Jean, Comte de Montfort, later Duc de Bretagne

Gobin de Grâce A French prisoner.

John II de Valois King of France (a conflation of the historic Philip VI with John II).

Prince Charles King John's eldest son, the Dauphin.

Duc de Lorraine

Prince Philippe King John's youngest son.

Villiers Norman lord sent as an envoy by Salisbury to the Dauphin.

Edward III rebuffs French demands for allegiance and **announces his intention to claim France** as his own.

As the English navy approaches, **the French King John boasts** of his strength.

King Edward and King John face off before the Battle of Crécy.

↑ **1**

↑ **4**

↑ **6**

Scenes 1–4

Scenes 5–6

↓ **2**

↓ **5**

After relieving the Scottish siege of Roxburgh Castle, **King Edward tries in vain to seduce the Countess of Salisbury**, who is also desired by the King of Scotland.

In a terrible sea battle at Sluys, **the French navy is routed**.

At the English court, King Edward III is discussing his claim to the French crown with the Comte d'Artois, who has joined the English side. When the Duc de Lorraine arrives from France to insist Edward swear allegiance to the French King John, Edward declares war. Meanwhile, the King of Scotland besieges the Countess of Salisbury in Roxburgh Castle. King Edward sends his son Prince Edward to France, and heads to Roxburgh himself. Enticed by the Countess's beauty, King Edward decides to stay.

As the king grows infatuated with the Countess, he asks his secretary Lodowick to write love letters to her. The king pressures her to yield to his desires, even though they are both married. She refuses, so he compels her father Warwick to intervene. Unable to deny the king, Warwick urges his daughter to comply. There is a distraction as young Prince Edward announces his readiness to lead the army for France, but the king soon resumes his amatory pursuit. The Countess reminds him that they are both married so the king promises to

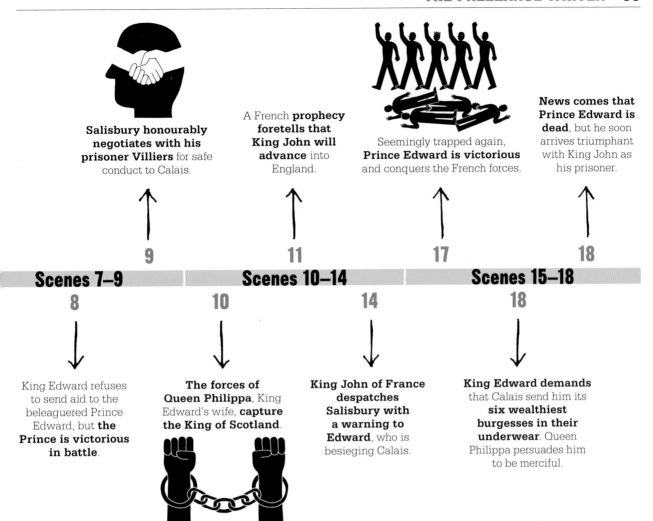

Salisbury honourably negotiates with his prisoner Villiers for safe conduct to Calais.

A French **prophecy foretells that King John will advance** into England.

Seemingly trapped again, **Prince Edward is victorious** and conquers the French forces.

News comes that Prince Edward is dead, but he soon arrives triumphant with King John as his prisoner.

9

11

17

18

Scenes 7–9

Scenes 10–14

Scenes 15–18

8

10

14

18

King Edward refuses to send aid to the beleaguered Prince Edward, but **the Prince is victorious in battle**.

The forces of Queen Philippa, King Edward's wife, **capture the King of Scotland**.

King John of France despatches Salisbury with a warning to Edward, who is besieging Calais.

King Edward demands that Calais send him its **six wealthiest burgesses in their underwear**. Queen Philippa persuades him to be merciful.

kill both their spouses. The Countess is horrified; the king finally sees sense and apologizes.

Off Sluys on the Belgian coast, the English rout the French navy, Prince Edward triumphs on land, and the French king, encamped at Crécy, tries to buy him off. When Prince Edward demands the crown instead, battle ensues. News reaches the king that his son is in danger. He refuses to send help, insisting that this is his son's chance to prove himself. Prince Edward returns triumphant and is knighted by the king. The king

besieges Calais while the Prince pursues King John. In Brittany, the Countess of Salisbury's husband offers the French prisoner Villiers freedom in exchange for a safe passage to Calais. A captain of Calais offers to surrender the town to the king, but the king insists he will only accept the surrender if six wealthy citizens are sent to him.

A prophecy that says John will appear in England seems favourable to the French. Faced with a large French army, Prince Edward turns down a French offer of mercy. Bad omens appear in the

sky and the French panic. The captured Salisbury is spared on the intervention of Villiers. Prince Edward is victorious and captures King John.

The six wealthy men of Calais are brought to the king. The queen urges mercy and he spares their lives. Salisbury arrives with the news that Prince Edward has been killed at Crécy. The king comforts the distraught queen, but suddenly, Prince Edward arrives, with King John as his prisoner. The excited Prince Edward promises more foreign adventures. »

IN CONTEXT

THEMES
Honour, kingship, valour, patriotism, brutality of war

SETTING
The royal court, London; Roxburgh Castle, Scottish borders; Flanders; Crécy, Poitiers, and Calais, France

SOURCES
1377 Jean Froissart's *Chronicles,* a French source for the early battles of the Hundred Years War.

1575 *The Palace of Pleasure,* by William Painter, features a story entitled "The Countesse of Salesberrie", on which the wooing scene is based.

1587 Raphael Holinshed's *Chronicles* is a source for the battles (although for dramatic reasons they have been compressed in time).

LEGACY
Early 1590s Date and place of first performance is not known.

1596 The play is published anonymously in London.

1623 The play is omitted from the First Folio, possibly because of political objections to its portrayal of the Scots.

1911 The Elizabethan Stage Society performs one scene at the Little Theatre, London.

2001 The Pacific Repertory Theatre performs the play at the Carmel Shakespeare Festival in California, US.

2002 The RSC performs the full play, to mixed reviews.

Edward III is the story of one of England's most formidable warrior kings, who ruled the country for half a century until his death in 1377.

The play was written in the early 1590s, around the same time as the *Henry VI* plays, but only in the last few decades has it been accepted among Shakespeare's works. Most editors now agree that Shakespeare did at least have a hand in some of the play but they generally believe that he was responsible for at most a few scenes, including Scenes 2 and 3, between Edward and the Countess of Salisbury, and Scene 12, in which Edward the Black Prince ruminates on death. Performances have been so few that, when the RSC staged it in 2002, they described it, rather inaccurately, as a "new" play by Shakespeare.

The story covers Edward III's defence of the kingdom against the Scottish King David II, and his wars in France, including the historical rout of the French navy at Sluys (1340), his victory over superior French forces at Crécy (1346), and finally the battle of Poitiers (1356) at which his young son, Edward,

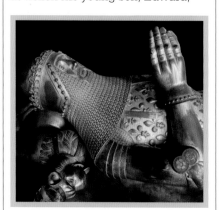

In the play, the Black Prince is a gung-ho adventurer, a portrayal that is probably close to the historical truth. His tomb in Canterbury Cathedral shows him resplendent in armour.

> Tell him the crown that he usurps is mine, And where he sets his foot he ought to kneel.
> **King Edward**
> Scene 1

the Black Prince, proved himself a hero. However, the portrait of Edward III presented in this play is very different from that of Shakespeare's other great warrior king, Henry V. While Henry V emerges as a dynamic young leader, inspiring his troops to victory with stirring speeches, Edward is anything but inspiring. No sooner has he, like Henry, sent the French ambassador packing with a declaration of war than we see him in Scotland in a far from heroic light.

Rough wooing
Arriving to lift the Scottish siege of Roxburgh Castle, Edward is entranced by the beautiful Countess of Salisbury, whose husband is fighting in France. He then embarks on a siege of his own to conquer her, and his tactics are not honourable. After his love letters, penned by his secretary Lodowick, are rejected, he resorts to power games, commanding her father to order her to submit to his desire. The strong-willed countess refuses, and desperately tells Edward that their spouses stand between them. Astoundingly, Edward offers to kill both of them,

saying, as if he is judge on their lives: "Thy beauty makes them guilty of their death" (3.157). The Countess is mortified, exclaiming: "O, perjured beauty! More corrupted judge!" (3.160). She tells him that there is a higher court, above the king – "the great star chamber o'er our heads" (3.161) – that will judge such a crime.

After this disturbing but memorable interlude, the countess is all but forgotten, and the play settles into a far more conventional to-and-fro of battles. However, the countess's absent husband, Salisbury, becomes a key focus for the sense of justice that runs through the play, along with his French counterpart, Villiers. Against the run of events, they both insist on behaving honourably.

Unsentimental leader

It is surprising just how negative a portrait this is of one of England's most dynamic monarchs, a king whose military victories turned England into a major power. The reason may have been due to contemporary Tudor politics. Edward III was a Plantagenet king, whose line ultimately came to an end with the first of the Tudors, a

Here flew a head dissevered from the trunk; There mangled arms and legs were tossed aloft.
French mariner
Scene 4

The Battle of Sluys is depicted in a French manuscript of 1400. The play omits the French king Philippe VI, who was defeated at Sluys. Instead, Philippe's son John loses the battle.

dynasty still keen to bolster its legitimacy in Shakespeare's day. Besides the unsavoury incident with the countess, Edward is seen as a tough, uncaring father. When Prince Edward, known to history as the Black Prince, is beleaguered in battle, Edward refuses help, saying, "Then will he win a world of honour too / If he by valour can redeem him thence. / If not, what remedy? We have more sons / Than one to comfort our declining age." (8.21–24).

Late in the play, news comes through that the young prince has apparently perished and his mother weeps in distress, but Edward's brand of comfort is to promise pitiless revenge. Moreover, when the citizens of Calais send him six leaders of the town as a gesture of submission, only the queen's intervention dissuades him from slaughtering them. There is a foretaste here of Shakespeare's other warrior-king Henry V, who threatens Calais with even more savage brutality. Although there are heroes in this play – Salisbury,

Villiers, and Prince Edward – it does not shy away from showing war as a very brutish business. A French mariner reports the sea battle of Sluys in gruesome terms: "Purple the sea whose channel filled as fast / With streaming gore that from the maimèd fell" (4.161–162).

Edward in *Edward III* is a far from attractive character, and yet the play ends, happily for him, with the young prince excited and eager for fresh challenges and Edward in calm control after a series of stunning military victories. With the French and Scottish kings his captives, and also the dauphin, he muses contentedly on their strange new unity: "God willing, then for England we'll be shipped, / Where in a happy hour I trust we shall / Arrive: three kings, two princes, and a queen." (18.242–244). ∎

WHAT ERROR DRIVES OUR EYES AND EARS AMISS?

THE COMEDY OF ERRORS (1594)

DRAMATIS PERSONAE

Egeon A merchant from Syracuse and father of the Antipholus twins. He is under sentence of death as the play begins.

Solinus Duke of Ephesus.

Antipholus of Ephesus Twin son of Egeon. He is a successful merchant, married to Adriana.

Antipholus of Syracuse Twin son of Egeon, who raised him. He has come to Ephesus to find his twin.

Dromio of Ephesus Servant of Antipholus of Ephesus and twin to Dromio of Syracuse. More put-upon and beaten than his Syracusan twin, his character is, understandably, less happy.

Dromio of Syracuse Servant of Antipholus of Syracuse and twin to Dromio of Ephesus. He has a lively wit and acts on his own initiative.

Adriana Wife of Antipholus of Ephesus. She is impatient with a marriage that restricts her liberty, and with an inequality between husband and wife that she resents.

Nell Adriana's kitchen-maid.

Luciana Sister of Adriana who, having seen a troubled marriage at close hand, is wary of marriage.

Emilia An abbess in Ephesus and, we later learn, the long-lost wife of Egeon.

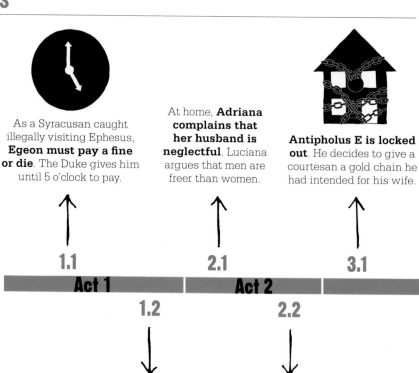

As a Syracusan caught illegally visiting Ephesus, **Egeon must pay a fine or die**. The Duke gives him until 5 o'clock to pay.

At home, **Adriana complains that her husband is neglectful**. Luciana argues that men are freer than women.

Antipholus E is locked out. He decides to give a courtesan a gold chain he had intended for his wife.

1.1   **2.1**   **3.1**

Act 1   **Act 2**

1.2   **2.2**

Egeon's sons **Antipholus and Dromio**, are warned to **conceal their Syracusan nationality**. Antipholus S is met by Dromio E who begs him to come home to dinner.

Adriana rebukes Antipholus S, thinking he's her tardy husband. He sees her sister, Luciana, and falls in love.

The city of Ephesus is at war with Syracuse. Syracusans visiting Ephesus illegally must pay a fine or be executed. One such is Egeon, a merchant just arrived. He tells Duke Solinus that he, his wife Emilia, their young twin sons, and their twin servants, were separated by a storm at sea years before. Egeon and his remaining son and servant returned to Syracuse, where he named the boys after their respective siblings. Once grown, Antipholus and Dromio as they were called, set off to seek their brother twins, but never returned. Now Egeon has risked death by coming to Ephesus in search of both sons and their servants. Moved by the tale, Duke Solinus gives Egeon a reprieve until five in the afternoon to raise the fine.

Unknown to Egeon, those he seeks have also just arrived. Sending Dromio to the inn with their money for safekeeping, Antipholus of Syracuse sets off to explore. Little does he know that the subjects of his own search are nearby. Antipholus of Ephesus, a thriving merchant, lives with his wife, Adriana, and her sister,

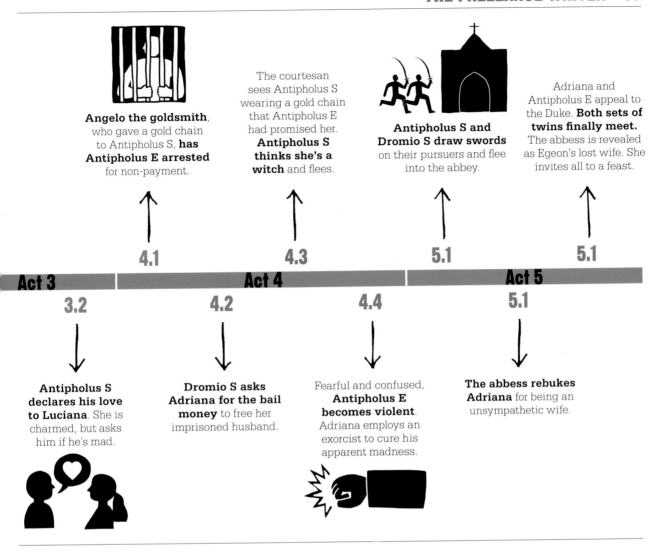

Angelo the goldsmith, who gave a gold chain to Antipholus S, **has Antipholus E arrested** for non-payment.

The courtesan sees Antipholus S wearing a gold chain that Antipholus E had promised her. **Antipholus S thinks she's a witch** and flees.

Antipholus S and Dromio S draw swords on their pursuers and flee into the abbey.

Adriana and Antipholus E appeal to the Duke. **Both sets of twins finally meet.** The abbess is revealed as Egeon's lost wife. She invites all to a feast.

4.1   **4.3**   **5.1**   **5.1**

Act 3   **Act 4**   **Act 5**

3.2   **4.2**   **4.4**   **5.1**

Antipholus S declares his love to Luciana. She is charmed, but asks him if he's mad.

Dromio S asks Adriana for the bail money to free her imprisoned husband.

Fearful and confused, **Antipholus E becomes violent**. Adriana employs an exorcist to cure his apparent madness.

The abbess rebukes Adriana for being an unsympathetic wife.

Luciana, both of whom resent the time he spends away from home visiting the tavern and a courtesan.

Furious that he's late again for dinner, Adriana spots Antipholus in the street and becomes angry with him. He responds surprisingly politely and seems unusually happy to eat with her. In fact, she has met her husband's twin, Antipholus of Syracuse, and he promptly falls in love with her sister. When her husband returns with friends, he finds the door to his home barred by someone claiming to be Dromio. He leaves, threatening revenge.

A series of mistaken encounters ensues. Antipholus of Ephesus sends Dromio of Ephesus for a rope to punish Adriana. But before the servant returns, a goldsmith arrests Antipholus of Ephesus for non-payment for a chain, which was delivered in error to his Syracusan brother. Dromio of Syracuse arrives and is sent to Adriana for the bail money. Dromio of Ephesus then returns with the rope.

Confused and frightened, Antipholus of Ephesus turns violent. Seeming mad, he's tied up with the rope, but escapes.

Meanwhile, the Syracusan twins attempt to flee the town. But, pursued by almost everybody in Ephesus, they take refuge in the abbey. As the fateful hour of 5 o'clock arrives, Adriana and Antipholus of Ephesus petition the Duke to mediate. While he hears their conflicting accounts, the abbess enters with the Syracusan twins and all becomes clear. When the twins recognize Egeon, the Abbess, in a final twist, reveals she is Emilia, Egeon's long-lost wife. So the family is reunited and the tale complete. »

IN CONTEXT

THEMES
Twinship, identity, marital and filial relationships, loss

SETTING
Port of Ephesus

SOURCES
1390 John Gower's English version of the Greek romance *Apollonius of Tyre* forms the basis of Egeon's and Emilia's frame narrative.

1595 Roman playwright Plautus's *Menaechmi* ("The Brothers Menaechmus") translated into English. A second play, *Amphitruo*, may have inspired Act 3, Scene 1.

LEGACY
1594 Performed at Gray's Inn, London.

1786 *Gli Equivoci*, an opera of the play, is staged in Vienna.

1938 Richard Rodgers and Lorenz Hart stage *The Boys from Syracuse*, a musical of the play, on Broadway, New York.

1938 Theodore Komisarjevski's production at Stratford-upon-Avon makes a fluid use of space that has a key influence on staging Shakespeare.

1963–97 Indian film-makers make five films based on the play's plot, most recently *Ulta Palta* starring Ramesh Aravind.

1976 Trevor Nunn's production for the RSC combines elements of farce, circus, and music hall.

2001 *The Kyogen of Errors*, a Japanese production of the play, tours the UK and USA.

The confusion at the heart of *The Comedy of Errors* is caused by a natural phenomenon, twinship, a subject that interested Shakespeare because he was the father of twins. Individuals like to think of themselves as unique, so identical twins are intriguing because they appear to duplicate identity. They suggest the possibility of one person being in two places at one time. And that can be both funny and frightening.

Shakespeare exploits both the comedy and the fear. He doubles the identical twins that he found in Plautus's *Menaechmi* by adding servant Dromios to the original twins. This nicely doubles the opportunity for farce as the play's mistimings gather pace. We're told that the servant twins have shared the lives of their masters since birth, which means that when the errors begin it's not just the master-servant relationship that comes under comic strain, clearly there are bonds of lifelong friendship and trust that are also tested.

Exploration of identity

Shakespeare's changes to his source material let him explore how far identity is influenced by others. We see the fear and isolation felt by each twin when even his servant-partner disputes his version of events. Each man appears to see and hear a slightly different world. Confusion over mistaken identity makes Antipholus of Syracuse want to leave town because the inconsistency he finds seems to confirm the place's reputation for witchcraft. It makes his twin brother so frustrated that he turns to violence, especially when his sanity is doubted. But this only convinces everyone that he is indeed mad. When identities and the bonds of trust between individuals are

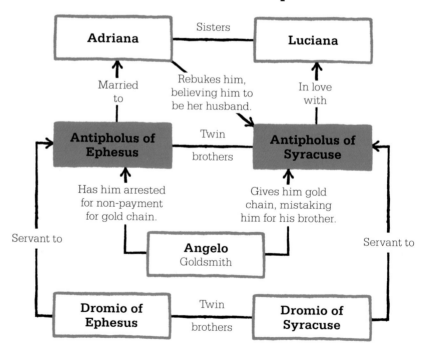

The twins' relationships

Adriana — Sisters — Luciana

Adriana: Married to / Rebukes him, believing him to be her husband. Luciana: In love with

Antipholus of Ephesus — Twin brothers — Antipholus of Syracuse

Has him arrested for non-payment for gold chain. / Gives him gold chain, mistaking him for his brother.

Angelo Goldsmith

Servant to / Servant to

Dromio of Ephesus — Twin brothers — Dromio of Syracuse

> I to the world am like
> a drop of water
> That in the ocean seeks
> another drop,
> Who, falling there to find
> his fellow forth,
> Unseen, inquisitive,
> confounds himself.
> **Antipholus of Syracuse**
> Act 1, Scene 2

threatened in this way, it becomes apparent how swiftly family and social relationships can fall apart.

Dramatic structure

Egeon's tragic story frames the comic action, and the day's grace given to the old man to redeem himself fixes the length of the play. The completion of the tale with the revelation that the Abbess is his long-lost wife, Emilia, brings a sense of wonder; because no hint of this is given. Emilia's return also completes a change of mood from threatened death to festive re-birth. The family is whole again. And so is their story.

Within this framing narrative, time goes adrift. As events move out of sequence, only the audience holds the narrative threads together. The farce builds up through scenes that almost mirror one another. And within these, Shakespeare's use of rapid one-line repartee maintains the momentum, creating a comic double act between master and servant. Even when they're arguing,

there's an obvious bond between them. The dialogue is so fast-paced and funny that there's little time to stop and think. For if anyone were to do that, the reason for the errors might come clear.

The love story between Luciana and Antipholus of Syracuse offers a brief respite from the chaos and a variation on the identity theme. In contrast to the anger all around, the gentle Antipholus woos the surprised Luciana with a lyricism that she clearly hasn't heard before.

Marriage bonds

Marriage, too, can be regarded as a type of twinship. Shakespeare draws attention to its responsibilities and strains by building up the role of Adriana, the Ephesian wife. His audience would know Saint Paul's "Letter to the Ephesians", which discusses the respective duties of husbands and wives, masters and servants; details that Luciana, Adriana's sister, is obviously versed in. Adriana, however, longs to lose herself in a fairer relationship, and says so at length, but to the wrong twin. Possibly her real husband wouldn't have listened to her so patiently. As the Abbess observes, if she criticizes too much she runs the risk of ruining everything about Antipholus that she loves.

The key props in the play – a gold chain and a rope – neatly symbolize its emphasis on bonds: of love and trust, and of punishment and control. The gold chain represents a husband's love, but is promised to the courtesan in an act of spite. When it's given to the wrong twin, his brother is arrested for debt. Finally, it finds the right Antipholus and, we hope, Adriana.

The last bond in the play is that of the Dromios who, reunited as brothers, leave as equals, hand-in-hand – to the audience's applause. ∎

The Kyogen of Errors

In 2001, the Mansaku Company of Japan performed *The Kyogen of Errors,* a Japanese-language production of the play, to English-speaking audiences. *Kyogen*, meaning "mad words", is a form of traditional Japanese theatre known for its earthy, comic style, for which Shakespearean slapstick is particularly suited, with language proving no barrier to farce.

At key moments, the audience was encouraged to join the comedy by chanting "*Ya-ya-koshi-ya!*" ("How complicated!"). In keeping with the traditions of Japanese *Noh* theatre, with which *Kyogen* is closely associated, each set of Antipholuses and Dromios wore identical masks – props that aided the play's visual complexities.

The success of the production showed how the themes in the play – marital relationships, loss, and identity – are so powerful and universal that they transcend even the most challenging of linguistic and cultural differences.

HUNTING HE LOVED, BUT LOVE HE LAUGHED TO SCORN
VENUS AND ADONIS (1592–1593)

IN CONTEXT

THEMES
Erotic desire, youth, longing, temptation

SETTING
Ancient Greece

SOURCES
8 CE Book X of Roman poet Ovid's *Metamorphoses,* in its original Latin, was probably used by Shakespeare.

1565–67 An English translation of Ovid's *Metamorphoses* by Arthur Golding was also drawn on for the poem.

LEGACY
1636 Reprinted at least 10 times in Shakespeare's lifetime, and another six times by 1636 – the most often reprinted work during his lifetime.

1817 Samuel Taylor Coleridge writes glowingly of the poem in his *Biographia Literaria*.

The poem *Venus and Adonis* retells the mythical tale of Venus, goddess of love, who woos and attempts to seduce the beautiful mortal youth, Adonis. Shakespeare announces the theme in the opening lines: "Even as the sun with purple-coloured face / Had ta'en his last leave of the weeping morn, / Rose-cheeked Adonis hied him to the chase. / Hunting he loved, but love he laughed to scorn."

Venus approaches Adonis, begs a kiss, drags him from his horse and tethers it to a tree, thrusts the boy to the ground, and smothers him with kisses. His bashfulness inflames her lust and, pinning him

Some scholars have speculated that Shakespeare may have seen a copy of Titian's painting *Venus and Adonis* (1554), in which the young hero seems to spurn the over-eager Venus.

to the ground, she tells him at length how lucky he should feel to be desired by one who was wooed by so great a figure as the god Mars. But Adonis, complaining that he's getting burnt by the midday sun, with much difficulty shakes her off. "Away he springs, and hasteth to his horse." (l.258). Tempted by a passing mare, however, the horse breaks away

and dashes into a wood with his mate. Venus renews her advances and takes Adonis by the hand, "A lily prisoned in a jail of snow" (l.362), saying that Adonis should take a lesson from his horse: "O, learn to love! The lesson is but plain, / And, once made perfect, never lost again." (ll.407–408).

Hunter hunted

She pretends to collapse before him. Guiltily he tries to bring her round and gives her a farewell kiss, which inflames her again, but he says he is unripe for love: "Before I know myself, seek not to know me."

(l. 525). His unwise offer of a kiss inflames her again. He tells her that he plans to go boar hunting, which causes her such pain that: "She sinketh down, still hanging by his neck. / He on her belly falls, she on her back." (ll.593–594).

Horrified that he may be killed, she advises him to hunt harmless animals such as hares. Adonis rebukes her for succumbing to lust: "Love comforteth, like sunshine after rain, / But lust's effect is tempest after sun." (ll.799–800).

At last he escapes, leaving her to bemoan her fate. Next morning, hearing sounds of hunting, she » dashes to see what is happening. She spies "the hunted boar" (l.900), sees Adonis's exhausted and wounded hounds, and bemoans his suspected fate.

Deluded into supposing that he is still alive she reproaches herself for being too fearful but, coming upon his body, speaks an elegy for him and prophesies that henceforward sorrow will always attend upon love. Adonis's body melts away and she vows to cherish the purple flower that springs up in its place. Finally, she returns to Cyprus in her dove-drawn chariot, planning to seclude herself away in perpetual mourning.

Publication and date

Venus and Adonis first appeared in print in 1593. London's theatres were closed that year and for much of the following year because of an outbreak of plague, and it seems likely that Shakespeare, who was already an established playwright, had time on his hands. The poem was published by Richard Field, a well-known London printer. Field,

who was also from Stratford-upon-Avon, went on to publish *The Rape of Lucrece*. *Venus and Adonis* was the first book to bear Shakespeare's name as author.

The first edition bore a Latin motto from the poems *Amores* ("The Loves") by the Roman poet Ovid: "Vilia miretur vulgus; mihi flavus Apollo pocula Castalia plena ministret aqua" – "let low-minded people admire vile things, but for me let Apollo supply goblets full of the water of the Muses".

Dedication

The poem bears a dedication to Henry Wriothesley, 3rd Earl of Southampton, a precocious and talented nobleman who was only 17 at the time. The formal dedication reads, "Right Honourable, I know not how I shall offend in dedicating my unpolished lines to your lordship, nor how the world will censure me for choosing so strong a prop to support so weak a burden. Only, if your honour seem but pleased, I account myself highly praised, and vow to take advantage of all idle hours till I have honoured you with

Ovid wrote his narrative poem *Metamorphoses* in the first decade CE. Running to 15 books and covering 250 myths, it would have given the schoolboy Shakespeare a thorough grounding in classical mythology.

some graver labour. But if the first heir of my invention prove deformed, I shall be sorry it had so noble a godfather, and never after ear [till] so barren a land for fear it yield me still so bad a harvest. I leave it to your honourable survey, and your honour to your heart's content; which I wish may always answer your own wish and the world's hopeful expectation. Your honour's in all duty, William Shakespeare." Shakespeare also dedicated his other narrative poem, *The Rape of Lucrece*, published in the following year, to Southampton.

Source

Shakespeare based *Venus and Adonis* on an episode from one of his favourite books, the long poem *Metamorphoses* ("Changes") by Ovid, which he would have studied

With this she seizeth on his sweating palm, The precedent of pith and livelihood, And, trembling in her passion, calls it balm – Earth's sovereign salve to do a goddess good.
Venus and Adonis
ll.25–28

O, what a sight it was wistly to view How she came stealing to the wayward boy, To note the fighting conflict of her hue, How white and red each other did destroy!
Venus and Adonis
ll.343–346

at school and which he refers to and quotes from many times in his plays. He even brings a copy of the poems on stage in his early tragedy *Titus Andronicus* and in his late romance *Cymbeline*. Shakespeare seems to have referred both to the original and to an English translation by Arthur Golding. But while Ovid tells the tale in only 75 lines, Shakespeare expands it to 1,194 lines of verse. He modifies both the characterization and the events of the original tale. In Ovid's version, the youthful Adonis returns Venus's love, but Shakespeare turns him into a bashful adolescent who shies away from the goddess's lustful advances. He also expands the story; the most substantial addition is the episode (ll.259–324) in which Adonis's horse lusts after a mare and gallops after her into the forest, frustrating Adonis's attempts to escape from Venus's clutches.

Style and reception

The poem is written in six-line stanzas. Each line is an iambic pentameter, meaning that it has ten syllables and every other syllable is stressed: for example "She looks upon his lips, and they are pale" (l.1123). The lines are rhymed in this order: a b a b c c, resembling the last six lines of a Shakespearean sonnet. The style is witty, narrating events with knowing detachment while also achieving lyrical beauty in the descriptive passages.

The poem was to be more frequently reprinted than any other of Shakespeare's works during his lifetime: nine times by 1610. It was especially popular with adolescents. In about 1600, Cambridge scholar Gabriel Harvey wrote that, "the younger sort take much pleasure in Shakespeare's *Venus and Adonis*, but his *Lucrece*, and his tragedy of *Hamlet Prince of Denmark*, have it

in them to please the wiser sort." *Venus and Adonis* acquired a reputation as soft porn due to lines such as these in which Venus tries to tempt Adonis with the delights of her body: "I'll be a park, and thou shalt be my deer. / Feed where thou wilt, on mountain or in dale; / Graze on my lips, and if those hills be dry, / Stray lower, where the pleasant fountains lie." (ll.231–234). In a play performed by Cambridge students early in the 17th century, a character boasts of how he woos his mistress with speeches larded with quotations from *Romeo and Juliet* and *Venus and Adonis*, and declares that he will "worship sweet master Shakespeare".

The poem's artificial style and digressive story line caused it to fall out of fashion until romantic poet and critic Samuel Taylor Coleridge's *Biographia Literaria* (1817) helped to restore its critical reputation. ■

In 2007, the Royal Shakespeare Company, in association with the Little Angel Theatre of Islington, London, gave a performance in which the poem was recited aloud while the story was acted out with puppets.

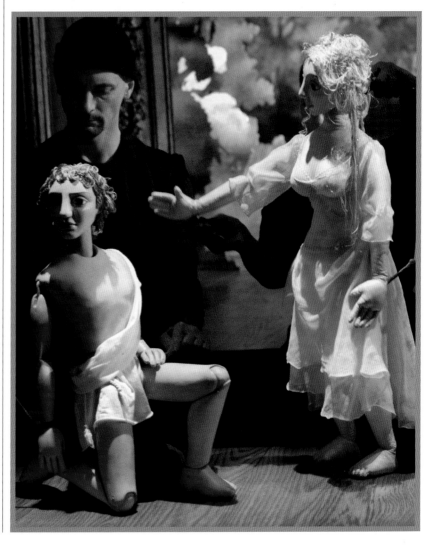

WHO BUYS A MINUTE'S MIRTH TO WAIL A WEEK

THE RAPE OF LUCRECE (1593–1594)

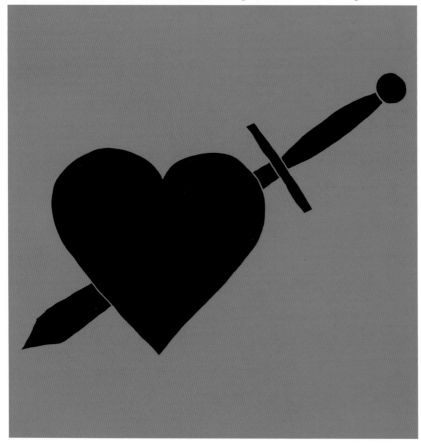

IN CONTEXT

THEMES
Lust, betrayal, honour

SETTING
Rome, 509 BCE

SOURCES
27–25 BCE *History of Rome* by the Roman historian Livy.

8 CE *The Book of Days* by the Roman poet Ovid.

LEGACY
1616 Six editions published by the time of Shakespeare's death attest to the poem's popularity.

1818 English poet Samuel Taylor Coleridge praises the dramatic qualities of the work.

1931 French playwright André Obey adapts the poem for the stage in *Le Viol de Lucrèce*.

1946 English composer Benjamin Britten writes an opera based on the poem.

The Rape of Lucrece is a poem that tells the classical story of the Roman general Tarquin, who desires and rapes Lucrece, the wife of his fellow warrior Collatinus (called Collatine in the poem). Shakespeare jumps straight into the action in the opening lines: "Lust-breathèd Tarquin leaves the Roman host / And to Collatium bears the lightless fire / Which, in pale embers hid, lurks to aspire / And girdle with embracing flames the waist / Of Collatine's fair love, Lucrece the chaste."

The narrator explains that Tarquin has left the Roman camp for Collatium because, on the previous night, the warriors had been boasting of the beauty and chastity of their wives. This has filled him with desire for Lucrece.

When he reaches Collatium, Lucrece welcomes him. He finds her even more beautiful than he had expected, praises her husband's valour, and goes to bed aching with desire for her. In a long soliloquy, Tarquin meditates about his intention to seduce Lucrece, aware of the horror and danger of what he intends to do, but unable to resist his evil impulses: "Here pale with fear he doth premeditate / The dangers of his loathsome enterprise, / And in his inward mind he doth debate / What following sorrow may on this arise." (ll.183–186).

A passage of vivid narrative describes how he makes his fearful way to the chamber where Lucrece lies sleeping: "Her breasts like ivory globes circled with blue, / A pair of maiden worlds unconquerèd, / Save of their lord no bearing yoke they knew, / And him by oath they truly honourèd." (ll.407–410).

When Lucrece awakes, Tarquin says he will kill her and her attendant slave unless she yields to him. She pleads with him in vain, and he rapes her: "with the nightly linen that she wears / He pens her piteous clamours in her head, / Cooling his hot face in the chastest tears / That ever modest eyes with sorrow shed." (ll.680–683).

She bears the load of lust he left behind,
And he the burden of a guilty mind.
The Rape of Lucrece
ll.734–735

A one-woman musical and dramatic performance based on the poem was given by Camille O'Sullivan in 2011. It toured Britain and Ireland under the auspices of the RSC.

Having done the deed, Tarquin creeps away in shame. From this point onwards, the poem concentrates on Lucrece. She addresses night, time, and opportunity in a series of laments, and curses Tarquin before deciding to kill herself for shame and to tell her husband what has happened. She calls her maid but does not confide in her. Lucrece writes to Collatine summoning him home and then meditates on a painting of the siege and fall of Troy, which is described at length. When Collatine arrives with her father and other lords, she tells them what has happened without at first naming Tarquin until all the men have vowed to avenge her. Then she suddenly stabs herself. "Even here she sheathèd in her harmless » breast / A harmful knife, that thence her soul unsheathed. / That blow did bail it from the deep unrest / Of that polluted prison where it breathed." (ll.1723–1726).

Her father and Collatine grieve over her body and Tarquin and all his family are banished from Rome.

Publication

Shakespeare seems to have thought of *The Rape of Lucrece* as a tragic companion piece to the ironically comic *Venus and Adonis*. In dedicating the earlier poem to the Earl of Southampton, he had promised that, if the Earl liked it, he would "take advantage of all idle hours till I have honoured you with some graver labour." *The Rape of Lucrece*, also dedicated to the earl, followed a year later, in 1594. Like the earlier poem, it was printed by Shakespeare's fellow Stratfordian Richard Field. (The title page calls it simply *Lucrece*, but the pages are headed with the longer title.)

Dedication

The dedication to this poem is written in much warmer terms than that to *Venus and Adonis*: "The love I dedicate to your lordship is without end, whereof this pamphlet without beginning is but a superfluous moiety. The warrant I have of your honourable disposition, not the worth of my untutored lines, makes it assured of acceptance. What I have done is yours; what I have to do is yours, being part in all I have, devoted yours. Were my worth greater my duty would show greater; meantime, as it is, it is bound to your lordship, to whom I wish long life still lengthened with all happiness. Your lordship's in all duty, William Shakespeare." Dedications could be mere formalities, intended to indicate

Italian artist Palma Giovane depicted the rape of Lucrece in this painting in about 1570. Many artists would have portrayed this famous tale in paintings that Shakespeare would have seen.

to potential purchasers that the author of a book had an eminent patron, and perhaps in the hope of a reward – two guineas (a little over £2) was a standard sum – from the dedicatee. But the warmth of affection – indeed, the "love… without end" – expressed here has understandably given rise to the suggestion that Shakespeare had a genuinely close friendship with the young, precociously talented, and remarkably good-looking aristocrat.

After the dedication comes "The Argument", a prose summary of the poem's action. The story it tells differs somewhat from that of the poem itself, and it may not have been written by Shakespeare.

Style and reception
The poem is written in the seven-line stanza form known as rhyme royal, which Shakespeare also uses in "A Lover's Complaint". Each line is an iambic pentameter – ten syllables in which, normally (though with variations), every other syllable is stressed, as, for example in line 6: "And girdle with embracing flames the waist". The lines rhyme a b a b b c c. The tone, unlike that of *Venus and Adonis*, is deadly serious throughout, and there are many digressions from the basic narrative.

The opening sequence, with its intense account of Tarquin's tormented state of mind as he approaches Lucrece's chamber, is the most vividly powerful. Shakespeare recalls the events and style of this poem in later writings, most memorably when Macbeth, on his way to murder King Duncan, speaks of "withered murder" which, "With Tarquin's ravishing strides, towards his design / Moves like a ghost." (*Macbeth* 2.1.52–56).

Like *Venus and Adonis*, the poem was popular right from its first publication. Six editions appeared in Shakespeare's lifetime, with another three by 1655. There are several admiring contemporary references to it. In 1818, the English poet Samuel Taylor Coleridge wrote of *The Rape of Lucrece* that the poem "gave ample proof of his possession of a most profound, energetic, and philosophical mind, without which he might have pleased, but could not have been a great dramatic poet".

The poem's rhetorical style fell out of fashion in later times, but more recently it has come to be admired for its profoundly dramatic quality and for its anticipations of Shakespeare's later work, especially in his plays based on Roman history and in *Macbeth*.

Britten's opera
In 1946, British composer Benjamin Britten wrote an opera based on Shakespeare's story. He was inspired on seeing a play adapted from the poem by French playwright André Obey. Britten's work is a "chamber opera" – an intimate work with 13 musicians and eight singers. ∎

Even here she sheathèd in her harmless breast
A harmful knife, that thence her soul unsheathed.
That blow did bail it from the deep unrest
Of that polluted prison where it breathed.
The Rape of Lucrece
ll.1723–1726

Classical tale

Like *Venus and Adonis*, *The Rape of Lucrece* is an example of a literary genre that flourished in the 1590s: long, classically based narrative poems telling stories of romantic love, often inspired in both tone and subject matter by the Roman poet Ovid, whose writings were much studied in grammar schools such as that of Stratford-upon-Avon.

Unlike *Venus and Adonis*, this time the subject matter is historical, not mythical. The events took place in 509 BCE and were already legendary by the time of the first surviving account, by the Roman historian Livy in his history of Rome published between 27 and 25 BCE. Shakespeare seems mainly to have used the account given by Ovid in his poem *Fasti*, known in English as *The Book of Days*, or *Chronicles*, first published in 8 CE. He seems also to have drawn on the Roman historian Livy and other sources. Shakespeare concentrates on the private rather than the political aspects of the story, and makes a little narrative material go a long way.

THE LORD CHAMBER MAN

1594–1603

LAIN'S

London theatres reopen in May after a **plague epidemic**. *Love's Labour's Lost* and *The Comedy of Errors* are written.

1594

Privateer Sir Francis Drake departs on his **final voyage**, a campaign against the Spanish Empire in the Caribbean.

1595

Spanish troops capture Calais. **Queen Elizabeth expels all Africans** from England.

1596

The Merry Wives of Windsor and *Henry IV, Part 2* are written. **Shakespeare buys New Place** as his Stratford family home.

1597

1595

Richard II, Romeo and Juliet, and *A Midsummer Night's Dream* are written.

1596

The Life and Death of King John, The Merchant of Venice, and *Henry IV Part 1* are written.

1596

The **Lord Mayor of London bans actors** from the city and tears down inn-theatres; the ban is lifted the following year.

1597

London theatres are closed for months when *The Isle of Dogs,* by Ben Jonson and Thomas Nashe is labelled seditious.

By the time the theatres reopened after the plague epidemic of 1592–94, the literary success Shakespeare had achieved with the publication of *Venus and Adonis* in 1594 helped him engineer a uniquely secure position in the theatre world.

With the theatres back in business, Lord Hunsdon, the Lord Chamberlain, reconstituted his theatre company as the Lord Chamberlain's Men. It brought together leading actors of the day, such as the tragedian Richard Burbage, who would launch some of Shakespeare's greatest roles; the clown William Kemp, who triumphed as the comic creation Falstaff; and Shakespeare himself. Crucially, the leading actors all owned shares in the company; Shakespeare had a 10 per cent stake.

That stake ensured Shakespeare had an income of between £200 and £700 a year – by no means a fortune, but far above any other playwright's earnings. Shakespeare chose to live frugally, renting various places to live in London, and by 1597, he had saved enough to buy his family a large house in Stratford – New Place. He went on to buy land nearby, and even a coat of arms.

Creative drive

Shakespeare's position in the company gave him a platform for his plays – and he made the most of it. In the two-year break caused by the plague, he had honed his poetic and dramatic skills, and over the next nine years, he wrote 17 plays, ranging from the romantic comedies *A Midsummer Night's Dream* and *Twelfth Night* to the

stirring history of *Henry V* and the tragedy of *Hamlet*. Many thousands packed the theatre to watch them.

Evidence for the dating of the early plays is limited, but reference to several of Shakespeare's plays is made by the little-known writer Francis Meres in a book called *Palladis Tamia: Wit's Treasury* published in 1598. Meres asserts that "Shakespeare among the English is the most excellent for the stage; for comedy, witness his *Gentlemen of Verona*, his *Errors*, his *Love Labour's Lost*, his *Love Labour's Won*, his *Midsummer's Night Dream*, and his *Merchant of Venice*; for tragedy, his *Richard II*, *Richard III*, *Henry IV*, *King John*, *Titus Andronicus*, and his *Romeo and Juliet*." Thus scholars have been given a date by which all of these plays must have been written.

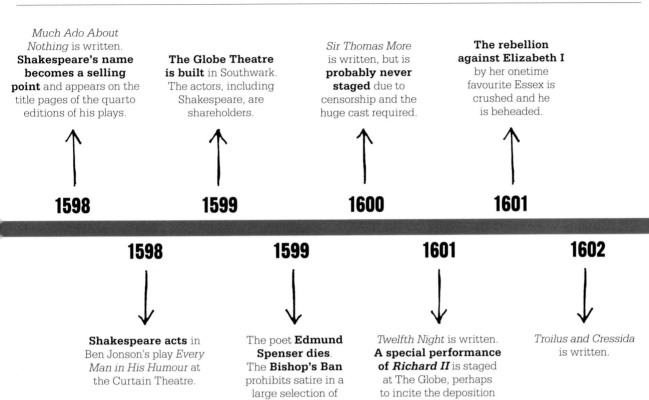

Much Ado About Nothing is written. **Shakespeare's name becomes a selling point** and appears on the title pages of the quarto editions of his plays.

The Globe Theatre is built in Southwark. The actors, including Shakespeare, are shareholders.

Sir Thomas More is written, but is **probably never staged** due to censorship and the huge cast required.

The rebellion against Elizabeth I by her onetime favourite Essex is crushed and he is beheaded.

1598   **1599**   **1600**   **1601**

1598   **1599**   **1601**   **1602**

Shakespeare acts in Ben Jonson's play *Every Man in His Humour* at the Curtain Theatre.

The poet **Edmund Spenser dies**. The **Bishop's Ban** prohibits satire in a large selection of literary works.

Twelfth Night is written. **A special performance of *Richard II*** is staged at The Globe, perhaps to incite the deposition of the Queen.

Troilus and Cressida is written.

Theatre on the edge

Although the Lord Chamberlain's men often performed before the queen, theatre life was precarious. The company was always playing cat-and-mouse with authorities keen to control what they saw as salacious entertainment, and theatres stayed on marginal land beyond the city walls. In 1598, the landlord of a Shoreditch playhouse known as The Theatre demanded a huge rise in rent, then decided to tear down the building altogether. Shakespeare's company secretly dismantled it beam by beam and carried the timbers over the river to Southwark to erect a new theatre, The Globe, which was owned by the company. The Globe was an instant triumph. In its opening year, 1599, it saw performances of *Julius Caesar*, *As You Like It*, *Henry V*, and *Hamlet*. The company's worries, however, went beyond capricious landlords. Theatre at this time could be political dynamite, and actors faced a constant battle to get scripts past the Master of the Revels, who vetted every play.

Dangerous times

Just how far this censorship went is clear from the cuts made to the script of *Sir Thomas More*. This play, which Shakespeare had a hand in but which has several authors, portrays the Chancellor of King Henry VIII, who refused to grant the king a divorce, in a favourable light. Some have argued that Shakespeare was a Catholic rebel, who stuffed his plays with coded symbols designed to evade the censor but convey a powerful message to anyone who understood them. If this is true, he was playing a risky game. It is true that the Lord Chamberlain's Men were not afraid of political controversy. On 7 February 1601, Sir Gelly Meyrick, acting on behalf of the Earl of Essex, commissioned a special performance of *Richard II* at The Globe, including the scenes in which the monarch is deposed and murdered – scenes too incendiary to publish at the time. The performance went ahead, and the very next day the Earl of Essex led a small army towards Whitehall Palace to bring down the queen and replace her with James VI of Scotland. Essex's revolution ended in farce and the Earl was executed. It could all have turned out badly for Shakespeare and the Chamberlain's Men, but somehow they managed to escape punishment. ∎

WHO CAN SEVER LOVE FROM CHARITY

LOVE'S LABOUR'S LOST (1594–1595)

DRAMATIS PERSONAE

Ferdinand King of Navarre.

Biron Lord attending on the king. He is surprised to fall in love with Rosaline.

Longueville Lord attending on the king. He woos Maria.

Dumaine Lord attending on the king. He woos Katharine.

Princess of France A diplomat, a skilled huntress, and a beauty. Later she becomes Queen of France.

Rosaline Lady attending on the princess. Biron falls for her.

Maria Lady attending on the princess. She falls in love with Longueville.

Katharine Lady attending on the princess. She falls in love with Dumaine.

Lord Boyet French lord attending on the princess who acts as a go-between.

Marcadé Messenger.

Don Adriano de Armado A pretentious Spaniard. He falls in love with Jaquenetta.

Mote Armado's clever page boy.

Costard Simple country fellow.

Jaquenetta A dairymaid.

Sir Nathaniel A curate.

Holofernes A schoolmaster who fills his speech with Latin (or an approximation of Latin).

Dull A simple constable. He understands very little.

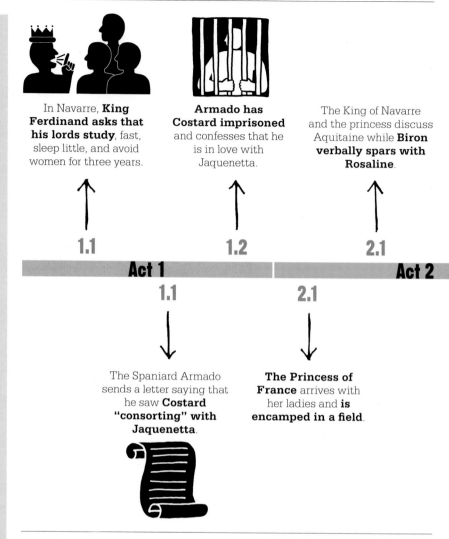

In Navarre, **King Ferdinand asks that his lords study**, fast, sleep little, and avoid women for three years.

1.1

Armado has Costard imprisoned and confesses that he is in love with Jaquenetta.

1.2

The King of Navarre and the princess discuss Aquitaine while **Biron verbally spars with Rosaline**.

2.1

Act 1   **Act 2**

1.1

The Spaniard Armado sends a letter saying that he saw **Costard "consorting" with Jaquenetta**.

2.1

The Princess of France arrives with her ladies and **is encamped in a field**.

At the court of Navarre, King Ferdinand tells his lords that, to be successful, they must study and renounce women for three years. Dumaine and Longueville agree but Biron is reluctant. The king agrees that he must make an exception for the Princess of France who is soon to arrive. Biron, seeing that rules can be bent, agrees to the oath. The pompous Armado has Costard imprisoned, saying that he saw him with Jaquenetta, and then reveals that he is in love with Jaquenetta. The Princess of France arrives. Her ladies each praise one of the lords so warmly that the princess swears they must be in love. The princess plays at being offended by her cool reception from the king. Biron and Rosaline spar verbally and Dumaine and Longueville ask Katharine and Maria's names. Boyet insists that the king is in love with the princess, and the ladies tease him for being a "love-monger".

Armado asks the boy Mote to sing to Jaquenetta for him, but Mote and Costard make fun of him. Armado sets Costard free on condition he takes a letter to

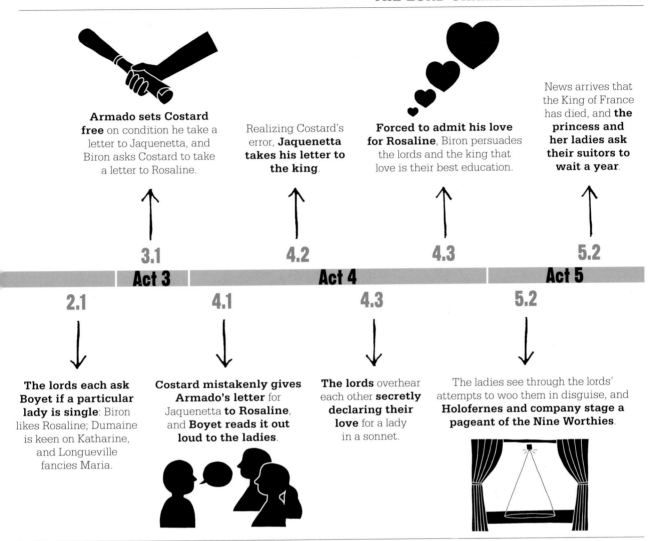

Armado sets Costard free on condition he take a letter to Jaquenetta, and Biron asks Costard to take a letter to Rosaline.

Realizing Costard's error, **Jaquenetta takes his letter to the king**.

Forced to admit his love for Rosaline, Biron persuades the lords and the king that love is their best education.

News arrives that the King of France has died, and **the princess and her ladies ask their suitors to wait a year**.

3.1

4.2

4.3

5.2

Act 3

Act 4

Act 5

2.1

4.1

4.3

5.2

The lords each ask Boyet if a particular lady is single: Biron likes Rosaline; Dumaine is keen on Katharine, and Longueville fancies Maria.

Costard mistakenly gives Armado's letter for Jaquenetta **to Rosaline, and Boyet reads it out loud to the ladies**.

The lords overhear each other **secretly declaring their love** for a lady in a sonnet.

The ladies see through the lords' attempts to woo them in disguise, and **Holofernes and company stage a pageant of the Nine Worthies**.

Jaquenetta. Biron also gives Costard a letter for Rosaline. Biron curses his foolishness in falling in love – and with a girl so deficient.

The princess and the ladies are hunting when Costard says he has a letter for Rosaline from Biron. The princess asks to see it and in his confusion, Costard gives Boyet Armado's letter. Boyet realizes it is meant for Jaquenetta, but the princess asks him to read it out loud. Boyet teases Rosaline bawdily about Biron and she responds in kind. Boyet indulges in an innuendo-laden exchange with Maria, joined by

Costard who doesn't quite get it all. Holofernes discusses the hunt with Dull and Nathaniel. Jaquenetta arrives with Costard and asks them to read the letter from Armado. It is, of course, Biron's letter to Rosaline and after Holofernes analyses the poem's merit they take it to the king.

Biron overhears the king composing a love sonnet. Biron and the king hear Longueville doing the same. Longueville hears Dumaine composing a sonnet. Longueville accuses Dumaine of breaking their agreement. The king accuses Longueville. Biron criticizes all

three. Costard arrives with Biron's letter to Rosaline. The quartet agrees to forget their pact and woo the ladies in earnest.

Armado, Holofernes, Nathaniel, Dull, and Mote are to entertain the party. They disguise themselves, but the ladies, forewarned, play them along. When the men return dressed as themselves, the ladies pretend not to recognize them. The lords decide to woo from now on only with honesty, but then news arrives that the princess's father has died. Her marriage is postponed, and the ladies prepare to depart. »

IN CONTEXT

THEMES
Romance, flirting, chastity, word-play, cycle of life

SETTING
Navarre – a kingdom between France and Spain

SOURCES
16th century The Italian tradition of *commedia dell' arte*, with stock characters, especially a pedant, a braggart, and a fool, appears to have been a source.

1586 *L'Académie Française* by Pierre de la Primaudaye, which appeared in English in about 1586, outlined philosophical thinking in the French court in the late 16th century, and may have been an influence on Shakespeare.

LEGACY
1597 A performance before the Queen (Elizabeth I) "this last Christmas" is referred to on the title page of the first edition.

1817 Literary critic William Hazlitt notes, "If we were to part with any of the author's comedies, it should be this."

1837 First performance since Shakespeare's time.

1946 A bold production by Peter Brook at the RSC based the play on the *fêtes galantes* (bucolic landscape) paintings of French artist Watteau.

2012 Deafinitely Theatre's production of *Love's Labour's Lost* at the Globe is the first full-length Shakespeare play entirely in sign language.

Love's *Labour's Lost* is the most conspicuously poetic of all Shakespeare's plays, with nearly two-thirds of the play in rhyming verse. Its clever word-play must have delighted the intellectual elite at the Elizabethan court, who counted this among their favourite Shakespeare plays.

However, the play's contemporary in-jokes have often been lost on audiences since then, and in the 18th and 19th centuries, it was the least performed of all Shakespeare's plays. Audiences watching the play can all too easily feel like the constable Dull, who, when the schoolteacher Holofernes comments, "Thou hast spoken no word all this while," replies, "Nor understood none neither, sir." (5.1.142–144).

The poetic knot-garden

In recent years, directors have found ways to release the play's witty comedy and sweet romance and make the most of its ingenious structure, likened by some to the elaborate Elizabethan knot garden that the pretentious Spaniard Armado alludes to in his letter to the king. It is a play that may be clever, but it also has a heart that

British director Kenneth Branagh made his movie version of *Love's Labour's Lost* (2000) a romantic 1930s Hollywood musical. Here, the young lords anticipate the arrival of the ladies.

These are barren tasks, too hard to keep –
Not to see ladies, study, fast, not sleep.
Biron
Act 1, Scene 1

goes beyond mere verbal tricks, as the surprisingly nuanced and affecting ending bears out.

The set-up is very simple. With the country at peace, the King of Navarre calls upon his lords to do nothing but study for three years – to eat little, to sleep little, and to renounce the company of women. The joke is, of course, that they haven't a hope of succeeding, least of all the king. As Biron, the least convinced of his lords, points out: "'Item: If any man be seen to talk with a woman within the term of three years, he shall endure such public shame as the rest of the court can possibly devise.' / This article, my liege, yourself must break; For well you know here comes in embassy / The French king's daughter with yourself to speak" (1.1.128–133). So already the king must make exception for the French king's daughter and her ladies – and as soon as this first exception is made, the whole plan quickly breaks down.

Much of the humour hinges on how the lords and the king pretend to each other that they are not falling under the romantic spell of the ladies, while the ladies amuse themselves watching the men squirm. The plot could hardly be simpler. Yet Shakespeare uses this straightforward story to create a gloriously intricate game of words. There is ample scope for a clever and merciless spoof of the pretentious wordplay of the day, which in many places is also downright obscene.

Finding love and self

The thrust of the play is clear enough: that it is absurd for men to cut themselves off from women and from love in order to find out about the world – women and love are the only true education. As Biron finally acknowledges: "From women's eyes this doctrine I derive. / They sparkle still the right Promethean fire. / They are the books, the arts, the academes / That show, contain, and nourish all the world" (4.3.326–329).

Shakespeare is keenly aware that love poetry is no substitute for real-life love, and, as later plays such as *Romeo and Juliet* and *As You Like It* show, young men who indulge in love poetry are often mistaking the idea of love for the real thing. This indulgence is

> Sir, he hath never fed of the dainties that are bred in a book; he hath not eat paper, as it were; he hath not drunk ink: his intellect is not replenished
> **Nathaniel**
> **Act 4, Scene 2**

the path taken by the King of Navarre, Biron, Dumaine, and Longueville, and so they are easily fooled by the ladies into paying court to the wrong girl when the ladies swap accessories.

The men are misguided enough, too, to think that they can disguise themselves to go wooing. The girls are not fooled – and only pretend not to know the lords when they come back as themselves. Finally, Biron realizes he must learn to be himself rather than act an image of love. In his succinct summary of the play, he says: "Let us once lose our oaths to find ourselves, / Or else we lose ourselves to keep our oaths." (4.3.337–338).

The final lesson

Unexpectedly, Shakespeare avoids giving us a neat happy ending. After Biron and the other men have been through this moment of self-discovery, they sit down to watch the pageant of the Nine Worthies presented by Holofernes, Nathaniel, Moth, Costard, and Armado. The women watch quietly, but in their

This orderly Elizabethan knot garden at Nyewood House in East Sussex, echoes the careful grouping of actors and the mannered patterns of speech of *Love's Labour's Lost*.

performances, the men mock so mercilessly that even the pedant Holofernes is moved to a heartfelt criticism, "This is not generous, not gentle, not humble" (5.2.622).

In the middle of the pageant, news arrives that the princess's father, the King of France, has suddenly died. The normal round of weddings that might tie up a comedy do not happen. Instead, the ladies each ask their suitors to wait a year, and to use that year to learn more about people and the world. Rosaline instructs Biron to tend the sick, and when he protests that there are no jokes in a hospital full of death, Rosaline reminds him that: "A jest's prosperity lies in the ear / Of him that hears it" (5.2.847–848). The play ends poignantly with haunting songs of the seasons, first the cuckoo for spring then the owl for winter. ∎

DOWN, DOWN I COME LIKE GLIST'RING PHAETHON

RICHARD II (1595)

DRAMATIS PERSONAE

King Richard II The rightful king of England.

John of Gaunt Duke of Lancaster, Bolingbroke's father, and Richard II's uncle.

Harry Bolingbroke Duke of Hereford, later King Henry IV by usurpation, cousin to Richard.

Thomas Mowbray Duke of Norfolk and Richard's ally, later banished for his quarrel with Bolingbroke.

Duke of Aumerle Duke of York's son, ally of Richard.

Duke of York Richard's uncle, and regent in his absence.

Queen Isabel Richard's wife.

Duchess of York The Duke of York's wife.

Earl of Northumberland An ally of Bolingbroke.

Bushy, Green, and Bagot Richard's followers, who are blamed for his bad policies.

Ross, Fitzwalter, and Willoughby Lords who join Bolingbroke's side.

Earl of Salisbury, Bishop of Carlisle Supporters of Richard.

Harry Percy Northumberland's son, also known as Hotspur.

Abbot of Westminster He joins a plot against Henry IV, but dies before he is arrested.

Sir Piers Exton Richard's murderer.

Bolingbroke accuses Mowbray of treason before the King and they challenge one another to **single combat**.

When John of Gaunt dies, Richard **seizes Bolingbroke's inheritance** and then leaves for Ireland. The disgusted nobles prepare to meet Bolingbroke who is returning to England.

York is heavily outnumbered and allows Bolingbroke and his troops to **enter Berkeley Castle**.

 1.1

 2.1   **2.3**

Act 1   **Act 2**

1.3   **2.2**

Richard interrupts the **trial by combat** between Mowbray and Bolingbroke, and **banishes them**.

The **Duke of York tries to raise an army** in the King's absence. Bushy, Bagot, and Green try to save themselves.

The play opens with an accusation of treason made by Bolingbroke against Mowbray. The latter stands accused of murdering the Duke of Gloucester, but John of Gaunt suspects that King Richard himself is implicated in the murder. Richard banishes Bolingbroke for 10 years, later commuted to six, but Mowbray is permanently exiled.

Bolingbroke wins popular sympathy as he leaves, while Richard alienates the people by levying high taxes. When Gaunt dies, Richard seizes all the land and wealth that by rights should pass to Gaunt's son, Bolingbroke. The nobles Ross, Willoughby, and Northumberland agree to meet Bolingbroke, who is to arrive back on English shores with an army.

While Richard is quelling a rebellion in Ireland the Queen is comforted by Bushy, Bagot, and Green. Then news is heard of Bolingbroke's return and the nobles' desertion. York, whom Richard left in charge, prepares for their attack.

At Berkeley Castle, York accuses Bolingbroke of treason. Bolingbroke insists that he was banished as

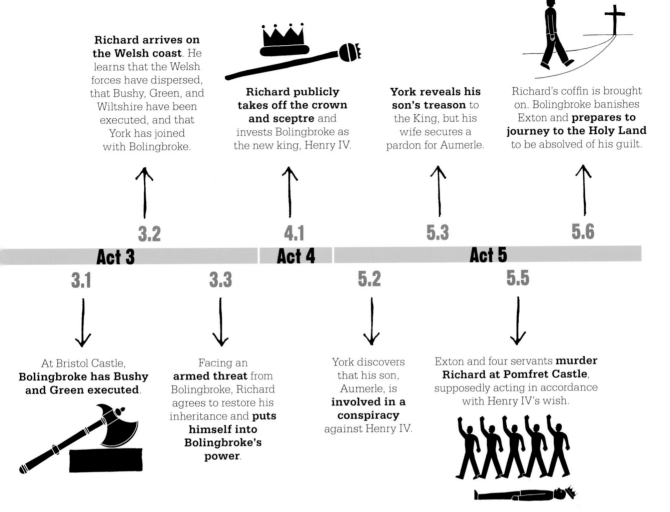

Richard arrives on the Welsh coast. He learns that the Welsh forces have dispersed, that Bushy, Green, and Wiltshire have been executed, and that York has joined with Bolingbroke.

Richard publicly takes off the crown and sceptre and invests Bolingbroke as the new king, Henry IV.

York reveals his son's treason to the King, but his wife secures a pardon for Aumerle.

Richard's coffin is brought on. Bolingbroke banishes Exton and **prepares to journey to the Holy Land** to be absolved of his guilt.

3.2   **4.1**   **5.3**   **5.6**

Act 3   **Act 4**   **Act 5**

3.1   **3.3**   **5.2**   **5.5**

At Bristol Castle, **Bolingbroke has Bushy and Green executed.**

Facing an **armed threat** from Bolingbroke, Richard agrees to restore his inheritance and **puts himself into Bolingbroke's power.**

York discovers that his son, Aumerle, is **involved in a conspiracy** against Henry IV.

Exton and four servants **murder Richard at Pomfret Castle,** supposedly acting in accordance with Henry IV's wish.

Hereford, not as the Duke of Lancaster, and that he has a right to defend his inheritance. York allows them to enter the castle.

Richard lands on the Welsh coast and greets the land joyfully. However, he despairs at the news brought by messengers. At Flint Castle, Bolingbroke demands that Richard repeal his banishment and restore his inheritance. Richard appears on the battlements and grants his request. Bolingbroke kneels to Richard but the power has shifted. Richard submits to travel to London with him.

York's son Aumerle is accused by Bagot of plotting Gloucester's death and being disloyal to Bolingbroke. Multiple challenges to fight ensue. York announces that Richard has named Bolingbroke his heir and is ready to resign his throne to him.

Richard is forced publicly to renounce the throne. He takes off his crown and sceptre but refuses to read the charges against him. Looking at his face in a mirror, he comments that "A brittle glory shineth in this face. As brittle as the glory is the face." (4.1.277–278). Bolingbroke has him taken to the

Tower. On the way, Richard meets his Queen and they say goodbye. York discovers that his son, Aumerle, is involved in a plot against Bolingbroke, now King Henry IV. He betrays him to the King, but the Duchess's eloquence manages to secure a pardon. Carlisle and the other conspirators will be executed.

Sir Piers Exton murders Richard at Pomfret Castle, and takes the body to Bolingbroke, expecting a reward, but the new King is deeply ashamed of the action. He has Exton banished, and sets off on a pilgrimage to the Holy Land. »

IN CONTEXT

THEMES
Kingship, betrayal, character flaws

SETTING
Locations in England and Wales during the reign of Richard II (1367–1400)

SOURCES
1587 Raphael Holinshed's *Chronicles of England, Scotland and Ireland.*

c.1592 Christopher Marlowe's play *Edward II.*

1595 Samuel Daniel's epic poem *The First Four Books of the Civil Wars.*

LEGACY
1601 Performed to rouse support for Essex's ill-fated rebellion against Elizabeth I.

1815 After two centuries of neglect, Edmund Kean revives the play in London, playing Richard as a courageous figure.

1937 English actor John Gielgud stages a production at Queen's Theatre, London, that emphasizes the play's poetry.

1971 English director Richard Cottrell's TV adaptation stars Ian McKellen as an effeminate, doomed Richard.

1995 Irish actress Fiona Shaw is cast as an androgynous Richard by director Deborah Warner at the National Theatre, London.

2009 Australian actress Cate Blanchett plays Richard at the Sydney Theatre, Australia.

When Richard observes of himself "Down, down I come like glist'ring Phaethon" (3.3.177), he offers a complex image of his own tragic fate. Phaethon was the son of Phoebus/Apollo, the sun-god of Greek mythology. According to legend, the youth stole his father's fiery chariot and drove it through the sky, but he could not keep control of the horses and caused terrible destruction to Earth. Jove hurled a thunderbolt at the chariot, and Phaethon plunged to his death.

Often interpreted as signifying the dangers of ambition, the myth initially seems more appropriate to the usurping Bolingbroke than to Richard, the divinely-appointed king of England, whose inherent majesty is often described in terms of the sun. Yet the myth was also used to condemn a failure of government, which is how Richard uses it, describing himself as, like Phaethon, "Wanting the manage of unruly jades" (3.3.178). The gardener will later confirm that it was Richard's inability to control his nobles that brought about his downfall: "We at time of year / Do wound the bark, the skin of our fruit trees, / Lest, being over-proud in sap and blood, / With too much riches it confound itself. / Had he done so to great and growing men, / They might have lived to bear, and he to taste, / Their fruits of duty." (3.4.58–64)

Power struggle

Richard's difficulties reflect the reality of 14th-century England, which saw a struggle between the nobles and the monarchy. At the start of the play, Richard cannot quell the argument between Bolingbroke and Mowbray because their obedience to the king matters less to them than personal honour. Indeed, the play's extraordinary

Ah, Richard! With the eyes of heavy mind I see thy glory, like a shooting star, Fall to the base earth from the firmament.
Earl of Salisbury
Act 2, Scene 4

language of sacramental kingship is partly driven by an awareness that the king is but one among a number of competing nobles who all have a claim to the throne.

Contemporary parallels

When Shakespeare wrote the play, the story of Richard II was a controversial one because of perceived analogies between his reign and that of Elizabeth I. The latter famously said to William Lambarde in 1601, "I am Richard II. Know ye not that?"

Like Richard, Elizabeth was perceived to be unduly influenced by court favourites, most notably the earls of Leicester and Essex. Like Richard, she had to contend with rebellion in Ireland, although she sent Essex to deal with it, rather than making the mistake of leaving the kingdom. She was also in the difficult position of lacking an heir. One of the accusations against Bushy, Bagot, and Green in Shakespeare's play is that they have prevented Richard from ensuring the succession. This is attributed not only to dissension between Richard and his Queen, but to his being "corrupted" in a homosexual sense, in a possible echo of Marlowe's *Edward II* where the king's sexual preferences are more explicitly divisive. Elizabeth did not have this particular charge to answer, but her failure to produce an heir – a consequence of her refusal to marry – encouraged ambitions among her powerful nobles, which would have been dissipated if the succession had been clearly determined. **»**

Richard compares himself to Phaethon, the youth of Greek myth who was struck from the skies. The fall is depicted here by Michelangelo, in an engraving Shakespeare may have seen.

Gaunt's speech

*This royal throne of kings,
    this sceptred isle,
This earth of majesty,
    this seat of Mars,
This other Eden,
    demi-paradise,
This fortress built by
    nature for herself
Against infection and
    the hand of war,
This happy breed of men,
    this little world,
This precious stone set
    in the silver sea,
Which serves it in the
    office of a wall,
Or as a moat defensive
    to a house
Against the envy of less
    happier lands;
This blessèd plot, this earth,
    this realm, this England*
(2.1.40–50)

John of Gaunt's speech is one of the most quoted in the Shakespearean canon, and was anthologized as early as 1600. Its imagery of England as walled in by the sea, protected by Nature, has been central to constructions of the nation, as has its imagery of England breeding warriors and kings. It provided titles for at least two British World War II films: David Lean's *This Happy Breed* (1944) and David MacDonald's *This England* (1941). That said, the speech's jingoism has also undergone some major reassessment, not least because "this England" subsumes within it the separate nations of Wales and Scotland. We should also remember that Gaunt's speech is uttered by a man on his death bed, who testifies to the ways in which "this England" has been ruined. It is an ideal that already does not exist.

Harry Bolingbroke v Richard II

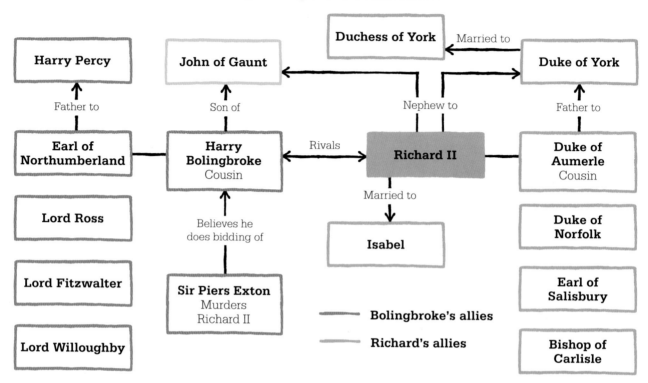

Harry Percy

John of Gaunt

Duchess of York — Married to → Duke of York

Father to ↑

Son of ↑

Nephew to

Father to ↑

Earl of Northumberland → Harry Bolingbroke — *Cousin* — Rivals → Richard II ← — Nephew to — Duke of York / Duke of Aumerle — *Cousin*

Rivals

Married to ↓

Lord Ross

Believes he does bidding of ↑

Isabel

Duke of Norfolk

Lord Fitzwalter

Sir Piers Exton — Murders Richard II

━━━ **Bolingbroke's allies**

━━━ **Richard's allies**

Earl of Salisbury

Lord Willoughby

Bishop of Carlisle

Shakespeare's play was implicated in the problems of his Queen when it was performed on the eve of a rebellion by the Earl of Essex, who had fallen out of favour following failures in Ireland. Supporters of Essex commissioned the Lord Chamberlain's Men to perform the play at the Globe on 7 February 1601. Presumably the deposition scene of Act 4 Scene 1 was included. It had been thought too seditious to be printed, and was absent from the published text until 1608. The next day, the Globe audience tried to stir up rebellion. However, Essex was denounced as a traitor and support dwindled. Shakespeare's company was investigated but not punished.

Self-fulfilling prophecy

While *Richard II* is a history play, it is entitled *The Tragedy of King Richard the Second*. Richard's image of himself as "glist'ring Phaethon" brings to mind the myth of the young god's fall, which has a tragic beauty to it, as Phaethon falls from the sky like a star to earth.

I live with bread, like you; feel want,
Taste grief, need friends.
Subjected thus,
How can you say to me
I am a king?
King Richard II
Act 3, Scene 2

The story reflects something similarly self-aggrandizing in Richard, whose fall inspires wonder and whose self-perception is echoed by other characters. Gaunt warns that "His rash, fierce blaze of riot cannot last" (2.1.33), while Salisbury laments: "Ah, Richard! With the eyes of heavy mind / I see thy glory, like a shooting star, / Fall to the base earth from the firmament" (2.4.18–20). Richard seems to be in love with this image of his own tragic fall and consciously tries to bring it about. Indeed, this is one of Shakespeare's few history plays with no battle scene, reflecting the ease with which Bolingbroke wins the crown. When he offers to "tell sad stories of the death of kings", Richard implicitly refers to the popular medieval definition of tragedy, the so-called *de casibus* tragedy, derived from

Boccaccio's *De Casibus Virorum Illustrium* (1355–74) (*Of the Fates of Famous Men*). The subjects all suffered a sudden descent from good fortune to adversity and death. When Richard calls for a mirror in which to read his downfall, he may have been alluding to a popular English collection of similar tales called *The Mirror for Magistrates*, which included *Richard II*.

A willing victim?

Clearly, Shakespeare's character imagines himself as a victim – of Bolingbroke, of the inherent nature of kingship, of fate, and perhaps of his own flaws. But more important than the cause of his tragic fall is the spectacle it makes, to the extent that Richard has been accused of "doom-eagerness", indulging in fantasies of his tragic abjection before they have become a political necessity. For example, Bolingbroke is ostensibly only pursuing repeal from banishment and restoration of inheritance, but Richard mentions deposition as early as Act 3 Scene 3, when he asks: "What must the King do now? Must he submit? / The King shall do it. Must he be deposed? / The King shall be contented. Must he lose / The name of King? A God's name, let it go" (3.3.142–145). Bolingbroke needs to do little more than stand there with an army looking menacing.

Playing the King

The king's pleasure in wordplay and his self-indulgent loquacity suggest Richard as an early forerunner for Hamlet. Along with Hamlet, this is one of the few Shakespearean tragic roles that has been played by women (most recently by Fiona Shaw and Cate Blanchett). Such casting can heighten the contrast between Richard's hyper-emotionalism, including a tendency to weep, and the pragmatism and self-control of Bolingbroke. Alternatively, casting a Richard and a Bolingbroke who look very like one another, or who share the roles between them, can also be effective, bringing out the play's exploration of what makes a king.

Some productions have had two actors play the roles of Richard and Bolingbroke on alternate nights, suggesting the arbitrariness of which man was king, and looking forwards to the Wars of the Roses, during which power would swing from the house of Lancaster to York, and back again. Shakespeare had already staged a series of plays on this theme: *Henry VI Parts One, Two,* and *Three,* and *Richard III*. In *Richard II*, he was returning to an action – the murder of a lawful king – that would change the perception of kingship. At the same time, however self-aggrandizing Richard appears, the play supports his argument that to be a king is inevitably to be the hero in a tragic cycle. ∎

A romantic engraving depicts Richard dying heroically at the hands of Piers Exton. The manner of Richard's murder is not known for certain. It is possible that he was starved to death.

A PAIR OF STAR-CROSSED LOVERS

ROMEO AND JULIET (1595)

DRAMATIS PERSONAE

MONTAGUES

Montague Head of the Montague household.

Romeo The romantically inclined son of Montague and Lady Montague.

Benvolio Romeo's cousin, a young peacemaker whose words go unheard.

Balthasar Romeo's servant.

CAPULETS

Capulet Head of the Capulet household. Juliet's father, at least 60 years old.

Lady Capulet Juliet's mother, around 26 years old.

Juliet Capulet and Lady Capulet's 13-year-old daughter.

Tybalt Juliet's cousin, a hot-tempered young man proud of his skill with a sword.

Nurse Juliet's old nurse, an affectionate and down-to-earth woman.

OTHERS

Mercutio Romeo's charismatic, witty, and bawdy friend.

Escalus The Prince of Verona.

Paris Escalus's kinsman, an arrogant, upright young man who expects to marry Juliet.

Friar Laurence Franciscan friar and apothecary, who marries Romeo and Juliet in secret.

Petruccio Follower of Tybalt.

After **the Montagues and Capulets brawl**, Capulet agrees to betroth his daughter Juliet to Paris and arranges a ball to celebrate.

Beneath Juliet's balcony, **Romeo overhears Juliet's avowal of love** for him.

Mercutio is killed by Tybalt, Romeo kills Tybalt and is banished by the Prince.

1.1

2.1

3.1

Act 1 **Act 2**

1.3

2.5

At the ball, masked **Romeo Montague is overwhelmed by Juliet's beauty**.

Romeo and Juliet are secretly married by Friar Laurence.

The chorus sets the scene as Verona, where two families feud. The play will last two hours, Chorus says, and tell the story of two of their children whose doomed love will end in death, reconciling the families at last.

The play then erupts onto the streets of Verona, and a brawl between the rival families, the Montagues and Capulets, is halted only by the intervention of the Prince of Verona. To appease the Prince, old Capulet agrees to marry his 13-year-old daughter Juliet to the Prince's young kinsman, Paris,

and arranges a masked ball to celebrate. Young Romeo Montague and his friends (including the wit Mercutio) sneak into the ball to get a glimpse of Rosaline Capulet, the object of Romeo's unrequited love – but Romeo is instead completely smitten by Rosaline's cousin Juliet.

Later that night, Romeo, lingering in the orchard below Juliet's balcony, overhears her declare that she loves him despite his family name, and he makes himself known to her. Ecstatic, the pair resolve to marry the following night. Friar Laurence and Juliet's

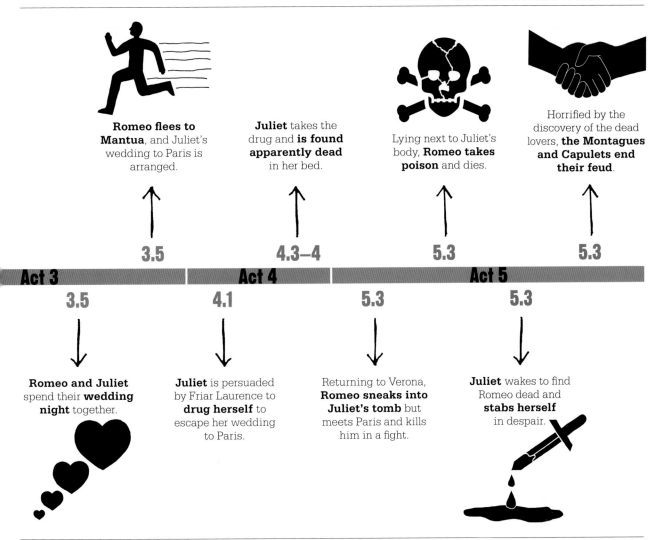

Romeo flees to Mantua, and Juliet's wedding to Paris is arranged.

3.5

Juliet takes the drug and **is found apparently dead** in her bed.

4.3–4

Lying next to Juliet's body, **Romeo takes poison** and dies.

5.3

Horrified by the discovery of the dead lovers, **the Montagues and Capulets end their feud**.

5.3

Act 3   Act 4   Act 5

3.5

Romeo and Juliet spend their **wedding night** together.

4.1

Juliet is persuaded by Friar Laurence to **drug herself** to escape her wedding to Paris.

5.3

Returning to Verona, **Romeo sneaks into Juliet's tomb** but meets Paris and kills him in a fight.

5.3

Juliet wakes to find Romeo dead and **stabs herself** in despair.

nurse agree to help them, hoping the union will end the feud. Next day in the street, Mercutio taunts Tybalt Capulet and the two begin to fence. But although only Romeo knows it, Tybalt is now his cousin-in-law and Romeo tries to break up the fight. Tybalt fatally wounds Mercutio. Romeo kills Tybalt in revenge, and the Prince banishes Romeo from Verona to Mantua.

Seeing Juliet distraught, though not knowing why, old Capulet decides her wedding to Paris must go ahead right away. Desperate, Juliet asks Friar Laurence for help.

The friar advises her to escape the wedding by taking a sleeping-draught, which will make her seem dead for 42 hours. The friar will send a message to Romeo in Mantua, who can then rescue her from the family tomb when she awakens. Juliet goes ahead with the plan, and is found apparently dead on the morning of the wedding.

The friar's message does not reach Romeo and he hears only of Juliet's death. Grief-stricken, Romeo rushes back to Verona and creeps into the Capulet tomb, where he meets Paris. The two

fight and Paris is killed. Romeo lays down beside Juliet's apparently lifeless body, takes poison, and dies. Not long after, Juliet regains consciousness and finds Romeo dead. She tries to take the poison from his lips with a kiss, but death eludes her, so she takes Romeo's dagger, stabs herself, and dies.

As the bodies are discovered, Friar Laurence explains the sorry situation to the Prince, who lambasts the families whose feuding has brought this tragedy. The old men shake hands and agree to end their enmity. »

IN CONTEXT

THEMES
Jealousy, loyalty, betrayal, romantic love, male friendship

SETTING
Verona, Italy

SOURCES
1562 Arthur Brooke's poem *The Tragical History of Romeus and Juliet.*

LEGACY
1679 English dramatist Thomas Otway resets the play in ancient Rome, with a happy ending that stresses the play's political dimensions.

1745 David Garrick and Spranger Barry perform rival versions at Drury Lane and Covent Garden in London.

1845 American Charlotte Cushman plays Romeo at the Haymarket, London, with her sister Susan as Juliet.

1935 Actors John Gielgud and Laurence Olivier alternate roles as Romeo and Mercutio in an acclaimed production at the New Theatre, London.

1938 Russian composer Sergei Prokofiev's ballet version opens in Brno, Czechoslovakia.

1957 Leonard Bernstein and Steven Sondheim's musical *West Side Story* moves the story to modern New York City.

1994 The exiled Macedonian Romany Company Pralipe stages a version in Bosnia with a Muslim Juliet and a Christian Romeo.

*R*omeo and Juliet is perhaps the most familiar of all Shakespeare's plays: a tale of two young lovers, doomed to be kept apart. There are many other stories of separated lovers, but the intensity of Romeo and Juliet's romance gives Shakespeare's drama an emotional charge that has resonated through the ages.

Romeo and Juliet fall in love instantly, marry the next day, and have one brief and precious night of love before they are forced asunder by their families' feud, and plunged into the spiral of events that brings them both to suicide. Few plays have ever captured so well the wild and heady energy of youthful emotion – not only its loves, but its rage, its vitality, and its volatility in a fractured world where elders fail to provide wise guidance. No wonder this play often seems to speak to contemporary youth with such startling immediacy.

Shakespeare makes the fate that awaits the lovers clear right from the start. In the short 14-line opening verse, the Chorus reveals the entire plot, telling us that the play is about two "star-crossed" lovers – lovers whose sad and conjoined fate is written in the

> Did my heart love till now?
> Forswear it, sight,
> For I ne'er saw true beauty
> till this night.
> **Romeo**
> Act 1, Scene 5

> That which we call a rose
> By any other word would
> smell as sweet.
> **Juliet**
> Act 2, Scene 1

stars – and that they will die before their parents see sense: "The fearful passage of their death-marked love / And the continuance of their parents' rage – / Which but their children's end, naught could remove – / Is now the two-hours' traffic of our stage;" (Prologue.9–12).

To modern audiences, used to films whose plots are constructed to keep the audience guessing, with plot twists right up until the end, this is a surprise, and today's reviewers might feel obliged to put in a spoiler alert. Far from spoiling the play for the audience, however, it gives the drive that makes *Romeo and Juliet* a compelling drama. We know exactly what is going to happen to the young lovers as they come together, even though they don't. We know that their love is doomed even as they embark on it with such beguiling charm, innocence, and optimism, and we can hardly turn away as they hurtle blindly towards their fateful end.

Indeed, it is the sense that their love is so powerful and inevitable that it can only end in death that has made their story captivating ever since the play was first performed in the 1590s. For

It is perhaps because we must see the pair as innocents that they are so young. Franco Zeffirelli picked up on this in his 1968 film version with Olivia Hussey, just 16 years old, as Juliet.

romantics, especially the young, the idea of love flying in the face of a cruel world is intoxicating.

Origins of the story

The basic story in which young lovers choose to die together rather than live apart is an ancient one. The Roman poet Ovid's *Metamorphoses*, for instance, contains the story of the separated lovers Pyramus and Thisbe, which Shakespeare parodied in his next play, *A Midsummer Night's Dream*. In the 3rd century CE, the story of *Ephesiaca*, by the Greek writer Xenophon of Ephesus, sees the 16-year-old Habrocomes and 14-year-old Anthia embark on a suicide pact.

The story of Romeo and Juliet in particular became popular in 16th-century Italy in versions such as Luigi da Porto's 1530 novel *Giulietta e Romeo*. The two feuding families in the story, the Montecchi (Montagues) of Verona and the Capeletti (Capulets) of Cremona, were historical, and the poet Dante writes of them in his *Purgatorio* as being at the centre of civil strife in 13th-century Italy. Shakespeare's immediate source, though, was an English version of the story written as a long poem in 1562 by Arthur Brooke entitled *The Tragical History of Romeus and Juliet*.

Shakespeare's changes

Many of the principal characters in *Romeo and Juliet* are much the same as in Brooke's poem, but Shakespeare's treatment of the story is very different. In *Romeo and Juliet*, the lovers have just one night together after their wedding; in Brooke's poem, Romeo visits Juliet every night for a month »

Elizabethan feuds

Romeo and Juliet was written at a time when England was as divided as it has ever been. King Henry VIII had split from the Roman Catholic church in 1533, and the wounds this had caused were still red raw. The Protestant regime of the reigning Queen Elizabeth I, Henry VIII's daughter, (pictured) was under attack from Catholics both from within the country and from abroad. The regime was fighting back, led by the queen's first minister Robert Cecil. Catholic recusants were hunted down ruthlessly by Cecil's henchmen, while agents of the Catholic Counter Reformation conspired to bring Protestant England back into the fold.

The younger generation, of which Shakespeare was one, were indeed caught between the warring factions – and it may be that *Romeo and Juliet* was intended as a reminder to them of the tragic consequences of their bitter conflict for their offspring. Romeo and Juliet could have found counterparts in England, with Protestants and Catholics replacing the Montagues and Capulets as the feuding neighbours.

The feuding houses of Verona

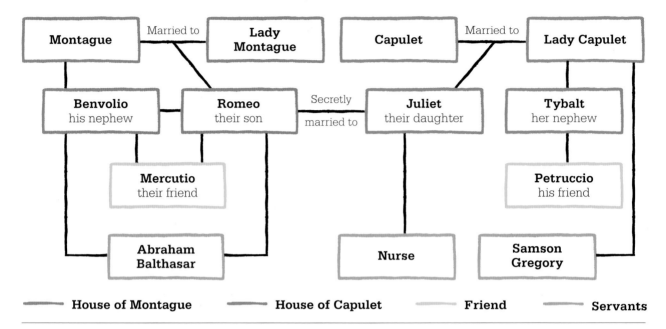

or two. Shakespeare's story is faster, and this serves to heighten the tragic brevity of the romance. Shakespeare has a very different attitude towards the lovers. Brooke thoroughly disapproves of them; they are "unfortunate lovers, thrilling themselves to unhonest desire, neglecting the authority

My bounty is as boundless
as the sea,
My love as deep. The more
I give to thee
The more I have, for both
are infinite.
Juliet
Act 2, Scene 1

and advice of parents and friends." Shakespeare, however, is on their side. In *Romeo and Juliet*, they are innocent victims – Juliet is just 13 – and in the beauty and ardour of their love, they soar far above their parents' bickering and bitterness. It is this large-hearted sympathy that gives Shakespeare such wide appeal, and made his message so subversive at the time.

While the characters in Brooke's poem are largely archetypes, in *Romeo and Juliet*, they are much more fleshed out and real. Shakespeare also brings minor characters such as the well-intentioned Friar Laurence and the chatterbox Nurse fully to life. Romeo's quick-witted and earthy friend Mercutio is entirely Shakespeare's creation, one of his most appealing. It is Mercutio's death in a sword-fight at the beginning of Act 3 that wrenches the mood of the play dramatically from comedy to tragedy.

A stage revolution

It is hard to appreciate today just how revolutionary Shakespeare was in bringing this story to the English stage. Italian novels were certainly becoming increasingly popular with the younger generation at the time – Shakespeare was not yet 30 when he wrote *Romeo and Juliet* – but no-one had put this kind of story on stage before. Previously, tragic drama had been mostly about noble lords and mighty warriors in grand settings. Here, the hero and heroine are just two ordinary contemporary teenagers, distinguished only by their love and their way with words, in an ordinary city that happens to be called Verona, but could be anywhere. The young Shakespeare's play was no slowly unfolding, grand epic as most earlier tragedies had been, but fast-paced, down, and dirty.

In the brief and measured verse with which the Chorus outlines the scenario, Shakespeare seems to be setting us up for the same cautionary tale of misbegotten love as appears in Brooke's version. But as soon as this cautionary rhyme is done, we are plunged into the anarchic reality of the feud, as the formal poetry gives way to a full-scale brawl on the streets of Verona. In the roughest of prose and with rude gestures, two pairs of servants, Samson and Gregory, Abraham and Balthasar, hurl bawdy threats at each other. Samson talks of cutting off the (maiden) heads of the Montague women.

Swords are drawn, fighting begins, and soon the young blades of the families enter the fray, followed quickly by old Capulet, feebly wielding his sword against the equally frail old Montague – as feebly, his much younger wife implies, as he now wields his marital "sword". This is an unruly world of macho posturing in which even the aged who should know better join in, and wisdom and guidance is left in the dubious hands of Friar Laurence and Juliet's nurse.

What's in a name?
In such a dysfunctional city, "name" is everything, and true substance and feeling is lost. But when Romeo and Juliet later embark on their romance, Juliet realizes a name can be a terrible trap, lamenting famously: "O Romeo, Romeo, wherefore [why] art thou Romeo? / ...That which we call a rose / By any other word would smell as sweet." (2.1.75–86) Juliet yearns for her love to

Contemporary audiences will have identified in Mercutio a portrait of the playwright Christopher Marlowe who, like Mercutio, died in a knife fight, in 1593. This illustration dates from 1903.

provide a way to transcend the trap of names: "Romeo, doff thy name, / And for thy name – which is no part of thee – / Take all myself." (2.1.89–91) But ultimately even their true love is not enough. "In what vile part of this anatomy / Doth my name lodge?" (3.4.105–106) Romeo asks Friar Laurence after his banishment, likewise realizing the poison in his name and desperate to rid himself of it. That name becomes his death sentence.

Posturing love
In Verona's world of false honour, even love, to begin with, is a posture. When Romeo first appears, wandering distractedly into the aftermath of the brawl, he is in love, not with Juliet – who he has yet to meet, – but with a Capulet girl called Rosaline. She is never fully seen, remaining as insubstantial as Romeo's love for her.

Fittingly, it seems, for a romance set in Italy, Romeo declares his love for Rosaline in a sonnet – a short »

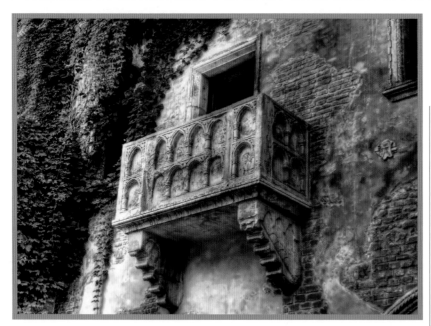

The balcony of a 14th-century building in Verona has been dubbed Juliet's balcony. The building may have belonged to the Capuleti family on whom the Capulets are based.

form of poem in 14 lines, which had been established by the 13th-century Italian poet Guittone of Arezzo and popularized by Petrarch. By the time of Shakespeare, sonnets had become the standard literary form for expressions of love, especially if unrequited – although Shakespeare was soon to invigorate the form with his own verses. Sonnets employed rhetorical devices including oxymoron – the putting together of contradictory words

such as "cold fire" and "loving hate". Romeo's sonnet to Rosaline is stuffed with conventional oxymorons: "Why, then, O brawling love, O loving hate, / O anything of nothing first create; / O heavy lightness, serious vanity, / Misshapen chaos of well-seeming forms, / Feather of lead, bright smoke, cold fire, sick health," (1.1.173–177).

Romeo has yet to learn that love, too, must break from these conventions to find something more truthful. Even when he sees Juliet for the first time, he speaks of her in formal couplets: "Did my heart love till now? Forswear it, sight, / For I ne'er saw true beauty till this night." (1.5.51–52).

Breaking convention
When Romeo and Juliet speak to each other for the first time, remarkably, they share the lines of a sonnet with breathless intensity, and the sonnet, conventionally the most personal and unspoken of verses, becomes a tender conversation. The final couplet is

shared between the two of them, as if to emphasize their miraculous connection and linked destiny: "**Juliet**: Saints do not move, though grant for prayers' sake. **Romeo**: Then move not while my prayer's effect I take. [He kisses her.]" (1.5.104–105).

From this point on, Romeo largely abandons rhyme when speaking to Juliet, and they both now speak mostly in blank verse, finding a new and more truthful way of interacting. It is the young Juliet who matures into this newer expression of love first, and Romeo is drawn in her wake.

The balcony scene
In the balcony scene, a stage metaphor for separated love, Romeo speaks to Juliet from the orchard below her balcony. The device of separating them on stage by the height of the balcony allows them to talk with a passion that would be impossible if they were together, as it could only lead to physicality.

Parting is such
sweet sorrow
That I shall say good night
till it be morrow.
Juliet
Act 2, Scene 1

A plague o' both
your houses.
They have made worms'
meat of me.
Mercutio
Act 3, Scene 1

Language of love

Shakespeare finds a new language of love that has a freshness and immediacy that was entirely new in English verse – rich in imagery, yet sincerely personal and new-minted by this earnest young couple, with rich poetic allusions such as Juliet's wish to be a falconer to lure Romeo back like a trained falcon replacing more formal metaphors. In his language, as in his story, Shakespeare moves on from the divisive conventions of the past to a new and more honest and profound mode of expression. Romeo and Juliet's lines resonate with real feeling. Rarely has young love been expressed with such tenderness and such beauty.

Yet that love is doomed from the start. Juliet urgently wishes for time to rush by to bring on the night, "the love-performing night" (3.2.5) that will allow them to be together. But the night is both a time of love and a symbol of death, and the urgent race into the dark is also a headlong charge into the galloping events that bring them to their tragic end.

Romeo and Juliet is full of oppositions – light versus dark, youth versus age, time running fast and time running slow, the moon versus the stars, love versus hate. Juliet describes Romeo to her nurse as "My only love sprung from my only hate" (1.5.137), as if the oxymorons of Romeo's sonnet to Rosaline have taken life.

As we were told it would, it is the darkness that wins out. Romeo and Juliet's love cannot win, for their romantic ideals prove no match for the force of their elders' quarrels. However, in death, they prove the catalyst that brings the quarrels to an abrupt end. Capulet reaches out to Montague "O brother Montague, give me thy hand" (5.3.295), as each praises the other's child. The Prince stands lamenting over their bodies: "A glooming peace this morning with it brings. / The sun for sorrow will not show his head." (5.3.304–305). Those left behind feel a profound shame. ∎

Adrienne Canterna choreographed and danced in the ballet *Romeo and Juliet*, directed by her husband Rasta Thomas. Their production mixed Prokofiev's score with modern music.

Adaptations

At least 30 operas and ballets have been adapted from Shakespeare's *Romeo and Juliet*, including Prokofiev's 1935 ballet *Romeo and Juliet* and Gounod's opera *Roméo et Juliette* (1867). Leonard Bernstein and Stephen Sondheim's 1957 stage musical *West Side Story* moves the action to New York's tough Upper West Side, where rival gangs, the Sharks and the Jets, clash. Many other stage shows have been adapted from Shakespeare's play, including French composer Gérard Presgurvic's musical spectacle *Roméo et Juliette: de la Haine à l'Amour* (2001).

More than 60 different film versions have been created, beginning with Clemence Maurice's 1900 production. One of the best known is Franco Zeffirelli's 1968 film, which made an impact with its beautiful teenage leads, including 16-year-old Olivia Hussey as Juliet in a controversial nude scene. Baz Luhrmann's *Romeo + Juliet* (1996, pictured above), starred Leonardo DiCaprio and Claire Danes, and set the action in a modern world of edgy youth on California's "Verona Beach".

THE COURSE OF TRUE LOVE NEVER DID RUN SMOOTH

A MIDSUMMER NIGHT'S DREAM (1595)

DRAMATIS PERSONAE

Theseus The Duke of Athens, conqueror of the Amazons.

Hippolyta The conquered queen of the Amazons, betrothed to Theseus.

Egeus Father of Hermia.

Hermia Short, fiery dark-haired daughter of Egeus, in love with Lysander.

Lysander Romantic and in love with Hermia.

Demetrius More hard-headed than Lysander, but also courting Hermia.

Helena Tall and fair-haired, in love with Demetrius.

Oberon King of the fairies.

Titania Queen of the fairies.

Robin Goodfellow A puck or mischievous sprite, also known just as Puck.

Peaseblossom, Cobweb, Mustardseed, and Mote Fairies who tend on Titania.

Peter Quince A carpenter who plays the Prologue.

Nick Bottom A weaver who plays Pyramus, whose head is transformed to that of an ass.

Francis Flute A bellows-mender who plays Thisbe.

Tom Snout A tinker who plays the Wall and worries that the lion will be too scary.

Snug A joiner, who plays Lion and is a slow-learner.

Robin Starveling A tailor who plays the Moon.

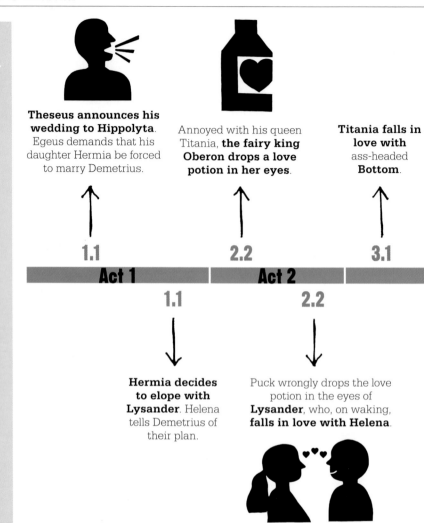

Theseus announces his wedding to Hippolyta. Egeus demands that his daughter Hermia be forced to marry Demetrius.

Annoyed with his queen Titania, **the fairy king Oberon drops a love potion in her eyes**.

Titania falls in love with ass-headed **Bottom**.

1.1

Act 1

2.2

Act 2

3.1

1.1

Hermia decides to elope with Lysander. Helena tells Demetrius of their plan.

2.2

Puck wrongly drops the love potion in the eyes of **Lysander**, who, on waking, **falls in love with Helena**.

In Athens, Theseus is preparing for his wedding to Hippolyta, the vanquished queen of the Amazons, when in bursts Egeus complaining that his daughter Hermia refuses to marry Demetrius. He says that she has been bewitched by Lysander. Theseus commands Hermia to marry Demetrius. Hermia and Lysander decide to elope and agree to meet the next night in the forest. Hermia confides in Helena. Helena is in love with Demetrius. To win Demetrius's love, Helena tells him of the elopement. A band of artisans resolve to meet in the forest to rehearse a play in honour of the wedding.

In the forest, the fairy king and queen, Oberon and Titania, quarrel over a changeling child. Oberon sends mischievous Puck to find the juice of a flower which, when placed in the eyes of a sleeper, makes them fall in love with the first person they see on waking. Oberon drops the juice on Titania's eyes. Demetrius and Helena pursue Hermia and Lysander into the forest. Oberon orders Puck to drop the juice in Demetrius's eyes so

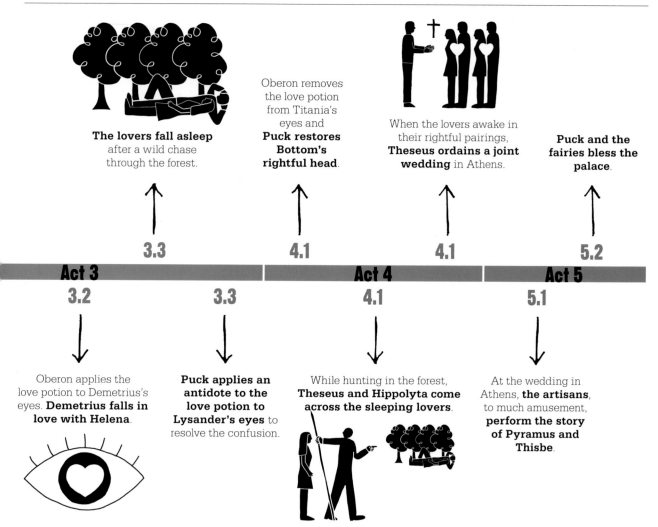

The lovers fall asleep after a wild chase through the forest.

Oberon removes the love potion from Titania's eyes and **Puck restores Bottom's rightful head**.

When the lovers awake in their rightful pairings, **Theseus ordains a joint wedding** in Athens.

Puck and the fairies bless the palace.

3.3   4.1   4.1   5.2

Act 3   **Act 4**   **Act 5**

3.2   3.3   4.1   5.1

Oberon applies the love potion to Demetrius's eyes. **Demetrius falls in love with Helena**.

Puck applies an antidote to the love potion to Lysander's eyes to resolve the confusion.

While hunting in the forest, **Theseus and Hippolyta come across the sleeping lovers**.

At the wedding in Athens, **the artisans**, to much amusement, **perform the story of Pyramus and Thisbe**.

that he falls in love Helena – but Puck mistakenly gives the juice to Lysander, who wakes and sees Helena and falls in love with her.

As the artisans rehearse, Puck changes the head of Bottom the weaver for that of a donkey. Bottom's companions flee, but Titania, sleeping nearby, awakes and falls in love with him. As the lovers appear, it is clear something is awry, and Oberon tries to make amends by applying the love juice to Demetrius's eyes. But when Demetrius falls in love with Helena, too, she thinks it is all a cruel joke.

The boys and girls fight and run through the forest before falling asleep. As they sleep, Puck removes the spell from Lysander's eyes.

Oberon removes the spell from Titania's eyes, and she is appalled when she wakes with Bottom in her arms. Oberon commands Puck to switch Bottom's head back, and Oberon and Titania are reconciled.

Theseus and Hippolyta, out hunting with Egeus, come upon the sleeping lovers. As the lovers awake, Hermia pairs with Lysander and Demetrius pairs with Helena. Theseus ordains that they shall join

him and Hippolyta in a three-way wedding. The artisans finish their rehearsal and all return to Athens.

After the wedding, the artisans perform their play *Pyramus and Thisbe*, about two parted lovers. In the play, Thisbe sees a lion and flees, dropping her mantle. Pyramus finds the mantle and stabs himself. Thisbe discovers Pyramus's body, so kills herself, too. The Court can barely contain its laughter, and as the play ends, Theseus calls an end to the revels. Puck leads a fairy procession through the palace. »

IN CONTEXT

THEMES
Love, identity, sense, and madness

SETTING
Mythical Athens, and a forest outside Athens

SOURCES
8 CE The poem *Metamorphoses* by the Roman poet Ovid, plus various Greek myths.

LEGACY
1604 The first recorded productions are at the court of King James I.

1662 A gutted adaptation is performed; English diarist Samuel Pepys describes it as "the most insipid, ridiculous play that I ever saw".

1692 English actor Thomas Betterton commissions Henry Purcell to write music for a version called *The Fairy Queen*.

1905 Austrian director Max Reinhardt stages the play in Berlin using a revolving set.

1914 British actor-director Harley Granville-Barker stages a controversial futuristic version.

1960 The play is adapted into an opera by British composer Benjamin Britten.

1970 Peter Brook's famous minimalist production for the RSC has a white box for a set.

2006 With a production originating in Chennai, Tamil Nadu, British theatre director Tim Supple turns the play into an Indian folk-tale.

A *Midsummer Night's Dream* is unique in Shakespeare's varied canon. Full of romance and poetry, humour and beauty, it is a flight of fantasy, a journey into a world of magic that explores love in all its tenderness, excitement, and danger. Its story has resonated across cultures, and the play is widely performed across the world.

The play is set not just on any night, but Midsummer Night. The summer solstice had a mystical significance dating back to ancient times. Shakespeare's England had pagan roots that ran far deeper than its Christian tradition, and this was the night when magic was felt to be in the air, and fairies and sprites were abroad. It is not that everyone believed in fairies, then. Edmund Spenser, who wrote his poem *The Faerie Queene* around this time, declared, "the truth is that there be no such things, nor yet the shadow of the things." Shakespeare simply uses the magic of this night to delve into the interplay between imagination and reality, madness and reason, love and common sense, and tell a story that is both an enchanting delight and a voyage into the dark places of the mind. Spenser's *Faerie Queen*, although set in fairyland, was about the real queen, Elizabeth I, and it is hard not to see Elizabeth, too, in the strong queens of the *Dream*, Titania and Hippolyta.

Wedding and marriage
It is not known for certain when *A Midsummer Night's Dream* was written, but some suggest that it was a play to celebrate a wedding,

Tim Supple's production for the RSC in 2006 set the action in India. The lines were spoken in a mix of English and six Indian languages. Here, Bottom bemoans his ass's head.

> O long and tedious night,
> Abate thy hours.
> **Helena**
> **Act 3, Scene 2**

possibly the wedding of the young Elizabeth de Vere to the Earl of Derby in 1595. Others dispute this idea, but the play does indeed seem to take the pattern of an elaborate masque. It begins with the announcement of a wedding – so often the endpoint of a drama – and finishes on the night of a triple wedding.

The weddings – in Athens, the world of reality – are brief scenes that frame the wild and spectacular journey into the fairy forest. There is a symmetry and movement between the world of lovers, fairies, and "mechanicals" that is like a marvellous dance, coming together in the magical torch-lit procession that ends the play. The play can be seen both as an exquisite wedding gift and an instruction on the true nature of love that the watching couple must learn before embarking on married life.

City and forest

A Midsummer Night's Dream has a triple structure. It begins in the city, journeys into the forest, and then returns to the city again. The city is the world of order, reason, and discipline, but order in this city has broken down. The characters must voyage into the wild in order to learn lessons for their real work.

In many ways, it is an interior journey – a journey of self-knowledge – but the journey is as much about society rediscovering what matters as it is a personal journey. Clearly, there is much to learn in Athens about marriage. At the opening of the play, Theseus explains how he won Hippolyta, the queen of the Amazons (a tribe of female warriors), by force: "Hippolyta, I have wooed thee with my sword, / And won thy love by doing thee injuries." (1.1.16–17).

Old Egeus calls for the death penalty if his daughter Hermia refuses to marry Demetrius. Even Theseus's "reprieve" only offers Hermia the choice of life in a nunnery instead. It is clear that Theseus and Egeus may have the law on their side, but their world of "reason" and "sense" has little understanding of human love and feelings. Indeed, Theseus's vision is entirely out of sympathy with imagination and poetry, as well as love, which he equates with a kind of madness: "The lunatic, the lover, and the poet / Are of imagination all compact" (5.1.7–8). Love, for Theseus, is a frantic delusion. Poetry is a frenzied rolling of the eye. »

> The lunatic, the lover,
> and the poet
> Are of imagination
> all compact.
> **Theseus**
> **Act 5, Scene 1**

An English idyll

The forest in *A Midsummer Night's Dream* is said to be outside Athens, but it is really an English wood, like the forest of Arden Shakespeare knew so well. The play can be seen to be a hymn to England, full of magic, yet down-to-earth and real – a reminder, perhaps, to distant rulers of what really matters.

The wild flowers Oberon, the king of the fairies, tells of are those of an English wood, brought to life with a tenderness and knowledge of a writer who had walked those woods since childhood. Shakespeare gives Oberon these words:
"I know a bank where the wild thyme blows, Where oxlips and the nodding violet grows, Quite over-canopied with luscious woodbine, With sweet musk-roses, and with eglantine" (2.1.250–253).

The fogs and sodden fields and the tired ploughman that the queen of the fairies, Titania, describe are scenes from England, not from Athens, and the artisans who put on the play are as solidly English as one can imagine.

> These are the forgeries of jealousy
> **Titania**
> **Act 2, Scene 1**

Parallels with Verona

In some ways, the Athens of Theseus is as unhealthy as the feuding Verona that brings such tragedy to *Romeo and Juliet* (which was written at much the same time). Like Romeo and Juliet, Hermia and Lysander are star-crossed lovers, doomed to separation by foolish and tyrannical parents. When Lysander laments that "The course of true love never did run smooth" (1.1.134), it is almost as if he is talking of Romeo and Juliet. The journey into the forest in *A Midsummer Night's Dream* is the journey the Montagues and Capulets needed to embark upon if Romeo and Juliet were to have a happy outcome.

A forest of the mind

The forest that the four lovers enter, along with the artisans, is a place of the imagination, a place of fantasy and dreams, where the normal order of things is turned upside down. Nowadays, psychologists might talk of the realm of the unconscious, and critics explore the psychological symbolism of the play and its expression of sexual desires and gender issues. In Shakespeare's time it is simply the world of dreams and faeries. Indeed, the whole play is presented as a dream that we have strayed into. As Puck says at the end: "If we shadows have offended, / Think but this, and all is mended: / That you have but slumbered here, / While these visions did appear; / And this weak and idle theme, / No more yielding but a dream" (Epilogue.1–6).

The forest of dreams is a place where normality is subverted. But it is more of a nightmare than a dream. Characters play parts,

> And though she be but little, she is fierce.
> **Helena**
> **Act 3, Scene 2**

wear masks and costumes, change roles, behave out of character, suffer delusions, swap status or lovers – and even, as in the case of Bottom the weaver, acquire the head of an ass. Here the world of reason and "common sense" – what is normally sensed – vanishes and nothing is certain. Identities continually shift and transform.

Troubled identity

The loss of identity is disturbing, often terrifying. What is love, when it can shift so easily? Isn't love attached to a person's identity? Hermia, the most constant of the lovers, begins to question who she

Adaptations

The play's unusual structure means it has not always been treated gently by adaptors. In the 17th century in particular, many productions took liberties, for example by staging the comic elements alone. The pageant-like nature of the play has inspired many to add music. One of the best was the *Fairy Queen* by English composer Henry Purcell (1692), which inserted exquisite musical masques between each scene. In 1842, Felix Mendelssohn wrote beautiful incidental music to a production that includes the famous Wedding March.

In the 20th century, adaptors have been more interested in the psychological and sexual symbolism. Peter Brook's 1970 version was performed in a plain white box, and focussed on the adult themes over spectacle. Benjamin Britten's 1960 opera had a fairy chorus of boy trebles as a chaste counterpoint to the libidinous adults. Film versions have included Max Reinhardt's epic and visually sumptuous rendering of 1935 and, more recently, Michael Hoffman's 1999 soap opera-like version set in Tuscany (pictured).

A Midsummer Night's Dream relationships

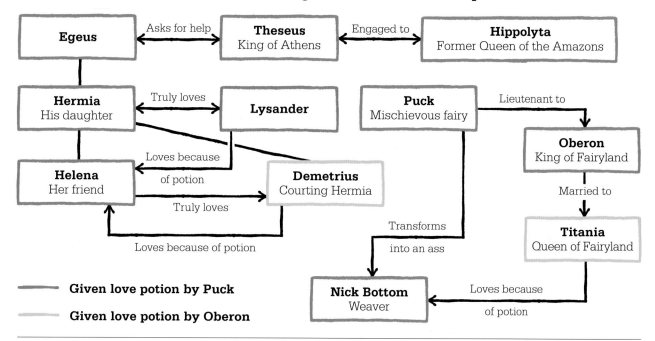

really is, as Lysander, who once professed to love her, suddenly seems to hate her – "Am I not Hermia? Are you not Lysander?" (3.2.274). Yet Helena lamented at the beginning of the play that she would have been happy if she could only be Hermia and so be loved by Demetrius – that she would give the world to be Hermia "translated".

In the forest, they are all "translated" under the influence of mischievous, shape-shifting Puck, and the effect is decidedly nightmarish. The magic love juices turn them this way and that, love to hate, hate to love, in an extreme fashion. Bottom is the most dramatically translated of all, yet he is the one who stays most constant. He may gain the head of an ass, but he is unfailingly courteous to Titania and to all the fairies who tend on him, and the relationship between him and Titania, though in some ways an illusion, is the gentlest and most tender in the play. Indeed, it is Bottom who has the sanest insight into love, telling Titania: "Methinks, mistress, you should have little reason / for that [loving me]. And yet, to say the truth, reason and love / keep little company together nowadays." (3.1.135–137).

Happy resolution

The artisans show the truest understanding of love, and pass through the madness of the forest with their identities intact. Even when they are playing characters in their play, they stay steadfastly themselves. Snout doesn't become the Wall, he simply, as Snout, "presents" it.

It is only fitting that these simple men bring the drama down to earth and good humour again at the end, leaving the realm of dreams to the fairies, with proper separation restored. At the end, everyone retires to bed, thankful to put this wild night behind them.

The fairies reinhabit the house as protective dreams: "But all the story of the night told over, / And all their minds transfigured so together, / More witnesseth than fancy's images, / And grows to something of great constancy; / But, howsoever, strange and admirable." (5.1.23–27). ∎

Now the hungry lion roars, And the wolf behowls the moon, Whilst the heavy ploughman snores, All with weary task fordone.
Puck
Act 5, Scene 2

THERE IS NO SURE FOUNDATION SET ON BLOOD

THE LIFE AND DEATH OF KING JOHN (1596)

DRAMATIS PERSONAE

King John King of England, he is vain, cruel and indecisive.

Queen Eleanor King John's mother.

Philip the Bastard Illegitimate son of John's eldest brother, Richard I. He is later renamed Sir Richard Plantagenet

King Philip of France He backs Arthur's claim to the English throne.

Louis the Dauphin King Philip's son.

Lady Blanche of Spain Niece of King John.

Cardinal Pandolf Papal legate.

Duke of Austria Previously killed Richard I, now defender of Arthur.

Arthur Son of John's elder brother, Geoffrey, later he becomes Duke of Brittaine.

Lady Constance Arthur's mother.

Prince Henry John's son, later King Henry III.

Hubert A loyal follower of King John.

Earl of Pembroke, Earl of Salisbury Nobles who rebel against John.

Lady Falconbridge Philip the Bastard's mother.

Robert Falconbridge Lady Falconbridge's legitimate son.

King Philip of France **challenges King John to renounce his throne** in favour of Arthur, but John defies him.

1.1

Cardinal Pandolf excommunicates King John for his defiance of the Pope. King Philip breaks their alliance.

3.1

The English side is victorious. John orders Hubert to murder Arthur.

3.3

Act 1	Act 2	Act 3

2.1

The French and English fight an inconclusive battle before the gates of Angers. **Peace is made** by the marriage of Blanche, John's niece, to King Philip's son, Louis.

3.2

In the battle with the French, **Philip the Bastard beheads the Duke of Austria** and **rescues Queen Eleanor** after she is captured by the French.

England and France prepare for war. Robert Falconbridge quarrels with his brother, Philip. They both claim to be the heir to their father's estate. Robert insists that his brother is the illegitimate son of Richard I, "the Lionheart". Queen Eleanor recognizes her son's features in Philip and renames him Sir Richard Plantagenet, although he continues to be known as the Bastard.

Outside the city of Angers (in France, but owned by the English), the French and English kings demand that the gates be opened to them. A battle is waged, with both sides claiming victory. Peace is made by the marriage of the dauphin to John's niece, Blanche, with all of England's French territories, except Angers, as her dowry. The arrival of Cardinal Pandolf, the Pope's legate, causes renewed conflict. When King John defies the Pope's authority, Pandolf excommunicates him. King Philip breaks his allegiance with England.

The Bastard decapitates the Duke of Austria (who had killed his father, Richard I), and rescues Queen Eleanor. Arthur is taken

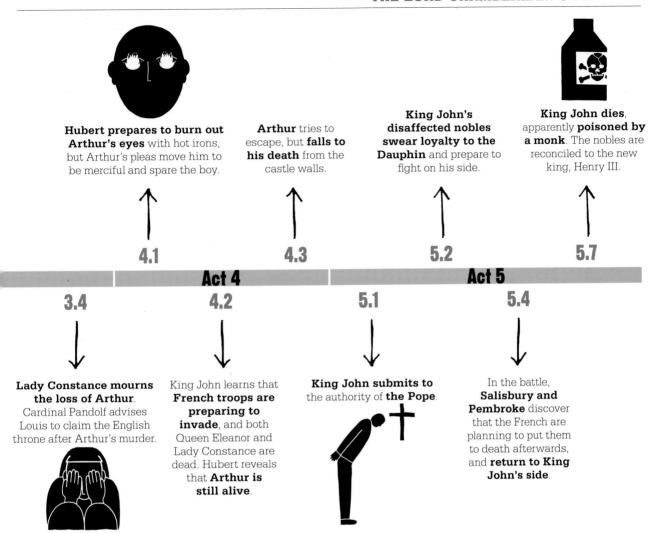

Hubert prepares to burn out Arthur's eyes with hot irons, but Arthur's pleas move him to be merciful and spare the boy.

Arthur tries to escape, but **falls to his death** from the castle walls.

King John's disaffected nobles swear loyalty to the Dauphin and prepare to fight on his side.

King John dies, apparently **poisoned by a monk**. The nobles are reconciled to the new king, Henry III.

4.1

4.3

5.2

5.7

Act 4

Act 5

3.4

4.2

5.1

5.4

Lady Constance mourns the loss of Arthur. Cardinal Pandolf advises Louis to claim the English throne after Arthur's murder.

King John learns that **French troops are preparing to invade**, and both Queen Eleanor and Lady Constance are dead. Hubert reveals that **Arthur is still alive**.

King John submits to the authority of **the Pope**.

In the battle, **Salisbury and Pembroke** discover that the French are planning to put them to death afterwards, and **return to King John's side**.

prisoner by King John and placed in the custody of Hubert, who is ordered to murder him. The Cardinal is cheered by the fact that King John will have to kill Arthur, which will turn the English against him. He recruits Louis the Dauphin to march on England.

Hubert cannot bring himself to kill Arthur and instead promises to tell King John that he is dead. John has had himself crowned for a second time. When the king announces that Arthur is dead of a sudden sickness, the nobles angrily renounce him. A messenger tells

the king that French troops are about to land on English soil. The Bastard brings in Peter of Pomfret who prophesies that John will give up the crown by noon on Ascension Day. John throws him in prison. John is relieved when Hubert confesses that the prince is still alive. But Arthur falls to his death. His body is found by Pembroke, Salisbury, and Bigot, who don't believe the death was accidental.

John submits to the authority of the Pope, on condition that Cardinal Pandolf disarm the French. It is Ascension Day when

John resigns his crown into Pandolf's hands, only to have it returned. The Bastard condemns this and insists that the king should continue to defy the dauphin. The latter is eager to fight, and refuses to be deflected by the Cardinal. The French are weakened by a loss of supplies and the defection of English nobles. As fortune turns in the favour of the English, King John is ill. He dies in the presence of his son, now King Henry III. English nobles offer their allegiance to the new king, and the Cardinal negotiates a truce. »

IN CONTEXT

THEMES
Inheritance, identity, kingship, loyalty

SETTING
The English court, Angers in France

SOURCES
1587 Holinshed's *Chronicles of England, Scotland, and Ireland*.

c.1589 Anonymously authored play *The Troublesome Reign of King John* may have been an influence on Shakespeare.

LEGACY
1737 First known performance at Theatre Royal, London.

1899 King John's death scene from Herbert Beerbohm Tree's production of *King John* represents the first example of Shakespeare on film.

1936 A Hindi film adaptation, *Saed-e-Havas* (*King John*) is made in India, directed by Sohrab Modi.

1953 At the Old Vic in London, Richard Burton plays a swashbuckling Bastard.

1980 The Weimar National Theatre in Germany stages an acclaimed production with a tough, uncompromising image of warfare.

2012 *King John* is staged in Armenian in London by the Gabriel Sundukyan National Academic Theatre. The production highlights the boisterous humour of the play, portraying King John as a clown-like figure.

When King John asserts that there is "No certain life achieved by others' death" (4.2.105), he alludes to his decision to kill Arthur – the young rival to his throne. Rather than confirming John's authority, the murder has undermined it, for England's nobles will no longer follow "the foot / That leaves the print of blood where'er it walks" (4.3.25–26).

Blood follows blood

The doctrine that blood follows blood, and that murdering other royal claimants does not secure one's grip upon the throne, resonates throughout Shakespeare's English history plays. For example, in *Richard II*, the murder of King Richard continues to generate new enemies for the usurper Henry IV. What is unusual about *King John*

The play includes John's disputes with his nobles, but omits the resolution – forcing him to sign the Magna Carta in 1215. John died a year later at Newark Castle, Nottinghamshire, shown here.

is the joke that is being played against the king when he makes this assertion, for, as the audience already knows, Arthur isn't really dead. The audience is allowed to think that John has won a lucky reprieve. But at the very moment when Hubert is hurrying after the earls to tell them that Arthur is not dead, they discover his body at the foot of the prison walls. This episode illustrates one of the distinct features of *King John*; why it appears to stand alone tonally as well as structurally.

The play undermines the ambitions and actions of the great, wrong-footing them at every turn. For example, the motives of the King of France may be morally suspect when he makes peace with England, as the Bastard points out, but an Anglo-French marriage at least prevents further bloodshed. However, Philip's vows of allegiance have barely been made before he is forced by Cardinal Pandolf to declare war once again. It seems impossible for the major characters to maintain a

THE LORD CHAMBERLAIN'S MAN 123

consistent policy on anything, and, as a result, the play struggles to achieve any kind of tragic effect (it may be worth noting that the term "Tragedy" is absent from the title). Tragedy depends on a kind of heroic consistency and self-assertion in the face of cosmic opposition or unlucky chance – and this is not the story of King John.

Disputed succession

John's assertion that "There is no sure foundation set on blood" (4.2.104) also relates to ideas of identity and inheritance. The play's opening dispute is about who stands next in line to the throne after the deaths of Richard and Geoffrey, Queen Eleanor's elder sons. There is disagreement about whether a son (Arthur) or a brother (John) should inherit, with even Eleanor implying that Arthur might have the superior claim.

The situation is made more complicated by the larger difficulty of determining paternity. This anxiety is focused on Philip the Bastard, who is proven to be the illegitimate son of Richard the Lionheart by physical resemblance. Philip is left in the position of choosing his identity – whether to inherit Sir Robert's estate, or suffer the stigma of illegitimacy

Mad world, mad kings, mad composition!
Philip the Bastard
Act 2, Scene 1

I am amazed, methinks, and lose my way Among the thorns and dangers of this world.
Philip the Bastard
Act 4, Scene 3

in order to be recognized as Richard's son. He chooses the latter, but the arbitrariness of his choice reinforces the point that "all men's children" (1.1.63) must doubt their paternity. In the verbal battle between Eleanor and Constance (2.1), both Arthur and Richard the Lionheart stand accused of being bastards.

It seems then that neither ruthless political action nor an unquestioned blood right to the throne are enough to render kingship secure. The play advises the necessity of maintaining loyalty, particularly among one's nobles. The new King Henry III is brought to tears by the sight of Salisbury, Pembroke, and Bigot kneeling before him. A cynical response to this display – given their betrayal of King John and then the dauphin – seems to be deliberately averted by the Bastard's final words, which emphasize the need for unity: "Naught shall make us rue / If England to itself do rest but true" (5.7.117–118). It is one of the play's deepest ironies that the man who carries the blood of Richard the Lionheart in his veins is denied the chance to rule the nation he loves more than its legitimate kings do. ∎

Philip The Bastard

Philip Falconbridge has more lines than any other character in *King John*, and is often described as the play's hero. Bastards in Shakespeare are usually villains (Don John, Iago, Edmund). The status of "bastard" was equated with a moral deficit, his inability to inherit wealth leaving him with a ruthless streak. However, the Bastard of *King John* is a comic figure: "Why, what a madcap hath heaven lent us here!" (1.1.84). He acts as both a satirical chorus, exposing the protagonists' true motives, and a heroic figure. In Maria Aberg's 2012 production for the RSC, Philip's gender was changed, and he was played with a mixture of tenderness and scorn by Pippa Nixon (above, left).

Philip is aware of the irony of a bastard defending the moral order, and at the end of the play Salisbury advises the new King Henry that it is his duty "to set a form upon that indigest" (5.7.26). That Philip speaks the play's final lines may testify to his charisma and rapport with the audience, or to the difficulty that subsequent kings will find in imposing this ideal "form".

IF YOU PRICK US, DO WE NOT BLEED?

THE MERCHANT OF VENICE (1596)

DRAMATIS PERSONAE

Antonio A merchant of Venice, he guarantees a loan to his friend Bassanio "with a pound of my flesh".

Bassanio Antonio's friend, and suitor to Portia.

Leonardo A servant to Bassanio.

Graziano, Salerio, Solanio Friends of Antonio and Bassanio.

Lorenzo Friend of Antonio and Bassanio, in love with Jessica.

Shylock A rich Jewish moneylender, father of Jessica.

Jessica Daughter of Shylock, in love with Lorenzo.

Tubal A Jew, Shylock's friend.

Lancelot A clown and servant to Shylock.

Gobbo Father of Lancelot.

Portia A rich heiress. She disguises herself as a doctor of law, "Balthasar", to save Antonio's life.

Nerissa Portia's maid, in love with Graziano.

Balthasar, Stefano Portia's servants. Later, the names of Portia and Nerissa in disguise.

Prince of Morocco Suitor to Portia.

Prince of Aragon Suitor to Portia.

Duke of Venice He must uphold Venetian law.

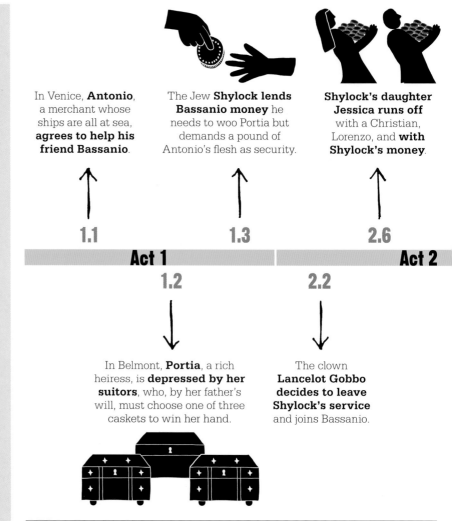

In Venice, **Antonio**, a merchant whose ships are all at sea, **agrees to help his friend Bassanio**.

1.1

The Jew **Shylock lends Bassanio money** he needs to woo Portia but demands a pound of Antonio's flesh as security.

1.3

Shylock's daughter **Jessica runs off** with a Christian, Lorenzo, and **with Shylock's money**.

2.6

Act 1 | **Act 2**

1.2

In Belmont, **Portia**, a rich heiress, is **depressed by her suitors**, who, by her father's will, must choose one of three caskets to win her hand.

2.2

The clown **Lancelot Gobbo decides to leave Shylock's service** and joins Bassanio.

In Venice, the merchant Antonio is sad, but agrees to help his friend Bassanio raise the money he needs to woo the beautiful heiress Portia. In Belmont, meanwhile, Portia is sad too. By her father's will, she must marry the man who chooses the correct one of three caskets – gold, silver, and lead. When Shylock hesitates to lend Bassanio money, Bassanio promises Antonio as guarantor. Shylock sees a chance of revenge on Antonio, who has previously mocked him. He stipulates that the bond be a pound of Antonio's flesh.

In Belmont, the Prince of Morocco arrives to try his luck with Portia. In Venice, Shylock's servant Lancelot decides to leave his master and serve Bassanio. Shylock's daughter Jessica is sad that Lancelot is leaving and decides to run away. She gives Lancelot a message for Lorenzo, who is staying with Bassanio. Shylock is invited to dinner with Bassanio, and while he's out, Jessica steals his money and escapes to Belmont disguised as a boy. In Belmont, the Princes of Morocco and Aragon fail the casket test, choosing gold and silver.

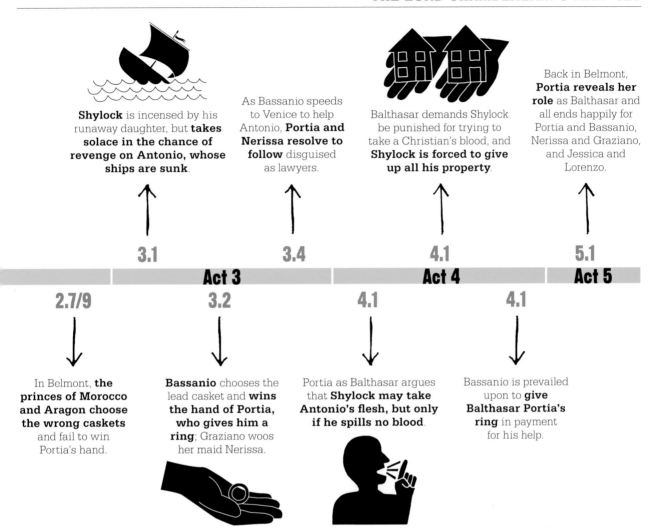

Shylock is incensed by his runaway daughter, but **takes solace in the chance of revenge on Antonio, whose ships are sunk**.

As Bassanio speeds to Venice to help Antonio, **Portia and Nerissa resolve to follow** disguised as lawyers.

Balthasar demands Shylock be punished for trying to take a Christian's blood, and **Shylock is forced to give up all his property**.

Back in Belmont, **Portia reveals her role** as Balthasar and all ends happily for Portia and Bassanio, Nerissa and Graziano, and Jessica and Lorenzo.

3.1

3.4

4.1

5.1

Act 3

Act 4

Act 5

2.7/9

3.2

4.1

4.1

In Belmont, **the princes of Morocco and Aragon choose the wrong caskets** and fail to win Portia's hand.

Bassanio chooses the lead casket and **wins the hand of Portia, who gives him a ring**; Graziano woos her maid Nerissa.

Portia as Balthasar argues that **Shylock may take Antonio's flesh, but only if he spills no blood**.

Bassanio is prevailed upon to **give Balthasar Portia's ring** in payment for his help.

In Belmont, Portia asks Bassanio to delay choosing caskets to prolong their time together. But to his and Portia's joy, he chooses the lead casket containing a portrait of Portia. Bassanio's friend Graziano and Portia's maid Nerissa decide to marry. This happiness is marred by news that Shylock is claiming his flesh from Antonio. Portia offers to repay the debt "twenty times over", and Bassanio sets off for Venice. Portia follows Bassanio disguised as a male lawyer, accompanied by Nerissa disguised as "his" clerk.

In a Venice courtroom, Shylock demands his pound of flesh. Balthasar (Portia in disguise) arrives to adjudicate. Balthasar says Shylock should be merciful, but the law is in his favour. Shylock delightedly prepares to take his pound of flesh. Then Balthasar informs him that in doing so he may not spill Antonio's blood. Stunned, Shylock accepts Bassanio's money. But Balthasar is relentless. As an alien threatening a Venetian, she tells Shylock, he faces the death penalty, which can only be averted by giving up all his

wealth. The Duke pardons him, providing he pay half his wealth to Antonio. Antonio simply asks that Shylock give the money to Jessica and Lorenzo on his death. Balthasar asks in payment from Bassanio only the ring Portia gave him.

Lorenzo and Jessica bask in their love as Portia and Nerissa return. The girls berate Bassanio and Graziano for giving their rings to other women. Antonio defends them, and Portia and Nerissa admit the truth. Portia tells Antonio his boats are safe, and Nerissa gives Lorenzo and Jessica Shylock's new will. »

IN CONTEXT

THEMES
Prejudice, revenge, justice, money, love

SETTING
Venice and the fictional town of Belmont, in Italy

SOURCES
The main elements of the plot, the flesh-bond and the story of the caskets, are taken from folk tales. The character Shylock is inspired by the following:

14th century Italian Giovanni Fiorentino's collection of tales *Il Pecorone* ("The Dunce").

1589 Christopher Marlowe's *The Jew of Malta*.

LEGACY
1605 The play is performed for James I on Shrove Tuesday.

1959 Tyrone Guthrie directs a production in Israel, with Aharon Meskin as Shylock. The action is moved to the present day, portraying Shylock as a capitalist financier.

1970 At the National Theatre, London, Laurence Olivier portrays Shylock as a Jew trying too hard to assimilate, as the action is moved to Venice in the 1880s.

1992 In his book *Shylock*, critic John Gross feels there is "a permanent chill in the air" in the play's treatment of Jews.

2004 A film adaptation directed by Michael Radford casts Al Pacino as Shylock, Jeremy Irons as Antonio, and Lynn Collions as Portia.

F ew of Shakespeare's plays have caused quite as much disquiet as *The Merchant of Venice*. The story is a blend of two old folk tales – that of the mean moneylender who demands an extreme payment, a pound of flesh, from his creditor, and that of the young princess who finds her true love through the test of three caskets. *The Merchant of Venice* has a happy ending for most, with the young lovers united, and in Portia, Shakespeare creates an appealing heroine, humble and loving yet brilliant and incisive in the court scene. But the moneylender Shylock, whose Jewishness is so crucial to his portrayal, and for whom the play does not end well, continues to arouse deep anxiety among audiences and performers.

The stereotypical Jew

The anxiety hinges on whether the play is anti-Semitic. A rapacious, skinflint moneylender, Shylock certainly conforms to a negative

In the 16th-century, Venetian Jews were confined to a ghetto, and Shylock would have been forced to live here. In this early 17th-century map of Venice, the ghetto is marked with a star.

stereotype of a Jewish character that was already well used by the time Shakespeare wrote his play around 1597. Indeed, Christopher Marlowe had a huge hit with such negative stereotypes around 1590 with *The Jew of Malta*. There are clear parallels between Shylock and Marlowe's Jew, Barabas, who, like Shylock, is a widowed father with a single beautiful daughter who rejects her father's "misplaced" Judaism and converts to Christianity. It is likely that neither playwright was writing from direct experience, however, since Jews had been banned from England long before. As a result, both Barabas and Shylock are perhaps best seen as stock villains.

There is no doubt that *The Merchant of Venice* has done a great deal to reinforce negative stereotypes of Jews over the centuries. Originally, perhaps, this was in a mostly comic vein, with Shylock played as a pantomime baddy. But more disturbingly, *The Merchant of Venice* was staged deliberately in Nazi Germany in the late 1930s to help justify the attacks on Jews. Critics, however, have been divided over whether this can be blamed on Shakespeare, or those who misuse the play. Many critics defend Shakespeare against the charge of anti-Semitism by underlining the play's nuances. Others have suggested that we should bear in mind the context of Shakespeare's age, when few people had the political and racial awareness we do now. Shakespeare was writing, as when he wrote of Othello, about storybook figures in tales from abroad. The problem, perhaps, is more for us today – how do we deal with characters such as Shylock with our awareness of the dangers such stereotypes pose?

The victim of prejudice

Since the Holocaust, most stagings of the play have been acutely aware of the dangers of portraying Shylock simply as a villain and have instead looked at the character more as a tragic victim of racial and religious prejudice. Shylock is seen as an outsider who is abused by the Christians of Venice, robbed and abandoned by his daughter, and finally humiliated by the loss of his fortune and good name and forced to convert to Christianity. Such is Shakespeare's skill as a playwright that this tragedy can be found in the play. In a famously telling speech, Shylock rails against the abuse he has suffered: "I am a Jew. Hath not a Jew eyes? Hath not a Jew hands, organs, dimensions, senses, affections, passions; fed with the same food, hurt with the same weapons, subject to the same diseases, healed by the same means, warmed and cooled by the same winter and summer as a Christian is? If you prick us, do we not bleed?" (3.1.54–59).

This speech is often quoted out of context as a heartfelt cry against racial prejudice – or the bitter cry of

Dustin Hoffman took on the role of Shylock in a 1989 production directed by Peter Hall. Hoffman portrayed the moneylender as a good man driven beyond endurance by mistreatment.

anger of the whole Hebrew race. But perhaps it is not quite so simple as that. When Shylock says, "If you prick us, do we not bleed?" he is not just saying that Jews have the same blood, but also referring to the common test for a witch, which was to prick the thumbs to see if they bleed. **»**

In sooth, I know not why I am so sad.
It wearies me, you say it wearies you
Antonio
Act 1, Scene 1

But love is blind, and lovers cannot see
The pretty follies that themselves commit
Jessica
Act 2, Scene 6

Tell me where is fancy bred,
Or in the heart, or in the head?
Singer
Act 3, Scene 2

Is this speech a plea for human rights or a justification for revenge – another stereotype of Jewish villainy? Either way, Shakespeare's audiences may have been surprised by how much they were moved by the words he placed in the mouth of the play's stock villain.

The melancholic merchant

Shylock often draws so much attention from critics that he is sometimes assumed to be the merchant in the play's title. But of course Shylock is a moneylender, not a merchant. The merchant of the title is Antonio. He plays a comparatively peripheral role in a play that is, in the main, a comedy about the nature of love.

In the very first line of the play, Antonio laments: "In sooth, I know not why I am so sad." His friends try to find an explanation for his sadness, but there is none. In a telling parallel, Portia opens the very next scene saying: "By my troth, Nerissa, my little body is aweary of this great world."

There is something that has cast a gloom over the world, and the comic journey of the play is to lift this gloom through the redeeming power of love, just as it is in *Twelfth Night,* in which it is Viola's task to lift the gloom into which Orsino and Olivia have sunk. In both plays, the heroines, Portia and Viola, must dress as men to win through, released by their disguise to reveal their true

This night, methinks is but the daylight sick.
Portia
Act 5, Scene 1

brilliance. In both plays, too, a misanthrope – Malvolio in *Twelfth Night* and Shylock in *The Merchant of Venice* – is left out of the general happiness at the play's end.

So what is the reason for this gloom? It may be no accident that Shakespeare's play is set in Venice, the commercial capital of Europe at the time, and the play focuses on a merchant. It is perhaps the restless quest for money and the commodification of relationships that has robbed the world of joy. When his daughter Jessica leaves, what is uppermost in Shylock's mind is the financial cost, and the plot of the play hinges on Bassanio's need to borrow money to even woo Portia.

The value of life

In the test of the three caskets, Portia will not find true love in the precious gold or silver caskets, but only the poor lead casket. When Bassanio makes the right choice of the lead casket, Portia explains that she has herself has little monetary value: "the full sum of me / Is sum of

Darko Tresnjak's 2007 production had a futuristic setting. At the end, it hints that the marriages will not turn out well, so it is not only Shylock (F Murray Abraham) who will suffer.

something which, to term in gross, / Is an unlessoned girl, unschooled, unpractiséd, / Happy in this, she is not yet so old" (3.2.157–160).

For Shylock, this would make her utterly worthless. For him, without money, there is no life. "Nay, take my life and all," he wails when the Duke threatens to take all his wealth in punishment for his crime, "you take my life / When you do take the means whereby I live." (4.1.373–374).

But the Christians in Venice are perhaps only slightly less obsessed with the making and spending of money. To achieve a happy ending, all the couples must leave the commercial world of Venice behind entirely and escape to the paradise of Portia's home in Belmont. Only there can Lorenzo and Jessica see that the real riches are in the beauties of the night and music: "the floor of heaven / Is thick inlaid with patens of bright gold." (5.1.58–59). It is also in Belmont that Antonio receives the happy news that his ships are safe, after Portia assures him with a letter that she has mysteriously acquired. But this happiness has come at a cost.

The friends in Venice

```
  Graziano  ←── Friends ──  Antonio  ── Friends ──→  Lorenzo

     ↕                         ↑                        ↕
Love each other            Friends   Guarantees    Love each other
                                     Bassanio's
  Nerissa                              debt          Jessica

                                                        │
  Lady-in-                                        Daughter to
  waiting                                                │
  and          Bassanio              Shylock  ←─────────┘
  confidante

              Owes money to ──→

              Defeats in court ──→

  Portia
```

────── Christian   ────── Jewish

Back in Venice, Shylock is a lonely and broken man, humiliated and vilified, with most of his money gone, his renegade daughter absent and waiting upon his death, when she will inherit what wealth of his remains. Elizabethan audiences may have seen this outcome as just deserts for the Jew. But Shakespeare manages to portray Shylock's fall as an all too human event. ∎

Demonized Jewry

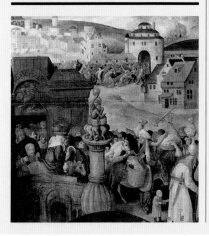

Jews had been banished from England since 1290, and they remained banished until 1655, when the Jewish scholar Manasseh ben Israel gained Oliver Cromwell's assent for Jews to return. There were a handful of Jews in London in Elizabethan times, but none would have been able to profess their religion openly, on pain of death. London Jews in the 1590s were mostly Marranos – descendants of forced Jewish converts from Portugal and Spain – including the queen's doctor Rodrigo Lopez, who was hung, drawn, and quartered in 1594, accused of conspiring to poison the Queen. Some scholars believe Lopez was the inspiration for Shylock, but there was no shortage of negative role models for Shakespeare to draw on, not least Marlowe's Barabas. With the Christian ban on usury, Jews had long been forced into the role of moneylenders. Prejudice was rife, partly because Jews were blamed by Christians for the betrayal of Christ. Jews were demonized in many ways – blamed for spreading the plague and associated with witches.

HONOUR IS A MERE SCUTCHEON

HENRY IV PART 1 (1596–1597)

DRAMATIS PERSONAE

Henry IV King of England, also known as Bolingbroke.

Harry, Prince of Wales Eldest son of the King, also known as Hal.

Earl of Worcester Leader of the rebel warlords.

Percy, Earl of Northumberland The Earl of Worcester's elder brother and fellow rebel.

Henry Percy Son of Northumberland, also known as Hotspur.

Kate Lady Percy, Hotspur's wife.

Sir John Falstaff A disreputable knight, and drinking companion of Prince Hal.

Mistress Quickly Hostess of the Boar's Head Tavern in Eastcheap, London.

Owain Glyndŵr A Welsh lord and Lady Mortimer's father.

Lady Mortimer Glyndŵr's daughter and Mortimer's wife.

Lord Edmund Mortimer Earl of March, Hotspur's brother in law.

Sir Richard Vernon A rebel executed after the Battle of Shrewsbury.

Sir Walter Blunt A noble loyal to the king, who dies fighting the Percys.

Ned Poins A follower of Falstaff.

Henry learns that **rebellion in the north and west** will postpone his crusade to the Holy Land.

1.1

Hal speaks in soliloquy **of his rebellious reputation** and long-term plan to reform himself.

1.2

At Gad's Hill, **Hal and Poins steal** back the stolen money **from Falstaff** and company.

2.1

Act 1

1.2

Ned Poins recruits Falstaff to rob travellers and pilgrims at Gad's Hill in Kent.

1.3

The barons **Worcester and Northumberland recruit the enthusiastic Hotspur** to their rebel cause.

The troubles that plague Henry IV's reign begin with his overthrow and murder of Richard II in the earlier play of that name. Plagued by guilt, which he longs to expiate with a crusade to the Holy Land, Henry is kept frustratingly at home by the threat of rebellion in Wales and in the north.

In Wales, the warlord Owain Glyndŵr has thrown his forces behind the claim of Glyndŵr's son-in-law, Edmund Mortimer, to be Richard's rightful heir. In the north, those barons who helped Henry to the throne, led by the Earl of Northumberland, fear his appropriation of their feudal rights. Henry has already demanded the Scottish prisoners captured for ransom by Hotspur. Faced with Henry's ultimatum, the fiery Hotspur vents his fury. The barons harness the young man's anger by recruiting him to their cause. Stung by Henry's ingratitude, they plan to join with Mortimer and the Scots against him.

Henry's son, Prince Hal, adds to his father's woes. He sidesteps all responsibility as Prince of Wales and wastes his time in the seamy

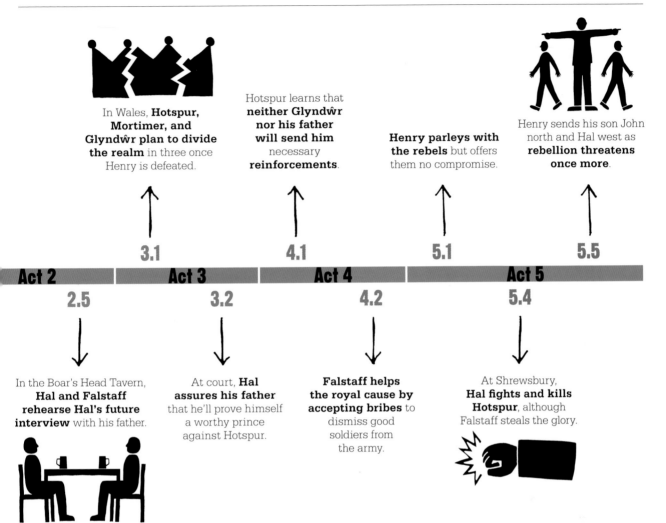

In Wales, **Hotspur, Mortimer, and Glyndŵr plan to divide the realm** in three once Henry is defeated.

Hotspur learns that **neither Glyndŵr nor his father will send him** necessary **reinforcements**.

Henry parleys with the rebels but offers them no compromise.

Henry sends his son John north and Hal west as **rebellion threatens once more**.

3.1

4.1

5.1

5.5

Act 2   Act 3   Act 4   Act 5

2.5

3.2

4.2

5.4

In the Boar's Head Tavern, **Hal and Falstaff rehearse Hal's future interview** with his father.

At court, **Hal assures his father** that he'll prove himself a worthy prince against Hotspur.

Falstaff helps the royal cause by accepting bribes to dismiss good soldiers from the army.

At Shrewsbury, **Hal fights and kills Hotspur**, although Falstaff steals the glory.

---

underworld of Eastcheap. There his surrogate father, Sir John Falstaff, holds sway over a tavern-court of drunkards, thieves, and prostitutes. Hal joins in the revelry, but only, he tells us, to shine the brighter when, like the prodigal son, he turns away from fleshly pursuits to take up his royal role.

Hal's eventual return to face his father is rehearsed in the tavern where, speaking as Hal, Falstaff defends his own licentiousness as a celebration of life. But Hal, speaking as his father, calls such vice life-threatening, and admits

he'll banish Falstaff one fine day. He seems to speak both as the king and as himself in this.

With the rebellion gathering pace, Hal returns to court and plays the tavern scene for real. When he promises to defeat Hotspur and appropriate his honours, Henry is reassured, finally seeing something of his own ambition in his son. Together they meet the rebels in a parley. Hal offers to fight Hotspur in single combat but the unbending Henry refuses, dismissing the rebels' claim of broken promises and repeating his demands.

The two sides fight at the Battle of Shrewsbury, where Hal fights Hotspur one-to-one. After killing his rival, the prince praises his nobility. Then, seeing the body of Falstaff, he grieves the loss of his less noble friend. True to form however, Falstaff is feigning. Once Hal has left, the wily knight sees the chance for profit and takes the body of Hotspur off as his own kill. Meeting Hal as he goes, Falstaff persuades the Prince to condone the lie. Meanwhile, news of further rebellion leaves the resolution of Henry IV's political difficulties to Part 2. »

IN CONTEXT

THEMES
Deception, usurpation, honour, disorder

SETTING
Court of Henry IV, and the Boar's Head Tavern; rebel camps in England and Wales; Shrewsbury

SOURCES
1587 Holinshed's *Chronicles of England, Scotland, and Ireland*.

1594 *The Famous Victories of Henry V*, an anonymous play probably known to Shakespeare.

1595 Samuel Daniel's poem "The First Four Books of the Civil War Between the Two Houses of York and Lancaster".

LEGACY
1597–1613 The play is a big success – five quarto editions of the text are published.

1600 References to parts 1 and 2 as "The Hotspur" and "Sir John Falstaff" attest to the popularity of these characters.

1642–60 Falstaff is kept on stage during the Puritan period in a drollery entitled "The Bouncing Knight".

1951 Richard Burton plays a heroic Hal in a Stratford-upon-Avon production.

1966 Orson Welles directs and stars in *Chimes at Midnight*, an artistic film adaptation.

1982 Trevor Nunn's RSC set presents Henry's England as a precarious wooden scaffolding.

There is little honour in the deposition of a king. The crown that Henry IV wears is one he took from the weak King Richard II, with the help of a group of independent warlords led by the Earl of Northumberland. Now he wants to unite England as a nation marching "all one way" (1.1.15). Unfortunately, this means replacing those same warlords' feudal powers with a centralized form of rule, and they are not pleased. Their threatened rebellion challenges Henry in the north and the west.

Henry doubly needs the support of these barons – not only to defend the borders but, importantly, to maintain his right to rule. He cannot claim to have inherited the throne. His right depends on might, and therefore on their support. Henry's dilemma as king is how legitimately he can quell their rebellion when his legitimacy is derived from rebellion itself.

Politics and chivalry
Shakespeare reinvents Henry here as a Renaissance prince rather than the medieval monarch that he was. His attempt to forge a nation-state under the crown, which was in fact a later Tudor project, is the strategy

I'll so offend to make offence a skill, Redeeming time when men think least I will.
Prince Hal
Act 1, Scene 2

So shaken as we are, so wan with care
King Henry
Act 1, Scene 1

of a politician. Such shrewd tactics cut clean across the chivalric code of honour with its escutcheons (shields bearing coats of arms) and heraldic etiquette on which the court of his predecessor, Richard II, was built.

Among the rebels, Richard is remembered as the perfect king. They conveniently forget his self-interested neglect of England, and now heap blame on his usurper for destroying the ideal. This illusion of chivalry fires the imagination of young Hotspur to pursue honour wherever it lies: "To pluck bright honour from the pale-faced moon… And pluck up drownèd honour by the locks." (1.3.200, 203). But the fact that it is unreachable shows how vulnerable it is.

Old men and the young
The play presents the conflict between this imagined past and Henry's coldly realistic present through a series of real and surrogate father-son relationships. Northumberland and Worcester, those powerful warlords who want to reinstate the past, are happy to recruit their valiant young kinsman Hotspur to the cause. They see a political naivety in his idealism that they can use. But they keep him well away from policy decisions

and, doubting the king's word, deny him the details of Henry's terms for peace. In the end, though, it is Northumberland who can't be trusted. He and Glyndŵr fail to send Hotspur essential reinforcements before the battle at Shrewsbury. Typically, Hotspur puts a brave face on this, arguing that it adds a "larger dare to our great enterprise" (4.1.78). But single-minded valour is no substitute for political strategy. And the consequence is fatal.

Henry sees in Hotspur the man he'll never be. He represents the knightly virtue that Henry stepped away from when he seized the crown. In this respect he is Henry's lost ideal, and the son that he would wish for: "A son who is the theme of honour's tongue" (1.1.80). His own son, Prince Hal, is a rebellious youth whom Henry needs to conform, for a noble heir would let him reinstate the line of legitimate inheritance that he himself usurped, and restore England's true order.

For the present, Hal chooses disorder. He spends his days far from the uneasy court, in the stews of the Eastcheap taverns, where excess, licentiousness, and dissipation are the norm. The whole is epitomized in the expansive and unconstrained fleshiness of Falstaff, the emblem of physical, moral, and spiritual disorder and of occasionally »

An RSC production in 1951 saw Richard Burton (centre), play an aloof, heroic Hal. Critics remarked upon Burton's eyes, which seemed to hold a vision of Hal's own destiny.

Censorship

Sir John Falstaff (above right, played by Antony Sher in a 2014 RSC production) is one of Shakespeare's bawdiest dramatic creations. His comic profanities were part of a long tradition of stage swearing. However, by the late 16th century, this was increasingly offending Puritan sensibilities. Shakespeare had already got into trouble by originally naming the character Sir John Oldcastle, which was also the name of a Protestant martyr. The outraged lord chamberlain (a descendant of Oldcastle's) forced Shakespeare to change the name and apologize.

Players came under pressure to clean up their language, then the 1606 "Act to Restrain the Abuses of Players" formally banned all onstage ribaldry and cursing. From then on, the plays were purged of any off-colour or irreligious language, a legacy that continued into the 20th century. The most drastic clean-up was, perhaps, the 1818 *Family Shakespeare* edited by the Reverend Thomas Bowdler, whose cuts were so severe that some plays, in particular *Othello*, were rendered nonsensical.

letting go. If Hotspur is true honour then Falstaff, as his name suggests, is its opposite. He sees honour as an empty word, a symbol that serves no material good. In this respect, Falstaff is a parody of Henry. Wit and low cunning are his tools, as political craft is the king's. And both of them are thieves.

Three worlds

Shakespeare constructed his own narrative using details from Holinshed's account of Henry's "unquiet reign" but much of the plot is his own invention. The result is a tightly structured, three-part story focusing on the relationships between a troubled monarch, his ambitious warlords, and his wayward heir. This gives us three clearly defined worlds in the court, the rebel camp, and the Boar's Head Tavern. The first two present events in historical time while the third, a wholly invented comic alternative to recorded history, acts as a foil. It's both a rebel space, and a topsy-turvy court, and offers a subversive commentary on the two. Falstaff's principles are the same as Henry's but applied to the realm of private

> But sirrah, there's no room for faith, truth, nor honesty in this bosom of thine; it is all filled up with guts and midriff.
> **Prince Hal**
> Act 3, Scene 3

In a rowdy Boar's Head Tavern, Falstaff (Roger Allam) plays the lute as Hal (Jamie Parker) dances in this 2010 production at the Globe Theatre.

life, as we see in the second scene (1.2). Some directors have made this clear in the scene transition, as the court figures leave by passing through the entering tavern folk, and Falstaff sits on what was Henry's throne. Where the court is factional and serious, in the tavern laws are joyously broken and honour mocked. And while the infestations of Eastcheap parody the dis-ease of Henry's court, in Falstaff they indicate a greed for pleasure more than power.

Hal's destiny

Hal may prefer to spend his time in Eastcheap, but he's not entirely unlike his royal father. His appearance as the wayward prince is part of a long-term plan, as he tells us privately at the scene's close. He's wasting time with the common people in order to reform

himself when the moment's right. He'll shine the brighter because of what he seemed to be. Critics are divided as to how we might respond to this, and much depends on individual performance. Should princes know their subjects' lives in order to govern better? If so, then Hal's calculation is wise. It shows him following a path between Hotspur's unquestioning pursuit of honour and Falstaff's selfish dismissal of it. The opposite view is that Hal is as crafty as his father and knows precisely how to make a show. In a world where chivalry is dying and honour a "mere scutcheon" (5.1.140), Hal deploys the tactics of a politician.

> 66

I can teach thee, coz, to shame
the devil – By telling the truth
Hotspur
Act 3, Scene 1

> 99

The Eastcheap world extends Hal's range of roles. Mimicking the tavern drawer (barman), he shows that he can "drink with any tinker in his own language" (2.5.18–19). The multi-layered tavern scene (2.5) draws the clearest parallels between kingship and acting when he and Falstaff rehearse Hal's interview with his father. Playing the king with a cushion for a crown, Hal responds to Falstaff's appeal against banishment with simple honesty: "I do; I will" (2.5.486). The moment is rich with possibilities, not least that Hal speaks for himself here and the threat of banishment is real. The knocking at the door that follows underlines the cold reality of Hal's words: that time will intrude upon this comic world and judgment will catch up with them all.

This parallel between politics and performance is acknowledged by the king himself when he and his son meet for real. He tells Hal that, as Bolingbroke, he rationed his appearances, and was so courteous in public that he soon had Richard's audience in his hands. He fears that the Prince is too familiar with his people and will be as vulnerable as Richard was. But Hal already has his plan. He assures his father that, as Henry used Richard, so he will use Hotspur and appropriate his reputation for himself: "Percy is but my factor, good my lord, / To engross up glorious deeds on my behalf" (3.2.147–148). Hal's language of commodity sounds more like a Renaissance merchant than a medieval knight. The politician prince will fashion his heroic image out of Hotspur's coat of arms.

The two meet at Shrewsbury in battle. On stage, it's a chance to thrill the audience with swordplay. The opponents are equally matched and by the end almost admire each other's fighting skills; this makes Hotspur's death all the more poignant, as Hal admits: "Fare thee well, great heart…When that this body did contain a spirit, / A kingdom for it was too small a bound" (5.4.86, 88–89).

Ambiguous ending

As Hal turns to leave, he sees Falstaff's body nearby and bids a brief farewell to his surrogate father. But once he's gone, the fat knight rises from the ground in high indignation at Hal's farewell. This comic coda alters the tone of the ending. We laugh, happy that Falstaff only pretends death. But we are also invited to consider Falstaff's feigning as a comment on Henry's tactical success. For the king used decoys in the battle, men dressed as him and carrying his escutcheon. It's a ploy that only confirms the rebels' view of him as a counterfeit king.

When Falstaff then heaves Hotspur's body on his back and goes off to spin tales of how he killed the hero, we watch story-telling take up what's left of chivalry. And as Hal meets Falstaff taking off the body, he agrees to "gild" (5.4.155), the old man's lie, which makes for an ambiguous, downbeat ending. It's a sign that Hal has yet to separate himself from his former life, and both his less-than-honourable father figures. ∎

Prince Hal is caught between, and is under pressure from, the "three worlds" of the play – the tavern and his surrogate family, the royal court and duty to his father, and the rebel camp, where Hotspur represents an ideal of knightly honour Hal knows he cannot attain.

Royal Court

Prince Hal

Boar's Head Tavern

Hotspur

WIVES

MAY BE MERRY, AND YET

HONEST TOO

THE MERRY WIVES OF WINDSOR
(1597–1598)

DRAMATIS PERSONAE

Mistress Margaret Page
The first "wife".

Master George Page
Margaret's husband.

Anne Page Their daughter.

William Page Their young son, a schoolboy.

Mistress Alice Ford
The second "wife".

Master Frank Ford Alice's husband, sometimes disguised as Brooke.

John, Robert Ford's servants.

The Host of the Garter Inn

Sir Hugh Evans
A Welsh parson.

Doctor Caius A French physician.

John Rugby His servant.

Mistress Quickly
Housekeeper of Doctor Caius, and Anne Page's go-between.

Robert Shallow
A justice of the peace.

Master Abraham Slender
Nephew of Robert Shallow, Anne's unlikely suitor.

Master Fenton
A young gentleman, Anne Page's lover.

Peter Simple
Slender's servant.

Sir John Falstaff The fat knight of the *Henry IV* plays. He is lodging at the Garter Inn.

Bardolph, Pistol, Nim
Followers of Falstaff.

After Justice **Shallow** pompously **threatens legal action** against Falstaff, Falstaff gleefully admits poaching deer.

In need of money, **Falstaff** resolves **to seduce mistresses Page and Ford**, who he thinks fancy him.

Mistresses Page and Ford find they have both received the same letter from Falstaff. They **decide to play along and bankrupt him**.

↑ **1.1**   ↑ **1.3**   ↑ **2.1**

Act 1

1.1   **1.3**

↓   ↓

Shallow instructs his nephew **Slender to court young Anne Page**, who is due to inherit 700 crowns.

Caius finds out from Mistress Quickly that parson **Evans** is backing Slender's suit of Anne and **challenges him to a duel**.

In Windsor, Justice Shallow threatens Falstaff for poaching deer. Falstaff cheerily admits his misdemeanours and trouble is averted. Shallow's nephew Slender is advised to marry young Anne Page for her money. At the Garter Inn, Falstaff laments his lack of funds, and plans to send letters to mistresses Page and Ford in a bid to get at their husbands' money.

Dr Caius is enraged when he sees a letter from parson Evans backing Slender's hopes to marry Anne Page. Caius is hoping to marry Anne himself.

Young Fenton then arrives, also hoping to marry Anne. Mistresses Page and Ford receive identical love letters from Falstaff and decide to teach the fat knight a lesson. Pistol, annoyed by being sacked by Falstaff, tells Ford about Falstaff's letter to his wife, while Nim tells Page. Page is not bothered, but the enraged Ford disguises himself as "Brooke" to meet Falstaff at the Garter Inn.

Mistress Ford invites Falstaff to her house when her husband is out. Brooke pretends to be a suitor of Mistress Ford himself and offers to

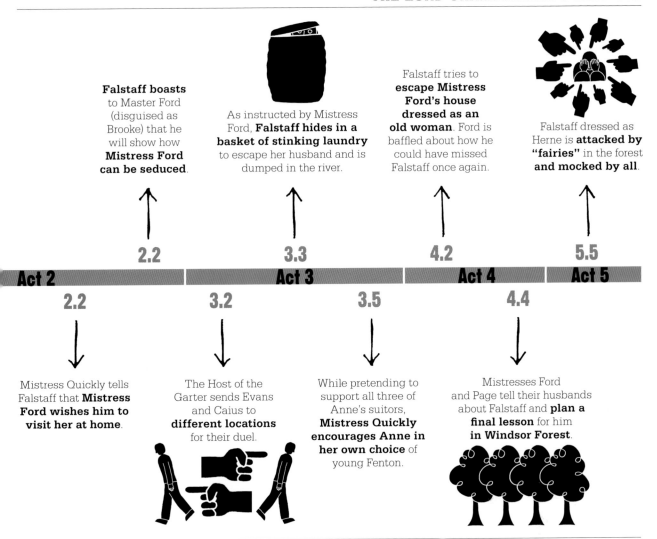

Falstaff boasts to Master Ford (disguised as Brooke) that he will show how **Mistress Ford can be seduced**.

2.2

As instructed by Mistress Ford, **Falstaff hides in a basket of stinking laundry** to escape her husband and is dumped in the river.

3.3

Falstaff tries to **escape Mistress Ford's house dressed as an old woman**. Ford is baffled about how he could have missed Falstaff once again.

4.2

Falstaff dressed as Herne is **attacked by "fairies"** in the forest **and mocked by all**.

5.5

Act 2 · **Act 3** · **Act 4** · **Act 5**

2.2

Mistress Quickly tells Falstaff that **Mistress Ford wishes him to visit her at home**.

3.2

The Host of the Garter sends Evans and Caius to **different locations** for their duel.

3.5

While pretending to support all three of Anne's suitors, **Mistress Quickly encourages Anne in her own choice** of young Fenton.

4.4

Mistresses Ford and Page tell their husbands about Falstaff and **plan a final lesson** for him **in Windsor Forest**.

---

pay Falstaff to seduce his wife on his behalf. Unaware of the plans the mistresses Ford and Page have for Falstaff, Ford angrily follows him on his assignation with Mistress Ford. As Ford comes home, Mistress Ford (as planned) tells Falstaff to hide in a basket of filthy linen, which is then dumped in the river. Recovering later at the Garter, Falstaff is told by Mistress Quickly that it was all a big mistake and Mistress Ford wants to meet again. Ford (as Brooke) finds out. At Mistress Ford's house, Falstaff is persuaded to dress as an

old woman in order to escape Ford, but Ford thinks it's his hated aunt and beats him black and blue.

Mistresses Ford and Page tell their husbands what has been going on, and together they plot Falstaff's final humiliation. They invite him to dress as the mythical stag spirit Herne the Hunter, and to meet them at night in the forest. Page arranges for Slender to elope with Anne, while Mistress Page, unaware, arranges for Caius to elope with Anne. Meanwhile, Anne elopes with Fenton. Page tells Slender that Anne will be in the

forest dressed in white. Mistress Page tells Caius that Anne will be in the forest dressed in green.

In the forest, Falstaff is terrified by "fairies" (really children trained by Evans), who pinch him while Pistol and Nim tease him with burning tapers. Caius runs off with a boy dressed in green and Slender with a boy dressed in white. The wives reveal their pranks to Falstaff who admits he has been made a complete ass – as Caius and Slender return to acknowledge that they too have been made fools of. Fenton arrives, married to Anne. »

IN CONTEXT

THEMES
Love, fidelity, forgiveness

SETTING
Windsor, a town on the River Thames near London

SOURCES
There are no direct sources for the play, which was largely a spin-off from the *Henry IV* plays. It is one of the very few of Shakespeare's plays to be set wholly in England, and much of the comedy draws from English in-jokes of the period.

LEGACY
1597 The play was probably first performed in April before Elizabeth I at Windsor.

1623 The Folio version purges the play's "profanities".

1786 A Russian adaptation, by Catherine the Great herself, is one of the rare non-English successes of the play.

1799 Italian court composer Antonio Salieri adapts the play as an opera, as does Guiseppe Verdi in 1893.

1902 A spectacular London production celebrates the coronation of Edward VII.

1985 British theatre director Bill Alexander stages an RSC "new Elizabethan" production set in 1950s suburbia.

2012 The play is performed in Kiswahili at the Globe to Globe Festival in London, which hosted 37 productions of Shakespeare's plays in 37 different languages.

The Merry Wives Of Windsor is one of the most enjoyed but least celebrated of Shakespeare's plays. Its tale of a lovable rogue getting his comeuppance at the hands of the women he hopes to take advantage of is a comic formula that has been recycled again and again, in everything from Restoration comedies to stage farces and TV sitcoms. The rogue is, of course, Shakespeare's unique creation, the "fat knight" Sir John Falstaff.

Suburban comedy

The remarkable thing, however, is that Shakespeare's play was one of the originals, the blueprint for all these later comedies. At the time Shakespeare wrote *The Merry Wives*, plays were mostly about aristocratic, mythical, or heroic figures. The idea of a comedy about the foibles of a "suburban" middle class was unheard of. Although younger English playwrights such as John Fletcher and Ben Jonson quickly followed with sharp "city" satires, the suburban comedy was Shakespeare's idea.

A story goes that Elizabeth I so liked the character of Sir John Falstaff in *Henry IV part 2* that she wanted to see "Falstaff in love", and

…here will be an old abusing of God's patience and the King's English!
Mistress Quickly
Act 1, Scene 4

Why then, the world's mine oyster,
Which I with sword will open.
Pistol
Act 2, Scene 2

The Merry Wives was Shakespeare's rather off-beat response. There is no reliable source for this story, however. Another speculative theory is that the play was performed in front of the queen in April 1597 in Windsor, prior to the annual feast for the knights of the Garter at Windsor Castle, or that *The Merry Wives* makes good the promise in the epilogue for *Henry IV Part 2* to "continue the story, with Sir John in it".

The fat knight's frolics

Scholars have debated the question of when in Falstaff's life the story is set. It's clearly before his reported death in *Henry V*, but is it before his drinking days in Eastcheap with Prince Hal in *Henry IV*, or after? It probably doesn't matter, because Shakespeare omits any reference to 15th-century historical events in *The Merry Wives* – it really feels as if Falstaff has been plucked from his own century and dropped amid the citizens of Shakespeare's time.

Falstaff is definitely the star of the play, and the comedy comes from this rambunctious character, who drops into the dull world of Windsor life and causes chaos. He imagines he is going to lord it over this provincial backwater with his knighthood and his eloquence but he's in for a surprise. The very biddable housewives who he thinks will make easy pickings, mistresses Page and Ford, quickly turn the tables on him and he is humiliated again and again.

What makes Falstaff so appealing is the manner in which he bounces back from each setback with irrepressible optimism. Even at the end, when made a complete fool in the forest, he has a comeback – "Have I lived to stand at the taunt of one that makes fritters of English?" (5.5.141–142). Throughout the play, his wit shines while all the other men mangle language so badly that it is often impossible for modern audiences to follow.

Mangled words

There are malapropisms and mispronunciations galore – and they are frequently bawdy. Mistress Quickly laments, "she does so take

on with her men; they mistook their erection" (presumably meaning "direction"), to which Falstaff ruefully responds, "So did I mine, to build upon a foolish woman's promise" (3.5.39–40). While when Hugh Evans is teaching the boy William his Latin, he talks of the "focative" case, not the vocative, saying, "Remember, William, focative is caret" – to which Mistress Quickly knowingly replies, "And that's a good root." (4.1.48–49).

Most of the play is about the wives asserting their control over the town. They are not easily fooled, and they are worthy of more respect than their husbands give them. They show, too, that they have a great sense of fun. But having fun does not make them disreputable; they do not have to be melancholy nuns or unattractive prudes to be good wives. As Mistress Page says, "Wives may be merry, and yet honest, too." (4.2.95).

In this 2008 production at the Globe Theatre, London, Christopher Benjamin's self-deluding Falstaff fancies he sees the "leer of invitation".

A triumph for love

Yet even as the wives come out on top with their husband's apologies and Falstaff's humiliation, they are caught by surprise, as Fenton and Anne show the real victor to be love. While the wives have been off teaching the men a lesson and the Pages have been trying to set up their daughter Anne in marriages she doesn't want, Anne has eloped with Fenton. "You would have married [Anne], most shamefully, / Where there was no proportion held in love" (5.5.213–214), Fenton tells them, and stresses how their love match will save Anne from "A thousand irreligious cursèd hours / Which forcèd marriage would have brought upon her." (5.5.221–222). The message still resonates today. ■

WE HAVE HEARD THE CHIMES AT MIDNIGHT

HENRY IV PART 2 (1597–1598)

DRAMATIS PERSONAE

Rumour Presenter of the play.

Henry IV King of England.

Prince Harry Eldest son of the king, known as **Hal** and later **Henry V**.

Earls of Warwick, Surrey, and Westmoreland; Harcourt, Gower, Sir John Blunt Supporters of the king.

Prince John of Lancaster; Humphrey, Duke of Gloucester; Thomas, Duke of Clarence Hal's brothers.

Lord Chief Justice of England Falstaff's nemesis.

Percy, Earl of Northumberland Rebel warlord.

Scrope, Archbishop of York; Lord Bardolph; Lord Mowbray; Lord Hastings; Sir John Coleville Rebellious nobles.

Sir John Falstaff Drinking companion of Hal.

Ned Poins, Bardolph, Ensign Pistol Followers of Falstaff.

Mistress Quickly Hostess of the Boar's Head Tavern.

Doll Tearsheet A prostitute.

Kate The widow of Henry Percy, Hotspur.

Robert Shallow Justice of the Peace in Gloucestershire.

Silence A colleague of Shallow.

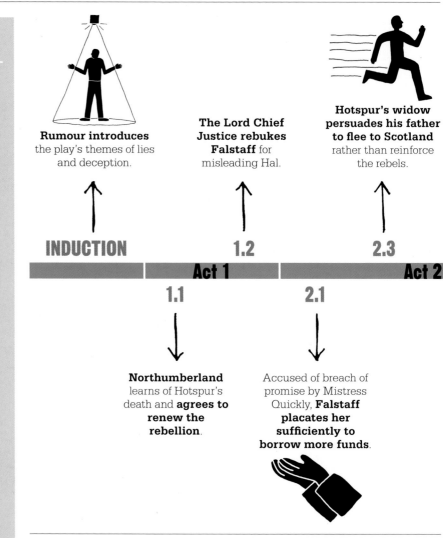

Rumour introduces the play's themes of lies and deception.

INDUCTION

1.1

Northumberland learns of Hotspur's death and **agrees to renew the rebellion**.

The Lord Chief Justice rebukes Falstaff for misleading Hal.

1.2

Act 1

2.1

Accused of breach of promise by Mistress Quickly, **Falstaff placates her sufficiently to borrow more funds**.

Hotspur's widow persuades his father to flee to Scotland rather than reinforce the rebels.

2.3

Act 2

The presenter Rumour begins the play by revealing the lie that's on its way to old Northumberland: that Hotspur has defeated King Henry's forces at the Battle of Shrewsbury. This happy news reaches him moments before it is contradicted by the truth: that Hotspur was killed, the rebels routed, and the king's men are marching north towards him. Despite his grief, Northumberland agrees to join the Archbishop of York's forces in a renewed fight. By the time the forces gather, however,

Northumberland has fled to Scotland and left his fellow rebels vulnerable. They agree to a parley, and present their grievances to Prince John who promises redress on behalf of his father. Although Mowbray remains unsure, the other lords dismiss their troops and prepare for peace. No sooner have their men dispersed than John arrests the rebels for high treason and condemns them all to death.

Deception also flourishes elsewhere. Falstaff should be with Prince John in the north but consumption, physical and

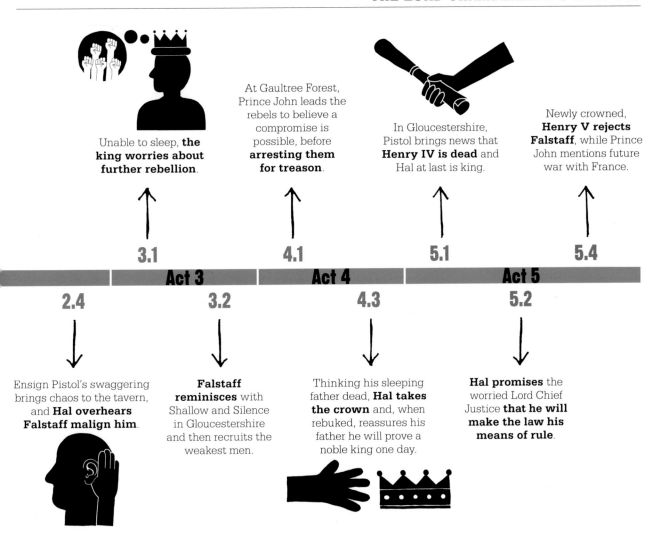

Unable to sleep, **the king worries about further rebellion**.

At Gaultree Forest, Prince John leads the rebels to believe a compromise is possible, before **arresting them for treason**.

In Gloucestershire, Pistol brings news that **Henry IV is dead** and Hal at last is king.

Newly crowned, **Henry V rejects Falstaff**, while Prince John mentions future war with France.

3.1 **4.1** **5.1** **5.4**

2.4 Act 3 **3.2** Act 4 **4.3** Act 5 **5.2**

Ensign Pistol's swaggering brings chaos to the tavern, and **Hal overhears Falstaff malign him**.

Falstaff reminisces with Shallow and Silence in Gloucestershire and then recruits the weakest men.

Thinking his sleeping father dead, **Hal takes the crown** and, when rebuked, reassures his father he will prove a noble king one day.

Hal promises the worried Lord Chief Justice **that he will make the law his means of rule**.

financial, keeps him in London. There the Lord Chief Justice rebukes him for dishonourably misleading Prince Hal, and Mistress Quickly has him arrested for debt. He mollifies her with further empty promises and borrows more; and then maligns Prince Hal, who overhears these potential words of treason. Amid the rising noise and chaos of the Eastcheap underworld, a sudden call to his father's sickbed delivers a timely rebuke to the wayward Prince for this irresponsible waste of time.

Sensing his own mortality, Falstaff seeks comfort from Doll Tearsheet before departing for duty. He is tasked with a recruiting drive in Gloucestershire. But since Falstaff takes bribes to exempt certain conscripts, his fighting force retains the poorest men in every sense.

At court, the wakeful king is troubled by his betrayal of those same warlords who helped him to the crown, and by fears for the future once the unpredictable Hal is king. He asks that the crown lie on his pillow as he sleeps. When Hal arrives and takes the crown

believing the king has died, the king is all the more convinced his son desires his death. Hal assures his father that he dreads that event, and promises that, when it comes, it will herald a just reign.

Henry dies, and Falstaff hopes for influence at court. But Hal keeps his word. Promising the Lord Chief Justice to defend the law, he dismisses Falstaff when his old friend hails him at the coronation. As Falstaff is arrested for debt, Prince John mentions a rumoured war with France and we know that Agincourt beckons. »

IN CONTEXT

THEMES
Time's decay, loyalty and betrayal, misremembering

SETTING
Court of Henry IV; Boar's Head Tavern, London; Gloucestershire; Gaultree Forest, Yorkshire

SOURCES
1587 Holinshed's *Chronicles of England, Scotland, and Ireland.*

1594 *The Famous Victories of Henry V*, an anonymous play probably known to Shakespeare.

1595 Samuel Daniel's poem "The First Four Books of the Civil War Between the Two Houses of York and Lancaster."

LEGACY
Since *Henry IV Part 2* is rarely played as a solo drama, most of the performance history is shared with Part 1.

Early 1700s Actor-manager Thomas Betterton's adaptation extends the popular role of Falstaff on the London stage.

1821 The play is performed as part of the coronation celebrations for George IV.

1945 Laurence Olivier plays a memorable Justice Shallow at the New Theatre, London.

1966 Orson Welles' film *The Chimes at Midnight* focuses on Hal's father-son relationship with Falstaff and the King.

2012 BBC's "Hollow Crown" series casts Simon Russell Beale as a melancholy Falstaff.

Falstaff remembers hearing London's church clocks chiming midnight when, as a student at the Inns of Court, he burned the candle at both ends. In those days, the lateness of the hour signalled a young man's liberty. Now, remembered in old age, it marks the end of things. With their blend of warmth and wistfulness Falstaff's words capture perfectly the bitter-sweet quality of this play, in which for king, rebels, and common folk alike, midnight chimes finality and judgment.

The title *Henry IV Part 2* leads us to expect a sequel to Part 1, and to a degree it is. As the title page to the 1600 quarto promises, we are to see again the comic knight John Falstaff, meet his new companion, Pistol, and follow the history to Henry's death and the coronation of the hero-king Henry V. It was a winning combination for the Elizabethan audience who had delighted in Part 1. But while there is comedy in Part 2, the mood is darker, and the historical events are less valiant, tainted as they are with political trickery.

O thoughts of men accursed! Past and to come seems best; things present, worst.
Archbishop of York
Act 1, Scene 3

The play appears to have been written for an audience that has seen Part 1, and it therefore uses similarities between the two in narrative and structure to make the differences stand out. While this play looks forwards to the coronation of Henry V, its main focus is retrospective. It revisits issues and relationships from Part 1 and reflects on them at a slower pace and in a more nuanced way.

Subjects to time
The three worlds of Part 1 – the court, the tavern, and the rebels – now feel the debilitating effects of time and mortality. Plump Jack Falstaff, Hal's father-substitute and tavern-king, is in physical decline: his first words in Part 2 are to enquire about the health of his urine. The king himself swaps the robe of majesty for a nightgown as sleepless anxiety about rebellion and his inheritance contributes to his deteriorating health. And the rebels, too, admit that their long dispute with the king has made

In an intriguing theatrical dynamic, a dotard Falstaff was played by British actor Timothy West alongside a cynical Prince Hal, played by West's son Samuel, at the Old Vic, London, in 1997.

From the medieval kings to Elizabeth I

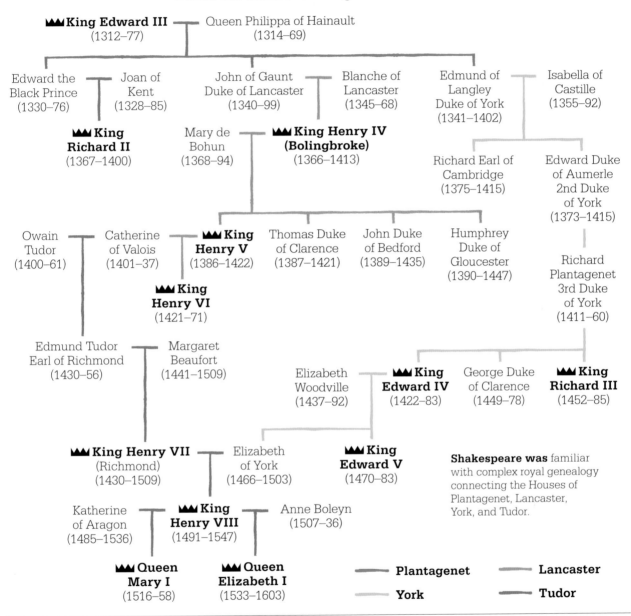

Shakespeare was familiar with complex royal genealogy connecting the Houses of Plantagenet, Lancaster, York, and Tudor.

— Plantagenet   — Lancaster

— York   — Tudor

---

them ill: "we are all diseased, / And with our surfeiting and wanton hours / Have brought ourselves into a burning fever, / And we must bleed for it" (4.1.54–57). Even when the central scenes take us to Gloucestershire, where pippin apples and fine game are on the menu, England appears as a society

in its twilight years where elderly men ponder sheep prices and tally the deaths of old friends.

   Not even Hal is untouched by this pervasive malaise. He admits when he first appears that he is "exceeding weary" (2.2.1) and seems bored with his wastrel life. Keeping up the image of the wayward

scapegrace has become harder since his father's illness, and the prince confides to Poins that his heart "bleeds inwardly" (2.2.41) for the king. He is concerned, too, about how his friends perceive him. He knows that Falstaff hopes for future influence at court, but now he learns that Poins, his close »

> Sir John, Sir John, I am well acquainted with your manner of wrenching the true cause the false way.
> **Lord Chief Justice**
> **Act 2, Scene 1**

companion, might have misused their friendship by claiming that his sister Nell and Hal will marry. Though Poins dismisses this as Falstaff's lie, there is a new unease in Eastcheap.

Time is running out, flesh is weak, and dreams decay. This vulnerability to time and its deceptions is described in the Induction to the play, which is spoken by the figure of Rumour, possibly wearing a robe decorated with tongues. He not only reveals the lie about Hotspur's death, but says that the greater danger comes from the lies we tell ourselves: "smooth comforts false, worse than true wrongs" (Induction.40–41).

Looking back

Characters spend much time revisiting and revising the past in this play, and almost unthinkingly rework history to suit the present. For example, the barons justify their continued rebellion with reference to the death of Richard II, and promises made but not fulfilled by Henry since becoming king. They overlook their own complicity in Henry's rise to power and dangerously underestimate how far the king will go to "wipe his tables clean" (4.1.199). Fearful and unable to sleep, Henry also looks back at that time and marvels at how easily the barons seem to switch allegiance. In doing so, he forgets how he, too, betrayed a king.

Meanwhile, profiting from the lie that he killed Hotspur, Falstaff has recast himself as a gentleman and adopted airs and graces he can ill afford. He is confronted in the street by the Lord Chief Justice who is unamused by the wit with which the fat knight usually extricates himself from trouble. Now Justice

> God knows, my son,
> By what bypaths and indirect crook'd ways
> I met this crown
> **King Henry**
> **Act 4, Scene 3**

itself warns Falstaff that time is short and judgment inevitable. At the play's end this same Justice will imprison Falstaff for debt.

The rebels also find that time is not on their side. Northumberland hears the falsehood of his son's victory before learning of his death, and news of his own departure for Scotland reaches his fellow barons too late for remedy. Prince John takes advantage of this weakened position to spring his trap. Although Mowbray is uneasy, the other rebel leaders trust the Prince's word and rashly dismiss their forces before

---

Language and place

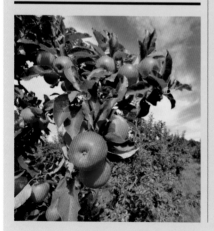

The Eastcheap tavern is a place of transit through which pass characters whom Shakespeare identifies by their idiosyncrasies of speech: Ensign Pistol's empty bombast; Mistress Quickly's sentimental picturing of the past; Bardolph's monosyllabic utterances, and Doll's abuse.

In contrast, Gloucestershire folk are rooted to and identified by place: John Doit of Staffordshire; Will Squeal, a Cotswold man; Clement Perkes o'th'Hill. Unlike Eastcheap, there is a deep sense of continuity in the country, and of events driven more by the seasons than by man. Falstaff contaminates this English idyll. In a telling moment, Feeble, a woman's tailor, speaks out against Falstaff's corrupt recruiting practices and declares that he is proud to die for King and country: "No man's too good to serve's prince… Faith, I'll bear no base mind." (3.2.234–235,238). Feeble's simple integrity puts Falstaff's enterprise to shame. It also rejects the calculating baseness of mind that ultimately derives from the very king whom Feeble would give his life for.

Thinking his sleeping father (David Yelland) dead, Hal (Tom Mison) tries on the crown for size in this 2011 production directed by Sir Peter Hall.

away. In his earlier words, he described his father as using the crown like armour, to serve himself. Now he says to the king that it is he, the king, who has protected the crown and suffered in its service. Henry takes up this flattering falsehood when he describes himself as meeting rather than seizing the crown, as if he took no active part in usurping Richard II. And Hal confirms the fiction that the crown has rightfully passed to Henry when he casts himself as its true inheritor: "You won it, wore it, kept it, gave it me; / Then plain and right must my possession be" (4.3.350–351). This revision by father and son of the central problem of Henry's reign exemplifies Shakespeare's major theme in the play – that of re-reading the past.

Having placated his father with this promise of loyalty, the prince receives his advice. Once king, says Henry, Hal should bring the people together in a foreign war.

Sombre finale
Shakespeare closes the play in the minor key. Falstaff is finally dismissed when Hal establishes his power in the rule of law. His rejection of his old friend is the final playing out of that promised moment from the comic tavern play in Part 1. Hal's new regal style now silences Falstaff's familiar greeting: "I know thee not, old man" (5.5.47). And when John mentions rumours of war, we remember Henry's deathbed advice to his son. We know this war will end with victory at Agincourt and see Hal fulfil his father's project of uniting the nation under the crown, however briefly. ∎

before establishing the details of his promised redress. Once the lords are powerless, John condemns them all to death. Timing is everything. As Lord Hastings puts it, "We are time's subjects, and time bids be gone" (1.3.110). Thanks to Prince John's tactics, by the middle of the play, all of Henry's enemies are gone.

Inheritance
Shakespeare alters history to implicate the king in this deception by tasking his son with the trick. The chronicles ascribe it to one of his nobles. In political terms, John has acted wisely in avoiding bloodshed. Yet, as the scene closes, his insistence that "God, and not we, hath safely fought today" (4.1.347) recasts his political stratagem as a battlefield victory by infusing it with honour that it hardly deserves. John has evidently inherited his father's calculation. He is, in Falstaff's words, a "sober-blooded boy" (4.2.84–85), lacking a sense of humour or taste for drink. In his lengthy praise of sack, or sherry, the fat knight says that Hal,

who also shares his father's cold-bloodedness, has warmed it with the wine of tavern life.

Hal shows his ability to sidestep the kind of confrontation that his brother seems to relish when he eventually meets the king. Henry has placed the crown beside him on his pillow and, mistaking sleep for death, Hal has briefly tried it on. Now it sits between them as they talk. The prince tells Henry what he wants to hear, but he does so by reworking slightly what happened when he briefly took the crown

My father is gone wild into his grave
Prince Harry
Act 5, Scene 2

OUT ON THEE, SEEMING! I WILL WRITE AGAINST IT

MUCH ADO ABOUT NOTHING (1598–1599)

DRAMATIS PERSONAE

Leonato Governor of Messina and father of Hero.

Hero Leonato's daughter and only heir.

Don Pedro Prince of Aragon, returned from war, possibly against Don John.

Don John Illegitimate brother of Don Pedro to whom he's grudgingly reconciled.

Claudio A young count who has distinguished himself in military action.

Benedick A lord of Padua also serving under Don Pedro; a professed bachelor.

Beatrice Niece of Leonato and cousin to Hero.

Borachio A follower of Don John who invents a plot to thwart Claudio's marriage to Hero.

Margaret A gentlewoman attending on Hero who plays a dubious role in Borachio's plot.

Ursula A gentlewoman attending on Hero, who helps to trick Beatrice into admitting her love for Benedick.

Friar Francis He arranges for Hero to fake her death.

Antonio Leonato's brother.

Conrad A follower of Don John, he is arrested with Borachio and forced to confess.

Dogberry Master Constable of the Watch, he tries to imitate his betters.

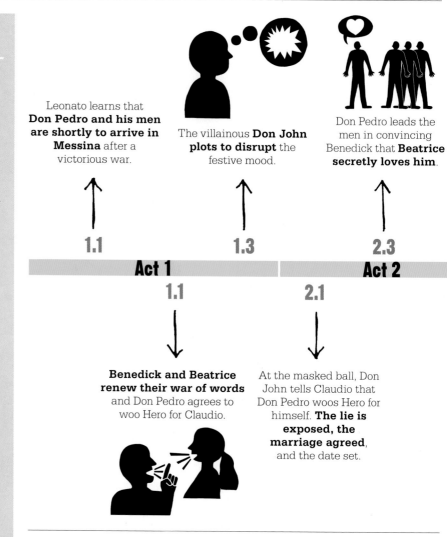

Leonato learns that **Don Pedro and his men are shortly to arrive in Messina** after a victorious war.

1.1

The villainous **Don John plots to disrupt** the festive mood.

1.3

Don Pedro leads the men in convincing Benedick that **Beatrice secretly loves him**.

2.3

Act 1   **Act 2**

1.1

Benedick and Beatrice renew their war of words and Don Pedro agrees to woo Hero for Claudio.

2.1

At the masked ball, Don John tells Claudio that Don Pedro woos Hero for himself. **The lie is exposed, the marriage agreed**, and the date set.

News comes to Leonato, Governor of Messina, that the victorious Don Pedro of Aragon will shortly return from war and that Claudio, a young member of his company, has distinguished himself in battle. Beatrice's playful enquiry after another officer, Benedick, sets the theme of their love-hate relationship. The couple's witty banter cuts through the welcoming formalities and sharply contrasts with Claudio's nascent adoration of Hero, Leonato's only heir. Claudio confesses this infatuation to Don Pedro and Benedick, as if seeking reassurance. But while Benedick, the avowed bachelor, ridicules idealized love, Don Pedro offers to win Hero's hand for Claudio at that evening's masked ball. With their identities disguised, the maskers indulge in innuendo, sexual banter, retribution, and deceit. And Don John, seizing the chance to play mischievously on Claudio's insecurities, insinuates that Don Pedro is wooing Hero for himself.

The lie is exposed, the match is made and, delighted, Leonato gives his blessing. All that remains is for

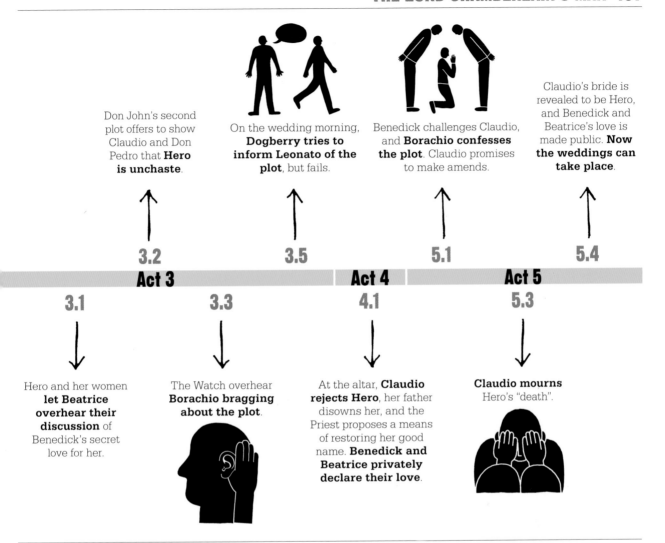

Don John's second plot offers to show Claudio and Don Pedro that **Hero is unchaste**.

On the wedding morning, **Dogberry tries to inform Leonato of the plot**, but fails.

Benedick challenges Claudio, and **Borachio confesses the plot**. Claudio promises to make amends.

Claudio's bride is revealed to be Hero, and Benedick and Beatrice's love is made public. **Now the weddings can take place**.

3.2   **3.5**   **5.1**   **5.4**

Act 3   Act 4   Act 5

3.1   **3.3**   **4.1**   **5.3**

Hero and her women **let Beatrice overhear their discussion** of Benedick's secret love for her.

The Watch overhear **Borachio bragging about the plot**.

At the altar, **Claudio rejects Hero**, her father disowns her, and the Priest proposes a means of restoring her good name. **Benedick and Beatrice privately declare their love**.

Claudio mourns Hero's "death".

Claudio and Hero to speak to one another for the first time. While they whisper together, Beatrice fends off a throwaway marriage proposal from Don Pedro.

Until the wedding, Don Pedro takes up matchmaking. Detecting compatibility in opposites, he decides to trick Beatrice and Benedick into admitting they love each other. Two scenes are set: Benedick eavesdrops as Don Pedro, Claudio, and Leonato discuss Beatrice's feelings. Meanwhile, she overhears Hero and Ursula revealing Benedick's love.

Borachio feeds Don John's malevolence with a plot to thwart the marriage. He'll speak to Margaret, dressed as Hero, at her window the night before the wedding, while Don John ensures that Claudio and Don Pedro witness the encounter. At the altar, Claudio cruelly rejects Hero, claiming that she's no longer pure. Hero faints. Claudio and Don Pedro leave. Unlike Leonato, the Priest believes in Hero's innocence and proposes a rescue plan. Benedick stays behind, concerned for Hero and Beatrice.

Overwhelmed by emotion, he and Beatrice confess their love. She then asks him to kill Claudio.

The duel does not take place because by chance the bumbling watchmen have overheard Borachio bragging about the plot. They bring the truth to light and clear Hero's name. Believing her to be dead as the Priest suggests, Claudio agrees to mourn at her "tomb" and to marry her "cousin", sight unseen. When this lady unveils, she is, in fact, Hero. The play ends with news of Don John's arrest, and a dance before the double wedding. »

IN CONTEXT

THEMES
Social codes and status, love, marriage, deception

SETTING
Messina, a port city in Sicily under Spanish rule

SOURCES
There are no direct sources. The Hero plot, based on an old tale, is indirectly indebted to:

1516 Ludovico Ariosto's *Orlando Furioso* (Italian verse translated into English, 1591)

1554 Matteo Bandello's *Novelle* (Italian prose adapted into French, 1569).

LEGACY
1613 The play is staged to celebrate the marriage of King James's daughter Elizabeth.

1662 William Davenant's *The Law Against Lovers* combines parts of *Much Ado About Nothing* and *Measure for Measure*. The play influences many Restoration comedies.

1861 Hector Berlioz's opera *Béatrice et Bénédict* portrays the witty sparring of the eponymous older couple in sparklingly jazzy syncopations.

1993 Kenneth Branagh's film moves the play to the Tuscan hills, giving it an easy-going holiday atmosphere.

1996 Michael Boyd's RSC production makes great use of mirrors, frames, and portraits to bring out the theme of appearance versus reality.

Much Ado About Nothing presents "seeming" in several guises. The wordplay on nothing/noting in the title would have alerted the play's first audience to the theme of observation. And the messenger's reports in the first scene make it clear that Messina is a society where appearances matter. But what's built on appearance, report, and hearsay is fragile, open to conflicting interpretations, and easily destroyed.

Appearing and observing

Both love stories in the play hinge on appearance and observation. Claudio has fallen in love with Hero because she seems to him a sweet, modest young woman. But he's unsure of his own judgment and seeks confirmation from the older Benedick and Don Pedro. Benedick differentiates between noting Hero and looking at her. His replies draw attention to the subjectivity of perception, as simply looking at her does not reveal any extraordinary

Friendship is constant
in all other things
Save in the office and
affairs of love.
Therefore all hearts in love
use their own tongues.
Let every eye negotiate
for itself,
And trust no agent.
Claudio
Act 2, Scene 1

And there shall appear such seeming truth of Hero's disloyalty that jealousy shall be called assurance.
Borachio
Act 2, Scene 2

traits in the young woman; Claudio's noting, however, marks her as priceless: "Can the world buy such a jewel?" (1.1.171). With no assurance for his budding love from Benedick, Claudio is reluctant to reveal his admiration for Hero to Don Pedro. Only when the Prince insists that he's serious in thinking "the lady is very well worthy" (1.1.207–208) does Claudio admit his love.

The courtship of Claudio and Hero follows a very formal pattern. First the lovers admire each other from a distance. Claudio does not even woo Hero himself, but leaves this to the Prince. The lovers do not speak to each other until their elders have agreed on the marriage and Leonato has given his blessing. Even at this point, Hero doesn't have any lines, although the text suggests that she takes the liberty of kissing Claudio in public.

Constrained by the formality of their courtship, Claudio and Hero hardly know each other. It's not surprising, therefore, that Claudio's faith in Hero is easily shaken when Don John tells him that his brother has wooed her for himself. Claudio does not doubt for a minute that Hero has accepted Don Pedro. The report is quickly revealed as false and laughingly dismissed by the Prince and Leonato. But Don John is still determined to prevent the marriage and, thanks to Borachio's plot, he makes it appear to Claudio and Don Pedro that Hero entertained a man on the night before the wedding. Mistaking Margaret for Hero, Claudio is instantly convinced that she is unfaithful and his idolising adoration quickly turns into hatred and disgust.

The formal, stylized nature of the courtship finds its counterpart in Claudio's public rejection of Hero in the disrupted wedding ceremony. As in the scene at Hero's window, Claudio misinterprets what he observes. Having rejected Hero as a "rotten orange" (4.1.32), he's convinced that "Her blush is guiltiness, not modesty" (4.1.42). Incapable of seeing her as the person she really is, Claudio falls from one extreme: Hero as chaste, pure, and innocent, to another: Hero as loose and wanton. The way she appears to him is determined by what others want him to believe. So it's no surprise that when, eventually, Borachio confesses the plot, Claudio instantly reverts to the first image he had of her.

Tricks and truths

While appearances give the love story of Claudio and Hero an almost tragic turn, they are put to comic use in the love story of Beatrice and Benedick. Here are two people who seem to detest nothing so much as each other. Yet we cannot help feeling that behind their battle of words they are hiding wounds caused by rejected love, hints of which can be heard in their banter: "You always end with a jade's trick. / I know you of old" (1.1.138–139).

Their friends are convinced that they will make a perfect couple and, in the two eavesdropping scenes, use report and hearsay to trick them into admitting their love. Claudio, Don Pedro, and Leonato paint the picture of a Beatrice desperately in love. But they think it best for her not to admit it for fear of being mocked by an unfeeling Benedick. Convinced that the three men tell the truth, because "The conference was sadly borne" (2.3.210), Benedick is determined that Beatrice's love will be requited. Even the prospect of being mocked by his friends for changing his mind about marriage does not deter him.

Hero and Ursula, in turn, praise Benedick as "the only man of Italy" (3.1.92). They reproach Beatrice for being proud and disdainful since, as a confirmed bachelor, she always finds things to criticize in even »

For his 1993 film, Kenneth Branagh cut the text to keep the action moving. A star-studded cast included Kate Beckinsale, Emma Thompson (front), and Branagh (second from right).

the most perfect of men. If she learned of Benedick's love, then she would "make sport at it" (3.1.59). Sobered by this criticism, Beatrice is prepared for "taming my wild heart to thy [Benedick's] loving hand" (3.1.112). Benedick can confirm that Beatrice is fair, virtuous, and wise, and Beatrice does not need reports of Benedick's merits to know that he is deserving. It is clear to us that, unlike Hero and Claudio, Beatrice and Benedick know each other well.

Language and reality
The play's language is characterized by wordplay, banter, and repartee. Beatrice and Benedick are involved in linguistic fencing matches from the moment they meet in the play: "**Benedick**: What, my dear Lady Disdain! Are you yet living?
Beatrice: Is it possible disdain should die while she hath such meet food to feed it as Signor Benedick?" (1.1.112–115). Conversation between Don Pedro and his men is predominantly light-hearted, blokeish joking, especially

But manhood is melted into courtesies, valour into compliment, and men are only turned into tongue, and trim ones, too.
Beatrice
Act 4, Scene 1

about Benedick's mistrust of women and rejection of marriage: "**Don Pedro**: 'In time the savage bull doth bear the yoke.'
Benedick: The savage bull may, but if ever the sensible Benedick bear it, pluck off the bull's horns and set them in my forehead, and let me be vilely painted…'Here you may see Benedick, the married man'." (1.1.243–250). This expresses the

deeply rooted fear in Messina society of being cuckolded. Even Leonato jokes about the legitimacy of his daughter. Where marriage brings fears of cuckoldry, Don John's accusation against Hero is readily believed. In the wedding scene, the language switches from jests to calculated insults as Claudio uses the very form of the marriage service to reject and humiliate Hero. The studied nature of his rejection is matched in the formal mourning ceremony at Hero's tomb. The readiness with which Don Pedro and Claudio dismiss the musicians and leave for a second wedding can make us wonder how much of Claudio's grief is merely "seeming".

Language is also used as a means of establishing social equality. In her conversations with men, Beatrice uses witty repartee to meet them on an equal footing. Both Margaret and Dogberry see language as having the potential to bring them level with their masters. Margaret's brief conversation with Benedick (5.2), a dialogue that

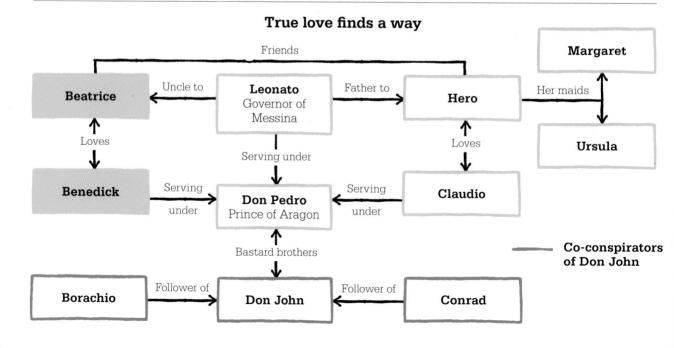

True love finds a way

The banter between Benedick and Beatrice is central to the play's charm. In the 2007 production at London's National Theatre, Simon Russell Beale and Zoe Wanamaker played the pair.

condenses many of the play's concerns about class and gender conflict, reveals her desire to move up socially. In the RSC production in 1996, she was caught at this point by Benedick with one of Hero's dresses. Access to these outward signs of social status makes her a threat in a society that depends so much on signs. However, Constable Dogberry's efforts to sound like his betters fail miserably. He epitomises a society distracted by surfaces, where words are easily divorced from their meaning.

Pairs and frames

The play is structured around pairs: Leonato and his brother Antonio; Claudio and Don Pedro; Borachio and Conrad; Dogberry and Verges. And Messina is a society where marriage is the rule. Don Pedro's scheme to make Beatrice and Benedick pair up, therefore, is not purely comic. It brings firmly into line two individuals who otherwise stand out uncomfortably against

> And when I lived
> I was your other wife;
> And when you loved
> you were my other husband.
> **Hero**
> Act 5, Scene 4

Messina's values in their preference for the bachelor life. Claudio and Hero are easily reconciled once her innocence is proven. But Beatrice and Benedick seem determined not to admit their love. In her final lines, Beatrice hints that she might yet refuse to be neatly paired off. Most productions follow the editorial tradition and attribute the reply, "Peace! I will stop your mouth" (5.4.97) to Benedick, as he kisses Beatrice. But the Quarto and Folio texts give this line to Leonato, who may be using his patriarchal authority to bring Beatrice to heel. Like *The Taming of the Shrew*, there is ambiguity in the ending.

By the end of the play, Don Pedro is the only single man left. Without an heir, he leaves his estate vulnerable to the plotting of others such as his bastard brother Don John. A born outsider, John refuses all efforts to be framed in Messina's codes. In a world of wordplay he guards his silence: "I am not of many words" (1.1.150). Refusing to perform, he is what he seems. News of his recapture darkens the festive mood. In the 1990 RSC production, he stood at the edge of the stage, and stared at Don Pedro as if reigniting the conflict suggested at the beginning of the play. ∎

> One Hero died defiled,
> but I do live,
> And surely as I live,
> I am a maid.
> **Hero**
> Act 5, Scene 4

ONCE MORE UNTO THE BREACH DEAR FRIENDS, ONCE MORE

HENRY V (1599)

DRAMATIS PERSONAE

Chorus Sets the scene for each of the Acts.

Henry V Once Prince Hal, now a soldier monarch.

Duke of Exeter Henry's uncle.

Dukes of Gloucester and Clarence The king's brothers.

Duke of York, and Earls of Salisbury, Westmorland, and Warwick English nobles.

Archbishop of Canterbury and Bishop of Ely Church prelates.

Earl of Cambridge, Lord Scroop, Sir Thomas Grey Traitors.

Fluellen, Gower Officers in Henry's army.

John Bates, Alexander Court and Michael Williams English soldiers.

Pistol, Nim, and Bardolph The Eastcheapers, former drinking friends of Prince Hal.

Nell Quickly A tavern hostess, wife of Pistol.

Charles VI King of France.

Louis the Dauphin Son of Charles VI.

Montjoy French herald and envoy to Henry at Agincourt.

Ambassador He delivers the gift of tennis balls to Henry.

Isabel Queen of France.

Catherine The King of France's daughter.

Alice Catherine's attendant.

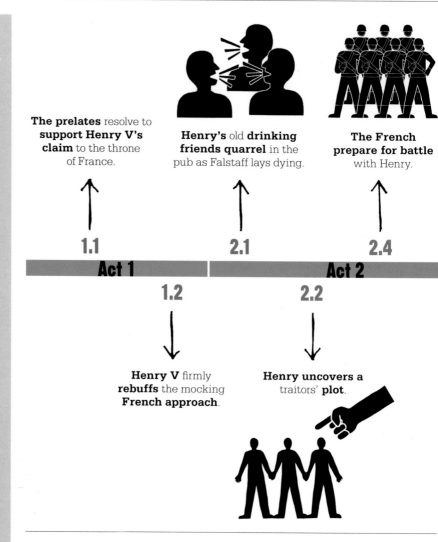

The prelates resolve to **support Henry V's claim** to the throne of France.

Henry's old **drinking friends quarrel** in the pub as Falstaff lays dying.

The French prepare for battle with Henry.

1.1

Act 1

1.2

Henry V firmly **rebuffs** the mocking **French approach**.

2.1

2.4

Act 2

2.2

Henry uncovers a traitors' **plot**.

The Chorus pleads with the audience to overlook the theatre's limitations and to picture the epic events to come. King Henry V, reformed from his wild youth, is assured by the Archbishop of Canterbury that his claim to the French throne is just. When the French ambassador brings him a mocking gift of tennis balls, Henry's riposte is that he will strike the French crown out of play.

In Southampton, the Chorus describes how the youth of England are eager to fight, but warns that there are three traitors. Henry's old drinking pals meet in a tavern. Bardolph stirs up trouble between Nim and Pistol, now married to Nim's former betrothed, hostess Nell Quickly. Henry unmasks the traitors and sends them for execution. Nell describes the death of old Falstaff, broken by Henry's rejection of him, and the three pals embark for France with Henry.

In France, the French king, Charles VI, and his son, the Dauphin, prepare for battle, mocking the wild youth of Henry. Henry's ambassador Exeter warns the French against resistance.

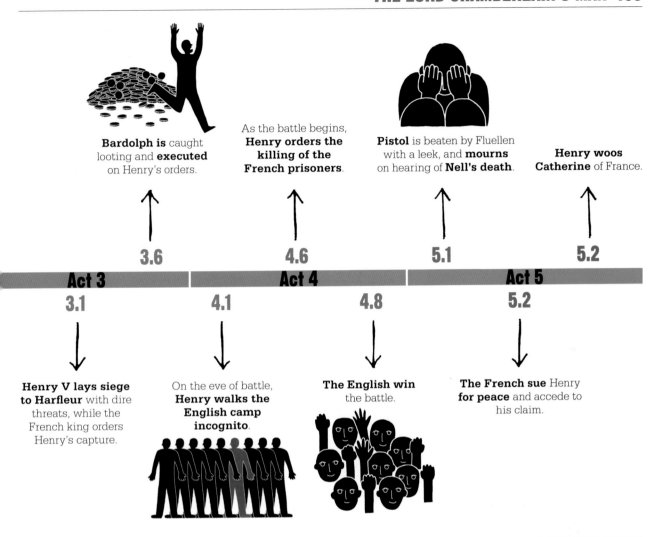

Bardolph is caught looting and **executed** on Henry's orders.

As the battle begins, **Henry orders the killing of the French prisoners**.

Pistol is beaten by Fluellen with a leek, and **mourns** on hearing of **Nell's death**.

Henry woos Catherine of France.

3.6

4.6

5.1

5.2

Act 3   **Act 4**   **Act 5**

3.1   **4.1**   **4.8**   **5.2**

Henry V lays siege to Harfleur with dire threats, while the French king orders Henry's capture.

On the eve of battle, **Henry walks the English camp incognito**.

The English win the battle.

The French sue Henry **for peace** and accede to his claim.

In France, Henry launches an attack on Harfleur and threatens dire repercussions if the townspeople do not yield. Meanwhile, Bardolph and his associates argue about joining the fight. In the French palace, the French king's daughter Catherine tries to learn English. The king rails against Henry while the Dauphin condemns French women for fraternizing with the English.

In the English camp, Bardolph is caught looting and executed on Henry's orders. Henry refuses an embassy from the French to persuade him to withdraw. Henry, disguised as Henry Le Roy, argues the rights and wrongs of the battle with the soldier Williams. The next morning, Henry, his army outnumbered 5 to 1, gives a speech pledging that those who fight with him will be forever remembered on this, St Crispin's Day.

As the French attack again, Henry orders the slaughter of French prisoners to free up the men guarding them. Gower reports that the French have slain English boys, and Henry swears the French no mercy. Henry wins the day, with 10,000 French slain and only three English lords. Henry prepares to return to England victorious.

In the French palace, Charles receives Henry. Henry agrees to peace only if his demands are met – including the hand of Princess Catherine. Henry starts to woo the French princess in a conversation made difficult by his poor French and her poor English. It ends with Henry kissing her. The Chorus recounts how destiny unfolds as Henry and Catherine's son becomes Henry VI and how his courtiers lost France again. »

IN CONTEXT

THEMES
War, patriotism, kingship

SETTING
London and Southampton in England; the palace of the French king; Harfleur and Agincourt in France

SOURCES
1577 Edward Halle's *Union of the Two Noble and Illustrious Families of Lancaster and York*.

1587 The key source is the *Chronicles of England, Scotland, and Ireland* edited by Ralph Holinshed.

LEGACY
1738 The first performance of the full play for 130 years is staged in London as Britain goes to war with France again.

1897 Frank Benson plays a heroic Henry in Stratford-upon-Avon, notably pole-vaulting onto the walls of Harfleur.

1944 Laurence Olivier directs and stars in a film version of the play. Part-funded by the British government, it stresses the patriotism of the play.

1986 Michael Bogdanov tours with a left-leaning version for the English Shakespeare Company, portraying Henry as a cold cynic.

1989 Kenneth Branagh's film adaptation brings a gritty reality to the battle scenes.

2003 Nicholas Hytner makes his debut as National Theatre Director setting *Henry V* in contemporary Iraq.

Henry V is often described as Shakespeare's war play. Unlike most of his plays, there is no unfolding of complex personal journeys or relationships. It appears to be a simple, thrilling story of how the heroic young soldier-king Henry V triumphs at Agincourt against all the odds, packed with stirring war poetry.

In the past, many regarded it as Shakespeare's most patriotic play – a glorification of a high point in England's history, when a small

Consideration like an angel came
And whipped th'offending Adam out of him
Archbishop of Canterbury
Act 1, Scene 1

"band" of Englishmen defeated a large army of the cream of French knighthood. At the centre of it all is an uplifting portrait of a matchless hero, leading his men to an unlikely victory. Speeches have often been culled from the play to inspire troops at moments of crisis. Most famously, British Prime Minister Winston Churchill echoed Henry's speech "We few, we happy few…" (4.3.60) in his broadcast telling the public of the debt owed to the "few" fighter pilots who saved the country in the Battle of Britain of 1940.

Changing perspectives
Attitudes towards the play have changed considerably through time, along with attitudes to war and nationalist fervour. Critics and theatre directors now treat the play much more warily than in the past. They often look for a subversive political message that parodies militarism – staging the play not

Laurence Olivier's morale-boosting film, made during World War II, left out some of Henry's more vicious acts, such as the hanging of Bardolph, to portray Henry as a heroic figure.

> I see you stand like greyhounds in the slips, Straining upon the start. The game's afoot.
> Follow your spirit, and upon this charge
> Cry, 'God for Harry! England and Saint George!'
>
> **Henry V**
> Act 3, Scene 1

in historical England, for instance, but in charged contemporary situations, such as the war in Iraq. Or they look to focus on the human cost of war implicit in the play. Many critics have gone further, and suggested that *Henry V* has been misread. Far from glorifying war, they say, the play is a complex exploration of the miseries of war and the power of propaganda.

What is clear is that the play is by no means a simple narrative of Henry's big moment. It tells the story from at least four different perspectives. Not only is there the straight sequence of scenes that places Henry at the thick of things; there is also the Chorus, which prepares us for each act; there are the trials and tribulations of the Eastcheapers; and there are the tough experiences of the ordinary soldiers. There is even a French perspective. These multiple viewpoints suggest there is much more going on than merely Henry's heroism, as each interweaves with the central Henry narrative.

Proclaiming Henry

The Chorus that opens the play puts the illusory theatre experience at the forefront, with its evocative mentions of "this wooden O" – the term often used for the round, timber-framed playhouses of Shakespeare's time, one of which has been accurately reconstructed today in the form of the Globe Theatre. The Chorus apologizes for the theatre's limitations in staging such an epic story, but the apology is uplifting: "O for a muse of fire that would ascend / The brightest heaven of invention: / A kingdom for a stage, princes to act, / And monarchs to behold the swelling scene." (Prologue-1–4).

The Chorus may be saying sorry, but at the same time, he is whipping up the crowd for the coming event with no less fervour than Henry will do when he later rouses his troops with his famous Crispin's Day speech. "Can this cock-pit hold / The vasty fields of France?" the Chorus asks (Prologue.11–12). The words conjure the same illusion as Henry will when he, beginning with the same false modesty, rouses his men with the promise of great memories for the future. »

> Would I were in an alehouse in London. I would give all my fame for a pot of ale, and safety.
>
> **Boy**
> Act 3 Scene 2

Historical Agincourt

The focus of *Henry V* is the Battle of Agincourt, a landmark English victory in a series of conflicts known as the Hundred Years War, which lasted from 1337 until 1453. It was fought between the English and French ruling families, the Plantagenets and the Valois, for control of the French throne.

The battle took place on 25 October 1415 near present-day Azincourt in northern France. Henry V did indeed fight in the battle. The outnumbered English forces possessed both technology and luck. Henry's archers could shoot up to six arrows a minute using the longbow, whereas the French possessed the slower, heavier crossbow, and, weighed down with armour, had chosen a muddy field for their attack.

The battle was not as one-sided as Shakespeare makes out, although the killing of the prisoners did take place. Neither was the impact of the battle as decisive as the play suggests. It took five more years of war before Henry reached a settlement with the French. He died at the age of 35 before ever becoming king of France.

> O God of battles, steel my
> soldiers' hearts.
> Possess them not with fear.
> Take from them now.
> **Henry V**
> **Act 4, Scene 1**

Beyond the banner

What follows the Chorus's prologue is not scenes of heroism but a shady debate between England's two church leaders. These men of the cloth do not discuss high moral matters, but a backstairs collusion to escape taxes by supporting Henry's claim to the French throne. If the church leaders' motives are so venal, maybe one should question their assessment that the erstwhile tearaway Prince Hal has had an almost religious conversion to the straight and narrow on becoming king: "Consideration like an angel came / And whipped th'offending Adam out of him." (1.1.29–30). Throughout the narrative, Henry presents himself as a Christian king, armed by God. After the seemingly miraculous triumph on the battlefield at Agincourt, he declines to take credit, offering the victory to God – "Take it God, / For it is none but thine." (4.8.111–112). But is this all image-building, part

In Kenneth Branagh's film version, the Battle of Agincourt takes place on a rain-drenched, muddy battlefield. In contrast to Olivier's earlier film, Branagh stressed the horrors of war.

of a necessary display of kingship? We never actually see Henry on the battlefield, nor do we ever hear of any strategic skill. Instead, Henry dazzles with rhetoric.

Henry the orator

Two speeches in particular show Shakespeare's language at its most muscular. The first is when Henry urges his men on outside the walls of Harfleur: "Once more unto the breach, dear friends, once more, / Or close the wall up with our English dead." (3.1.1–2). The second is his address before the battle, when he promises: "And Crispin Crispian shall ne'er go by / From this day to the ending of the world / But we in it shall be rememberèd, / We few, we happy few, we band of brothers" (4.3.57–60).

Ruthless leader

The picture presented of Henry is far from simply heroic. Shakespeare shows him to be not just an inspiring leader, but a tough, even brutal, one too. His way with justice is ruthless. The traitors are tricked into urging their own death sentence, while Henry brusquely confirms the death sentence on his drinking friend Bardolph for stealing from a church, despite pleas for clemency. Indeed, Henry's old Eastcheap pals – Bardolph, Nim, and Pistol – are as unheroic an image of soldiering as can be. Disreputable, lazy, cowardly, and argumentative, very often they seem to parody Henry's rhetoric, with Bardolph proclaiming, "On, on, on, on, on! To the breach! To the breach!" (3.2.1–2). In the prequel, *Henry IV*, these were entertaining characters, a comic counterpoint to the main action led by the irrepressible Sir John Falstaff. But in *Henry V*, much of the humour has drained away and the lovable rogues of the earlier play become victims, bearing the cost of war more than the other characters.

Falstaff dies without ever even appearing – a victim, so Mistress Quickly insists, of Henry's neglect: "The King has killed his heart" (2.1.84). Bardolph and Nim are hanged offstage for the same roguery that made them endearing in the earlier play. Finally, Mistress Quickly dies of the French malady (venereal disease), again offstage. Only Pistol survives, and even he is humiliated by being forced to eat leek by Fluellen. The juggernaut of Henry's heroic new age has rolled on and left these characters of an earlier time in its wake.

Henry the king

The portrait of a king in *Henry V*, then, is an ambiguous one, more so than the stirring speeches would suggest. What is certain is that Henry is no unthinking military leader. He has a keen insight into his role as king. As he explains to Bates and Williams when in disguise, "All his senses have but human conditions. His ceremonies laid by, in his nakedness he appears but a man" (4.1.103–105).

Henry knows that he is, underneath the crown, just a man. But he is keenly aware that, as king, he cannot behave as other men do. "We are no tyrant," he insists, "but a Christian king, / Unto whose grace our passion is as subject / As our wretches fettered in our prisons" (1.2.241–243). The image of his human emotions as a wretched prisoner in chains is disturbing, but his view of the need

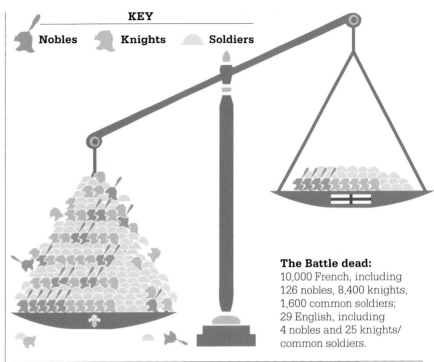

KEY

Nobles   Knights   Soldiers

The Battle dead:
10,000 French, including 126 nobles, 8,400 knights, 1,600 common soldiers; 29 English, including 4 nobles and 25 knights/ common soldiers.

for self-control and self-sacrifice is clear. The result is that Henry's personality remains largely hidden. He has just one moment of personal revelation – a long soliloquy at the end of his nightwalk about the camp – and even here his argument about the burdens of kingship seem more theoretical than emotional. Henry is a consummate actor, able to be whoever his people need him to be – from theologian with the bishops to common man with the soldiery, to charming, unschooled lover with the princess Catherine.

The Henriad

Henry V was the fourth play of the Henriad, a quartet of history plays, following *Richard II* and *Henry IV* Parts 1 and 2. Together with the first quartet (comprising *Henry VI* Parts 1, 2, and 3, and *Richard III*), it forms a complete chronology of English history from the time of Richard II (1377–99) to the time of Richard III (1483–85). *Henry V* provides a contrasting figure to the quartet's first king, Richard II, whose weaknesses are transformed into Henry's strengths. Richard smashes a mirror when he loses his throne. But as the English prepare for battle, the Chorus holds Henry up as "the mirror of all Christian kings" (2.0.6). Henry is our own reflection, the king we want him to be, which may explain why our view of this hero is so hard to pin down. ∎

Take it God,
For it is none but thine.
Henry V
Act 4, Scene 8

THERE IS A TIDE IN THE AFFAIRS OF MEN WHICH, TAKEN AT THE FLOOD, LEADS ON TO FORTUNE

JULIUS CAESAR (1599)

DRAMATIS PERSONAE

Julius Caesar A Roman general and senator who, having defeated the tyrant Pompey, is crowned emperor.

CAESAR'S SUPPORTERS

Mark Antony A senator and soldier who is loyal to Caesar. Antony is a manipulative man, able to turn the civilians against Brutus.

Calpurnia Wife of Caesar. She asks him not to visit the Capitol on the ides of March.

Octavius Caesar Nephew and adopted son of Julius Caesar, Octavius is the named heir to his uncle.

Lepidus One of the rulers of Rome after the assassination of Caesar.

Soothsayer A prophesier who warns Caesar to beware the ides of March.

CONSPIRATORS

Marcus Brutus A senator and staunch Republican, who is persuaded by Cassius to revolt against Caesar.

Caius Cassius Manipulative and greedy, he exploits Brutus's loyalty to the republic in order to overthrow Caesar.

Portia Loyal, loving, and trustworthy wife of Brutus.

Lucius Serving boy to Brutus.

Trebonius, Decius Brutus, Metullus Cimber, Cinna, Caius Ligarius Conspirators against Caesar.

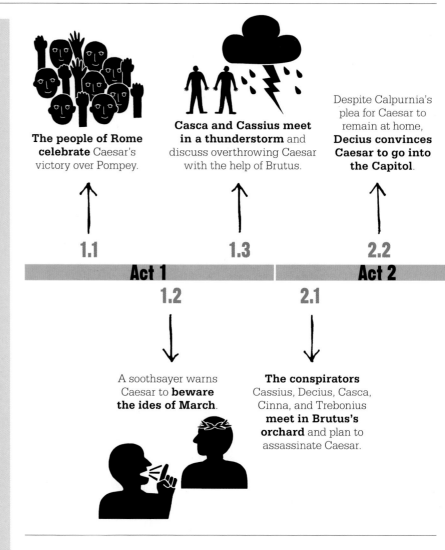

The people of Rome celebrate Caesar's victory over Pompey.

Casca and Cassius meet in a thunderstorm and discuss overthrowing Caesar with the help of Brutus.

Despite Calpurnia's plea for Caesar to remain at home, **Decius convinces Caesar to go into the Capitol**.

1.1

1.3

2.2

Act 1 **Act 2**

1.2

2.1

A soothsayer warns Caesar to **beware the ides of March**.

The conspirators Cassius, Decius, Casca, Cinna, and Trebonius **meet in Brutus's orchard** and plan to assassinate Caesar.

In Rome, the people celebrate a holiday, the Lupercal, and also rejoice in the triumph of Julius Caesar over the former leader, Pompey.

While greeting his followers, Caesar is warned by a soothsayer to beware the ides (15th) of March. Caesar ignores this warning and dismisses the soothsayer as a dreamer. As he leaves, Cassius draws Brutus aside to convince him that Caesar has become too self-important and that Brutus himself would be a better leader, being of equal standing and as respected by the public. After this, Cassius and Brutus learn from Casca that Caesar has been offered a crown three times, but refused it, albeit unconvincingly, each time. He finally accepts the offer, agreeing to become king and sole leader of Rome. Cassius, left alone, admits that he will use whatever deception necessary to convince Brutus to overthrow Caesar.

During a thunderstorm the night before Caesar is to be crowned Casca notes that many ill omens have appeared. The conspirators meet at Brutus's home and agree to

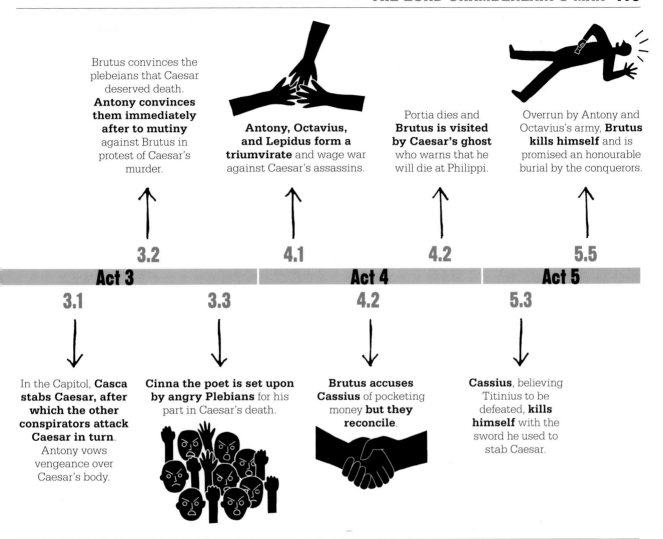

Brutus convinces the plebeians that Caesar deserved death. **Antony convinces them immediately after to mutiny** against Brutus in protest of Caesar's murder.

Antony, Octavius, and Lepidus form a triumvirate and wage war against Caesar's assassins.

Portia dies and **Brutus is visited by Caesar's ghost** who warns that he will die at Philippi.

Overrun by Antony and Octavius's army, **Brutus kills himself** and is promised an honourable burial by the conquerors.

3.2

4.1

4.2

5.5

Act 3

Act 4

Act 5

3.1

3.3

4.2

5.3

In the Capitol, **Casca stabs Caesar, after which the other conspirators attack Caesar in turn**. Antony vows vengeance over Caesar's body.

Cinna the poet is set upon by angry Plebians for his part in Caesar's death.

Brutus accuses Cassius of pocketing money **but they reconcile**.

Cassius, believing Titinius to be defeated, **kills himself** with the sword he used to stab Caesar.

murder Caesar in order to liberate the country from his dictatorship. Brutus has reservations, but he agrees that it must be done to put a stop to Caesar's ambition.

The next day, on the fateful ides of March, Caesar is convinced by Decius that he should go into the city, where he is stabbed by each of the conspirators. When the great soldier Mark Antony hears of this, he laments the death of Caesar, but he shows respect for the people who murdered him, asking them if he can give a speech to the people before

Caesar's funeral. Brutus agrees to let Antony do this, in spite of Cassius's warning that it would be dangerous to let him rally the public in Caesar's name.

After Brutus gives a speech to the people, Antony convinces them that Caesar was unjustly murdered by the conspirators, and that this injustice must be avenged. The people then take Caesar's body to be buried, and start a public mutiny. When Caesar's son Octavius returns to Rome, he and Antony start a war against Brutus and the conspirators.

Brutus sees the ghost of Caesar, and acknowledges that he will lose the battle. After he finds Cassius dead, Brutus asks his servant Lucius to hold his sword while he runs onto it and he dies. Finally, Antony and Octavius arrive as victors after the war, lamenting the fall of Brutus and noting that, despite his crime against Caesar, his intentions were the most honourable of all the conspirators. The play closes with Octavius promising to give Brutus a respectable funeral. »

IN CONTEXT

THEMES
Power, ambition, rebellion, civil war

SETTING
Ancient Rome

SOURCES
1579 Sir Thomas North's translation of Plutarch's *Lives of the Noble Grecians and Romans*.

LEGACY
1599 A performance at a Bankside theatre is mentioned in the diary of the Swiss traveller Thomas Platter the Younger. The theatre is likely to have been the Globe.

1898 British actor-manager Herbert Beerbohm Tree opens the first of his successful Shakespearean productions at Her Majesty's Theatre, London, with a lavish Julius Caesar.

1937 At the age of 22, Orson Welles stages a heavily edited, modern-dress adaptation set within a European fascist context at the Mercury Theatre in New York.

1977 While imprisoned on Robben Island, South Africa, Nelson Mandela marks on his copy of the play Caesar's words "cowards die many times before their deaths" as an inspirational passage.

2013 An all-female production at the Donmar Warehouse in London, directed by Phyllida Lloyd, sets the action in a contemporary women's prison.

The first of Shakespeare's Roman plays, *Julius Caesar* is a tale of ambition, political manipulation, and duty. The true tragic figure of the play is Brutus, whose actions proceed from a noble desire to serve Rome. Brutus's struggle between love for Caesar and fear of his despotism make him a sympathetic and honourable tragic figure.

Following the events laid out in Plutarch's history, the play charts the events leading up to Caesar's assassination and the civil war that breaks out thereafter. The senators' concerns about Caesar's leadership echoed anxieties about the aged and heirless Queen Elizabeth in 1599, when the play was first performed. Her inheritance and legacy were not to be discussed, let alone satirized, but could be approached sideways via history.

Shakespeare brings an acute sense of humanity to the story. His historical figures are not simply biographical documentations of the lives of noble Romans. Rather, the characters experience hardship and

Why, man, he doth bestride
the narrow world
Like a Colossus, and
we petty men
Walk under his huge legs,
and peep about
To find ourselves
dishonourable graves.
Cassius
Act 1, Scene 2

O conspiracy,
Sham'st thou to show thy
dang'rous brow by night,
When evils are most free?
Brutus
Act 2, Scene 1

anxiety, which makes them more morally ambiguous than Plutarch's counterparts. For instance, it is not clear whether Caesar would have mutated into the tyrant that Brutus fears before his assassination, nor that Cassius is a categorically self-interested man, nor even that Ocatvius will make a suitable successor to his adopted father. Such ambiguity has led the American historian Garry Wills to argue that the play has no villains and is, therefore, unique among Shakespeare's tragedies.

Seductive rhetoric

Power in this play does not come from strength, honour, or military prowess. Instead, power is linked to manipulative and calculated rhetoric. Without the support of the people, the senators cannot avoid civil unrest, and how to convince, placate, and organize the civilians in Rome is a major preoccupation of the leaders. It is this that motivates Brutus's address to the people after Caesar's death and Antony's speech about Caesar's reputation.

Antony's oft-quoted speech beginning "Friends, Romans, countrymen" (3.2.74) is a carefully crafted piece of rhetoric calculated

A 1953 film adaptation by director Joseph Mankiewicz starred Marlon Brando as Antony. Brando received coaching in declaiming Shakespearean verse from co-star John Gielgud.

to inspire suspicion of Brutus and respect for the late Caesar. Antony accuses the public who so recently celebrated Caesar's triumph at the Lupercal of being "brutish beasts", an echo of Brutus's name. Antony suggests that his enemy is a liar, simultaneously touting Caesar as a peerless hero. With this speech, and with his reading of Caesar's will, Antony gains the support of the civilians, thereby exploiting their new hatred of Caesar's murderers to justify civil war.

With this support, Antony unleashes havoc in the streets. Rebellions and rioting lead to the assassination of Cinna, the poet. There is no accountability for such violent crimes because the civilians act out of anger and fear. Antony understands this, but chooses to spur on the people's distrust of the conspirators to further his own interests. With persuasive rhetorical flourishes, the senators also manipulate one another. In the

same way that Antony persuades the people that the conspirators are treasonous murderers, so too Cassius convinces Brutus that Caesar must be removed from office. The most potent piece of rhetoric is the cry made by the conspirators after Caesar's death: "Liberty! Freedom! Tyranny is dead!" (3.1.77). Intangible ideals are cleverly used to justify the horror of

Caesar's assassination. Rhetoric and persuasion are integral to the political tacticians in Rome, so it is with a scathing voice that Cassius declares, "For who so firm that cannot be seduced?" (1.2.312).

Women unheeded

The women in this masculine political Rome are presented as supportive, stoic wives. Both »

Contemporary twist

The director Gregory Doran staged a politically provocative adaptation of the play in 2012. With a black cast and set in an unspecified African country, this production of *Julius Caesar* drew inspiration from contemporary political tyranny in its depiction of a nation familiar with despots, civil war, superstition, poverty, and disease. The actions of 20th-century dictators such as Idi Amin and Bokassa, and, more recently, Robert Mugabe, together with the unfolding of the Arab Spring in 2010, collectively informed this interpretation.

Ray Fearon's Antony was a charismatic, manipulative man whose speech to the citizens was delivered on a raised platform over the bloodied body of Caesar, played by Jeffery Kissoon. Brutus was played as a fiercely honourable but naive man by Patterson Joseph. Caesar's own tyranny was skilfully echoed by a giant statue of the leader, designed by Michael Vale, resembling icons of dictatorship in the 20th century. The production was adapted for the screen later that year.

Brutus's wife Portia and Caesar's wife Calpurnia exist to temper the passions, albeit unsuccessfully, of their husbands. Neither politician shares his misgivings with his wife, nor does either one heed the wifely warnings of danger.

Calpurnia appeals to Caesar's regard for reputation and honour to ask him to remain at home on the ides of March. By contrast, Portia wounds her own thigh, proving herself an equal to her husband through noble suffering. She takes her own life by swallowing hot coals, setting the bar of honour very high for Brutus's death.

Like the men in this world, the women craft their speech. Portia urges her husband to reveal his anxieties in a series of questions using the rule of listing in threes: "Is Brutus sick? and is it physical / To walk unbracèd and suck up the humours / Of the dank morning? What, is Brutus sick? / And will he steal out of his wholesome bed / To dare the vile contagion of the night, / And tempt the rheumy and unpurgèd air / To add unto his sickness? No, my Brutus, / You have some sick offence within your mind, / Which by the right and virtue of my place / I ought to know of." (2.1.260–269).

Although Brutus promises to be more open with his wife, she remains ignorant of the plot against Caesar. This echoes Calpurnia's lack of influence over Caesar.

Masters of fate?

For the conspirators at the start of the play, time and opportunity work in their favour. Caesar is not yet an emperor, nor has he morphed into a tyrant. Before he can become either, Brutus believes it is in the interests of the people and state to dispatch him: "There is a tide in the affairs of men / Which, taken at the flood, leads on to fortune; / Omitted, all the voyage of their life / Is bound in shallows and in miseries. / On such a full sea are we now afloat, / And we must take the current when it serves, / Or lose our ventures" (4.2.270–276).

Cowards die many times before their deaths; The valiant never taste of death but once.
Julius Caesar
Act 2, Scene 2

When he speaks of riding the tide of opportunity, Brutus suggests that fate has a degree of flexibility to it and that to make the most of opportunities leads on to fortune. This is a theory he takes from Cassius who argues that autonomy is the route to success: "Men at sometime were masters of their fates. / The fault, dear Brutus, is not in our stars, / But in ourselves, that we are underlings." (1.2.140–142).

Brutus's belief in destiny explains his willingness to accept his defeat at Philippi. Although he took the opportunity to remove Caesar, it is the ghost and retribution of that same enemy that brings about Brutus's fall. In other words, fate intervenes to punish the conspirators. If fate leads these men to their inevitable ends, how can there be, and what is the purpose of, free will? This question consumes Brutus and Cassius, as well as proving fatal to Caesar. Although Shakespeare does not provide a resolution to the conflict between fate and free will,

The knives are out for Caesar in this 2014 production at the Globe Theatre, with George Irving as Caesar, and Anthony Howell as Cassius.

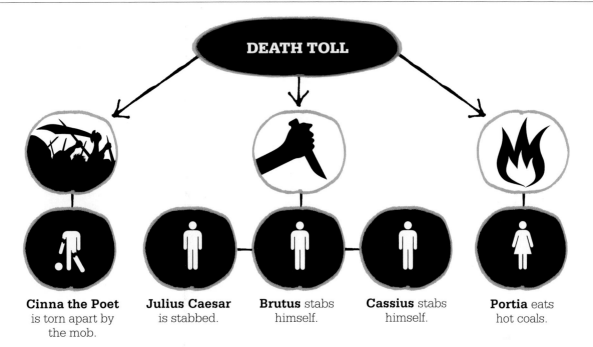

DEATH TOLL

Cinna the Poet is torn apart by the mob.

Julius Caesar is stabbed.

Brutus stabs himself.

Cassius stabs himself.

Portia eats hot coals.

there is an overwhelming sense of destiny throughout the play, specifically with the many omens that appear during the action.

Ominous portents

Casca expounds on the unnatural events that led up to the ides of March during an equally ominous thunderstorm. Fire drops from the sky, men walk around the streets in flames, lions stalk the Roman roads, and nightingales sing at midday. Casca claims "I believe they are portentous things" (1.3.31).

The signs of doom, as Cassius and Brutus choose to interpret them, echo the Soothsayer's warning to Caesar to "Beware the ides of March" (1.2.25). Caesar ignores the omen by dismissing the Soothsayer, while the conspirators take the omens as a sign to attack Caesar, rather than a warning about impending turmoil should they proceed. Both Caesar and Brutus misinterpret such signs and go on to make decisions with tragic

consequences. It is no accident that, when Casca expostulates about portents, the senator Cicero responds with a statement that rings true for every individual in this tragedy: "Indeed it is a strange-disposèd time; / But men may construe things after their fashion, / Clean from the purpose of the things themselves" (1.3.33–35). There is, in other words, a greater force at work fore-warning these men of their destinies, but the

I love the name of honour more than I fear death.
Brutus
Act 1, Scene 2

power to interpret and act on those warnings lies with the individual. Ultimately, Brutus takes advantage of chances thrown his way, and yet still ends in defeat. Octavius and Mark Antony will overcome Brutus, just as Brutus took advantage of Caesar's decision to ignore caution on the ides of March.

The intricacies of fate aside, the play makes clear the respect that these men have for one another. Brutus's love for Caesar prevents him from overcoming his guilt at Phillippi; Caesar's trust in Brutus prompts him to exclaim "*et tu, Bruté?*" [you, too, Brutus?] (3.1.77) upon his murder; Cassius is loyal to Brutus despite taking advantage of his integrity; and Antony respects Brutus who, in his opinion, "was the noblest Roman of them all" (5.5.67). They recognize nobility in one another. This is what separates this tragedy from others, including *King Lear*, *Hamlet*, and *Macbeth*, because every character is capable and deserving of redemption. ■

ALL THE WORLD'S A STAGE

AND ALL THE MEN AND WOMEN

MERELY PLAYERS

AS YOU LIKE IT (1599–1600)

DRAMATIS PERSONAE

Duke Senior Older brother of Duke Frederick, living in exile in the Forest of Arden.

Rosalind Duke Senior's daughter. Later disguised as Ganymede.

Amiens One of Duke Senior's lords, a talented singer.

Jaques One of Duke Senior's lords, a melancholy philosopher.

Duke Frederick Father to Celia, he usurps his brother.

Celia Daughter of Duke Frederick and Rosalind's cousin. Later, she disguises herself as Aliena.

Touchstone A court fool.

Le Beau A courtier.

Charles A wrestler.

Oliver Oldest son of Sir Rowland de Bois.

Orlando Younger brother of Oliver, kept uneducated.

Jaques de Boys Younger brother of Oliver.

Adam Former servant of Sir Rowland de Bois.

Corin An old shepherd.

Silvius A young shepherd in love with Phoebe.

Phoebe A young shepherdess, disdainful of Silvius.

William A countryman and rival in love for Audrey with Touchstone.

Audrey A goatherd, she is betrothed to Touchstone.

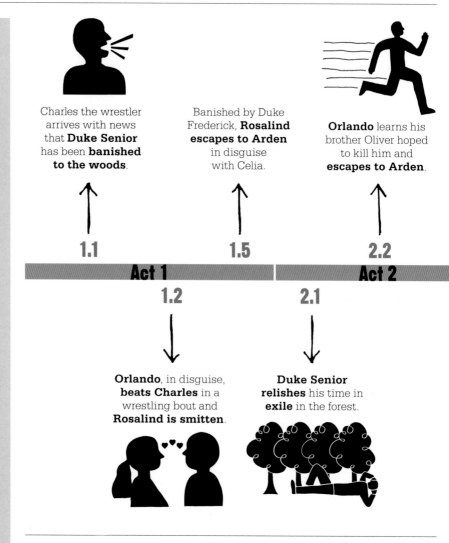

Charles the wrestler arrives with news that **Duke Senior** has been **banished to the woods**.

1.1

Banished by Duke Frederick, **Rosalind escapes to Arden** in disguise with Celia.

1.5

Orlando learns his brother Oliver hoped to kill him and **escapes to Arden**.

2.2

Act 1 · **Act 2**

1.2

Orlando, in disguise, **beats Charles** in a wrestling bout and **Rosalind is smitten**.

2.1

Duke Senior relishes his time in **exile** in the forest.

Since their father's death, Orlando has been kept at home and denied education by his older brother Oliver. When Oliver hears that Orlando plans to fight Charles the wrestler, Oliver tells Charles to kill him. At court, Rosalind laments her father, Duke Senior's, banishment. With her cousin Celia, she watches the wrestling match and both are taken with Orlando, who surprisingly beats Charles. Orlando falls in love with Rosalind, but has to escape to the forest with old Adam, pursued by Oliver. Celia's father, Duke Frederick, feels threatened by Rosalind's popularity and exiles her. Rosalind dresses as the boy Ganymede and flees to the forest with Celia and Touchstone, the fool. In the forest, Duke Senior and his lords, including the gloomy Jaques, enjoy the simple life.

Duke Frederick organizes a pursuit of Rosalind and Celia. In the forest, Rosalind and Celia witness Silvius telling the old shepherd Corin of his unrequited love for Phoebe. Faint with hunger, Orlando meets Duke Senior's men and draws his sword. They offer him supper

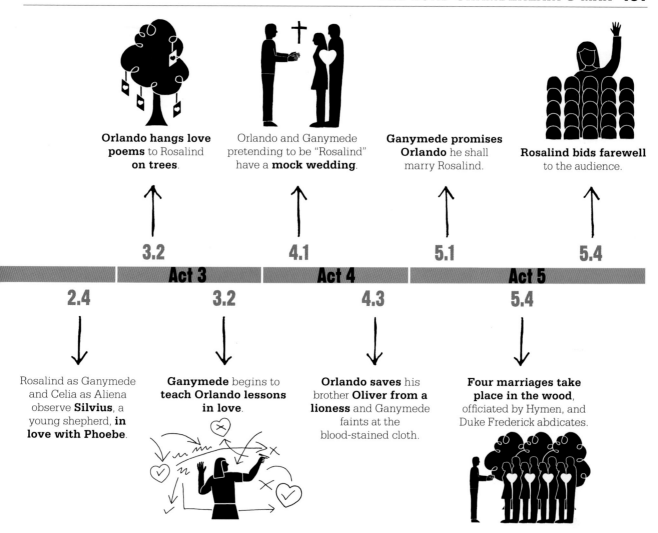

Orlando hangs love poems to Rosalind **on trees.**

Orlando and Ganymede pretending to be "Rosalind" have a **mock wedding.**

Ganymede promises Orlando he shall marry Rosalind.

Rosalind bids farewell to the audience.

3.2

4.1

5.1

5.4

Act 3   **Act 4**   **Act 5**

2.4   **3.2**   **4.3**   **5.4**

Rosalind as Ganymede and Celia as Aliena observe **Silvius,** a young shepherd, **in love with Phoebe.**

Ganymede begins to **teach Orlando lessons in love.**

Orlando saves his brother **Oliver from a lioness** and Ganymede faints at the blood-stained cloth.

Four marriages take place in the wood, officiated by Hymen, and Duke Frederick abdicates.

and he joins their band. Orlando, pining for Rosalind, hangs poems to her on the trees. Touchstone and Corin compare lifestyles. Rosalind finds Orlando's poems and when he appears, she, still disguised as Ganymede, teaches him how to woo her as Rosalind. Rosalind as Ganymede and Celia as Aliena come across Phoebe. Rosalind/Ganymede suggests Phoebe should be thankful for Silvius's love; but instead Phoebe falls for Ganymede.

Rosalind/Ganymede pretending to be Rosalind goes through a mock wedding with Orlando presided over by Aliena as the vicar. Orlando leaves promising to return in the afternoon. He fails to return but Rosalind is distracted by an anguished love letter from Phoebe to Ganymede. Oliver suddenly arrives with a blood-stained cloth. It seems that Orlando found him under a tree about to be attacked by wild beasts and saved his life, only to be injured by a lioness. Oliver is now reconciled with Orlando, and the cloth is a message from Orlando to Rosalind. Rosalind swoons. Touchstone scares off William, his rival for Audrey's

affections. Oliver and Alien decide to marry. Orlando is impatient to be with the real Rosalind and Ganymede promises he will make Rosalind appear by magic so they can be married. He also promises Silvius that he will marry Phoebe.

On the big day, Ganymede and Aliena slip out to return with Hymen as Rosalind and Celia. Four wedding ceremonies are performed by Hyman. News arrives that Duke Frederick has become a hermit, leaving the dukedom to Duke Senior. The actor playing Rosalind bids adieu to the audience. »

IN CONTEXT

THEMES
Love, romance, mortality

SETTING
**The French court
and the Forest of
Ardennes (in Belgium)
or Arden (in England)**

SOURCES
1590 Thomas Lodge's prose
tale *Rosalynde*.

LEGACY
1603 *As You Like It* may
have been performed for
King James I.

1723 Charles Johnson's
filleted version, *Love in a
Forest*, appears, with scenes
from other Shakespeare
plays added.

1741–57 Irish actress Peg
Woffington plays Rosalind on
the London stage for 16 years.

1879 A production at
Stratford-upon-Avon features
a freshly killed deer from a
Warwickshire forest.

1961 British director Michael
Elliott's production for the
RSC stars Vanessa Redgrave
as a boyish Rosalind.

1977 German director Peter
Stein stages a large-scale
promenade production in Berlin.

1996 Kenneth Branagh's film
version relocates the action
to a European colony in
19th-century Japan.

2013 A contemporary youth
version by Maria Aberg for the
RSC features music by folk
musician Laura Marling.

A s You Like It is one of
Shakespeare's most
enduringly popular plays.
It forays into the beautiful Forest of
Arden for an interlude full of light
romance and wit, philosophical
speculation, and broad comedy. In
the clever, ardent, playful Rosalind,
who spends her time in Arden
dressed as the boy Ganymede, it
has an engaging central character.

Strangely, though, very little
happens in *As You Like It*. Two
young people, Rosalind and
Orlando, run away to the Forest of
Arden to escape difficult relatives
– Rosalind fleeing her uncle Duke
Frederick, who usurped the power
of her father (who's already fled to
the forest), and Orlando from his
brother Oliver, who connives to have
him killed, form a rather paper-thin
plot. In the forest, Rosalind, dressed
as Ganymede, teaches Orlando the
ways of love and meets various folk.
After a few misunderstandings,
Rosalind and Orlando get married,
along with three other couples who
also found romance in the forest, and
all family differences are resolved.
And this is all that happens.

> What passion hangs these
> weights upon my tongue?
> I cannot speak to her, yet she
> urged conference.
> **Orlando**
> **Act 1, Scene 2**

Romantic nonsense?

The Irish playwright George
Bernard Shaw thought the play
so flimsy that he dismissed it as
a silly crowd-pleaser. The title
"As You Like It", Shaw suggested,
was just Shakespeare throwing
back at the audience their taste
for such romantic nonsense. But
although *As You Like It* has had
a chequered historical reception,
most critics now agree that
Shaw missed the point. It is
really a clever, sophisticated play.
While it is more wholeheartedly
entertaining perhaps than any
other of Shakespeare's plays, it
is still packed full of ideas and
insights into life and love. The
title, far from being a throwaway,
is perhaps both a celebration of
the joy of theatre, and an invitation
to be open-minded. As the Royal
Shakespeare Company put it,
"Gender roles, nature, and politics
are confused in a play that reflects
on how bewildering yet utterly
pleasurable life can be."

In 1950, Hollywood star Katharine
Hepburn took on the part of Rosalind.
She said of the role that it is "one of the
great tests of how good an actress you
are, and I wanted to find out".

I did not entreat to have
her stay.
It was your pleasure,
and your own remorse.
Celia
Act 1, Scene 3

There may not be much plot, but there is a feast of romance and comedy – poems and songs, wit and banter, all spilling from characters' lips with continual invention. It is an intellectual and poetic picnic to which the audience is invited to spend a couple of hours for their pleasure and mental stimulation. Nothing much happens because nothing is meant to happen. Just as time is briefly suspended for the characters in Arden – "There's / no clock in the forest," (3.2.294–295) says Orlando – so it is also for the audience watching the play as they go on a holiday in the theatre. It's a chance to mentally recharge and rethink – to "fleet the / time carelessly" (1.1.112–113) – away from the pressures of ordinary life.

Country vs city

As You Like It is structured in three parts. It begins in the court or city, where unsolvable problems arise; it journeys into nature or a fantasy world, where the problems are untangled; and then returns to the court, the real world at the end with the problems resolved. In fact, *As You Like It* ends before the final return to court, but with Duke Frederick's sudden change of heart offstage at the end, it's clear only Jaques will stay in the forest.

It is the nature section, in the Forest of Arden, that dominates most of the play: for this reason, it is often described as a "pastoral comedy". Pastoral literature was very much in vogue at the time – British critic Frank Kermode described *As You Like It* as "the most topical of the comedies", because it is most engaged with

Hugh Thomson's 1915 illustration of Act 1, Scene 3, in which Celia and Rosalind contemplate leaving the court, hints at the move to the idyllic forest in the finery of the peacocks' feathers.

the intellectual interests of the age. The word "pastoral" refers literally to the shepherd's life. It is not about real shepherds but an idealization – a harmonious "Arcadia". Shepherds don't look after sheep in pastoral literature; instead they are poets, »

Music is a key part of the pastoral merriment of *As You Like It*, as in this production at the Delacorte Theater, New York (2012). There are more songs in the play than any other of Shakespeare's.

philosophers, and singers. The pastoral world is an imaginary golden age or Garden of Eden, a peaceful and uncorrupted place where harmony can be rediscovered away from the strife and pressures of everyday reality.

Pastoral literature in Shakespeare's time was very highbrow. It was prose and poetry, full of lovelorn shepherds and disdainful girls, and characters with fancy classical names who were quite clearly courtiers on

holiday rather than real country folk. Despite its focus on the simple life, it was nothing much to do with real nature. In *As You Like It*, Shakespeare turns the pastoral into popular entertainment for the stage. He continually subverts the form, letting realism bleed into its idealized world and gently satirizing the genre's conventions. In one scene, for instance, Orlando is seen pinning poems to trees in true poet-shepherd style; in the very next

scene, the real old shepherd Corin is talking about his hands filthy with sheep grease.

The countryside continually interweaves the ideal and the real, the classical with the native England. Even the name of the forest, Arden, has this ambiguity. In Shakespeare's original source, Thomas Lodge's novel *Rosalynde* (1590), the setting was the Ardennes, a hilly region bordering France and Belgium. In some editions of the play, the Belgian spelling "Ardenne" is kept – and Shakespeare retains French names for characters such as Jaques and Amiens – but in other editions the forest is called Arden. Arden was a real woodland near Shakespeare's childhood home in Warwickshire, and it is also the family name of his grandmother, Mary Arden. Aptly, whether by coincidence or design, the name "Arden" also echoes both Ar-cadia and E-den.

A shepherd's life

The origins of pastoral literature date back to writers such as the Greeks Hesiod (c.750–650 BCE) and Theocritus (c.270 BCE) and, most famously, the Roman poet Virgil (70–19 BCE) in his *Eclogues*. They all wrote of golden ages and rural idylls. The genre was rediscovered in Europe during the Renaissance, and in Elizabethan England, the idea of the pastoral became popular among intellectuals and poets. A key work was Edmund Spenser's much-imitated *The Shephearde's Calender*, first published in 1579. Others include Sir Philip Sidney's long prose work

Arcadia and Christopher Marlowe's romantic poem *The Passionate Shepherd to His Love*, published in 1599.

Pastoral literature often contained subversive messages, and was intended to be held up as a mirror to the contemporary world. At the time *As You Like It* was written, satire had recently been banned by the Church. The play may contain reference to this ban in Celia's line: "since the little wit / that fools have silenced, the little foolery that / wise men have makes a great show." (1.2.84–86)

O wonderful,
wonderful, and most
wonderful–wonderful,
and yet again wonderful,
and after that out of
all whooping!
Celia
Act 3, Scene 2

Ambiguous Rosalind

At the very heart of the play's ambiguity is the character of Rosalind. In the forest, Rosalind dresses as a boy and takes the very classical name, Ganymede – the name of a beautiful Trojan boy in Greek myth. On the Elizabethan stage, she would have been played by a boy actor, and the play has fun with her constantly switching gender identities. At one point, Rosalind, disguised as Ganymede, pretends to be "Rosalind" to teach Orlando how to love. So at this moment on stage, there would have been a boy actor playing a girl who is playing a boy playing a girl! Meanwhile, Orlando is in love not with the pretend Rosalind played by Ganymede but the "real" Rosalind who is at that moment playing Ganymede playing Rosalind. And Phoebe – a girl's role also played by a boy actor – is in love with Ganymede, mistakenly thinking her a boy, when "he" is in fact a girl played by a boy! Much of the entertainment in the play comes from seeing how adeptly it manages these confusions and, at the end, resolves them.

Critics have talked a great deal about gender issues in *As You Like It* and the undercurrents of homoeroticism in, for instance, Phoebe's love for Ganymede/Rosalind, Celia's for Rosalind, and Orlando's flirtation with Ganymede. Indeed, the Ganymede of Greek myth was a beautiful boy who became Zeus's lover and was a byword for erotic relationships between men and young boys. In the play's epilogue, "Rosalind" has fun with the ambiguity of her gender. She partly steps out of her role, and as a boy actor toys with the audience, offering a kiss to "as many of you as had beards that pleased". Shakespeare's play is a celebration of all kinds of love and sexual possibilities, as the title implies.

True love

Beneath the role-playing and gender-switching, a portrait of the reality of love appears. When Orlando says he will die for love, Rosalind as Ganymede at once points out the flaws in this romantic nonsense. "Men have died from time to time for love, and worms have eaten them,"

No, no, Orlando; men are
April when they woo,
December when they wed.
Maids are May when they are
maids, but the sky changes
when they are wives.
Rosalind
Act 4, Scene 1

she says in her somewhat down-to-earth fashion, "but not for love" (4.1.99–101).

But Rosalind is not a cynic like Jaques, who doesn't believe in love. At this very moment, she is "fathom deep" in love with Orlando (4.1.196) and "cannot be out / of »

The idyllic countryside setting in Shakespeare's source novel *Rosalynde* was the Ardennes in Belgium (below). Shakespeare's forest may also be partly inspired by the Arden forest in England.

The seven ages of man

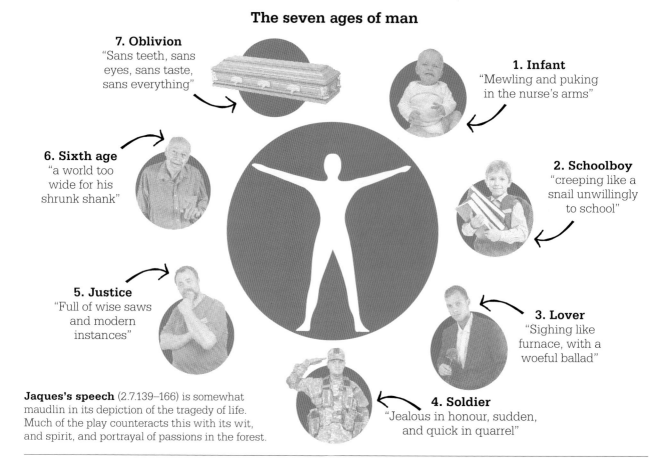

7. Oblivion
"Sans teeth, sans eyes, sans taste, sans everything"

1. Infant
"Mewling and puking in the nurse's arms"

6. Sixth age
"a world too wide for his shrunk shank"

2. Schoolboy
"creeping like a snail unwillingly to school"

5. Justice
"Full of wise saws and modern instances"

3. Lover
"Sighing like furnace, with a woeful ballad"

4. Soldier
"Jealous in honour, sudden, and quick in quarrel"

Jaques's speech (2.7.139–166) is somewhat maudlin in its depiction of the tragedy of life. Much of the play counteracts this with its wit, and spirit, and portrayal of passions in the forest.

the sight" of him (4.1.205–206). Indeed, she is more in love with him at this moment than he is with her, despite his protestations and poems. At this moment, Orlando is more in love with love than with Rosalind, and she must remain as Ganymede to teach him how to love her for real. She is high-spirited, insightful, witty, and passionate – but she can only stop playing Ganymede when Orlando stops playing at love.

Love is dressed in many guises in the play. Curmudgeonly Touchstone suddenly finds his heart with Audrey. The once-mean brother Oliver falls in love at first sight with Celia. Even Silvius's absurd poems and declarations bear fruit with Phoebe. Yet beneath it all, love is shown to be real and important.

The world's a stage

The best known speech in *As You Like It* is Jaques's speech, which begins: "All the world's a stage, / And all the men and women merely players. / They have their exits and their entrances, / And one man in his time plays many parts" (2.7.139–142).

The speech suggests that we are all merely playing parts, and describes the seven stages of life, from infancy to decrepit old age. This simple metaphor for life is often quoted out of context, and taken as Shakespeare's theme for the whole play and its theatricality. Its message about the pointless artificiality of life seems strangely bleak, though. Indeed, it's not so different from desolate Macbeth's

view when he says, "Life's but a walking shadow, a poor player / That struts and frets his hour upon the stage / And then is heard no more. It is a tale / Told by an idiot, full of sound and fury, / Signifying nothing." (*Macbeth* 5.5.23–27).

But of course the speaker is Jaques, whose name, as the jester Touchstone slyly reminds us in dubbing him "Monsieur What-ye-call't" (3.3.66), is pronounced "jakes", Elizabethan slang for toilet. It's a reminder that Jaques might well be talking "crap". In fact, in the character of Jaques, Shakespeare is making fun of a stereotype of Elizabethan times – the melancholy young philosopher with his fashionably jaded outlook on life. In his meandering observations,

> I will weary you then no longer with idle talking.
> **Rosalind**
> **Act 5, Scene 2**

Jaques is perhaps missing the point just as much as Orlando with his poems on trees. At the very instant Jaques finishes his speech with his bleak summary of old age as "second childishness and mere oblivion", on comes old Adam, carried on Orlando's back, decrepit old age personified. It's a funny moment, and a clear sign we shouldn't take Jaques too seriously. In some ways, neither does Jaques himself, for he relishes the bite of his own sardonic wit too much to be truly gloomy. For all his cynicism, he seems to positively enjoy being miserable. This is his life choice – as valid, perhaps, as any other. When the couples wed, and all is forgiven, the glut of happiness and "dancing measures" are too much for Jaques. Instead, despite entreaties, he chooses to go into exile once more, joining Duke Frederick in a hermit's cave.

It is Rosalind who has the final word, stepping forward to erase the boundary between character and actor, stage and audience, offering an invitation to leave this theatrical diversion, "as you like it": "I am sure, as many as have good beards, or good faces, or sweet breaths will for my kind offer, when I make curtsy, bid me farewell" (Epilogue). ∎

James Thomas Watts, a Victorian landscape artist, captured a forest idyll in his painting of Celia, Rosalind, and Touchstone in the forest. Country idylls were popular subjects in Victorian art.

Playing Rosalind

After its initial success at the Globe in 1599, *As You Like It* fell almost entirely out of fashion in the 17th century, and it was not until 1740 that the play was properly performed again by Charles Macklin at Drury Lane in London. In Macklin's production, Hannah Pritchard was unaffectedly lively as Rosalind and the role has been a favourite ever since.

Actors who have played Rosalind include Edith Evans, Katherine Hepburn, Vanessa Redgrave (pictured), Maggie Smith, and Fiona Shaw. Theatre company Cheek by Jowl's 1991 production had an all-male cast, with Adrian Lester as Rosalind.

There have been three major films of the play, each very different. Paul Czinner's whimsical 1936 version, with German Elisabeth Bergner as Rosalind, was an early sound film of the Shakespeare play. Christine Edzard's edgy 1992 version dressed Rosalind in jeans and hoodie in London's "cardboard city" for down and outs. Kenneth Branagh's lush 2007 film was set in 19th-century Japan and starred Romola Garai.

THE SLINGS AND ARROWS OF OUTRAGEOUS FORTUNE

HAMLET (1599–1601)

DRAMATIS PERSONAE

Hamlet Son of the dead king and Prince of Denmark. He is the nephew and step-son of King Claudius.

Claudius The newly crowned Danish king who marries his brother's widow, Gertrude.

Fortinbras Nephew of the Norwegian king and successor to the Danish throne. He seeks vengeance against Denmark for his father's murder.

Polonius Courtier and trusted adviser to Claudius. Father to Ophelia and Laertes.

Gertrude Mother to Hamlet and former wife of the deceased King Hamlet. She is now the wife of Claudius and Queen of Denmark.

Laertes Son of Polonius and brother to Ophelia. Laertes has been studying in France, but returns to Denmark to avenge Polonius's death.

Rosencrantz and Guildenstern University companions of Hamlet, whom he distrusts.

Ophelia Daughter of Polonius and sister to Laertes.

Horatio Trusted friend of Hamlet, to whom Hamlet reveals his plans.

Ghost of Hamlet's father It orders Hamlet to avenge his father's death.

Four players They perform in Hamlet's play.

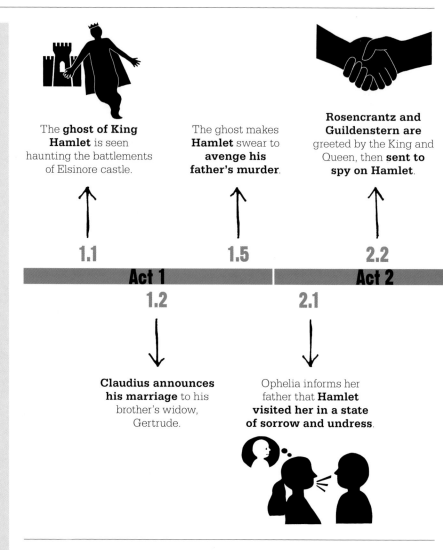

The **ghost of King Hamlet** is seen haunting the battlements of Elsinore castle.

The ghost makes **Hamlet** swear to **avenge his father's murder**.

Rosencrantz and Guildenstern are greeted by the King and Queen, then **sent to spy on Hamlet**.

1.1 **1.5** **2.2**

Act 1 **Act 2**

1.2 **2.1**

Claudius announces his marriage to his brother's widow, Gertrude.

Ophelia informs her father that **Hamlet visited her in a state of sorrow and undress**.

In Elsinore castle in Denmark, King Claudius grieves for the death of the former king, his brother. He hastily marries Gertrude, the dead king's widow, and sends messengers to Norway, Denmark's feuding neighbour, to prevent an invasion by the Norwegian Prince Fortinbras. Gertrude's son, Hamlet, is also grieving for the king, his father. Horatio, a companion, informs Hamlet that the ghost of his father has appeared on the battlements at night, and takes him to see for himself. The ghost tells Hamlet that

Hamlet's father was murdered by his uncle. Hamlet swears to avenge his father. However, unsure if he can believe the ghost, Hamlet feigns madness to distract his peers while he discovers the truth.

The courtier Polonius interprets Hamlet's strange behaviour as a symptom of love for Ophelia. After informing the King of this, they use Ophelia to spy on Hamlet. Hamlet guesses what she is doing and cruelly denies any affection for her.

To help assuage Hamlet's grief the King and Queen send for Rosencrantz and Guildenstern,

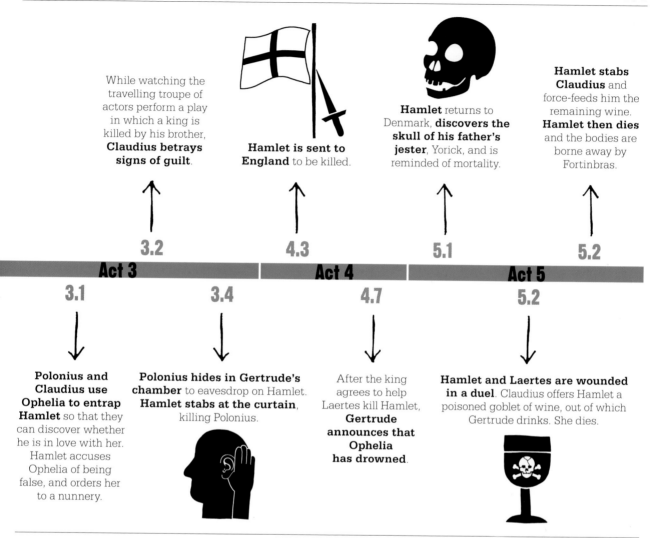

While watching the travelling troupe of actors perform a play in which a king is killed by his brother, **Claudius betrays signs of guilt**.

3.2

Hamlet is sent to **England** to be killed.

4.3

Hamlet returns to Denmark, **discovers the skull of his father's jester**, Yorick, and is reminded of mortality.

5.1

Hamlet stabs Claudius and force-feeds him the remaining wine. **Hamlet then dies** and the bodies are borne away by Fortinbras.

5.2

Act 3 **Act 4** **Act 5**

3.1

Polonius and Claudius use Ophelia to entrap Hamlet so that they can discover whether he is in love with her. Hamlet accuses Ophelia of being false, and orders her to a nunnery.

3.4

Polonius hides in Gertrude's chamber to eavesdrop on Hamlet. **Hamlet stabs at the curtain**, killing Polonius.

4.7

After the king agrees to help Laertes kill Hamlet, **Gertrude announces that Ophelia has drowned**.

5.2

Hamlet and Laertes are wounded in a duel. Claudius offers Hamlet a poisoned goblet of wine, out of which Gertrude drinks. She dies.

---

his old college friends, whom he now distrusts. Instead, he focuses on the arrival at court of travelling players, and orders them to perform a play in which a king is murdered by his brother. Hamlet sees that King Claudius is affected by the play, and takes this as proof of guilt.

On his way to Gertrude's chamber, Hamlet overhears the King in prayer, confessing to the murder. Meanwhile, Polonius hides behind an arras (a tapestry) in Gertrude's chamber to spy on Hamlet. Hamlet berates his mother for remarrying. Polonius calls for

help and Hamlet, believing the voice to be the King's, stabs at the tapestry and kills Polonius.

The King punishes Hamlet by sending him to England with Rosencrantz and Guildenstern with the intention of having him killed on arrival. On the journey, they are attacked by pirates. Hamlet escapes and returns to Denmark.

Laertes arrives in Elsinore and demands vengeance for the murder of Polonius. Grief-stricken by the murder, Ophelia loses her mind and drowns in a brook, spurring on Laertes's hatred for Hamlet.

Horatio and Hamlet witness Ophelia's burial. Hamlet reveals himself to the mourners and challenges Laertes to a duel. Laertes injures Hamlet with a poisoned blade, after which he is himself mortally wounded with the same blade. Gertrude drinks poisoned wine intended for Hamlet and dies, causing Laertes to accuse Claudius of murder. Hamlet stabs the King and forces the remaining poisoned wine down his throat before himself dying in the arms of Horatio. Fortinbras and his troops arrive to bear away the bodies. »

IN CONTEXT

THEMES
Revenge, betrayal, honour, mortality

SETTING
Elsinore in Denmark

SOURCES
c.1185 "Amleth", by Danish historian Saxo Grammaticus is the story of a legendary Danish prince whose uncle killed the king and married the queen.

1580 French poet François de Belleforest retells the story in his *Histoires Tragiques*, translated into English in 1608.

LEGACY
1602 The first recorded performance is on 26 July.

1742 English actor David Garrick becomes the most famous Hamlet of his day.

1827 Irish actress Harriet Smithson plays Ophelia at the Odéon, Paris; the play is a great success in France.

1919 Poet T S Eliot argues that the character Hamlet is an artistic failure.

1948 English actor Laurence Olivier's screen adaptation has dark, Freudian undertones.

1964 Grigori Kozintsev directs a Soviet film of the play.

1996 British actor Kenneth Branagh directs a film version that runs for over four hours.

2001 Director Peter Brook directs a multilingual *Hamlet* in Paris with actors speaking Japanese and Swahili.

Hamlet is Shakespeare's longest play, with perhaps the most challenging lead role. It is also his most enduringly popular tragedy. The play is a story of kingship, war, madness, and revenge. It is also a story that centres on a troubled man whose responsibilities to his father and to his kingdom are diametrically opposed to his instincts and temperament. Unlike its source text about the legendary Danish king Amleth, which is described as a romance, Hamlet is undeniably a tragedy – *The Tragedy of Hamlet, the Prince of Denmark*, as it is listed in the First Folio. Shakespeare retains the details about Amleth's feigned madness and need for revenge, but adds new information, such as naming the ghost – also called Hamlet – and adding a companion for the hero in the form of Horatio. Shakespeare also adds two other sons seeking revenge for their fathers' deaths: Laertes and Fortinbras.

A 2000 film adaptation starring Ethan Hawke sets *Hamlet* in New York City. The ghost is an apparition on CCTV, and the play-within-the-play takes the form of a video game.

> But I have that within which passeth show – These but the trappings and the suits of woe.
> **Hamlet**
> **Act 1, Scene 2**

Hamlet has been read as the story of an ill-fated hero, a victim of fate and "outrageous fortune", as well as one about a mentally unstable, indecisive young man. In both readings, the character and the world he inhabits are overwhelmed by melancholy and corruption.

Prince of Denmark

Hamlet is a man of 30; he is a son, a nephew, a lover, a courtier, and a university student of Wittenberg. As the only male heir to the former king, Hamlet should have ascended immediately to the throne. That his uncle, Claudius, takes the crown is largely because of Gertrude's "o'er-hasty" (2.2.57) marriage, as the character herself describes it. The result is that, when the audience first meets Hamlet, he has been robbed of his father, all trust in his mother, and the throne to which he is entitled. It is not surprising, therefore, that he should be quiet, resentful, and moody in his first appearance.

Claudius calls his subjects together to discuss Fortinbras, Laertes, and Hamlet, respectively. His priorities, in order of significance, are relations political, social, and domestic. Although this may seem justifiable, prioritizing Laertes and his wish to travel abroad above Hamlet's obvious grief seems irresponsible and callous in Hamlet's eyes. This explains the bitterness of his opening words in the play, which are a response to

> O, vengeance! Why, what an ass am I? Ay, sure this is most brave, That I, the son of the dear murderèd, Prompted to my revenge by heaven and hell, Must, like a whore, unpack my heart with words And fall a-cursing like a very drab, A scullion!
>
> **Hamlet**
> **Act 2, Scene 2**

Elsinore castle, the setting for the play, is in fact Kronborg, an ancient fortress on the Danish island of Zealand. It was rebuilt in the 1580s and appears here as it did in Shakespeare's day.

Claudius calling him "son": "A little more than kin and less than kind" (1.2.65).

Despite his dark mood and sombre appearance, Hamlet commands love and respect from his peers. He is the first person Horatio thinks to tell about the appearance of the ghost, and it is Hamlet, not the king, whom the players first greet at court. In the play's closing scene, Horatio states that Hamlet has "a noble heart" (5.2.311), echoing Ophelia's early claim that he has "a noble mind" (3.1.153). In fact, Ophelia speaks of Hamlet as though he is a symbol of hope, calling him "Th'expectancy and rose of the fair state, / The glass of fashion and the mould of form, / Th'observed of all observers" (3.1.155–157).

Unstable Hamlet

Hamlet is also described in less positive terms. He is full of "turbulent and dangerous lunacy" »

Prayer scene

During the 19th century, scholars and actors went to great lengths to excuse Hamlet of wickedness in his pursuit of vengeance. The prayer scene, in which Claudius confesses his guilt and Hamlet stalls his vengeance, was removed from the play until the 1880s. At this moment, Hamlet begins to speak in violent and disturbing terms of damnation, a topic of great debate both in the 16th and 19th centuries. Wishing to damn someone to eternal hellfire is not a Christian sentiment, and whether or not such an attitude might be thought justifiable in Hamlet's search for vengeance, Victorian audiences did not wish to hear these words spoken on the stage.

Notable modern performances of the scene include David Tennant's Hamlet (2009, above). This hit stage production was filmed for a special TV version by the BBC. Hovering his dagger above the head of Patrick Stewart's Claudius, in the film version, he delivers the speech as a voiceover rather than directly to the audience.

(3.1.4), "melancholy" and "unmanly grief", with "A heart unfortified, a mind impatient" (1.2.96). He is, in other words, unstable and rash.

Although Hamlet elicits respect for his nobility and receives censure for his attitude, he has a distinctive need to offer other people advice. He tells Ophelia to choose a nunnery over marriage; he advises the players on their acting techniques, and he reprimands Laertes for weeping at Ophelia's funeral. What makes Hamlet think he has more right to mourn than Laertes, her brother? From what experience, and with what authority does he lecture the actors on stagecraft? And from what motive does he send Ophelia off to a convent?

The play's the thing

The ghost has informed Hamlet that his father was murdered with a poison administered into his ear while asleep in his orchard. This very same scenario is played out in *The Mousetrap*, the play Hamlet chooses to stage before the King and Queen. The Player King's brother emerges from the shadows of an orchard to pour poison into

A poster advertizes the 1868 grand opera *Hamlet* by French composer Ambroise Thomas. The story became popular in France after a translation by adventure novelist Alexandre Dumas.

the Player King's ear. Hamlet has chosen drama as the medium through which to test the truth of the ghost's story. First, he explains to the players that the function of plays and acting is, "to hold, as 'twere, the mirror up to nature, to show virtue her own feature, scorn her own image, and the very age and body of the time his form and pressure" (3.2.21–24). Drama is, in Hamlet's view, a way of revealing truths about real life. It is with this logic that he claims that a play will

"catch the conscience of the King" (2.2.607). The power of drama to move individuals to tears, guilt, and happiness is powerfully explored both here and in the scene in which the chief player delivers a speech to Hamlet about the fall of Troy. This monologue focuses on the intensity of the grief of Hecuba, whose husband, Priam, has been slaughtered by the Greek enemy. Hamlet is clearly moved by the extent of Hecuba's sorrow and by the actor's ability to engage emotionally with the speech. He considers both himself and his mother inadequate in comparison, because Gertrude fails to mourn for her husband's death, and Hamlet struggles to motivate himself to seek revenge.

Mother complex

It is no accident, then, that Hamlet's *Mousetrap* is not entirely motivated by the discovery of Claudius's guilt. He is also using

Poor Yorick

One subject that is inseparable from the play concerns the nature of existence. Perhaps the most iconic image in Shakespearian tragedy is that of Hamlet admiring Yorick's skull. This is the moment when Hamlet recognizes the reality of death. He contemplates the difference between the living head of his father's jester, with its lips, tongue and wit, and the grotesque remnants of his body.

Yorick's skull is given to Hamlet by a gravedigger, who is able to see humour in the tragedy. He speaks in a pragmatic way about whether Ophelia (an alleged

suicide case) merits a Christian burial, and casually digs up bones from graves to clear space. In a play in which all is contemplated by Hamlet, the gravedigger is a welcome voice that trivializes the otherwise overwhelming subject of death.

In 1930, G Wilson Knight argued that Hamlet's fixation with death poisons everyone around him, and that it is he who triggers the entire tragedy. Though Hamlet claims to be a victim of fortune, it can be argued that he is ultimately responsible for his own fate.

> ...but, O, what form of prayer
> Can serve my turn? 'Forgive
> me my foul murder'?
> That cannot be, since
> I am still possessed
> Of those effects for which
> I did the murder –
> My crown, mine own
> ambition, and my queen.
> May one be pardoned and
> retain th'offence?
> **Claudius**
> **Act 3, Scene 3**

the play to test his mother's conscience. Indeed, much of Hamlet's melancholy stems from anger with his mother, whose marriage to Claudius he thinks incestuous. The Player Queen makes a speech about fidelity, in which she swears never to remarry in the event of her husband's death: "The instances that second marriage move / Are base respects of thrift, but none of love. / A second time I kill my husband dead / When second husband kisses me in bed" (3.2.173–176).

With this play-within-the-play, Hamlet seizes control of events by taking up arms against his troubles in a way that is otherwise rare in the course of the action of

the play proper, during which he is often paralysed by indecision, a character flaw that proves fatal.

Outrageous fortune?

Hamlet is not a man in a good position. He has left university at the age of 30 and returned to live at home; his father has died and he cannot reconcile with his mother after her remarriage; and he is forced to take on the responsibility of avenging his father's murder in secret. Although Hamlet's famous question is "to be or not to be" (3.1.58), it is the question he asks immediately after that haunts him more than anything: "Whether 'tis nobler in the mind to suffer / The slings and arrows of outrageous fortune, / Or to take arms against a sea of troubles, / And, by opposing, end them" (3.1.59–62).

Hamlet chooses to suffer the outrageous fortune that he believes is an external attack rather than an internal conflict. Assuming the position of a self-confessed victim of fate, much like Romeo, Hamlet

shakes off responsibility for his actions, namely delaying revenge, murdering Polonius, rejecting Ophelia, and having Rosencrantz and Guildenstern executed. In the play's final act, Hamlet speaks of providence and the inevitability of his defeating the King. If, however, the so-called outrageous fortune is removed from the equation, what is left is a series of bad decisions that have ill consequences. »

> You are the Queen, your
> husband's brother's wife.
> But – would you were not so
> – you are my mother.
> **Hamlet**
> **Act 3, Scene 4**

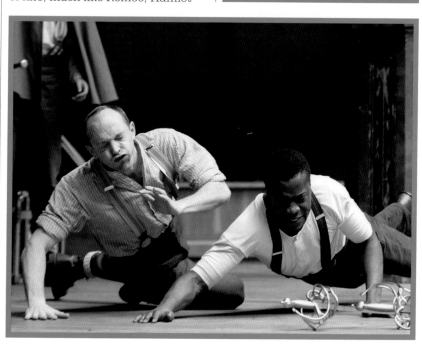

Hamlet (right, Ladi Emeruwa) fights with Claudius (left, John Dougall) in a production by the Globe Theatre that was set to play in 205 countries during a world tour between 2014 and 2016.

The tragedy spirals out of control because the characters within the world of Denmark make poor choices that lead to a catalogue of even worse outcomes. Not only does Hamlet defer taking revenge on Claudius, but he accidentally stabs Polonius, which leads Laertes to seek vengeance against him. He rejects Ophelia in such a humiliating and devastating way that, when she learns of her father's murder at the hands of her former lover, she loses her sanity and, potentially, her dignity. Polonius, too, is no blameless character. He exhibits poor judgement when he dispatches a spy to France to trail his son, when he convinces Ophelia to trap Hamlet, and especially when he proposes hiding behind the arras in order to eavesdrop on Gertrude's

> O, what a rash and bloody deed is this!
> **Gertrude**
> **Act 3, Scene 4**

conversation with her son. Add to these tragic events Ophelia's accidental drowning, Claudius's poisoning of the wine goblet, Gertrude accidentally drinking it, and Laertes being wounded by his own poisoned blade, and this tragic world is riddled with fateful accidents. Both the characters' choices and their fortunes do indeed seem outrageous.

Revenge

First and foremost, Hamlet is a tale of revenge. The revenge motif repeats throughout the play, not just in having three avengers all seeking the same thing, but in the terrible cycle of destruction and grief that proceeds from any desire to exact vengeance on an enemy.

As a revenge story, *Hamlet* follows conventions established by the English playwright Thomas Kyd in *The Spanish Tragedy* (1587), which was one of the most popular revenge tragedies of the period. Shakespeare includes a ghost, a play-within-a-play, and a deathly object in the form of Yorick's skull, to echo the revenge tradition. The

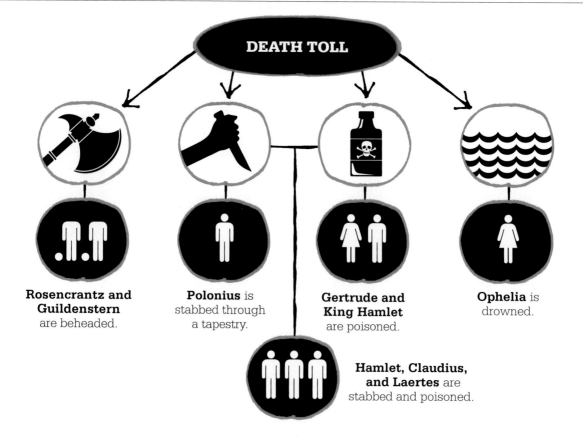

DEATH TOLL

Rosencrantz and Guildenstern are beheaded.

Polonius is stabbed through a tapestry.

Gertrude and King Hamlet are poisoned.

Ophelia is drowned.

Hamlet, Claudius, and Laertes are stabbed and poisoned.

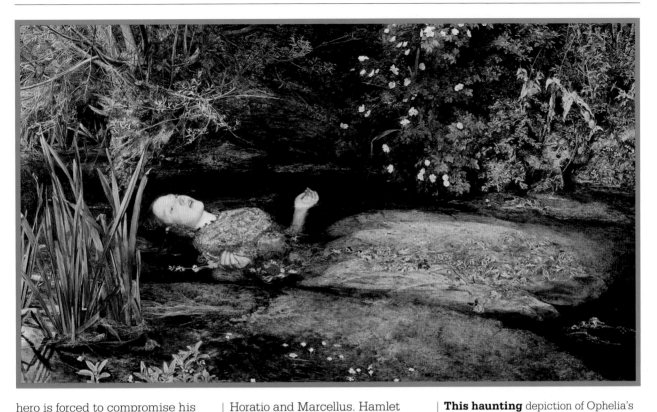

hero is forced to compromise his own conscience in order to carry out an attack on the original criminal, in this case Claudius.

As well as their brutality, revenge tragedies were known for their meta-theatrical jokes, which Shakespeare incorporates into his play when the ghost calls out to

Now cracks a noble heart. Good night, sweet prince, And flights of angels sing thee to thy rest.
Horatio
Act 5, Scene 2

Horatio and Marcellus. Hamlet refers to the ghost as "old mole" and "this fellow in the cellarage" (1.5.153), which draws a knowing audience's attention to the actor calling from beneath the stage floor, rather than any disembodied, spectral voice. However, Hamlet is no simple revenge hero: he is torn between hatred for his uncle, love for his father, disgust for his mother, and distrust of the ghost. He deliberately delays his attack on Claudius, choosing instead to ruminate on his actions and on his existence. Hamlet's approach places him in direct contrast with Laertes and Fortinbras, who also seek revenge against their fathers' murderers. When news of Polonius's death reaches Laertes, he flies in the face of all custom and duty in order to challenge the king, risking his own reputation by committing treason. Unlike Hamlet, Laertes

This haunting depiction of Ophelia's death was painted by British artist John Everett Millais in 1852. The floating flowers correspond to the play's description of her garland.

does not delay and even swears to "dare damnation" (4.5.131) in order to have revenge on Polonius's murderer. Although his behaviour is rash and is exploited by the king, who also wishes Hamlet dead, Laertes's motivation and intent are not dissimilar to those of Hamlet. The third avenger is Fortinbras, whose own father was murdered by Hamlet's father, the former king. Whereas Hamlet delays and Laertes rushes in, Fortinbras tactfully assembles his army and plans to invade Denmark, making his vengeance political rather than personal. Laertes and Fortinbras lack Hamlet's tragic flaw – the doubt and indecision that lead Hamlet inexorably to his fate. ■

YOUTH'S A STUFF WILL NOT ENDURE

TWELFTH NIGHT (1601)

DRAMATIS PERSONAE

Orsino Duke of Illyria, in love with Olivia.

Viola A young lady shipwrecked in Illyria, disguised as Cesario, a male page, in order to win favour with Orsino.

Sebastian Twin brother of Viola, whom she believes to have drowned at sea.

Antonio Sea captain and companion of Sebastian. He is arrested, but eventually forgiven.

Captain The captain of Viola's wrecked ship.

Olivia A beautiful countess, in mourning for her father and brother, she woos Cesario and later marries Sebastian.

Maria Olivia's feisty maid, who is the author of the plot to humiliate Malvolio.

Sir Toby Belch Olivia's reprobate kinsman, who plays pranks on the dimwitted Sir Andrew.

Sir Andrew Aguecheek A rich but ineffectual young man, would-be suitor to Olivia.

Malvolio Olivia's puritanical and pedantic steward.

Feste Olivia's jester, a wit and gifted impersonator, who verbally spars with the people of his household. He acts as a commentator on events.

Valentine and Curio Gentlemen attending to Orsino.

Orsino laments that **Olivia spurns his love** because she is mourning her brother.

1.1

Viola as Cesario is sent by Orsino to Olivia to plead his love, but **Olivia falls for Cesario**.

1.5

In revenge against the killjoy steward, **Maria and her friends fool Malvolio** into thinking Olivia loves him.

2.2

Act 1 **Act 2**

1.2

Washed up in Illyria by a tempest, **Viola dresses as a man** to enter the service of Orsino.

2.1

Viola's twin brother **Sebastian**, thought to be drowned, **reaches Illyria**.

Spurned by the beautiful Olivia, Orsino of Illyria begs for sad music to reflect his lovelorn state. Viola is shipwrecked on the shores of Illyria. Convinced her twin brother Sebastian has drowned and that she is alone, she decides to dress as a boy and join Orsino's service. Meanwhile, Olivia's reprobate cousin Sir Toby and her maidservant Maria persuade rich but dim Sir Andrew to pay court to Olivia. Orsino sends Viola (as Cesario) to Olivia as a messenger of his love. But Viola is already in love with Orsino herself.

Feste the clown tries to cajole Olivia out of her mourning, but is rebuked by her puritanical steward Malvolio. They are interrupted by the arrival of Cesario. But Cesario's ingenious pleading of Orsino's case, falls on deaf ears as Olivia is smitten by Cesario. When Cesario goes, Olivia sends Malvolio after to tell him he has left a ring behind.

Viola's twin Sebastian arrives in Illyria, saved by his companion Antonio. Thinking Viola dead, Sebastian resolves to try Orsino's court. When Malvolio gives Viola Olivia's ring, she realizes Olivia has

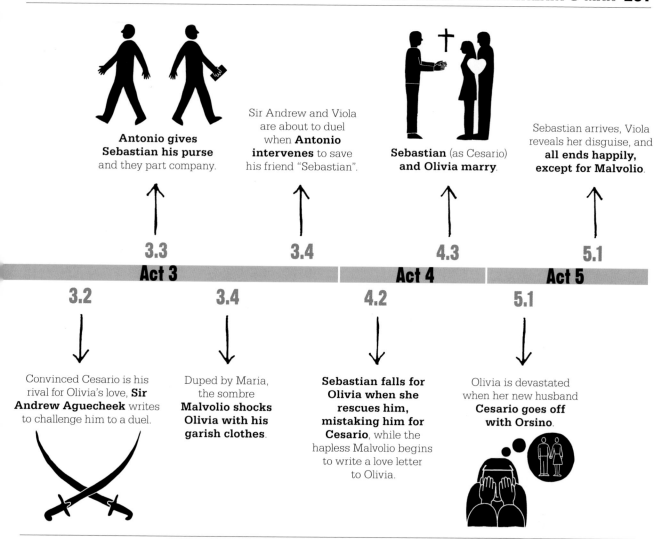

Antonio gives Sebastian his purse and they part company.

Sir Andrew and Viola are about to duel when **Antonio intervenes** to save his friend "Sebastian".

Sebastian (as Cesario) **and Olivia marry**.

Sebastian arrives, Viola reveals her disguise, and **all ends happily, except for Malvolio**.

3.3   **3.4**   **4.3**   **5.1**

Act 3   **Act 4**   **Act 5**

3.2   **3.4**   **4.2**   **5.1**

Convinced Cesario is his rival for Olivia's love, **Sir Andrew Aguecheek** writes to challenge him to a duel.

Duped by Maria, the sombre **Malvolio shocks Olivia with his garish clothes**.

Sebastian falls for Olivia when she rescues him, mistaking him for Cesario, while the hapless Malvolio begins to write a love letter to Olivia.

Olivia is devastated when her new husband **Cesario goes off with Orsino**.

---

fallen for Cesario. Sir Toby and his friends are partying when the killjoy Malvolio complains about the noise. As he leaves, they plot their revenge on him, forging love letters from Olivia to Malvolio, which he discovers and believes are genuine.

At Orsino's request, Viola dressed as Cesario returns to Olivia, who tells Cesario she loves him. Sir Toby works on Sir Andrew to challenge Cesario to a duel. Antonio tells Sebastian he has enemies at Orsino's court, so they decide to part. Convinced by Maria that Olivia wants him to dress

colourfully, Malvolio changes his normally drab clothes for yellow stockings. Sir Andrew delivers a challenge to Cesario. Just as the two draw swords, Antonio intervenes to rescue Cesario, thinking him to be Sebastian, but Cesario denies knowing him.

Thinking him to be Cesario, Sir Toby attacks Sebastian, but he is rescued by Olivia, who also thinks him to be Cesario. Olivia proposes marriage to Sebastian, thinking him Cesario, and Sebastian, already in love with Olivia, accepts. Hauled before Orsino as a pirate, Antonio

is deeply hurt that Cesario, who he thinks is Sebastian, denies their friendship. Olivia arrives and claims Cesario as hers. To Olivia's shock, Cesario aligns herself with Orsino, so Olivia summons the priest to verify they are married. Suddenly, Sebastian arrives and greets Antonio with passionate relief, as everyone else stands amazed by his likeness to Cesario.

All is revealed. Orsino acknowledges his love for Cesario and proposes marriage. The trick on Malvolio is revealed, and Malvolio pledges his revenge. »

IN CONTEXT

THEMES
Mistaken identity, gender swapping, love

SETTING
Illyria, the name for a province on the Adriatic (present-day Croatia and Slovenia) in Roman times

SOURCES
1531 A risqué Italian play called *Gl'ingannati* (The Deceived Ones).

1581 English author Barnabe Rich's *Farewell to the Military Profession*.

LEGACY
1602 The play is performed on 2 February at the Middle Temple in London.

1741 A Drury Lane production revives the full play with Hannah Pritchard as Viola.

1897 William Poel puts on the play at the Middle Temple in an Elizabethan style.

1912 Harley Granville-Barker's modern production in black and silver has a vivid portrayal of Viola by Lillah McCarthy.

1955 John Gielgud's production at Stratford-upon-Avon stars Laurence Olivier and Vivien Leigh.

1968 The rock-musical *Your Own Thing* opens in New York. It sets the action of *Twelfth Night* in the modern day.

1996 Director Trevor Nunn sets the action in the 19th century for his film adaptation, with Imogen Stubbs as Viola.

*T*welfth Night, or What You Will is a comedy in which genders are swapped and identities mistaken. It has an appealing heroine, Viola, the shipwrecked girl who finds true love dressed as a boy, but there is also a dark side in the tormenting of the puritanical steward Malvolio.

An unruly night

The first half of the play's full title refers to the eve of the 12th Day of Christmas, 5 January. This is the Feast of the Epiphany, when, according to tradition, the Magi, the three wise men, arrived with their gifts for the infant Christ. In Elizabethan England, Twelfth Night was the last day of the Christmas holidays, and its associations were as much pagan as Christian. It was one last riot of feasting, drinking, games, and theatre masques, before returning to work. It was a time of "misrule" when normal rules were briefly subverted: masters became servants and servants became masters; and, in the tradition of the Roman winter feast of Saturnalia, men dressed as girls and vice versa. Often, a large cake was made. Whoever got the slice with a bean or coin in it became the Lord of Misrule for the night.

It is thought that Shakespeare's play was written to be performed as a Twelfth Night entertainment. The first recorded performance took place in private at Middle Temple Hall, one of the law school Inns of Court, on 2 February 1602. But the play is full of allusions to Twelfth Night. In this topsy-turvy world, servants get above themselves, girls dress as boys, and identities are mixed up. Viola, presumably in a nod to the Roman Saturnalia, calls herself Cesario when she dresses as a boy. And throughout the play, Feste the clown, whose very name suggests a feast, refers often to wise men and fools. Indeed, he is in some ways, the only sane one in the play.

Pre-Raphaelite artist Walter Howell Deverell painted Act 2, Scene 4, in which Feste sings a song that ponders the cruelty of love. The song begins "Come away, come away death".

Lovers and suitors

Feste — The Fool

Fabian

Viola (Cesario) ← Twins → Sebastian

Malvolio

Countess Olivia

Duke Orsino

Sir Andrew Aguecheek

Servants to

Loves

Loves

Marries

Suitors of

Loves

Uncle to

Maid to

Servants to

Sir Tony Belch

Friends

Maria

Valentine

Curio

— Male   — Female   ⋯ Female dressed as male

A sad place

There is something of the fairy tale in *Twelfth Night*. The play begins with a girl shipwrecked and alone in a strange country, Illyria, after a terrible storm. (We only find much later that her name is Viola.) It is a country sunk, absurdly, in gloom. The Duke of Illyria wallows in the melancholy of his love for the beautiful Olivia, a fashionable affliction in Elizabethan England. He morbidly pleads for such an excess of music that it will spoil his taste for it: "If music be the food of love, play on, / Give me excess of it, that, surfeiting, / The appetite may sicken and so die. / That strain again! it had a dying fall" (1.1.1–4).

Meanwhile, the Countess Olivia, the object of his affections, is even more gloomy. She is deep in mourning for her brother, and has pledged to remain veiled for seven years. She has given her household to the charge of her cheerless steward Malvolio, who sees it as

Many a good hanging prevents a bad marriage
Feste
Act 1, Scene 5

his task to ensure that nobody has any fun. Both Orsino and Olivia have locked themselves away in their dark places of melancholy – just as, ironically, Malvolio will be locked in a dark cell when the prank played on him goes all too well.

This melancholy is in some ways a madness that has engulfed Illyria. Olivia and Orsino are both foolish in the theatrical excess of their sadness, as Feste shows:

"**Feste**: Good madonna, why mournest thou?
Olivia: Good fool, for my brother's death.
Feste: I think his soul is in hell, madonna.
Olivia: I know his soul is in heaven, fool.
Feste: The more fool, madonna, to mourn for your brother's soul being in heaven." (1.5.62–67).

The bringer of joy

Viola's role is to break this spell of melancholy and bring joy and true love back into this world, just like the revel spirit of Twelfth Night. At the time, many puritans frowned upon the festivities of Christmas (they succeeded in banning it in 1647) and railed against the riotous excess of the theatre, so there may have been a political message here.

Viola, of course, has her own bereavement to contend with. When she comes ashore in Illyria, she is convinced that her brother has drowned and that she is » entirely alone in the world. Her reaction is not to go into mourning like Olivia, but to take action.

Viola's choice to dress up to look like her brother is a strange one, but it leads to comic and romantic possibilities. It allows Viola close to her beloved Orsino, yet prevents her from revealing her love. It also opens the way for the chaos caused by mistaken identities as her brother Sebastian turns up.

> She sat like patience on a monument, Smiling at grief.
> **Viola**
> Act 2, Scene 4

In a comic subplot, which ultimately turns a little dark, Shakespeare adds two foolish suitors: the roguish Sir Toby Belch and the rather silly Sir Andrew Aguecheek, who, along with the cheeky Maria, plot to humiliate Malvolio.

A woman's part

From the start, Orsino is strangely drawn to his young serving boy. He puts it down to Cesario's youth: "they shall yet belie thy happy years / That say thou art a man. Diana's lip / Is not more smooth and rubious; thy small pipe / Is as the maiden's organ, shrill and sound, / And all is semblative a woman's part" (1.4.30–34). To Orsino, locked in his self-love, Cesario simply looks and sounds like a woman – but the lingering over physical details and the innuendo suggest there is a more ambiguous attraction. And of course the gender boundaries are blurred even more as Viola was originally played by a boy actor. Viola's situation becomes even

more tricky when she visits Olivia as Cesario. Olivia soon lowers her veil for the young "boy". After just one meeting, she is so eager for him to return that she sends Malvolio after him with a ring that she pretends Cesario has dropped. On the face of it, she thinks Cesario's effeminate looks must be because he is a gentleman. But like Orsino, she lingers just a little too long on Cesario's attractions: "Thy tongue, thy face, thy limbs, actions, and spirit / Do give thee five-fold blazon" (1.5.282–284). Her desperation comes across as comic after her mourning reticence, but it seems more like lust than love.

Untying the knot

Meanwhile, Viola has fallen in love with Orsino, and the situation has become impossible. She describes herself as a "monster", neither man nor woman: "As I am man, / My state is desperate for my master's love. / As I am woman, now, alas the day, / What thriftless sighs shall poor Olivia breathe." (2.2.36–39).

> Then come kiss me, sweet and twenty. Youth's a stuff will not endure.
> **Feste**
> Act 2, Scene 3

> One face, one voice,
> one habit, and two persons,
> A natural perspective,
> that is and is not.
>
> **Orsino**
> Act 5, Scene 1

Viola laments that it has become "too hard a knot for me t'untie" (2.2.41). But we have just seen exactly how the knot will be loosened, for Viola's twin Sebastian has turned up, not drowned after all. While Viola's genuine distress becomes ever more poignant, the play becomes a comedy for us, because we know how it will all work out. We laugh as Sebastian is mistaken for Cesario and Cesario for Sebastian, causing comic confusion.

All seems about to turn dark, however, when Olivia, soon after marrying Sebastian believing him to be Cesario, comes to Orsino – only to find that Cesario, in what seems a terrible betrayal, denies all knowledge of the wedding and pledges allegiance to the baffled Orsino. Within moments, all is revealed as Sebastian and Cesario appear together, and everyone stands in wonder as their remarkable likeness appears: "One face, one voice, one habit, and two persons, / A natural perspective, that is and is not." (5.1.213–214).

The solution is simple. Olivia stays married to Sebastian, and Viola can reveal herself as a woman and marry her love Orsino. It is neat, but the ambiguities of gender haven't quite vanished. As Sebastian says to Olivia, "You are betrothed to a maid and a man" (5.1.261), while as Orsino and Viola leave the stage together at the end of the play to be married, Viola is still dressed as a boy, described by Orsino as his "master's mistress".

Gender bending

It is perhaps not surprising that many critics have explored *Twelfth Night* for homoeroticism. Indeed, because Sebastian and Antonio express their love for each other so ardently, many modern theatre productions have played theirs as a homosexual relationship, and looked for similar undertones in Olivia's relationship with Cesario.

Yet notions of sexuality were different in Shakespeare's time. Close relationships between two men could be considered the ideal of friendship. Shakespeare may be exploring our double nature: the elements of "man" and "woman" in all of us. As Orsino says: "Cesario, come – / For so you shall be while you are a man; / But when in other habits you are seen, / Orsino's mistress, and his fancy's queen." (5.1.381–384). The play's subtitle, "What You Will", may be a message for us all to embrace love wherever we may find it. ∎

The 2006 film *She's the Man* moved the action to an American school called Illyria. Viola enters her brother's school pretending to be male in order to play with the boys' soccer team.

Malvolio

Malvolio is a dark shadow version of the story of *Twelfth Night*, his name a twisted part anagram of both Olivia and Viola's names, meaning in Italian "evil" (mal) and "I desire" (volio). Malvolio's inner world turns ever bleaker as the outer world wakes up to pleasure, and this puritan who believes everyone else is foolish is shown to be the real fool.

Sir Toby, Maria, and their friends conspire to trick Malvolio into believing that Olivia is in love with him – and he, pompous and self-deluding, all too easily falls prey to their games. They fool this sombre puritan into dressing up in garish jesterlike clothes (including yellow cross garters) and smiling inanely at Olivia, who employed him because of his seriousness. He foolishly thinks the letter's words, "Some are born great, some achieve greatness, and some have greatness thrust upon 'em" (2.5.140–141) must be for him. Yet the joke can begin to seem cruel – and in his final humiliation, when the trick is exposed, we almost sympathize with his parting words, "I'll be revenged on the whole pack of you" (5.1.374).

WAR AND LECHERY CONFOUND ALL

TROILUS AND CRESSIDA (1602)

DRAMATIS PERSONAE

THE TROJANS

Priam King of Troy.

Hector Eldest son of Priam and leader of the Trojan army.

Paris Brother to Hector and Troilus, Paris has taken Helen as a lover, precipitating war.

Troilus A Trojan warrior, and youngest brother to Hector and Paris. He falls in love with Cressida.

Pandarus Courtier and uncle to Cressida.

Andromache Wife of Hector.

Cassandra Sister to Hector, Paris, and Troilus. Cassandra has the gift of foresight and predicts the fall of Troy.

THE GREEKS

Helen Wife of Menelaus of Greece, and lover of Paris.

Agamemnon Respected general in the Greek army.

Ulysses A philosopher.

Nestor A wise old man.

Achilles A legendary warrior and pride of the Greek army.

Ajax and Diomedes Greek warriors.

Cressida Pledges love for Troilus but later proves faithless.

Calchas Father of Cressida. He has joined the Greeks.

Patroclus Achilles' companion.

Thersites Commentator on the war.

Seven years after the Trojan War began, **Pandarus** makes **attempts to woo Cressida on behalf of Troilus**.

Hector sends a **challenge to the Greeks**. Ulysses and the generals plot to humiliate Achilles by choosing Ajax to fight with Hector.

Troilus and Cressida are brought together by Pandarus, who encourages them to **consummate their love**.

1.1   **1.3**   **3.2**

Act 1	Act 2	

1.2   **2.2**

Cressida feigns indifference to Troilus, calling him a "sneaking fellow". However, she **secretly admits to loving him**.

The **Trojans** decide **against returning Helen to the Greeks**.

A prologue announces that the story begins seven years into the Trojan War. Troilus, son of King Priam of Troy, the younger brother of Hector and Paris, is in love with Cressida, the daughter of a traitor. He employs her uncle, Pandarus, to woo her for him. Cressida appears dismissive of Troilus, but secretly admits to being attracted to him.

Outside the Trojan walls, the Greek camp is disorderly. Achilles refuses to fight, and Menelaus, their leader, lacks credibility as a warrior. Meanwhile, in Troy, courtiers debate the purpose and expense of the long war with the Greek army. Hector concedes that Helen, whose abduction started the war, must not be returned to the Greeks.

Hector sends a message to the Greek army challenging any warrior to a duel. Ulysses uses the challenge to humiliate Achilles by announcing that the dull-witted Ajax should fight Hector. Ajax is related to the Trojan princes by his mother, who is the sister of Priam.

Back in Troy, Troilus successfully woos Cressida in Pandarus's home, where they

Troilus gives Cressida his sleeve as a token of faithfulness. In return she gives him her glove. **Diomedes takes Cressida away from Troy**, promising Troilus to treat her as she deserves.

Diomedes and Cressida meet and are overheard by Troilus, Ulysses, and Thersites. Cressida gives Diomedes Troilus's sleeve and promises to meet him the next night.

Troilus fights with Ajax and Diomedes. Hector and Achilles fight.

Troilus announces Hector's death and claims that revenge against the Greeks will compensate for their loss.

↑ **4.5**   ↑ **5.2**   ↑ **5.6**   ↑ **5.10**

Act 3   **Act 4**   **Act 5**

3.3   **4.7**   **5.3**   **5.9**

↓   ↓   ↓   ↓

Calchas begs Agamemnon to **exchange Antenor for Cressida**. Diomedes is sent to Troy to negotiate.

Hector and Ajax fight in a **duel** of honour, in which they draw. Achilles is angered. Troilus asks Ulysses to take him to Cressida's tent.

Troilus refuses to hear Pandarus and **tears up a letter** he brings **from Cressida**.

Hector is attacked and **killed by Achilles** and the Myrmidons.

---

spend an evening together. During the night, Calchas makes a deal with the Greek leader Agamemnon to exchange a Trojan prisoner of war, Antenor, for his daughter, allowing Cressida to join her father at the Greek camp. A messenger, Diomedes, brings news of the exchange to Troilus who is forced to hand over Cressida.

When she is returned, Cressida is greeted, not unwillingly, with kisses by the Greek army. This prompts Ulysses to conclude that she is a flirtatious, dangerous woman.

On the day of the duel, Ajax and Hector fight, reaching an amicable draw. Achilles takes a dislike to Hector and swears to kill him. At night, after the fight, Troilus follows Ulysses to Cressida's tent, where she is also overheard by Thersites. Before Troilus can reveal himself, he spots Cressida and Diomedes becoming intimate. Cressida offers Diomedes a sleeve, which was a token of love given to her by Troilus. Heartbroken and disillusioned, Troilus swears vengeance on Diomedes and denounces Cressida as false and unfaithful.

The next morning, in spite of the warnings of his wife and sister, Hector fights Achilles. He wins the battle, and the defeat wounds Achilles's pride, prompting him to murder Hector with the Myrmidons, his gang of Greek soldiers. Troy is forced to watch as Achilles drags Hector's body around the battlefield, and Troilus resigns himself to seek revenge for his brother's murder. The play ends as Pandarus is rejected by Troilus, and is left a cynical old man who promises to bequeath nothing but diseases to future generations. »

IN CONTEXT

THEMES
**Lust, war, betrayal,
honour, heroism**

SETTING
Troy, 12th century BCE

SOURCES
1598 *The Iliad*, Homer's epic
poem of the Trojan Wars,
translated into English by
George Chapman.

1385–86 *Troilus and Criseyde*
by English poet Geoffrey
Chaucer.

1460–1500 *The Testament of
Cresseid* by Scottish poet
Robert Henryson, an imagined
sequel to Chaucer's tale.

LEGACY
1609 The play is described
in the Quarto as a comedy.

1679 English poet John
Dryden revises the play so
that the lovers die along with
Diomedes, and Cressida is
faithful to Troilus.

1898 Shakespeare's version is
is staged in Munich, the first
known performance anywhere
since Shakespeare's time.

1938 The play is staged in
London by Michael Macowan
as a work of anti-war
propaganda, with Thersites
as a cynical war reporter.

2012 Two acting companies
perform the play at Stratford.
The RSC play the Greeks and
a New York-based company
play the Trojans. The contrast
in styles highlights cultural
differences between the sides.

*T*roilus and Cressida is a play
about war and lust. Thought
of as a problem play with
an intellectual tone, it is challenging
to read and to perform. In the 17th
century, English poet John Dryden
claimed that the play was a "heap
of rubbish", while modern responses
tend to focus on the bitterness of
the characters. Critic A D Nuttall
called it a "sick, clever play".

The play is based on an epic
tale of legendary men including
Achilles, Hector, Ajax, Ulysses,
Paris, and Menelaus. Shakespeare,
however, challenges the reputations
of these figures by deconstructing
the idea of a "hero". Paris is a vain
and selfish youth, Achilles a love-
sick rebel, Ajax a witless brute, and
Menelaus a cuckold and a laughing
stock. Troilus, a great warrior, is a
melancholy lover, motivated entirely
by his infatuation with Cressida.
The only symbol of heroism is
Hector, who longs to face a worthy
hero. However, Hector is murdered
by Achilles's men while unarmed.
With these amorous, apathetic, and
dishonourable soldiers, Shakespeare
satirizes heroism in war.

Women are angels, wooing;
Things won are done. Joy's
soul lies in the doing.
That she beloved knows
naught that knows not this:
Men price the thing ungained
more than it is.
Cressida
Act 1, Scene 2

In a 2009 production at the Globe,
London, Laura Pyper played Cressida as
a teenager in the process of discovering
herself and working out how to survive
in a world of men and war.

To add to this dearth of honour,
the original cause of the crisis is a
woman who barely seems worth
the effort. The characters spend
three acts debating Helen's virtue
and the purpose of keeping her in
Troy at the expense of soldiers'
lives. When Helen appears finally
in Act 3, she speaks little and
makes exclamations about lovesickness: "Let thy song be love.
'This love will undo us all.' / O
Cupid, Cupid, Cupid!" (3.1.106–107).

These are not the words of a
woman for whom thousands of
Trojans and Greeks have sacrificed
their lives. Helen and Paris
represent the lecherous, selfish
nature of love in this corrupt Troy.
Helen's infidelity to her husband
and decadent behaviour with Paris
also mirror Cressida's disloyalty to
Troilus. As Thersites reminds the
audience, the world is filled with
nothing but "Lechery, lechery, still /
wars and lechery!" (5.2.196–197).

Our firebrand brother,
Paris, burns us all.
Cry, Trojans, cry! Ah Helen,
and ah woe!
Cry, cry 'Troy burns!'
– or else let Helen go.
Cassandra
Act 2, Scene 2

The nature of value

During a debate about Helen, the Trojans – Paris, Hector, and Troilus – discuss her in terms of worth: "**Hector**: Brother, she is not worth what she doth cost / The holding. **Troilus**: What's aught but as 'tis valued? **Hector**: But value dwells not in particular will. / It holds his estimate and dignity / As well wherein 'tis precious of itself / As in the prizer" (2.2.50–55).

Troilus argues that something becomes valuable when its cost is high. Cressida understands that Troilus thinks this way, so she refuses his advances in order to seem more valuable in his eyes. However, Hector claims that something has to have an intrinsic value in order to be prized. It is only Paris's obsession with Helen that makes her worthy of Troy's allegiance, rather than any inherent

In a 2006 production by German director Peter Stein, the battle scenes were staged on a steeply raked stage that allowed the audience to follow several fights simultaneously.

worth in herself. This sobering fact makes the trauma of warfare in this play seem entirely pointless. This is doubly true for the Greek army, which has no respect for its leader, Menelaus, and his motivation for seeking vengeance on Troy.

Despite Hector's belief that Helen is a disproportionately expensive commodity, it is in the interest of Troy to protect her honour, and that of the men whose lives were lost in her name. The economics may be askew in this city, but in Hector's ideal world, value and worth must be earned. It is this that makes his death at the hands of Achilles, whose heroic worth is entirely unmerited, especially tragic. Both Troilus and Hector, who hold idealistic views about love and war, respectively, are disillusioned by the play's end. Neither Helen nor Cressida turns out to be "worth" anything beyond the tears and pain they cause to others, and Hector's own value is desecrated by Achilles.

In the politically and morally ugly world that Shakespeare shows, the realist is the vulgar, illegitimate,

and deformed commentator, Thersites, who understands the real value and cost of war. He cuts through the high rhetoric of honour, and degree used by the Greek generals with one fundamental truth: "All the argument is a whore and a cuckold. / A good quarrel to draw emulous factions and bleed to death upon" (2.3.71–73). Again, "value" and "worth" are skewed and corrupted by lust and a hunger for war and glory.

The lovers and their go-between, Pandarus, predict their own reputations in posterity, in the »

Words, words, mere words, no matter from the heart.
Troilus
Act 5, Scene 3

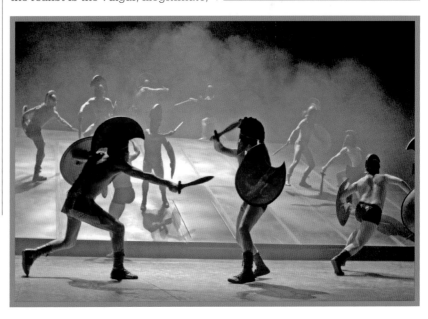

same way that the war itself has become a legendary quarrel about Helen of Troy. Familiarity with the story makes the scene in which the lovers pledge eternal faithfulness a moment of ironic foresight. Troilus swears to be so constant to his love that the analogy "as True as Troilus" shall be coined. In turn, Cressida vows that, should she break her promise, she will inspire future generations to cry "as false

as Cressid". Pandarus seals the vow by exclaiming: "[...] let all pitiful / goers-between be called to the world's end after my / name: call them all panders. Let all constant men be / Troiluses, all false women Cressids, and all brokers- / between panders. Say 'Amen'" (3.2.196–200).

Although these outcomes are inevitable, Shakespeare offers the characters the chance to change their fates. Pandarus deliberately

involves himself in the affairs of his niece and Troilus, even when they wish him gone. At no point is he forced or cajoled into becoming their go-between. Troilus chooses to hand over Cressida to Diomedes: something he does not have to do. As a warrior and prince, he ought to be more concerned about his kingdom than his lover, like Hector who actively chooses battle over the pleas of his wife, Andromache.

Trojans v Greeks

Cressida seemingly embraces her move to the Greek camp, allowing the generals and soldiers to kiss her in a way that prompts Ulysses to doubt her virtue. Although Cressida struggles with guilt about betraying Troilus, she fails to reject Diomedes; she encourages him. These decisions are made freely, and imply that the characters, rather than fate or destiny, are responsible for their own tragedies.

I am a bastard, too. I love bastards. I am bastard begot, bastard instructed, bastard in mind, bastard in valour, in everything illegitimate.
Thersites
Act 5, Scene 8

Which genre?

When it first appeared in print in 1609, the play was announced as *The Historie of Troylus and Cresseida*. An introduction by the publisher claimed that the play was a comedy. To further complicate matters, the First Folio lists the play under the tragedies. However, the only character to die during the play's action is the heroic Hector. The play is cynical in tone but, with its subversive depiction of legendary warriors and of the character of Helen, it seems to have a mischievous, darkly comic heart.

While there is humour in the situations these characters find themselves in, the play is riddled with despair and disappointment. Ulysses discusses the importance of order in the army and attempts to teach Achilles about honour and reputation, but all in vain. Achilles would prefer to cheat his way to glory by murdering Hector like a coward, rather than fight battles. Shakespeare forces the audience to experience Troilus's pain as he witnesses Cressida offer her new

For their 2012 production, the Ngakao Toa theatre company moved the action to the tribal Maori wars of pre-European New Zealand. The play starts with a *haka*, or war dance.

lover the very token that he gave to her in exchange for her fidelity. At that moment Troilus loses faith in love and loyalty. There is nothing comical about this sentiment.

In the late 19th century, the British scholar Frederick Boas re-categorized the text as a "problem play", meaning that it is comic in structure but tragic in tone and subject matter. Irish playwright George Bernard Shaw sparked scholarly interest in the play in 1884 when he argued that the subject matter "starts at the twentieth century". In other words, it is a modern play expressing the concerns of a new age. It is self-consciously cynical, and it refuses to provide the audience with characters and events that satisfy our sense of justice. As such, it is seen as one of Shakespeare's most bitter and disillusioned plays. ∎

I SCORN TO CHANGE MY STATE WITH KINGS'

SHAKESPEARE'S SONNETS (1593–1603)

IN CONTEXT

THEMES
Romantic love, platonic love, jealousy, religion, sex

SOURCES
14th century Italian poet Francesco Petrarch writes some of the first sonnets, expressing unrequited love for an unavailable muse.

LEGACY
18th century After more than a century of neglect, Shakespeare's sonnets are championed by the Romantic poets John Keats and William Wordsworth.

1889 *The Portrait of Mr. W. H.*, a story by Oscar Wilde, is published. It suggests that the sonnets are addressed to a boy player called Willie Hughes. A longer version appears in 1921, 21 years after Wilde's death.

1958 British composer Benjamin Britten's Nocturne for tenor and orchestra ends with a setting of Sonnet 43.

1960s–1980s The words "art made tongue-tied by authority" in No 66 become a slogan for resistance to censorship in communist eastern Europe.

1961 British singer Cleo Laine records jazz settings of sonnets composed by her husband, Johnny Dankworth.

2012 Canadian musician Rufus Wainwright records his own settings of some of the sonnets, including No 29.

The word sonnet comes from the Italian *sonetto*, meaning a little sound. In Shakespeare's time, it could be used to refer to any short poem, but now it is limited to poems of 14 lines with a particular rhyme scheme.

Structure of a sonnet

A typical Shakespearean sonnet has 14 lines, and each line is an iambic pentameter – that is, it has 10 syllables made up of five units (known as feet) in each of which an unstressed syllable is followed by a stressed one, as in "And **look** up**on** my**self** and **curse** my **fate**" (Sonnet 29). The lines have the following rhyming pattern: a b a b a b c d c d e f e f g g.

Using Sonnet 29 (see box below) as a typical example, close examination shows that the poem does not follow the pattern exactly. For instance, it would be natural to stress the first, not the second syllable of the first line, and in the third line it is natural to stress both "deaf" and the first syllable of "heaven". The second and fourth lines fit the regular pattern. Variations like these enable the poet to avoid a simple jog-trot

'Gainst death and all oblivious enmity Shall you pace forth; your praise shall still find room Even in the eyes of all posterity That wear this world out to the ending doom.
Sonnet 55

rhythm and to draw a reader's attention to especially significant words or phrases.

This sonnet has a clear structure, which is created partly by its rhyme scheme. The first four lines (known as a quatrain) establish a situation: the poet is unhappy. The next four lines elaborate on this by giving reasons for his unhappiness. It is common for sonnets to change direction in the ninth line; this is known as the volta (Italian for "turn"). Here, the poet thinks of

Sonnet 29

When, in disgrace with fortune and men's eyes,
I all alone beweep my outcast state,
And trouble deaf heaven with my bootless cries,
And look upon myself and curse my fate,
Wishing me like to one more rich in hope,
Featured like him, like him with friends possessed,
Desiring this man's art and that man's scope,
With what I most enjoy contented least:
Yet in these thoughts myself almost despising,
Haply I think on thee, and then my state,
Like to the lark at break of day arising
From sullen earth, sings hymns at heaven's gate;
  For thy sweet love remembered such wealth brings
  That then I scorn to change my state with kings'.

his friend, or lover ("thee"), which cheers him up, and his happiness is conveyed partly by the image of the lark rising from earth to heaven and singing as it goes; line 11 has an extra syllable in "arising", which leads with no pause to the next line (an effect known as enjambement, a running over of the sense from one line to the next). The poet's new happiness is conveyed partly by the emphatic rhythm of "sings hymns at heaven's gate", where it is natural to stress both "sings" and "hymns". Then the new situation is summed up in the final couplet, with stresses on both syllables in "sweet love" and "such wealth", and the poem comes to a triumphant conclusion with the emphatic rhythms of its last line and the contrast between the poet's new state of happiness in love with that even of kings.

Not all the sonnets have as clear a structure as this one.

Italian sonnets

The first sonnets came from medieval Italy, most famously written by Francesco Petrarch (1304–74). Typically they express hopeless love for an inaccessible and idealized beloved. Shakespeare refers to Petrarch in Romeo and

So long as men can breathe or eyes can see,
So long lives this, and this gives life to thee.
Sonnet 18

The Italian poet Francesco Petrarca (commonly known in English as Petrarch) wrote a series of sonnets addressed to a woman named Laura, whom Petrarch admired from afar.

Juliet when Mercutio, thinking that Romeo is still in love with Rosaline, says "Now is he for the numbers [verse rhythms] that Petrarch flowed in" (2.3.36–37).

The first English sonnets were written by Sir Thomas Wyatt and the Earl of Surrey in the middle of the 16th century. Their poems were included in a popular book known as *Tottel's Miscellany*, also called *Songs and Sonnets*, first published in 1557. Shakespeare refers to this in *The Merry Wives of Windsor*, in which a bashful young man, Abraham Slender, wishes he had a copy of it to hand to help him in his wooing of Mistress Anne Page. He says "I had rather than forty shillings I had my book of songs and sonnets here" (1.1.181–182).

What are sonnets about?

Typically, sonnets are poems of romantic love, often directly addressed to an object of love, but over the centuries poets have used the sonnet form for many different purposes. It has also been common to write a collection or sequence of interconnected sonnets all addressed to the same real or imagined person. For example, English poet and soldier Sir Philip Sidney wrote poems addressed to his beloved calling himself "Astrophil" and her "Stella". Sidney's collection was published as *Astrophil and Stella* in 1591, five years after his death, and many other poets imitated it in a spate of sonnets from 1591 to 1597.

In later Elizabethan times, the sonnet form came frequently to be used for religious verse – love poems addressed to God, as it were. Shakespeare's contemporary, poet and cleric John Donne (1572–1631) wrote a number of Holy Sonnets, and one of Shakespeare's sonnets, No 146, is a religious poem. **»**

Happy air, remain here with your living rays:
and you, clear running stream, why can't I exchange my path for yours?
**Petrarch
Sonnet 227**

Sonnet form in the plays

Few of Shakespeare's sonnets appeared in print until 1609, but he had often used the sonnet form before this date. Parts of his plays, especially but not only in the early part of his career, are written in the form of a sonnet. An obvious example is the Prologue to Romeo and Juliet. Shakespeare also uses sonnet form within the dialogue of that play, most conspicuously in the first lines that Romeo and Juliet speak to each other (see box, below).

The first reference to the sonnets comes in 1598, when Francis Meres, in a book on contemporary and other writers called *Palladis Tamia*, or *Wit's Treasury*, cryptically mentions "Shakespeare's sonnets among his private friends", implying that he had written poems of love or friendship that came to be known about at least within a circle of intimates. The following year, versions of two sonnets – Nos 138 and 144 – made it into print without

So shalt thou feed on death, that feeds on men, And death once dead, there's no more dying then.
Sonnet 146

his permission in a book called *The Passionate Pilgrim*, which also includes three extracts from *Love's Labour's Lost* and other short poems that may or may not be by Shakespeare.

In 1609, a collection of 154 sonnets called *Shakespeare's Sonnets* appeared in print. The 154 sonnets are followed by a longer poem, "A Lover's Complaint" (p.224).

It is not clear whether Shakespeare himself intended the collection to be published, and there are a number of strange features about it. The title page reads not, as might have been expected, "Sonnets, by William Shakespeare", but "Shakespeare's Sonnets, never before imprinted", which seems to imply both that someone else was publishing them on his behalf and that people had known of their existence, and looked forward to their publication, for some time.

"Mr W. H."

Even stranger is the fact that the book's dedication appears not over the author's name, as is the case with the poems *Venus and Adonis* and *The Rape of Lucrece*, but over the initials "T. T." of its publisher, Thomas Thorpe. The dedication, laid out in the manner of a tombstone, is puzzling in other ways, notably in that the dedicatee is also identified only by his initials. It reads: "To the onlie begetter of these insuing sonnets Mr W. H. all happinesse and that eternity promised by our ever-living poet wisheth the well-wishing adventurer in setting forth."

That thou are blamed shall not be thy defect, For slander's mark was ever yet the fair. The ornament of beauty is suspect
Sonnet 70

Romeo and Juliet's first words

Romeo
If I profane with my unworthiest hand
This holy shrine, the gentler sin is this:
My lips, two blushing pilgrims, ready stand
To smooth that rough touch with a tender kiss.
Juliet
Good pilgrim, you do wrong your hand too much,
Which mannerly devotion shows in this.
For saints have hands that pilgrims' hands do touch,
And palm to palm is holy palmers' kiss.
Romeo
Have not saints lips, and holy palmers, too?
Juliet
Ay, pilgrim, lips that they must use in prayer.
Romeo
O, then, dear saint, let lips do what hands do:
They pray; grant thou, lest faith turn to despair.
Juliet
Saints do not move, though grant for prayers' sake.
Romeo
Then move not while my prayer's effect I take. [*He kisses her.*]

The question of who is meant by "Mr W. H." is a long-standing mystery in literary history. Some of the sonnets are clearly addressed to a man, or boy ("sweet boy", No 108, "my lovely boy", No 126), and it has often been supposed that Thorpe is thinking of this person as the "begetter" of the sonnets. Two candidates are Henry Wriothesley, Earl of Southampton, dedicatee of the narrative poems, and William Herbert, Earl of Pembroke, dedicatee of the First Folio of 1623. But neither man was properly addressed as "Mr" and Southampton's initials are "H. W.", not "W. H.". Also, "begetter" might simply mean the person who supplied the manuscript. Nobody really knows what Thorpe meant – and trying to work it out now is, according to poet W H Auden, "an idiot's job".

There is good reason to believe that Shakespeare wrote his sonnets, sometimes singly, sometimes in interrelated batches, over a long period of time. Probably the first sonnet he wrote – maybe

Let not my love be called idolatry,
Nor my belovèd as an idol show,
Since all alike my songs
and praises be
To one, of one, still such,
and ever so.
Sonnet 105

Sonnet 145 may have been written by a young Shakespeare as he courted his future wife, Anne Hathaway. She came from a prosperous family and lived in this home outside Stratford-upon-Avon.

even his first attempt at verse – is No 145 (see p.220 for the full poem), irregular in that it is written in octosyllabics, that is, eight-syllabled lines instead of the usual ten. The reason it is believed to have been written so early is partly that it is light in tone and not very sophisticated in technique, but mainly that in the last two lines the words "hate" and "away" pun on the name of the woman he married when he was 18, Anne Hathaway. It is a wooing poem.

It looks as if Shakespeare himself put the poems into the order in which they are printed. Some stand alone as independent poems, but »

Henry Wriothesley, 3rd Earl of Southampton, painted here in his teens around 1590, has been proposed as the unnamed young man to whom Sonnets 1–126 are addressed.

Many other poems in this group could equally well relate to a man or a woman.

The Dark Lady

The last 26 poems include all those that are clearly addressed to a woman, with whom the poet clearly has a difficult sexual relationship. Some of these sonnets indicate that she is dark in colouring, and even in character, that she is a rival of the poet in his love for his friend, and that the poet loves her against his better judgement. For this reason, they have come to be known as the Dark Lady sonnets, and many fruitless attempts have been made to identify a woman of the period who might fit the bill.

All aspects of love

Although all the sonnets are written in the same form, with only minor variations, they are extremely varied in style and ease of understanding. The poems also

others are related to one another in subject matter and fall naturally into groups of varying length.

The first 17 appear to be addressed to a young man who is very dear to the writer but whom he is encouraging to marry and to have children. Other poems up to No 126 also relate to one or more young men with whom the poet has a close and loving, though not necessarily sexual, relationship.

When my love swears that she is made of truth I do believe her though I know she lies, That she might think me some untutored youth Unlearnéd in the world's false subtleties.
Sonnet 138

run the whole gamut of love, from romantic idealism to brutal sexual realism. For this reason, it is difficult to read them in one sitting.

They include some of the most beautiful and popular love poems in English, some of which might equally be addressed to a male or a female, young or not so young. They tell of the power of love and of friendship to convey happiness, to transcend time, to confer a kind of immortality on the loved one. "Shall I compare thee to a summer's day? / Thou art more lovely and more temperate", says the poet in No 18, while No 116 is a great hymn to love (see p.221, opposite).

Other poems are very different in tone and the emotion they inspire in the reader. Some speak of rivalry: "Two loves I have, of comfort and despair, / Which like two spirits do suggest me still. / The better angel is a man right fair, / The worser spirit a woman coloured ill." (No 144). Some poems tell of disillusionment and self-deception in love: "When my love swears that she is made of truth / I do believe her though I know she lies." (No 138).

Sonnet 145

Those lips that love's own hand did make
Breathed forth the sound that said "I hate"
To me that languished for her sake;
But when she saw my woeful state,
Straight in her heart did mercy come,
Chiding that tongue that ever sweet
Was used in giving gentle doom,
And taught it thus anew to greet:
"I hate" she altered with an end
That followed it as gentle day
Doth follow night, who like a fiend,
From heaven to hell is flown away.
   "I hate" from hate away she threw,
   And saved my life, saying "not you".

Sonnet 116

Let me not to the marriage of true minds
Admit impediments. Love is not love
Which alters when it alteration finds,
Or bends with the remover to remove.
O no, it is an ever-fixèd mark
That looks on tempests and is never shaken;
It is the star to every wand'ring barque,
Whose worth's unknown, although his height be taken.
Love's not time's fool, though rosy lips and cheeks
Within his bending sickle's compass come;
Love alters not with his brief hours and weeks,
But bears it out even to the edge of doom.
    If this be error and upon me proved,
    I never writ, nor no man ever loved.

No 147 makes the point bluntly: "For I have sworn thee fair, and thought thee bright, / Who art as black as hell, as dark as night."

The poet's complicated relationship with love is explored in the sonnets. In No 149, the poet abases himself before the beloved: "Canst thou, O cruel, say I love thee not / When I against myself with thee partake?" In No 147, he writes with self-disgust of his enthralment to someone he feels is unworthy of him: "My love is as a fever, longing still / For that which longer nurseth the disease."

No 129 expresses shame at having yielded to lustful desire: "Th'expense of spirit in a waste of shame / Is lust in action".

However, there is also celebration of bodily desires. In No 146, the poet writes that the soul can be enriched by bodily decay: "Then, soul, live thou upon thy servant's loss, / Buy terms divine in selling hours of dross." In No 151, he says with exultant obscenity that: "thou betraying me, I do betray / My nobler part to my gross body's treason. / My soul doth tell my body that he may / Triumph in love; flesh stays no farther reason, / But rising at thy name doth point out thee / As his triumphant prize." »

In 2009, American director Robert Wilson and Canadian songwriter Rufus Wainwright produced a pop-opera, setting 25 of Shakespeare's sonnets (in German) to a variety of musical styles.

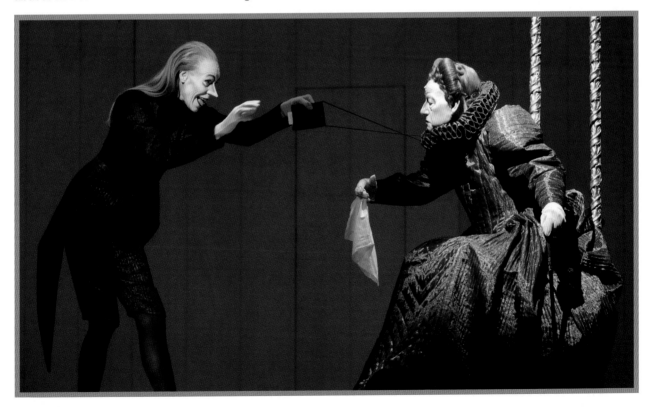

In the closing lines of No 151, the poet leaves no doubt about what part of the body he means by "flesh": "Proud of this prize, / He is contented thy poor drudge to be, / To stand in thy affairs, fall by thy side. / No want of conscience hold it that I call / Her 'love' for whose dear love I rise and fall."

Reputation

Unlike the narrative poems *Venus and Adonis* and *The Rape of Lucrece*, the sonnets were not a publishing success, and the 1609 edition was not reprinted. The sonnets (like the other poems) were not included in the First Folio of 1623. They did not appear in print again until 1640, in a book published by John Benson that omits eight of them, changes their order, alters pronouns in three of them so that they appear to refer to a woman rather than to a boy or a man, mangles others, gives some of them titles such as "An Invitation to Marriage" and "The Picture of True Love", and adds poems by other writers. After this, the sonnets were largely ignored for close on 150 years, with the result that critics such as John Dryden, Alexander Pope, and Samuel Johnson have nothing to say about them.

Only in the late 18th century did the sonnets come back into circulation. The English Romantic poet-critics John Keats and William Wordsworth both took the sonnets seriously and were influenced by them in their own work. Keats is said to have kept a bust of Shakespeare next to his desk for inspiration. In a letter to the painter Benjamin Robert Haydon, dated 10 May 1817, Keats wrote:

He was naturally learned; he needed not the spectacles of books to read nature. He looked inwards, and found her there.
John Dryden
(1631–1700)

Painted between 1595 and 1610, the Cobbe Portrait is believed to be the only image of Shakespeare drawn from life. It was probably commissioned by his patron and muse Henry Wriothesley.

Shakespeare's love poems still strike a chord with lovers across the world. Sonnets 116 and 141, in particular, are often read at marriages and civil partnership ceremonies.

"I remember your saying that you had notions of a good Genius presiding over you. I have of late had the same thought – for things which I do half at Random are afterwards confirmed by my judgment in a dozen features of Propriety. Is it too daring to fancy Shakespeare this Presider?"

Wordsworth, who was critical of certain aspects of the poetry in Shakespeare's plays, famously wrote of the sonnet form that "with this key / Shakespeare unlocked his heart". If so, responded fellow poet Robert Browning "the less Shakespeare he." Commenting on this exchange, Auden held that the artist is always both unlocking his heart and dramatic.

Victorian disapproval

Especially but not only in the Victorian period, the poems' reputation has suffered from homophobic distaste for the fact that some of them are love poems from one male person to another. This has also made some readers prefer to think that in them Shakespeare is writing of imagined situations rather than from personal experience. Nevertheless, the most obviously romantic of them have exerted strong appeal. They have frequently appeared in poetic anthologies.

Adapting the sonnets

Many attempts, all unsuccessful, have been made to rearrange the poems into an order that appears to be more meaningful than the original. The density of style of many of the poems makes them difficult to set to music, but there have been successful settings of a few of them in a variety of musical styles by musicians as diverse as the classical composer Benjamin Britten, the jazz arranger Johnny Dankworth, and the singer-songwriter Rufus Wainwright. ∎

Religion and merit

The religious references in Shakespeare's sonnets reflect both sides of a central doctrinal dispute of his time. The reformist Martin Luther (above) held that the key to salvation lay in faith alone. This contrasted with Catholic doctrine, which held that good works, prayers, pilgrimages, or the purchase of indulgences could increase an individual's chances of salvation. The poet takes from both traditions when dealing with the value of individual merit.

Sonnet 88 opens with the lines "When thou shalt be disposed to set me light / And place my merit in the eye of scorn". Here, he appears to take the reformist line, holding that his merit is worthless.

However, in No 108, merit is raised in a different way: "What's new to speak, what now to register, / That may express my love or thy dear merit?" Here, the poet seems to think merit far from worthless. Moreover, he follows with "Nothing, sweet boy; but yet like prayers divine / I must each day say o'er the very same", alluding to the Catholic practice of repeating the same prayers daily.

THAT FALSE FIRE WHICH IN HIS CHEEK SO GLOWED
A LOVER'S COMPLAINT (1609)

IN CONTEXT

THEMES
Love, betrayal

LEGACY
1790 Irish Shakespearean scholar Edmond Malone suggests that the language of the poem indicates that Shakespeare may have been attempting to emulate Edmund Spenser, author of *The Faerie Queen*.

1991 In his book *Motives of Woe*, John Kerrigan notes that the poem's narrative triangle of a young woman, older man, and seductive suitor mirrors a similar triangle in the sonnets.

2007 Brian Vickers argues that "A Lover's Complaint" was not written by Shakespeare, but by John Davies of Hereford. His conclusion is based on computer analysis of the poem's vocabulary. As a result, it is omitted from the RSC's *Complete Works*. However, Vickers' methods have since been questioned.

In the 1609 volume *Shakespeare's Sonnets*, the final item was printed with a separate heading saying that it too is by Shakespeare. It is a 329-line poem called "A Lover's Complaint", written, like *The Rape of Lucrece*, in the seven-line stanza form known as rhyme royal. It was not uncommon for collections of sonnets to conclude with a complaint, or lament, of a woman forsaken by her lover. Here, a nameless young woman, abandoned by her irresistibly attractive but faithless young man, also unnamed, bemoans her plight.

The poem is very different from the sonnets. It is written in a self-consciously old-fashioned and artificial style and employs a series of distancing perspectives. A narrator merely sets the scene. After saying that he has seen a love-lorn lass "Tearing of papers, breaking rings a-twain, / Storming her world with sorrow's winds and rain", he departs to let her tell her story to "A reverend man that grazed his cattle nigh". But this man also fades out of sight as the girl tells a story of seduction and abandonment. Her complaint contains within itself another

what a hell of witchcraft lies
In the small orb of
one particular tear!
A Lover's Complaint

long complaint, her lover's ultimately successful speech of seduction ending with the tears of desire that brought about her downfall: "O father, what a hell of witchcraft lies / In the small orb of one particular tear!"

She fell, she says, and she would fall again in the face of such eloquent persuasion: "O that infected moisture of his eye, / O that false fire which in his cheek so glowed, / O that forced thunder from his heart did fly, / O that sad breath his spongy lungs bestowed, / O all that borrowed motion seeming owed / Would yet again betray the fore-betrayed, / And new pervert a reconcilèd maid." ∎

TRUTH AND BEAUTY BURIED BE

THE PHOENIX AND TURTLE (1601)

IN CONTEXT

THEME
The death of ideal love

LEGACY
Many critics consider the poem's ambiguities unresolvable, but various attempts have been made to decode its allegorical nature.

1878 A B Grosart suggests that the poem refers to a relationship between Queen Elizabeth I and the Earl of Essex, who rebelled against the Crown and was executed in 1601. The phoenix was the queen's personal badge.

1930s American scholar Clara Longworth proposes that it reveals Catholic sympathies. Others have suggested that the birds are Catholic martyrs.

2006 Peter Ackroyd suggests that the poem may have been written for the wedding in 1586 of the sister of Lord Strange, for whose company Shakespeare was working.

In 1601, in a book by Robert Chester called *Love's Martyr: or Rosalind's Complaint*, appeared a poem by Shakespeare called "The Phoenix and Turtle".

The poem falls into three parts of mounting intensity. First, it summons a convocation of benevolent birds, with a swan as priest, to celebrate the funeral rites of a phoenix and a dove who have fled "In a mutual flame from hence". ("Turtle" here means a turtledove.) The birds sing an anthem in which the death of the lovers is seen as marking the death of "love and constancy": "So they loved as love in twain / Had the essence but in one, / Two distincts, division none. / Number there in love was slain." Their mutual love was such that "either was the other's mine". In the third section, Love makes a funeral song: "To the phoenix and the dove, / Co-supremes and stars of love, / As chorus to their tragic scene."

The funeral song, known as a threnos, or threnody, is written in an even more incantatory style than what has gone before. Its five stanzas have three rhyming lines, whose tone is grave simplicity: "Beauty, truth, and rarity, / Grace in all simplicity, / Here enclosed in cinders lie. / Death is now the phoenix' nest, / And the turtle's loyal breast / To eternity doth rest. / Leaving no posterity / 'Twas not their infirmity, / It was married chastity. / Truth may seem but cannot be, / Beauty brag, but 'tis not she. / Truth and beauty buried be. / To this urn let these repair / That are either true or fair. / For these dead birds sigh a prayer."

This strange, mystically beautiful poem probably had meanings for its original readers that are lost to us. Many unsuccessful attempts have been made to interpret it as a religious allegory or a celebration of the love of a real married couple. ∎

Truth may seem but cannot be, Beauty brag, but 'tis not she.
The Phoenix and Turtle

WITH SELFSAME HAND, SELF REASONS, AND SELF RIGHT, WOULD SHARK ON YOU
SIR THOMAS MORE (1603–1604)

IN CONTEXT

THEMES
Justice, religion, moral fortitude

SETTING
London

SOURCES
c.1575 Nicholas Harpsfield's biography of More, *The life and death of Sr Thomas Moore*.

1587 Holinshed's *Chronicles of England, Scotland, and Ireland*.

LEGACY
1590s There is no record of any staging of the play in the 16th or 17th centuries.

1922 The first known performance of the play is a University of London student production.

1960 An adaptation appears on Austrian public radio.

1983 The BBC produces a radio version of the play, with Ian McKellen in the title role.

2005 Nigel Cooke stars in an RSC production of the play.

I n 1753, the British Museum acquired a remarkable bequest from the bookseller John Murray. It was a manuscript called "The Booke of Sir Thomas Moore" and is a working draft of the play *Sir Thomas More* dating from around 1600. The manuscript contains the only known examples of writing in Shakespeare's hand, aside from a handful of signatures.

The manuscript is believed to show revisions to the text for a play originally written by Anthony Munday and, maybe, Henry Chettle, after it had been submitted to the official censor Edmund Tilney. The manuscript shows both Tilney's interventions and the hands of at

The fool of flesh must with her frail flesh die
More
Scene 17

least four writers, including Chettle, Thomas Heywood, Thomas Dekker, and Shakespeare, not to mention an editor, known simply as Hand C.

The power of the censor
The subject of the play was a sensitive one: the Catholic martyr Sir Thomas More (1478–1535). More rose from comparatively humble beginnings to become King Henry VIII's chancellor. He was an opponent of the Protestant Reformation and strongly against Henry's split from the Catholic church. In 1535, he was executed for treason for his quiet refusal to go along with the annulment of Henry's marriage to Catherine of Aragon and his subsequent marriage to Anne Boleyn.

Anne Boleyn was the mother of the reigning queen, Elizabeth I, so a play that was favourable to More would be seen as undermining Elizabeth's legitimacy. This made More a bold choice of subject matter, and it is not surprising that the play was probably never performed in the queen's lifetime. The writers are careful to steer around the issue of Anne's marriage, and Henry VIII is never mentioned by name. The brunt of Tilney's demands for cuts

The German artist Hans Holbein captured More's intelligence and dignity in this extraordinarily vivid portrait of 1527, painted when More was a rising star at Henry's court.

came in the first third of the play where Londoners riot against foreigners. He appears to have been most concerned over public order.

An unwieldy play

The play's failure to reach the stage may have been due to practical as well as political reasons. It has 59 speaking parts, which would have severely taxed any theatre company, with many actors playing three or more roles. Probably only the roles of Sir Thomas More and perhaps the Earls of Shrewsbury and Surrey, could have been played by actors with no other parts.

More's life is split into three parts – his rise, his chancellorship, and his fall. The early part of the play shows More as Sheriff of London, and stresses his wisdom and moderation. When a group of Londoners rise in rebellion against foreigners in their midst, More ends the riot with quiet persuasion.

It is thought that the key scene in this part of the play was written by Shakespeare. It seems likely that Shakespeare had not seen the rest of the play and was simply given a brief by the editor, since there are characters he just names as "other" or even "o", and the entry of More is confused. But what he writes stands out in a generally mediocre play.

Tolerance for foreigners

In Shakespeare's script, More calmly stands before the rioters in St Martin's Gate. He makes a passionate plea for the tolerance of refugees. Painting a poignant picture of the foreigners (strangers)

bullied out by the rioters, More tells them that this brings only the idea that bullying prevails: "Imagine that you see the wretched strangers, / Their babies at their backs, with their poor luggage, / Plodding to th' ports and coasts for transportation, / And that you sit as kings in your desires…What had you got? I'll tell you: you had taught / How insolence and strong hand should prevail." (6.84–87, 90–91).

More asks what will stop bullies preying on them. "With selfsame hand, self reasons, and self right, / Would shark on you, and men like ravenous fishes / Would feed on one another." (6.95–97).

Moreover, More goes on, if the king is driven to banish the rioters themselves, surely they would expect to be treated decently abroad: "Would you be pleased / To find a nation of such barbarous temper" (6.145–146).

More carries his constancy through to his own death. He cannot change his mind and sign the articles that recognize Anne Boleyn and her heirs as legitimate. Yet he calmly accepts his fate. "No eye salute my trunk with a sad tear", More says to end the play as the axeman prepares to behead him, "Our birth to heaven should be thus: void of fear." ∎

THE K
MAN
1603–1613

NG'S

Shakespeare writes *Measure for Measure* and *Othello*.

The **Treaty of London** ends England's war with Spain. Shakespeare is living in lodgings near St Paul's Cathedral.

The **Gunpowder Plot** to blow up Parliament is **foiled**. Ben Jonson's *Volpone* is first performed at The Globe.

Pericles, Prince of Tyre is written, and is performed at the Globe Theatre.

1603   **1604**   **1605**   **1607**

1603   **1605**   **1606**   **1607**

Queen Elizabeth I dies and is succeeded by her cousin James VI of Scotland as James I of England.

King Lear and *Timon of Athens* are written. The lead in *Lear* is created for the King's Men's lead tragic actor, Richard Burbage.

Macbeth, *Antony and Cleopatra*, and *All's Well That Ends Well* are written.

Monteverdi's opera *L'Orfeo* is performed in Mantua, Lombardy (in present-day Italy).

On 24 March 1603, Queen Elizabeth I died after 45 years on the throne. She was succeeded by her cousin James VI of Scotland, son of Mary Queen of Scots, whom Elizabeth had beheaded 16 years earlier. One of James's first acts on becoming king was to give Shakespeare's company a royal patent to make them the King's Men.

By royal command
This was a financial boost for the troupe, but it also added pressure. Now they not only had to please the general public; they had to please the king and his courtiers, too. In the 13 years between James becoming king and Shakespeare's death, the King's Men performed for the court 187 times – more than once a month.

Around this time, Shakespeare's style changed. He moved away from the crowd-pleasing comedies, romances, and histories of the later years of Elizabeth's reign. Now he wrote fewer plays, but they were grander and darker. In the first three years of James's reign, he wrote just six plays, five of which were ambitious tragedies – *Othello*, *King Lear*, *Macbeth*, *Antony and Cleopatra*, and the uncompleted *Timon of Athens*. Even *Measure for Measure* was intense and morally challenging. While Shakespeare was writing these great works, the company had his impressive back-catalogue to keep the theatres full.

Escape to Stratford?
Nobody knows quite how Shakespeare spent his time during these years. One of the

few things we do know is that, by 1604, he was renting a room in the house of a Huguenot called Christopher Mountjoy. We know this because Mountjoy got into a bitter lawsuit with his son-in-law and Shakespeare is mentioned in the legal documents.

Living perpetually in rented accommodation clearly brought its stresses. So it may be that Shakespeare, not under as much pressure as in his younger days, took every chance to go home to Stratford and write in a calmer environment. He may also have had to leave London when the plague returned.

On 5 November 1605, a very distant relative of Shakespeare, Robert Catesby, was involved in the most infamous Catholic attempt to bring down England's Protestant

Coriolanus is written. The new **Blackfriars Theatre opens**, but an outbreak of plague closes the theatres soon after.

Thomas Thorpe publishes a collection of 154 **sonnets** by Shakespeare.

The **King James Version**, a new English translation of the Bible, is published in London.

Henry VIII, or *All is True* and *The Two Noble Kinsmen* are written.

1608 **1609** **1611** **1613**

1609 **1610** **1612** **1613**

The Winter's Tale is written. Shakespeare's younger contemporary, **Ben Jonson**, is **critical** of the play.

Cymbeline and *The Tempest* are written. The latter is the probably the last play Shakespeare writes entirely by himself.

Thomas Shelton **translates** into English some of **Cervantes'** *Don Quixote*, which may have inspired Shakespeare's "lost" play, *Cardenio*.

James I's daughter Elizabeth marries Frederick V of Bohemia.

---

government, the Gunpowder Plot. The plot was foiled when a Catholic lord was given a secret warning and tipped off the authorities. They were told to search under the Houses of Parliament, and there they found Guido (Guy) Fawkes sitting on 36 barrels of gunpowder. Had Fawkes set them off, it would not only have blown up the Parliament buildings but the nearby Whitehall Palace and the royal family too. Practising Catholics were already in a minority by this time, and the clampdown on Catholics that followed effectively ended the Catholic challenge to government in England.

The last plays

The King's Men continued to prosper, and in 1608 were able to acquire a second theatre,

the Blackfriars. This new theatre was very different from the Globe – indoors and much smaller, so performances were almost entirely by candlelight. The company continued to perform at the Globe in summer, then they could play right through winter in the Blackfriars.

Shakespeare began to write plays suited to the more intimate space of the Blackfriars and its facility for spectacular theatrical effects, such as the storm and the flying spirits in *The Tempest* and the statue coming to life in *The Winter's Tale*. He was also collaborating with other writers again – Thomas Middleton (1580–1627) on *Timon of Athens* in 1606, George Wilkins (1576–1618) on *Pericles* in 1607, and John Fletcher (1579–1625) on the

lost play *Cardenio*, *All Is True* (*Henry VIII*), and *The Two Noble Kinsmen* in 1613.

The collaborations with Fletcher were Shakespeare's last plays. On 29 June 1613, the Globe Theatre caught fire during a performance of *Henry VIII* when a theatrical cannon misfired and set the roof thatch alight. Everybody escaped unhurt, but the theatre burned down. The Globe was rebuilt ready for the following summer, but it appears that it reopened without Shakespeare. All we know about his life from that point on is that he wrote nothing more and died just three years later at home in Stratford on 23 April 1616, within a month of signing a document saying he was in "perfect health". He was 52 years old. ∎

MAN, PROUD MAN DRESSED IN A LITTLE BRIEF AUTHORITY

MEASURE FOR MEASURE (1603–1604)

DRAMATIS PERSONAE

Duke Vincentio Governor of Vienna who disguises himself as a friar to observe how Angelo governs in his absence. He later proposes marriage to Isabella.

Angelo Duke Vincentio's deputy, who is given the opportunity to govern Vienna. He suggests that Claudio's death sentence could be overturned should his sister Isabella give up her chastity.

Escalus The Duke's aide, who oversees and criticizes Angelo's puritanical approach to government.

Claudio Isabella's brother, who is arrested and given a death sentence for getting his betrothed, Juliet, pregnant.

Isabella A novice nun who is called to plead for her brother's life. She is determined to save Claudio, as well as preserve her chastity.

Lucio A brash busy-body who delights in the scandals plaguing Vienna. He provokes the Duke's displeasure with his defamatory gossip, and is forced to marry a prostitute.

Mistress Overdone The keeper of the brothel who discovers that Angelo intends to close down her business.

Mariana Once betrothed to Angelo, but he refused to marry her. She takes Isabella's place in Angelo's bed, and so tricks him into marriage.

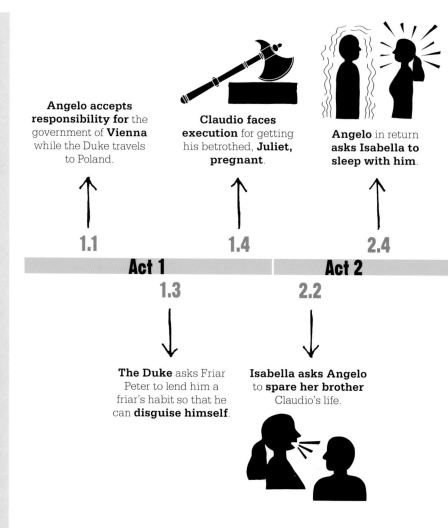

Angelo accepts responsibility for the government of **Vienna** while the Duke travels to Poland.

1.1

Act 1

1.3

The Duke asks Friar Peter to lend him a friar's habit so that he can **disguise himself**.

Claudio faces execution for getting his betrothed, **Juliet, pregnant**.

1.4

Angelo in return asks Isabella to sleep with him.

2.4

Act 2

2.2

Isabella asks Angelo to **spare her brother** Claudio's life.

Duke Vincentio hands power to his deputy Angelo and announces that he is leaving the country on business. During the 14 years the Duke has been in government, Vienna has become a lawless city, where pimps and prostitutes thrive. The Duke secretly plans to observe how the puritanical Angelo governs in his absence. He assumes the disguise of a friar in order to move around the city unrecognized.

Once in power, Angelo enforces forgotten laws. Claudio is arrested for getting his wife-to-be Juliet pregnant, and the pimps and bawds fear that they too will soon suffer. On hearing of Claudio's death sentence, his sister Isabella leaves the nunnery she was about to join to plead with Angelo to spare her brother's life.

Isabella is escorted by Lucio who encourages her to argue her brother's case. Angelo remains unmoved by Isabella's argument, but he asks her to return the next day. She comes unaccompanied and Angelo presents her with a chilling ultimatum: he will spare her brother's life on the condition

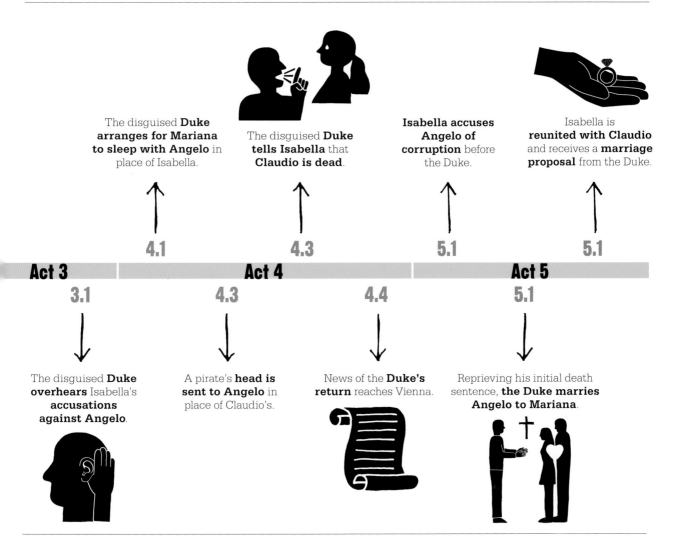

The disguised **Duke arranges for Mariana to sleep with Angelo** in place of Isabella.

4.1

The disguised **Duke tells Isabella** that **Claudio is dead**.

4.3

Isabella accuses Angelo of corruption before the Duke.

5.1

Isabella is **reunited with Claudio** and receives a **marriage proposal** from the Duke.

5.1

Act 3   **Act 4**   **Act 5**

3.1   **4.3**   **4.4**   **5.1**

The disguised **Duke overhears** Isabella's **accusations against Angelo**.

A pirate's **head is sent to Angelo** in place of Claudio's.

News of the **Duke's return** reaches Vienna.

Reprieving his initial death sentence, **the Duke marries Angelo to Mariana**.

that she sleeps with him. Isabella is distraught, but Angelo reminds her that no-one would believe her were she to report his proposal.

Isabella visits her brother in prison and tells him of Angelo's behaviour. Though Claudio is appalled, he questions her commitment to her chastity when his life is at stake. The disguised Duke overhears their conversation and ministers to each of them. He tells Isabella that all is not lost, and suggests a cunning solution. He will arrange for Mariana, Angelo's ex-fiancée, to sleep with him under

the cover of darkness, so that Angelo will believe he has slept with Isabella and spare Claudio.

The Duke's plan is successful but Angelo is still resolved to execute Claudio. The disguised Duke intervenes by having the head of a condemned prisoner sent to Angelo in place of Claudio's. The Duke does not share his plan with Isabella, leading her to believe that her brother has been beheaded.

Vincentio stages his return to Vienna, and praises Angelo for his good government. Isabella accuses Angelo of corruption; she has no

idea that the Duke has observed everything while in disguise. When Mariana confirms that it was she who slept with Angelo, the Duke, who has returned disguised as a friar once more, supports her story. The Duke is unmasked by Lucio and Angelo begs for execution; he is surprised when Mariana pleads to spare his life, and Isabella joins Mariana in her plea. The Duke grants their wish on the condition that Angelo marry Mariana. Having reunited Isabella with her brother, the Duke asks for her hand in marriage – twice! »

IN CONTEXT

THEMES
Justice, morality, power, sex

SETTING
Vienna

SOURCES
1565 Shakespeare may have been familiar with Giraldi Cinthio's Italian novella *Hecatommithi*. However, he introduced Mariana and the "bedtrick". In the source material, the Isabella figure sleeps with the Angelo character, and marries him.

1578 Shakespeare made use of George Whetstone's English tragicomedy *Promos and Cassandra*.

LEGACY
1818 The poet Samuel Taylor Coleridge writes of the play that it is "the most painful" of Shakespeare's works.

1836 Richard Wagner composes a two-act opera, *Das Liebesverbot* (The Ban of Love), which follows the story of *Measure for Measure*.

1950 In a thought-provoking twist, the director Peter Brook instructs the actress playing Isabella to pause for as long as possible before joining Mariana to plead for Angelo's life.

1970 In another approach to this problem play, Estelle Kohler's Isabella turns to the audience in despair following the Duke's proposals in John Barton's production staged at Stratford-upon-Avon.

In the opening scene, Duke Vincentio reveals to Escalus his plan to leave Vienna, lending Angelo "all the organs / Of our power" (1.1.20–21) to rule in his absence. He is keen to hear Escalus's opinion of his plan: "What think you of it?" (1.1.21). He is also eager to know his companion's estimation of Angelo himself: "What figure of us think you he will bear?" (1.1.15–16). In asking so many questions, the dramatist is readying his audience to observe, evaluate, and pass judgement upon Angelo's behaviour. Angelo's reaction to being "Dressed in a little brief authority" (2.2.121) will be a concern throughout the drama.

Shakespeare builds a sense of anticipation around Angelo's arrival. By the time Vincentio announces "Look where he comes" (1.1.24), the audience is sure to be curious about this mysterious figure with whom the Duke seems somewhat obsessed. Angelo shows respectful reticence at first to taking control of "Morality and mercy in Vienna" (1.1.44); he asks that "there be some more test made of [his] metal" (1.1.48) before he assumes this powerful role. Little does he realize that the Duke will be testing him throughout the rest of the drama.

> ## Some rise by sin, and some by virtue fall.
> **Escalus**
> Act 2, Scene 1

The virtuous character of Isabella is played here by Flora Robson in a production in 1933. In Whetstone's tale, she is a chaste maid; in Shakespeare's play, she is about to enter a nunnery.

Testing times
Angelo's job will not be easy, for law and order have all but disappeared in Vienna. Having passed responsibility to Angelo, the Duke confides in a friar that: "We have strict statutes a nd most biting laws, / The needful bits and curbs to headstrong weeds, / Which for this fourteen years we have let slip… / And Liberty plucks Justice by the nose, / The baby beats the nurse, and quite athwart / Goes all decorum." (1.3.19–31).

During the Duke's time, Vienna has become a city where criminality and prostitution are rife; and slanderous allegations are even made about the Duke's own behaviour: "Ere he would have hanged a man for the getting a hundred bastards, he would have paid for the nursing a thousand"

(3.1.380–383). The puritanical Angelo would seem a prime candidate for restoring moral order in a city that has become diseased. The Duke recognizes that having, neglected his authority for so long, he would prove a tyrant were he to try to enforce order anew; far better, he thinks, to have Angelo "in th'ambush of [his] name strike home" (1.3.41). While Angelo will in time prove to be a hypocrite, the Duke will prove a Machiavellian operator.

Abuse of power

Various characters pass comment on Angelo's character during the course of the play. The Duke notes that Angelo is "precise" (1.3.50), and that he "Stands at a guard with envy, scarce confesses / That his blood flows, or that his appetite / Is more to bread than stone." (1.3.51–53). The gossipy and salacious Lucio presents an image of Angelo that drains him of every

> The law hath not been dead, though it hath slept.
> **Angelo**
> Act 2, Scene 2

drop of blood and compassion: Lucio professes that "Some report a sea-maid spawned him, some that he was begot between two stockfishes. But it is certain that when he makes water his urine is congealed ice; that I know to be true." (3.1.372–375).

While Angelo may not be the monstrous figure of Lucio's imagination, he proves to have little

in the way of compassion when he sentences Claudio to death for having had sex with his wife-to-be outside of wedlock: "'Tis one thing to be tempted… / Another thing to fall" (2.1.17–18). His conviction would remain steadfast were it not for the sudden entrance of the virtuous Isabella into his life. Like Angelo, Isabella has a reputation for "stricture and firm abstinence" (1.3.12). Her first exchange with a nun expresses both her moral fortitude and her readiness to live by a strict set of rules; she is surprised to hear, for example, that the votarists of Saint Clare do not live by "a more strict restraint" (1.4.4). In different circumstances, Angelo and Isabella might find »

Early 17th-century Vienna, shown in this engraving, is described as a lawless and immoderate city in need of a firm hand. The neglectful Duke chooses exacting Angelo for the task.

Sweet sister, let me live.
Claudio
Act 3, Scene 1

that they have much in common, but the context in which they first meet is crucial in defining the dynamic of their relationship. Isabella finds herself before a figure of immense authority, and faces the challenge of persuading him to overturn the death sentence he has placed on her brother. Two strictly principled individuals must find it within themselves to forgive a sinful act. Shakespeare lends Isabella a powerfully persuasive voice. Her speeches suggest a keen intellect and a compassionate heart. She finds ways to prick Angelo's conscience, to unearth doubts and anxiety. "If he had been as you and you as he, / You would have slipped like him, but he, like you, / Would not have been so stern." (2.2.66–68). At other times her speeches remind Angelo of his shared humanity: "Go to your bosom; / Knock there, and ask your heart what it doth know / That's like my brother's fault?" (2.2.140–142). Ultimately, her words have the desired effect – to shame Angelo into reconsideration: "O, it is excellent / To have a giant's strength, but it is tyrannous / To use it like a giant." (2.2.109–111).

Persuasive power
The question for readers and audiences is whether it is Isabella's words alone, or also her physical appearance that affect Angelo? With Lucio and the Provost present, Angelo maintains his image of the stern authoritarian, but his behaviour alters dramatically when Isabella returns as instructed for their second meeting, in private. When she returns, Isabella promises to "bribe" (2.2.149) Angelo, but as she goes on to explain "Not with fond shekels of the tested gold, / Or stones, whose rate are either rich or poor / As fancy values them; but with true prayers, / That shall be up at heaven and enter there / Ere sunrise" (2.2.153–157). Is Isabella's "bribe" completely innocent, or is there a sense in which she manipulates her womanliness as Lucio has instructed her to? Her brother had confidence in her chances of getting his death sentence overturned because he believed that "in her youth / There is a prone and speechless dialect / Such as move men" (1.2.170–172).

Whether Isabella "moves" Angelo, or whether he discovers unknown passions within is a matter of debate. Either way, Angelo moves from being a law enforcer to a corrupt abuser of power: "I have begun, / And now I give my sensual race the rein. / Fit thy consent to my sharp appetite. / …Redeem thy brother / By yielding up thy body to my will, / Or else he must not only die the death, / But thy unkindness shall his death draw out / To ling'ring sufferance."

You bid me seek redemption of the devil.
Isabella
Act 5, Scene 1

(2.4.159–167). Having been indecently propositioned by Angelo, Isabella retorts: "I will proclaim thee, Angelo; look for't. / Sign me a present pardon for my brother, / Or with an outstretched throat I'll tell the world aloud / What man thou art." (2.4.151–154). However, she is in a vulnerable position – Angelo is a powerful man and she has no witnesses on whom to draw.

Power corrupts

Angelo's response is chilling. He replies: "Who will believe thee, Isabel? / My unsoiled name, th'austereness of my life, / My vouch against you, and my place i'th'state, / Will so your accusation overweigh." (2.4.154–157). Angelo calculates that his power makes

After reuniting Isabella
(Naomi Frederick) with her brother, Vincentio (Simon McBurney, who also directed this 2005 production) asks for her hand: "Say you will be mine" (5.1.491).

Isabella powerless. She knows that she is in the right, but to whom should she complain? Isabella is trapped. In the story from which Shakespeare borrowed for his play, the Isabella character does, in fact, sleep with the deputy, but Shakespeare's incarnation says "Then Isabel live chaste, and brother die." (2.4.184). Shakespeare provides her a way out of this situation through the comic device of the "bedtrick", by which Angelo sleeps with his ex-fiancée, believing it to be Isabella.

Having escaped Angelo's bed, Isabella now finds herself the subject of the Duke's desires when he recovers power. The Duke offers her his hand in marriage on two separate occasions at the close of the play: "Dear Isabel, / I have a motion much imports your good, / Whereto, if you'll a willing ear incline, / What's mine is yours, and what is yours is mine." (5.1.533–536). There is no response from Isabella. ∎

Problem play

Shakespeare does not have Isabella respond to the Duke. Is it to be assumed that Isabella is speechless and overcome with joy at the prospect of marrying this high ranking official, who has returned to Vienna and exercised his authority by helping to reveal Angelo's abuse of power? Or does Isabella's silence convey her distrust of men? Her brother hoped that she would lose her virginity to save his life; Angelo made her the focus of his lust; and the Duke allowed her to grieve over her brother's death when he knew him still to be alive. Opinion remains divided over whether Isabella should or should not take the Duke's hand at the close; her silence will always invite various interpretations.

Measure for Measure is often referred to today as being one of Shakespeare's "problem plays". Though the play ends with the prospect of three marriages, the atmosphere of the final scene, and the play in general, is far from buoyant and uplifting. This a dark comedy, shaped by Shakespeare to shock rather than enchant.

BEWARE
MY LORD OF JEALOUSY
IT IS THE GREEN-EY'D
MONSTER

OTHELLO (1603–1604)

DRAMATIS PERSONAE

Othello General in the Venetian army, also known as the Moor.

Iago Othello's "ancient", or standard-bearer, who is envious of Othello's position.

Desdemona Othello's bride, who is disowned by Brabanzio after her wedding. Her name means "ill-fated".

Cassio A lieutenant in the army, who is wrongly accused by Iago and Othello of committing adultery with Desdemona.

Emilia The sole companion of Desdemona and much neglected wife of Iago.

Roderigo A suitor to Desdemona, spurred on by Iago to seek vengeance against Othello.

Brabanzio The father of Desdemona and former companion of Othello.

Montano The governor of Cyprus, who is to decide Iago's fate at the end of the play.

Bianca A courtesan who adores Cassio. He does not reciprocate the affection.

Lodovico Venetian ambassador to Cyprus, cousin of Desdemona.

Graziano A noble Venetian who arrives in Cyprus with Lodovico.

A clown He argues in the street with Cassio.

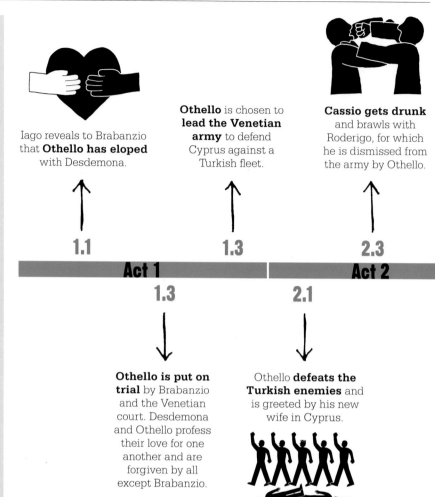

Iago reveals to Brabanzio that **Othello has eloped** with Desdemona.

Othello is chosen to **lead the Venetian army** to defend Cyprus against a Turkish fleet.

Cassio gets drunk and brawls with Roderigo, for which he is dismissed from the army by Othello.

1.1

1.3

2.3

Act 1

Act 2

1.3

2.1

Othello is put on trial by Brabanzio and the Venetian court. Desdemona and Othello profess their love for one another and are forgiven by all except Brabanzio.

Othello **defeats the Turkish enemies** and is greeted by his new wife in Cyprus.

With the help of the love-sick gentleman Roderigo, the soldier Iago plots to thwart the Moorish general of the Venetian army, Othello. Iago tells Brabanzio that his daughter, Desdemona, has eloped with Othello. Brabanzio demands justice from the Venetian court. After hearing Desdemona's defence, the law favours Othello, who must now speed to Cyprus to prevent a Turkish invasion. Desdemona insists upon meeting Othello in Cyprus once he has defeated the Turks.

Iago plagues Othello with suspicions about Desdemona's relationship with Cassio. In the meantime, Iago persuades Roderigo, who is in love with Desdemona, to challenge Cassio to a fight. Their brawl wakes Othello, who dismisses Cassio from the army. Cassio pleads with Desdemona to persuade Othello to forgive him, causing the Moor to suspect his wife of infidelity.

Iago has his wife Emilia steal a handkerchief that was given to Desdemona by Othello. He plants it in Cassio's bedchamber and

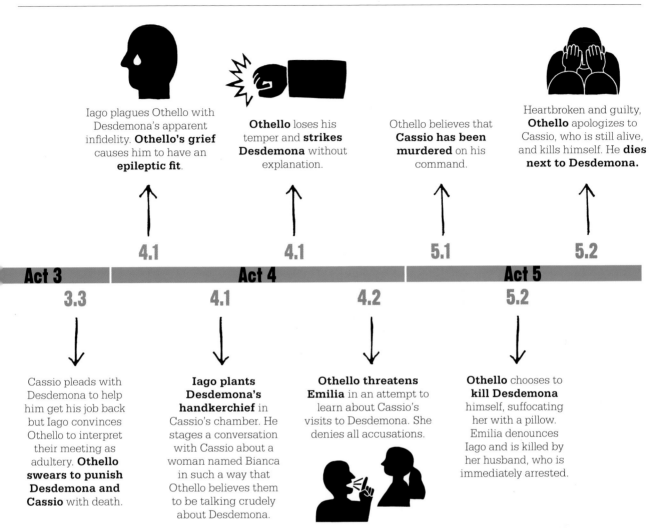

Iago plagues Othello with Desdemona's apparent infidelity. **Othello's grief** causes him to have an **epileptic fit**.

Othello loses his temper and **strikes Desdemona** without explanation.

Othello believes that **Cassio has been murdered** on his command.

Heartbroken and guilty, **Othello** apologizes to Cassio, who is still alive, and kills himself. He **dies next to Desdemona.**

4.1   4.1   5.1   5.2

Act 3   **Act 4**   **Act 5**

3.3   4.1   4.2   5.2

Cassio pleads with Desdemona to help him get his job back but Iago convinces Othello to interpret their meeting as adultery. **Othello swears to punish Desdemona and Cassio** with death.

Iago plants Desdemona's handkerchief in Cassio's chamber. He stages a conversation with Cassio about a woman named Bianca in such a way that Othello believes them to be talking crudely about Desdemona.

Othello threatens Emilia in an attempt to learn about Cassio's visits to Desdemona. She denies all accusations.

Othello chooses to **kill Desdemona** himself, suffocating her with a pillow. Emilia denounces Iago and is killed by her husband, who is immediately arrested.

weaves a plot to make Othello believe that Desdemona gave it to Cassio as a token of love.

Iago continues to weave his web of deceit around Othello, telling him that Cassio has admitted committing adultery with Desdemona. Othello is consumed by jealousy, refusing to speak with Desdemona. Othello suffers an epileptic fit, after which he resolves to kill Cassio and Desdemona.

When Desdemona's cousin, Lodovico, arrives as an ambassador from Venice, he sees Othello strike Desdemona in public. Roderigo

grows restless at his lack of progress in wooing Desdemona. Iago persuades him to kill Cassio. During their struggle, Cassio fatally wounds Roderigo, who confesses his part in Iago's plot.

At the same time, Othello wakes Desdemona from her sleep. He asks her to pray for forgiveness for what she has done. He can then murder her with a clear conscience. Desdemona swears her innocence, but he smothers her with a pillow, whereupon Emilia enters and accuses Othello of murder. Desdemona revives briefly, falsely

telling Emilia that she has killed herself. When the others enter the chamber to inform Othello of Roderigo's death, they discover Desdemona's body and demand an explanation. Emilia admits taking the handkerchief. Iago stabs Emilia to stop her betraying him further, whereupon Othello immediately repents of his actions. He asks forgiveness of all present, and out of rage drives his dagger into Iago who, although wounded, is not killed. Othello stabs himself and dies by Desdemona's side, leaving Cassio in control of the Venetian army. »

IN CONTEXT

THEMES
Jealousy, loyalty, betrayal, love

SETTING
16th-century Venice and Cyprus

SOURCES
1565 *Un Capitano Moro* (A Moorish Captain), a tale by the Italian author Giraldi Cinthio, which Shakespeare may have read in Italian, or in a French translation from 1583.

c.1600 Arrival of a Moorish delegation at the Elizabethan court to promote an Anglo-Moroccan alliance.

1603 The 1570 Turkish attack on Cyprus, documented in *The History of the Turks* by English historian Richard Knolles.

LEGACY
1604 The earliest recorded performance of *Othello* is held at Whitehall Palace.

1660 Margaret Hughes plays Desdemona, becoming the first woman to perform legally on the English stage.

1816 Gioachino Rossini's opera *Otello*, loosely based on Shakespeare, opens in Naples.

1825 Ira Aldridge is the first black actor to play Othello on the London stage.

1887 The opera *Otello* by Giuseppe Verdi is first performed in Milan.

1930 The black actor and singer Paul Robeson plays Othello at the Savoy in London.

Unlike the original story of "A Moorish Captain", which rarely mentions it, Shakespeare makes Othello extremely conscious of his race. Black characters in Elizabethan drama are often devilish, cruel individuals, like Aaron in *Titus Andronicus*. Othello is the first sympathetic black character on the Elizabethan stage. The audience sympathizes with his plight, and Desdemona clings desperately to her love for "the Moor".

Othello the Moor
Iago and Roderigo are openly vicious in their racial attacks on Othello. Othello is introduced to the audience through the eyes of Iago in crude racial and sexual terms. He is described as a "black ram" mounting Brabanzio's "white ewe" (1.1.88–89). When Shakespeare wrote the play, darkness of skin, along with physical deformity and non-Christian heritage, were popularly associated with immorality and savagery. Othello himself refers frequently to his black heritage, which he blames for making him quick to anger and to experience jealousy. Othello belies the stereotype in all his conduct except for his rage and suspicious nature, which prompt Emilia to accuse him of being "the blacker devil" (5.2.140).

Othello the military hero
Not everyone characterizes Othello in racial terms. He is often judged by his military prowess. Before he is called before it by Brabanzio's complaint, the court is in discussion about choosing Othello to lead the attack on the Turks off the coast of Cyprus. Shakespeare makes it clear that Othello's merit speaks for itself within the Venetian hierarchy. His calm level-headedness is

Nineteenth-century Irish painter Daniel Maclise captures a troubled marriage. Othello broods while Desdemona looks up at him pleadingly, clutching the cursed handkerchief.

> The Moor is of a free and
> open nature,
> That thinks men honest that
> but seem to be so,
> And will as tenderly be
> led by th' nose
> As asses are.
> **Iago**
> Act 1, Scene 3

evident when he defends himself against Brabanzio's accusations that he kidnapped Desdemona.

Othello's tone and experience, compared with Desdemona's rebelliousness and the fact that she still resides with her father, suggest a significant age gap between the couple. Nevertheless, Othello's love for Desdemona is sincere, and it is this sincerity that makes him vulnerable to Iago's machinations. Othello is brought down from a justified position of strength and respect to a savage, unjustified, and bitter end all because he could not control his jealousy. The respect and love with which the Venetians regard Othello is made clear by their shock when he is discovered with Desdemona's body at the end. This was not a man they imagined succumbing to anxiety, paranoia, and murder.

"Honest" Iago

Manipulative, cruel, and motivated by hatred and jealousy, Iago uses Roderigo's unrequited love for

Desdemona as a way of extorting money and extra hands to support his scheme to undermine Othello. Roderigo compulsively follows Iago's instructions in the hope that it will bring him closer to Desdemona. Iago also manipulates the audience by divulging his scheme in soliloquies. He justifies his contempt for Othello with two uncorroborated arguments: that Othello has slept with his wife, Emilia, and that Cassio has stolen his promotion to captain. Curiously, Iago's warning to Othello about the "green-eyed monster" is one that he cannot heed himself. It is a cruel irony that both Othello and Cassio hold Iago in the highest of esteem, bestowing on him the title "honest".

It is Iago who convinces Othello that Desdemona is false and Iago who suggests that Othello "strangle her in bed, even the bed she hath contaminated" (4.1.202–203).

Jealous Iago

When Othello swears to take vengeance on Cassio, he makes a vow that has a ritualistic flavour to it. He speaks in terms of oceans and the heavens, while Iago calls on the stars to witness his commitment to serving his master. »

> O, I ha' lost my reputation,
> I ha' lost the immortal part
> of myself, and what remains
> is bestial!
> **Cassio**
> Act 2, Scene 3

Ira Aldridge

In 1825, American actor Ira Aldridge became the first black person to play Othello on a London stage. Born in New York in 1807, Aldridge moved to Europe when he found acting opportunities hard to come by in his native country. He was just 18 years old when he first took the role of the Moor. Aldridge received favourable reviews for his performance, although the praise was tinged with racist assumptions. One critic wrote that he "delivers the most difficult passages with a degree of correctness that surprises the beholder", suggesting that the critic had been sceptical of a black actor's ability to perform such a feat.

Aldridge went on to play the title roles of *King Lear* and *Richard III* in a long career on the European stage. In an inversion of the usual practice with Othello, Aldridge would sometimes take on roles as white men, using make-up to "white up". Although he never returned to the US, Aldridge was seen as an inspirational figure among black American actors. He died in 1867 while on tour in Poland.

Set in a modern army, the award-winning 2013 National Theatre production in London imagined Iago (Rory Kinnear) and Othello (Adrian Lester) as long-time comrades.

A husband's jealousy

Strip away the Venetian court, the social hierarchy, and the military setting, and at the heart of this play is a story about a husband and wife separated by a malicious conman. With its grand opening scenes in the political world of law and warfare, the play's domestic focus may seem strikingly incongruous. Shakespeare narrows his focus gradually through the action so that the final scene takes place in a bedchamber. That the Venetian army, politicians, and lords spill into this same room reminds the audience how vulnerable the private life of a public figure like Othello truly is. To acknowledge that this tragedy is triggered by jealousy is to admit something fundamentally insecure about human trust and, most disturbingly, about love.

Where does this jealousy come from? After hearing her defence, Brabanzio disowns Desdemona and warns Othello that, having deceived her own father, she is likely also to be false to her husband. The seeds of suspicion are sown in Othello's imagination from the first act of the play. However, it is really Iago who baits and encourages Othello's mistrust of Desdemona. Iago's four most powerful words are "look to your wife" (3.3.201).

Jealousy and envy eat away at the core of this play. Brabanzio, Cassio, and Roderigo all experience some kind of envy that reflects and orbits the central jealousy between Iago and Othello. The image of a bright-eyed monster feeding and slowly growing fat is sickly and

The nature of this exchange, and the fact that Othello calls it a "sacred vow" (3.3.463), has led critics to characterize it as a sinister echo of the wedding ceremony between Othello and Desdemona, which the audience is not invited to see. As well as making Iago his accomplice in Cassio's murder, Othello promotes him to the position of lieutenant. Now Iago has replaced Desdemona, figuratively, and Cassio, literally, in Othello's life.

In spite of Iago's villainy, the character receives as much attention as Othello. Historically, actors have competed for audience acclaim when performing these roles. Othello's dependence on and vulnerability to Iago's deceit, coupled with Iago's ambiguous motivation and manipulative skill, make them a dynamic and even disturbing couple, who drag one another down into a pit of psychological horror because neither one can control his jealousy. From the 18th century on, leading actors performing the play began to double up and alternate the roles of Othello and Iago. In a famous example from the Victorian era, English actor Henry Irving and American actor Edwin Booth alternated roles in a production at the Lyceum Theatre in London.

> This fellow's of exceeding honesty, And knows all qualities with a learned spirit...
>
> **Othello**
> Act 3, Scene 3

disturbing. The monster is a demonic entity that possesses its host and takes over its life. Iago plants a small suspicion in his general's mind, feeding it slowly until Othello is physically incapacitated by an obsession with his wife's infidelity. Throughout the play, jealousy is described as wicked, a plague, and as something damned.

Othello's fervid imagination is tainted by carnal images, which manifest themselves in his use of bodily rhetoric. He speaks of Desdemona's flesh rotting and perishing, of other men "tast[ing] her sweet body" (3.3.351), and of Cassio stealing her lips so that she is "stolen". Othello accuses Desdemona of being a strumpet and whore. This preoccupation with carnal imagery culminates in an analogy in which he compares his wife's genitals to the gates of hell.

Many Shakespearean tragedies revolve around a character's central and unfixable flaw. In this case, the tragedy comes from green-eyed jealousy that was born, nursed, and nurtured in Othello's own imagination. The jealous "nature" that he argues was inherited from his Moorish ancestors becomes, by this logic, Othello's tragic flaw. The evil seeds that Iago sows thrive so virulently in Othello's mind and body that in the end there is nowhere else for them to grow but to reach out and destroy Desdemona.

This very specific tragic flaw has not always been considered a satisfying topic for a great tragedy. In the early 20th century, the British Shakespeare scholar A C Bradley complained that the tragic aspects of the play were

The American actor and singer Paul Robeson played Othello on the London stage in 1930, opposite Peggy Ashcroft as Desdemona. At the time, it was still rare for black actors to play the role.

overshadowed by its subject matter: a man who is sexually jealous of his wife. This, in Bradley's view, was something profoundly objectionable and morally repulsive. »

Portraying Othello

Critics have famously disagreed in their responses to the character of Othello. In 1937, the critic F R Leavis argued that the character is inherently savage, and only barely manages to cover his uncivilized nature until he gives in to instinct. On the other hand, romanticized readings of Othello characterize him as an honourable man rather than an unprincipled savage. In the 1870s and 80s, the Italian actor Tommaso Salvini interpreted the Moor as a hot-blooded and passionate but noble hero. He performed Othello's suicide by slitting his throat and dying with fierce bodily convulsions. Salvini performed the part in Italian, even on occasions when the rest of the cast spoke English, which led to him being known as the Italian Moor.

Prior to the late 20th century, Othello was played by white actors such as Orson Welles (pictured) wearing dark make-up, a practice now obsolete. An exception was in a racially inverted production in 1997 in Washington DC, when Patrick Stewart played a white Othello in a black nation.

Faithful wives

Both Emilia and Desdemona are depicted as women who loyally follow and obey their husbands. Desdemona's loyalty to Othello is clear in her submissiveness to his will. She follows him to Cyprus, tends to him when he appears to be ill, apologizes for being the object of his scorn even after he strikes her in public, and finally dies when he wishes her to. In a similar fashion, Emilia obeys Iago's will when she steals Desdemona's handkerchief at his bidding.

The difference between the women becomes apparent at the play's close when Desdemona refuses to name her murderer, and Emilia denounces Iago. But the result is the same – they are both murdered by their husbands and their faithfulness goes unrewarded. Desdemona's helplessness in the face of Othello's accusations and Iago's manipulation is counteracted by Emilia, whose love for her companion emboldens her to speak out against Othello and to accuse her husband of villainy even when Iago holds a dagger to her throat. It is Emilia who travels with Desdemona, comforts and supports her when she is abandoned by her father and, later, her husband. Emilia also encourages Desdemona to consider herself an equal to Othello. She asks "have not we affections, / Desires for sport, and frailty, as men have?" (4.3.99–100). In contrast to her husband's relationship with Othello, Emilia is fiercely loyal to Desdemona, and her dying words are spent in defence of her companion.

French tenor Roberto Alagna and Albanian soprano Inva Mula took the roles of Otello and Desdemona in a 2008 production of Verdi's *Otello*. The villain Iago is cast in a lower, baritone voice.

> Yet she must die, else she'll betray more men.
> **Othello**
> Act 5, Scene 2

While the women display loyalty to their men, the men themselves are far more concerned with appearances, which are a major driver in their actions. Cassio and Othello are both preoccupied with their reputations. Cassio's name is tainted by his late-night brawl with Roderigo, for which he is dismissed from his service under Othello. Cassio's lament for his reputation early in the play's action foreshadows Othello's far more sinister concern over his honour.

While the military men grow fearful over their honour, the women suffer attacks on their sexual reputations. Iago's accusations against Desdemona are sufficient to cast her entire character into doubt. This is echoed in Cassio's comments to Bianca. He calls her a "bauble", implying that her moral laxity makes her unworthy to be his bride.

Damnation

What does it mean to be damned? And what constitutes a damnable sin? These are questions that Shakespeare has his characters struggle with throughout the action of the play.

Othello frequently uses the word "damn" in reference to Desdemona, and even tells her that she is "double-damned" (4.2.38) by her deceit. Damnation is associated with hellfire and eternal punishment, which is suited to the Catholic characters of the play. Because of the dishonour and sinfulness of Desdemona's alleged infidelity, Othello considers it his duty to murder her "else she'll betray more men" (5.2.6). Her infidelity is what he calls "the cause" that spurs him on to seek her death.

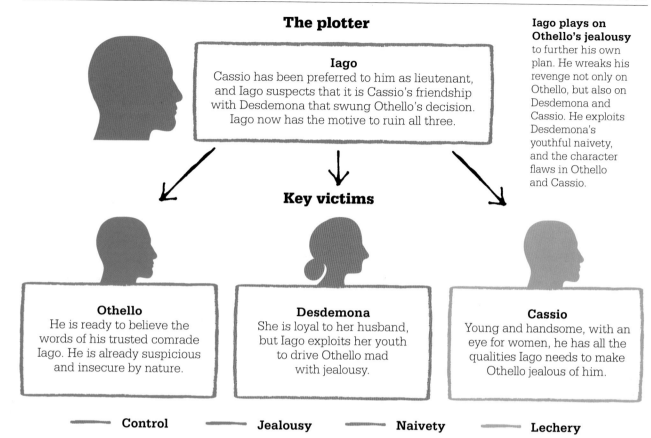

The plotter

Iago
Cassio has been preferred to him as lieutenant, and Iago suspects that it is Cassio's friendship with Desdemona that swung Othello's decision. Iago now has the motive to ruin all three.

Iago plays on Othello's jealousy to further his own plan. He wreaks his revenge not only on Othello, but also on Desdemona and Cassio. He exploits Desdemona's youthful naivety, and the character flaws in Othello and Cassio.

Key victims

Othello
He is ready to believe the words of his trusted comrade Iago. He is already suspicious and insecure by nature.

Desdemona
She is loyal to her husband, but Iago exploits her youth to drive Othello mad with jealousy.

Cassio
Young and handsome, with an eye for women, he has all the qualities Iago needs to make Othello jealous of him.

—— **Control** —— **Jealousy** —— **Naivety** —— **Lechery**

He requests that she pray so that he can preserve her immortal soul despite killing her body. This suggests that the murder is, in Othello's mind at least, an honour killing rather than a vengeful killing.

Honour is a word that creeps into the world of the characters. How can Othello be honourable if he is also a murderer? When the truth is eventually known to Othello, he calls for his own damnation, claiming that Desdemona is a "heavenly sight" while he is a "cursèd, cursèd slave" (5.2.283). The question on everyone's lips at the close of the play relates to Iago. What will happen to him now? Othello accuses him of being a "demi-devil" (5.2.307) and Lodovico calls him a

Villainy, villainy, villainy!
I think upon't, I think. I smell't.
O villainy!
Emilia
Act 5, Scene 2

"hellish villain" (5.2.378). Iago might have survived this tragedy, but his torment will begin now, first through earthly torture and then in everlasting hellfire. Survival may be his punishment.

The handkerchief
Othello's handkerchief, which is embroidered with strawberries, is a key instrument of his marital downfall. By attaching emotional significance to this small object, Othello makes himself vulnerable to Iago's scheming, and readily accepts the theory that Desdemona handed over this treasured gift to her "lover". The fact that Desdemona lies about misplacing it affirms her husband's suspicions about her infidelity.

This tiny prop comes to represent the tension and mistrust in Othello and Desdemona's marriage. So weighted is this object that, in 1693, the historian Thomas Rymer argued that the play ought to be called "The Tragedy of the Handkerchief". ∎

A MAN MORE SINNED AGAINST THAN SINNING

KING LEAR (1605–1606)

DRAMATIS PERSONAE

King Lear King of Britain.

Goneril Lear's eldest daughter, married to Albany, but becomes adulterously involved with Edmond.

Duke of Albany Goneril's husband.

Regan Lear's middle daughter, married to Cornwall, later pursues Edmond as her second husband.

Duke of Cornwall Regan's husband.

Cordelia Lear's youngest daughter, later becomes the Queen of France.

Duke of Burgundy Cordelia's first suitor.

King of France Cordelia's second suitor.

The Fool Lear's court jester, very close to Cordelia, whose absence he mourns.

Earl of Kent One of Lear's most loyal followers. Later disguises himself as a bluff servant called Caius.

Earl of Gloucester Another loyal follower of Lear, father to Edgar and Edmond.

Edmond The illegitimate son of Gloucester.

Edgar The eldest son and legitimate heir of Gloucester, later disinherited. Adopts a succession of disguises, including that of the mad beggar, Tom o' Bedlam.

Oswald Goneril's servant.

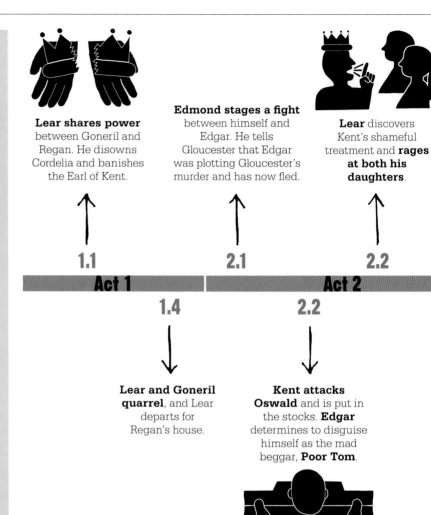

Lear shares power between Goneril and Regan. He disowns Cordelia and banishes the Earl of Kent.

Edmond stages a fight between himself and Edgar. He tells Gloucester that Edgar was plotting Gloucester's murder and has now fled.

Lear discovers Kent's shameful treatment and **rages at both his daughters**.

1.1

Act 1

2.1

2.2

Act 2

1.4

2.2

Lear and Goneril quarrel, and Lear departs for Regan's house.

Kent attacks Oswald and is put in the stocks. **Edgar** determines to disguise himself as the mad beggar, **Poor Tom**.

King Lear renounces his throne and divides the kingdom among his three daughters. He asks each to profess her love for him, so that he may decide who will gain the larger share. Goneril and Regan play along, but Cordelia refuses to flatter. She is banished, along with the Earl of Kent. The King of France offers marriage to Cordelia, and they depart for France. Kent adopts the disguise of the servant Caius.

Shortly after Cordelia's banishment, the Earl of Gloucester is estranged from his elder son,

Edgar. In a plot contrived by the illegitimate Edmond to steal his brother Edgar's inheritance, Gloucester is tricked into thinking that Edgar seeks to kill him and seize his land. Edgar is pursued by the law, but disguises himself as the beggar Poor Tom.

Lear takes up residence at the court of his eldest daughter, Goneril, and her husband, Albany, but she accuses her father of rowdy behaviour. Lear curses her with barrenness and leaves for Regan's house, only to find that she and her husband, Cornwall, are away from

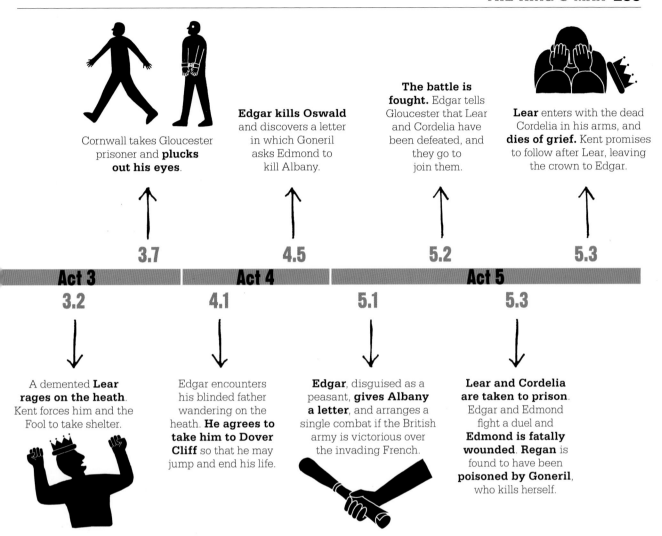

Cornwall takes Gloucester prisoner and **plucks out his eyes**.

3.7

Edgar kills Oswald and discovers a letter in which Goneril asks Edmond to kill Albany.

4.5

The battle is fought. Edgar tells Gloucester that Lear and Cordelia have been defeated, and they go to join them.

5.2

Lear enters with the dead Cordelia in his arms, and **dies of grief.** Kent promises to follow after Lear, leaving the crown to Edgar.

5.3

Act 3 | **Act 4** | **Act 5**

3.2

A demented **Lear rages on the heath**. Kent forces him and the Fool to take shelter.

4.1

Edgar encounters his blinded father wandering on the heath. **He agrees to take him to Dover Cliff** so that he may jump and end his life.

5.1

Edgar, disguised as a peasant, **gives Albany a letter**, and arranges a single combat if the British army is victorious over the invading French.

5.3

Lear and Cordelia are taken to prison. Edgar and Edmond fight a duel and **Edmond is fatally wounded. Regan** is found to have been **poisoned by Goneril**, who kills herself.

home, and that they have put Kent in the stocks. After a furious confrontation with both daughters, Lear rushes into a thunderstorm. Deranged with fury and grief, he and his Fool befriend Poor Tom.

Goneril and Regan plot to have their father killed, but Gloucester has the king secretly conveyed to safety at Dover, in the knowledge that Cordelia is returning with a French army to avenge her father. When Gloucester's actions are discovered, he has both his eyes plucked out by Cornwall (who is fatally wounded by his own

servant). Edgar leads the blinded Gloucester to what he pretents to be the edge of Dover Cliff so that he may end his life. When Gloucester falls forward onto level ground, Edgar convinces him that he has miraculously survived the jump.

Cordelia takes Lear into her protection. A battle ensues. Lear and Cordelia are defeated and imprisoned. Disguised as a knight, Edgar challenges Edmond to single combat. When Edmond is fatally wounded, Edgar reveals his identity. The jealousy between Goneril and Regan over Edmond

erupts into murder and suicide – Goneril poisons her sister, and then stabs herself. Edmond urges Albany to rescue Lear and Cordelia, but it is too late. Lear enters, carrying the dead Cordelia in his arms. Broken with grief, the King slips back into madness, failing to recognize Kent when he finally reveals his true identity. Just at the moment when Lear thinks that Cordelia might still be alive, he dies. Albany offers to divide the kingdom between Kent and Edgar, but Kent says that he will follow his master, leaving the crown to Edgar. »

IN CONTEXT

THEMES
Love, betrayal, bereavement and death

SETTING
Ancient Britain, approximately 800 BCE

SOURCES
12th century Geoffrey of Monmouth's *Historia Regum Britanniae* (*History of British Kings*).

1587 Raphael Holinshed's *Chronicles of England, Scotland, and Ireland.*

LEGACY
1681 Nahum Tate's *The History of King Lear ... Reviv'd with Alterations* adapts the play so that Cordelia survives and is betrothed to Edgar.

1851 In his novel *Moby Dick*, Herman Melville's Captain Ahab rages in the storm, a scene inspired by *King Lear.*

1957 The ballet *The Prince of the Pagodas* by choreographer John Cranko, with music by Benjamin Britten, borrows plot elements from *King Lear.*

1985 The film *Ran*, by director Akira Kurosawa, turns Lear into a samurai warlord.

1987 *Lear's Daughters*, a play by Elaine Feinstein, is a prequel to *King Lear.*

1991 Jane Smiley's novel *A Thousand Acres* moves the play's action to a farm in Iowa. The story is told from the perspective of Ginny (Goneril).

While *King Lear* is often considered the height of Shakespeare's achievement in tragedy, it also undermines many of the assumptions upon which his other tragedies were built. It lays waste to our ideals, producing a vision of nihilistic despair not unlike the plays of 20th-century Irish playwright Samuel Beckett. In this way, *King Lear* is both ancient (it is set in 800 BCE) and remarkably modern.

From the start, Shakespeare conceived of Lear in a mould that is significantly different from his other tragic heroes. Where the sources give the King's age as in his sixties, Shakespeare emphasizes Lear's decrepitude, insisting that he is more than 80 years of age and ready to "crawl toward death" (1.1.41). Modern productions often cast a significantly younger actor in the role. In 2014, a 53-year-old Simon Russell Beale played Lear

as a dangerously volatile figure, tyrannizing his daughters in the initial love test, and later stabbing the Fool to death in a frenzied attack. But neither in this production nor in the play as written is there any sense of how Lear's physical strength or rhetorical power might ever have served his subjects' interests, or indeed how he might once have inspired admiration and love. Goneril and Regan suggest that his lack of judgment in banishing Cordelia is not a single tragic error, associated with "the infirmity of his age", but a personality trait: "he hath ever but slenderly known himself" (1.1.292–293). Without any sense of Lear's former greatness, his descent into madness loses something of the grandeur and

Lear divides his kingdom between his three daughters. In this production at the Bad Hersfeld Festival, Germany (2012), Volker Lechtenbrink plays Lear and Kristin Hoelck is Cordelia.

> Meantime we shall express
> our darker purpose.
> Give me the map there.
> Know that we have divided
> In three our kingdom
> **King Lear**
> **Act 1, Scene 1**

sense of waste that it might have possessed in another Shakespearean tragedy.

Lear as tragic hero

Lear's description of himself as "a man / More sinned against than sinning" (3.2.59–60) hints at his passivity in the play. By comparison with Edmond, who plots his father's death and orders the deaths of Lear and Cordelia, Goneril, who will use her lover to kill her husband and who poisons her sister, and Cornwall, who plucks out Gloucester's eyes, Lear's acts of banishment (though they constitute a kind of social death) will come to seem relatively mild. Throughout acts three and four, when Hamlet or Macbeth are acting furiously to bring about their own destruction, Lear exists on the margins of the plot, in the liminal space of the heath. In his mental confusion, he identifies the behaviour of a mad beggar as the pattern for his own paternal betrayal, and muses on the dangers of female sexuality and the hypocrisy of the powerful. In this respect, *King Lear* is a remarkably philosophical tragedy, in which the plot pauses whenever it encounters the protagonist. Nothing that Lear does after the opening scene has any real impact on the action.

Sins of the father

So what "sins" might Lear be blamed for in that opening scene? For Shakespeare's audience, his act of "unburdening" himself by giving up his throne would have been deeply suspect. In a society with no expectation of retirement, the voluntary renunciation of power would have seemed to undermine the respect for age and male authority that was so deeply embedded in the culture. Kingship was also believed to be divinely appointed – hence it was an act of sacrilege to attempt to sever king from crown. Also potentially damaging is Lear's decision to divide the kingdom. Myths abounded about the catastrophic consequences of such division, leading to bloody civil war and fratricide, and Shakespeare was writing during the reign of James I, a king seeking to strengthen ties between his two hostile kingdoms, England and Scotland.

Ultimately, however, it is Lear's disavowal of Cordelia that brings the King to his knees. Lear estranges himself from the one »

> O madam, my old heart is
> cracked, it's cracked.
> **Gloucester**
> **Act 2, Scene 1**

Paul Scofield

In a 2004 poll of RSC actors, Paul Scofield's Lear was voted the greatest Shakespearean performance of all time. Then aged 40, Scofield appeared in Peter Brook's 1962 staging of *King Lear*. Critic Kenneth Tynan described Brook's production as revolutionary in its depiction of Lear not as "the booming, righteously indignant Titan of old, but an edgy, capricious old man, intensely difficult to live with". Scofield's Lear was a very human depiction of the king, for whom our pity is not automatically to be granted.

In 1971, Scofield played Lear in Brook's film adaptation of the play, and in 2002, having himself reached the age of 80, he starred in an acclaimed radio version.

Lear was one of many Shakespearean roles that Scofield took on in a career that spanned 65 years. He appeared infrequently on screen, despite many approaches from Hollywood, preferring the relative anonymity of the stage and radio, but won an Academy Award for his portrayal of Sir Thomas More in the 1966 film *A Man for All Seasons*.

Lear is accompanied by his Fool during the storm, illustrated here by Scottish artist William Dyce (1806–64). The Fool is the only character allowed to speak the truth to the king.

daughter whose love and reverence will be unaffected by his loss of status, unlike Goneril and Regan whose respect for their father exists only while he has power. If the kingdom had been divided in three, Cordelia might have served as a buffer between her two elder and ambitious sisters. Furthermore, banishment results in her becoming Queen of France, which leads her to seek to depose the rightful rulers of Britain with French troops. Though Shakespeare makes clear that her motive is "love, dear love, and our aged father's right" (4.3.28) rather than ambition, the fact remains that Lear has made his kingdom vulnerable.

It can certainly be argued that Lear's actions in the first scene set a destructive precedent. By failing to value the genuine love of Cordelia over the insincere flattery of her sisters, Lear encourages a character like Edmond to pursue his inheritance by faking filial love, and by slandering his brother. As though Lear's blindness were

Blow, winds, and crack your cheeks! Rage, blow, You cataracts and hurricanoes,
King Lear
Act 3, Scene 2

infectious, Gloucester fails to see through the deception and fatally places his trust in the wrong son. But in a larger sense, the tragedy sees suffering as something that exists outside any simple process of cause and effect, and as a fundamental part of the human condition. To be "a man / More sinned against than sinning" is not some kind of cosmic injustice, but the norm.

The basest beggar

Where *Hamlet* only pretends to consider "What a piece of work is a man", *King Lear* offers a profound meditation on this subject, and its conclusions are as melancholy as Hamlet might have wished them. Blinded Gloucester describes the mad Lear as a "ruined piece of nature", and when he tries to kiss Lear's hand, the King advises: "Here, wipe it first; it smells of mortality" (4.5.128–130). The play relentlessly confronts man's physical needs. Lear's madness coincides with the assault upon his body of extreme cold, wind, and rain. It is no coincidence that his wits are only restored once he has been brought into shelter, given fresh clothes, and allowed to sleep. Earlier on in the play, Lear had appeared to glimpse the troubling physical similarities that define all men, if they are deprived of the external trappings of class and wealth. When his daughters try to take away his knightly retinue, he counters: "O, reason not the need! Our basest beggars / Are in the poorest thing superfluous. / Allow not nature more than nature needs, / Man's life is cheap as beast's." (2.2.438–441).

But King Lear at this point has no idea what the life of the basest beggar might be, and it is with a kind of redemptive sadism that

> Unaccommodated man is no
> more but such a poor, bare,
> forked animal as thou art.
> **King Lear**
> Act 3, Scene 4

Shakespeare casts him out into
the wilderness to encounter one.
Poor Tom represents a misery
that Lear has never imagined – a
vagrant, tormented by demonic
voices, clothed only in a blanket,
and drinking from puddles mixed
with horse urine. Lear's response,
which is to take off his own clothes,
signifies his final descent into
madness. He now conspires in
the destruction of his familial and
social identity. But there is also a

sense of fellowship in the discovery
that in his nakedness he is no more
than "such a poor, bare, forked
animal, as thou art" (3.4.101–102).
In this respect, *King Lear* has
often been seen as a socialist
play, in that it forces the king to
acknowledge his similarity to the
lowest social class (even though
Edgar is actually an earl's son) and,
more importantly, to acknowledge
his own responsibility for Poor
Tom's condition: "O, I have ta'en /
Too little care of this" (3.4.32–33). In
a radical challenge to contemporary
politics, the play features both a
king and an earl calling for a
redistribution of wealth, "So
distribution should undo excess, /
And each man have enough"
(4.1.64–65).

More's the pity
If the play is initially driven by
the need to strip man down to
his bare essentials, as anticipated
by Cordelia's destructive use of
the term "Nothing", it then begins
to move towards the "something"

> I have no way, and therefore
> want no eyes.
> I stumbled when I saw
> **Earl of Gloucester**
> Act 4, Scene 1

upon which humanity is founded.
This "something" is the capacity to
feel pity. The play's most virtuous
characters, Edgar and Cordelia,
repeatedly tell us of their emotional
reaction to other people's suffering.
Edgar wonders at both Gloucester
and Lear: "O thou side-piercing
sight" (4.5.85); "my heart breaks at
it" (138); while Cordelia repeatedly
voices her pity for the father who
wronged her. Both characters
also attest to the efficacy of pity,
with Edgar being driven to rescue
his father from despair, and
Cordelia using her tears to gain
an army, before using the same
restorative drops to bring Lear
back to his senses.

By contrast, evil is defined
in the play as the absence of
pity, which leads in turn to an
absence of pitiful action. Goneril
and Regan allow Lear to wander
on the heath in a thunderstorm,
drawing forth language that
defines pity as that which
separates man from beast.
Thus, Cordelia observes, "Mine »

The blind Gloucester (right, Geoffrey
Freshwater) meets with the now-mad
Lear (left, Greg Hicks). Without his
sight, Gloucester finally realizes his
previous blindness towards Edmond.

enemy's dog, though he had bit me, should have stood / That night against my fire" (4.6.30–31).

That the play has limits to its own capacity for pity, however, is something critics have recently pointed out with regard to the treatment of Goneril and Regan. But perhaps the most violent reaction against the play has focused on the way in which its supposedly redemptive experience of suffering, and the value it places on pity, comes to nothing.

When Shakespeare's audience went to see *King Lear*, they were expecting, at worst, to endure the grief of his daughters' ingratitude and the physical deprivations of his homelessness. Gloucester's blinding was an added turn of the screw, derived from Sir Philip Sidney's prose romance, *The Countess of Pembroke's Arcadia* (1593). However, in all the other versions of the Lear story, including an earlier play *The True Chronicle Historie of King Leir* (*c.*1594), in which Shakespeare may even have

acted, good triumphs over evil in the final battle and Lear is restored to his throne. He dies of old age and is succeeded by Cordelia. Audience reactions must certainly have echoed Kent's sentiments "Is this the promised end?" (5.3.238), when not only do Lear and Cordelia lose the battle, but Cordelia is murdered, causing her father to die of grief.

A problematic end?

Subsequent critics, including Samuel Johnson, put on record their dismay with the play's ending. The 17th-century Poet Laureate Nahum Tate felt compelled to draft a new ending in which Cordelia survives. In Tate's version, a love story develops between Cordelia and Edgar, to whom she is betrothed at the end. It was this version of the tragedy that would be performed for nearly 150 years, to the detriment of Shakespeare's original version.

Tate was partly responding to the fact that much of the structure of *King Lear* is comic.

Howl, howl, howl, howl!
O, you are men of stones.
King Lear
Act 5, Scene 3

The double plot is a feature of comedy, usually allowing a broader perspective and the exploration of alternative themes – though the similarity of Gloucester's plight to that of Lear only serves to render the play more claustrophobic. The combat between the older and the younger generation, with the latter attempting to free itself from parental oppression particularly in matters of the heart, is also the stuff of comedy. The movement of exiled characters into a green

Lear's tangled web

In Jean-François Sivadier's 2007 production, the play was translated into tough, contemporary French. A physical production, its action was as uncompromising as its language.

world where they discover a truer relationship to nature and to their own humanity, before returning to civilization, is also a staple of the pastoral genre. Even the Fool naturally belongs in a play like *As You Like It* rather than a tragedy.

Agony of grief

But these romantic, comic expectations endure only to be smashed to pieces. When Lear enters, carrying dead Cordelia, some fantasy about how the world works is finally destroyed. It is not just the futility of it – after all their suffering, Lear and Gloucester cannot make use of anything they have learned, and are denied the chance to make amends to their children – it is rather that the play confronts the unavoidable destiny of bereavement and death, with no offer of consolation.

At the end of a Shakespearean tragedy, the hero's demise is usually carefully stage-managed, offering

him artistic control so that he may leave a final impression of greatness, but Lear dies in the middle of a thought – and not about himself but about Cordelia, whose death is so painful as to be incomprehensible: "Why should a dog, a horse, a rat have life, / And thou no breath at all? Thou'lt come no more. / Never, never, never, never, never." (5.3.282–284). Pity is revealed to be something that no one feels enough ("O, you are men of stones" (232)), and that

cannot rescue Lear from his agony of grief. No other play by Shakespeare offers such a bleak perspective on the tragic fact of human mortality.

Shakespeare's society was deeply Christian, with a system of religious practices a part of everyday life. Yet no one can comfort Lear, other than to will that he be spared further pain by not feeling. It is in this respect that *King Lear* remains perhaps Shakespeare's most devastating play. ∎

A feminist reading

In 1817, the English literary critic William Hazlitt argued that "that which aggravates the sense of sympathy in the reader, and of uncontrollable anguish in the swol'n heart of Lear, is the petrifying indifference, the cold, calculating, obdurate selfishness of his daughters." Since the late 20th century, however, feminist critics have taken issue with this reading, arguing that the childless Goneril at least has plenty of motivation to act as she does against her father. Lear's curse of sterility upon her in 1.4 has allowed actors to give greater

psychological depth to her character, and to make her an object of pity. Similarly, the incestuous intensity that defines Lear's possessiveness over Cordelia at the start of the play was a theme explored by the US writer Jane Smiley in her novel *A Thousand Acres* (1991). This retells the story from the perspective of Goneril. Ginny (Goneril) suffers flashbacks that reveal how her relationship with her father has been shaped by the sexual abuse she and her sister Rose (Regan) experienced from him in childhood.

THE MIDDLE OF HUMANITY THOU NEVER KNEW'ST, BUT THE EXTREMITY OF BOTH ENDS

TIMON OF ATHENS (1606)

DRAMATIS PERSONAE

Timon A prodigal Athenian lord who showers gifts upon his visitors. He falls into debt and discovers that no-one is prepared to help him. He leaves the city to live alone in the woods.

Apemantus A misanthropic philosopher with a talent for sarcasm. He warns Timon about the fickle flatterers feasting on his generosity.

Flavius Timon's faithful steward, who is troubled by his master's prodigality, and tries to warn him about his changing fortune.

Alcibiades An Athenian soldier who is banished from Athens. He plans his revenge and encounters Timon in the woods.

Phyrnia and Timandra Two prostitutes who accompany Alcibiades when he visits Timon in the woods. Timon offers them gold to spread sexual diseases.

Poet and Painter Two artists who visit Timon hoping to receive payment. They visit Timon in the woods when they hear that he has discovered gold.

An old Athenian He takes Timon's money after complaining that Timon's servant has been trying to seduce his daughter.

A fool He exchanges witticisms with servants.

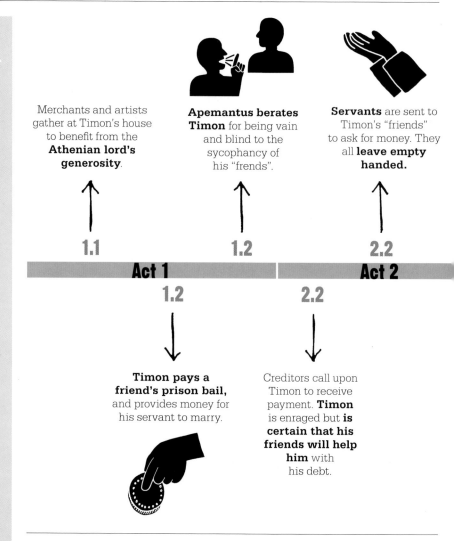

Merchants and artists gather at Timon's house to benefit from the **Athenian lord's generosity**.

Apemantus berates Timon for being vain and blind to the sycophancy of his "frends".

Servants are sent to Timon's "friends" to ask for money. They all **leave empty handed.**

1.1

Act 1

1.2

2.2

Act 2

1.2

2.2

Timon pays a friend's prison bail, and provides money for his servant to marry.

Creditors call upon Timon to receive payment. **Timon is enraged but is certain that his friends will help him** with his debt.

Artists and merchants gather at Timon's home to present him with gifts and seek his patronage. Timon is well known for his extravagant generosity. A poet at the gathering has written a fable in which a patron like Timon falls from fortune to find himself destitute. Timon receives the poet's work gladly, and pays bail to release one of his friends from prison, but will not accept any favours in return.

The satirist Apemantus tries to warn Timon that his "friends" are simply feeding off his generosity.

Flavius, a servant, reveals privately that Timon's wealth has been spent, and that he is running further into debt. Timon remains unperturbed, believing that his friends will come to his financial aid. However, when three of his "friends" are asked to lend money, they all refuse, making elaborate excuses to justify their lack of kindness. Hearing this news, Timon flies into a rage and decides to treat them to a feast. Believing Timon to be wealthy again, his friends are shocked when he serves them stones and warm

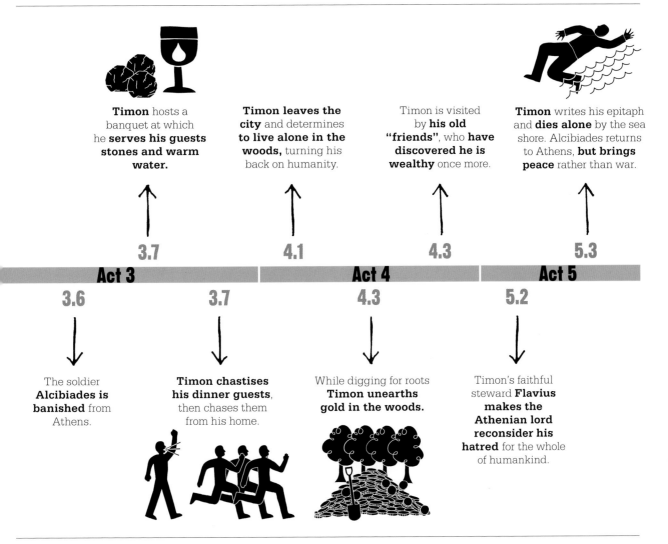

Timon hosts a banquet at which he **serves his guests stones and warm water.**

3.7

Timon leaves the city and determines **to live alone in the woods,** turning his back on humanity.

4.1

Timon is visited by **his old "friends"**, who **have discovered he is wealthy** once more.

4.3

Timon writes his epitaph and **dies alone** by the sea shore. Alcibiades returns to Athens, **but brings peace** rather than war.

5.3

Act 3   Act 4   Act 5

3.6

The soldier **Alcibiades is banished** from Athens.

3.7

Timon chastises his dinner guests, then chases them from his home.

4.3

While digging for roots **Timon unearths gold in the woods.**

5.2

Timon's faithful steward **Flavius makes the Athenian lord reconsider his hatred** for the whole of humankind.

---

water and forces them from his home, berating them for their falsity.

Timon leaves Athens for the woods and prays for the city's destruction. A vengeful soldier called Alcibiades enters the woods at the same time, intent upon destroying the city. He has been banished for attempting to save the life of a soldier who has been sentenced to death. When Timon reaches the woods, he digs for roots, but discovers gold, and news soon spreads to Athens that he is rich once again. Hating humankind

for the ingratitude he has been shown, Timon rails at his former friends, who now come to seek him (and his gold) in the woods. Timon provides the soldier Alcibiades with money to finance his attack on Athens, and gives money to whores to spread disease among citizens. Both Apemantus and Flavius visit Timon, and the Athenian lord reluctantly acknowledges Flavius's goodness, despite his hatred of humankind. He writes his epitaph and dies by the sea, as Alcibiades enters Athens, spares the city, and promises peace. »

That what he speaks is all in debt, he owes For every word.
Flavius
Act 1, Scene 2

IN CONTEXT

THEMES
Love, pride, wealth, vanity, hate, revenge, misanthropy

SETTING
Athens and woods outside the city

SOURCES
c.100 CE Plutarch's *Lives of the Noble Grecians and Romans.*

1566 William Painter's *Palace of Pleasure.*

1602 An anonymous play called *Timon.*

LEGACY
1678 English poet Thomas Shadwell creates an adaptation of Shakespeare's play titled *The History of Timon of Athens, the Manhater.*

1844 Karl Marx quotes the play in *Political Economy and Philosophy.* He is drawn to Shakespeare's description of gold as a "yellow slave".

1963 Duke Ellington composes a jazz score for Michael Langham's production at Stratford, Ontario, Canada.

1973 Peter Brook stages the play in French at the Bouffes du Nord Theatre in Paris.

1991 In a modern-dress production at the Young Vic, London, David Suchet's Timon hands out car keys to his guests as gifts.

2004 Oxford University Press publishes an edition of the play recognizing Shakespeare's collaboration with Thomas Middleton on this work.

imon is perhaps Shakespeare's most extreme characterization. He swings from being a lover of humankind to hating all of humanity. Timon's companion, the satirist Apemantus, finds it remarkably straightforward to sum up the Athenian lord's experience of life: "The middle of humanity thou never knewest, but the extremity of both ends" (4.3.302–303). Apemantus witnesses Timon's transformation from philanthropist to misanthropist, and provides a satirical commentary on the transition. At first, Apemantus watches as Timon showers the visitors to his home with lavish gifts and banquets, but then sees him hurling stones and gold at the people he had once held so dear.

In choosing to dramatize a life story that had previously been alluded to in the works of Plato, Aristophanes, Lucian, and Plutarch, Shakespeare created a play that focused upon man's relationship with "Yellow, glittering, precious gold" (4.3.26). As a generous gift-giver, Timon is never short of "friends" – "Methinks I could deal kingdoms to my friends, / And ne'er

Th'unkindest beast more kinder than mankind.
Timon
Act 4, Scene 1

be weary" (1.2.220–221). But once Timon's debts are revealed, none of his friends is prepared to show him the same generosity of spirit.

Blindness and vanity
Timon's story is not simply a tale of riches to rags. It is true to say that the play's structure is schematic, dividing into two contrasting parts, but Shakespeare's presentation of Timon himself is far from simplistic. The faithful steward Flavius reveals early in the play that Timon's coffers are already empty, and that he "owes" (1.2.198) for every word he speaks. Timon's extreme generosity

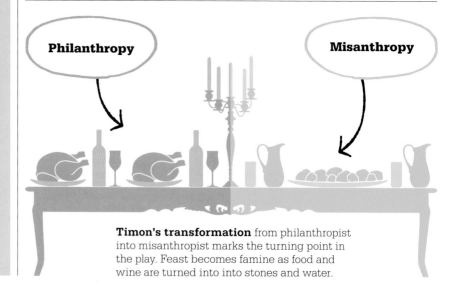

Timon's transformation from philanthropist into misanthropist marks the turning point in the play. Feast becomes famine as food and wine are turned into into stones and water.

is puzzling. On the one hand, he makes caring pronouncements, arguing that, "'Tis not enough to help the feeble up / But to support him after" (1.1.109–110). However, he also declares that "there's none / Can truly say he gives if he receives" (1.2.9–10). How can Timon's guests ever repay his generosity if he will not let them do so? Flavius suggests that Timon's "worst sin is he does too much good" (4.2.39), but Apemantus is keenly aware of the glass-faced flatterers who circle around Timon like vultures, and is frustrated by his blindness (and vanity): "It grieves me to see so many dip their meat in one man's blood; and all the madness is, he cheers them up, too" (1.2.39–41).

Retreat from humanity

Having learned that his "fortunes 'mong his friends can sink" (2.2.227), Timon turns his back on society and heads for the woods, where he concludes he will find "Th'unkindest beast more kinder than mankind" (4.1.36). Like King Lear, Timon discards his clothes, in an attempt to be free from the "disease" of false friendship and sugar-tongued sycophancy. Once outside the Athenian walls, Timon announces that he will bear nothing but nakedness from this detestable town. As a cursing misanthrope, Timon grows in lyrical prowess, spitting forth condemnatory verse, shaped to shock: "This yellow slave / Will knit and break religions, bless th'accursed, / Make the hoar leprosy adored, place thieves, / And give them title, knee, and approbation / With senators on the bench. This is it / That makes the wappered widow wed again. / She whom the spittle-house and ulcerous sores / Would cast the

gorge at, this embalms and spices / To th' April day again" (4.3.34–42).

Entrenched firmly at the other extreme of humanity, Timon's pronouncements are as savage and bilious as they had once been naive but well meaning. His hymns to hatred possess a strange music that is both hypnotic and somewhat overwhelming. Having looked to the gods and the mercenary soldier Alcibiades to wreak vengeance on Athens, Timon looks forward only to his own death: "My long sickness / Of health and living now begins to mend, / And nothing brings me all things" (5.2.71–73). Rather than remaining in a "dream of friendship", Timon prefers to rail through his "sickness". He dies at peace with himself, although still at war with humankind.

Few Shakespearean characters embody a nihilistic vision with the same commitment as Timon. This is one of Shakespeare's longest roles, and it provides actors with a challenge: to avoid presenting "the middle of humanity" and concentrate on capturing the "extremity of both ends" while retaining psychological realism for audiences. ∎

> Here lie I, Timon, who alive
> All living men did hate.
> Pass by and curse thy fill,
> but pass
> And stay not here thy gait.
> **Timon's epitaph**
> Act 5, Scene 5

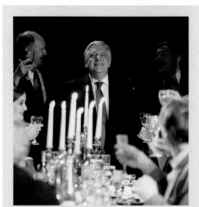

Timon the banker

A 2012 production at the National Theatre in London, set *Timon of Athens* in the financial district during the credit crunch. The action is imagined as a meltdown among the financial elite, played out to a backdrop of anti-capitalist protest. Timon's debts are a "liquidity crisis".

Timon, played by British actor Simon Russell Beale, is a vain philanthropist, who is fawned upon while his stock is high. He is a power player in a world where friendship is a commodity with a cash value. This production exemplified Karl Marx's characterization of the play as about the power of money. Timon's scorn is directed towards today's elite: "Your solemn masters are large-handed robbers and filch by law."

When Shakespeare wrote the play, England was going through a political crisis, and Guy Fawkes had recently been executed for his part in the Gunpowder Plot. In Hytner's production, protesters wear the Guy Fawkes masks popularized by the Internet-based Anonymous activist movement, and the play feels as relevant as ever.

BLOOD WILL HAVE BLOOD

MACBETH (1606)

DRAMATIS PERSONAE

Duncan King of Scotland. He is invited to Macbeth's castle and is murdered in his sleep.

Malcolm Duncan's son. He flees to England for fear of his life when his father is slain, but returns to defeat Macbeth, and to be crowned.

Macbeth A noble warrior and Thane of Glamis. He murders the king and begins a reign of terror. He is killed by Macduff as the witches prophesied.

Lady Macbeth Macbeth's wife. She encourages her husband to kill the king, but is later tormented by the part she played in his murder.

Banquo A close ally of Macbeth. He is murdered at Macbeth's command, but returns to haunt him.

Fleance Banquo's son, he flees from the hired murderers.

Macduff The Thane of Fife, and faithful supporter of King Duncan. He discovers the king's dead body, and incites rebellion against Macbeth.

Lady Macduff Macduff's wife. She is murdered, with her children, at Macbeth's order.

Witches Bearded hags who predict that Macbeth will become king. They also tell him the circumstances under which he will lose the crown and his life.

A Porter Keeper of the castle gate. A drunken, witty, cynic.

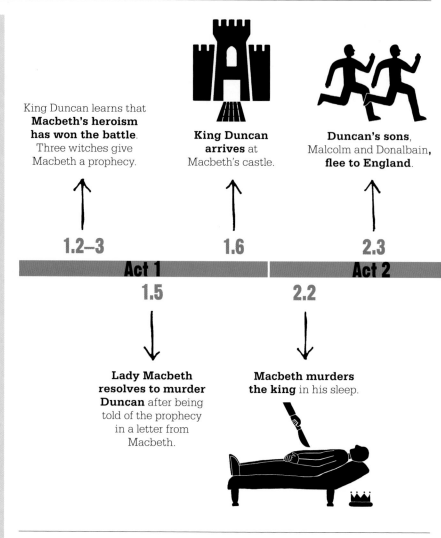

King Duncan learns that **Macbeth's heroism has won the battle**. Three witches give Macbeth a prophecy.

King Duncan arrives at Macbeth's castle.

Duncan's sons, Malcolm and Donalbain, **flee to England**.

1.2–3

1.6

2.3

Act 1

Act 2

1.5

2.2

Lady Macbeth resolves to murder Duncan after being told of the prophecy in a letter from Macbeth.

Macbeth murders the king in his sleep.

Three witches assemble on a heath for an encounter with Macbeth. Returning from victory on the battlefield Macbeth and Banquo meet these "weird sisters", who prophesy that Macbeth will become king and that Banquo's heirs will reign thereafter. Soon after, Macbeth receives word that he has been made Thane (clan chief) of Cawdor, which leads him to give credence to the witches' foresight. He shares his news with his wife, and she begins to plot to murder King Duncan so that Macbeth can become king.

News arrives that Duncan will visit the Macbeths' castle, and Lady Macbeth persuades her husband to kill him that night. She lays plans to drug the king's guards, so that Macbeth may slip into the king's chamber. As he makes his way there Macbeth sees a vision of a floating dagger signalling the way. Having murdered the king Macbeth returns to his wife with the bloody daggers still in his hands. Terrified that the murder has woken other sleepers Macbeth begins to panic until his wife calms him. As the couple leave to wash themselves

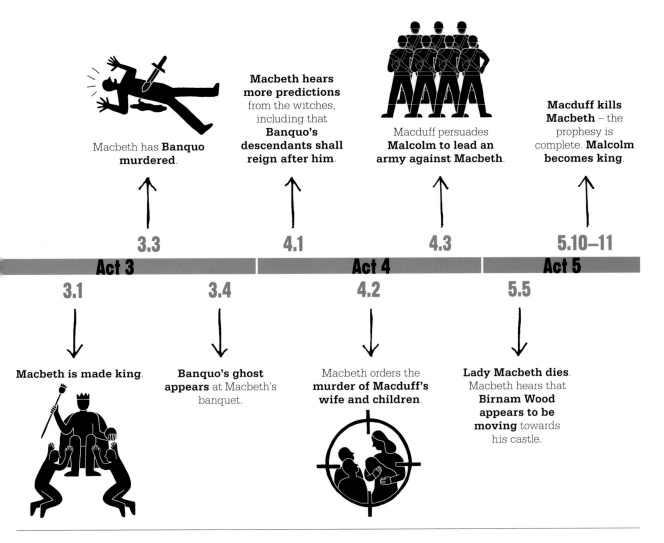

Macbeth has **Banquo murdered**.

Macbeth hears more predictions from the witches, including that **Banquo's descendants shall reign after him**.

Macduff persuades **Malcolm to lead an army against Macbeth**.

Macduff kills Macbeth – the prophesy is complete. **Malcolm becomes king**.

3.3

4.1

4.3

5.10–11

Act 3

Act 4

Act 5

3.1

3.4

4.2

5.5

Macbeth is made king.

Banquo's ghost appears at Macbeth's banquet.

Macbeth orders the **murder of Macduff's wife and children**.

Lady Macbeth dies. Macbeth hears that **Birnam Wood appears to be moving** towards his castle.

of the king's blood, a knocking is heard at the gate. The porter ushers in Macduff, who finds the king's body and raises the alarm. Macbeth murders the guards lest they wake. On hearing of their father's murder, the king's sons, Malcolm and Donalbain, leave for England.

Macbeth becomes king, though Banquo harbours secret fears that he murdered King Duncan. Fearing Banquo's suspicions, Macbeth arranges his murder, but Banquo's son Fleance escapes the killers. Macbeth is terrified when Banquo's ghost appears at a banquet he

holds that evening. Lady Macbeth tries to distract their dinner guests from her husband's strange behaviour, especially when he addresses an empty chair.

Macbeth returns to find the witches and is told that his throne is secure until Birnam Wood marches towards Dunsinane. He feels further reassured when told that he cannot be killed by anyone born of woman. On hearing that Macduff has travelled to England to persuade Malcolm to lead a rebel army, Macbeth orders the murder of Macduff's wife and children. This

terrible news reaches Macduff in England and strengthens his resolve to be revenged.

Lady Macbeth's guilt for Duncan's death leaks out when she is heard speaking of the murder in her sleep. While Macbeth believes that he can see a forest walking towards his castle, he hears that his wife has died. The moving wood is in fact an army carrying the branches of trees. In the battle that ensues, Macduff reveals that he was ripped from his mother's womb; the prophecy is complete, and Macbeth is killed. »

IN CONTEXT

THEMES
Ambition, kingship, fate, the supernatural, betrayal

SETTING
Scotland and England

SOURCES
1587 Raphael Holinshed's *Chronicles* describes the reigns of King Duncan and Macbeth and features a woodcut illustration of the weird sisters.

LEGACY
1664 William Davenant's adaptation of *Macbeth* includes flying witches.

1812 Famed Welsh actress Sarah Siddons performs Lady Macbeth for the last time.

1847 Giuseppe Verdi's opera *Macbeth* is first performed.

1913 Arthur Bourchier directs and stars in a German silent film version of the play.

1957 Akira Kurosawa's film *Throne of Blood*, transposes **Macbeth** to feudal Japan.

1967 The sci-fi TV series *Star Trek* uses *Macbeth* as material for two episodes.

1976 Ian McKellen and Judi Dench play the Macbeths at Stratford-upon-Avon.

2003 Vishal Bhardwaj directs *Maqbool* an Indian film adaptation of *Macbeth* set in the Mumbai underworld.

2004 The film *Harry Potter and The Prisoner of Azkaban* film features a chorus of the weird sisters' incantation.

The Macbeths risk everything to become king and queen of Scotland. In murdering King Duncan they are committing the greatest of sins: regicide. The couple are fully aware that their desire for the crown is criminal and diabolical, and yet they resolve upon this course of action that will bring calamity to them both. Like Richard III, the Macbeths discover to their despair that gaining the throne will not bring them contentment. Macbeth is convinced that he will only rest easy once he knows that he is safely in power: "To be thus is nothing / But to be safely thus" (3.1.49–50). To be "safely thus" would mean that there are no contenders for the throne left alive. The Macbeths find themselves trapped in a cycle of violence, haunted by their deed and the "horrible imaginings" (1.3.137) that ensue: "Blood will have blood" (3.4.121). The killing must continue.

Macbeth is literally and symbolically a dark play. About two-thirds of it takes place at night, lending the drama an eerie intensity. Ghosts walk at night; deadly deeds are committed under the cover of darkness; and night-time brings nightmares for those with a guilty conscience. The

So foul and fair a day
I have not seen.
Macbeth
Act 1, Scene 3

If it were done when 'tis done,
then 'twere well
It were done quickly.
Macbeth
Act 1, Scene 7

audience's relationship with Macbeth also darkens scene by scene as he falls from being a trusted warrior to becoming a Machiavellian murderer.

Traces of humanity are gradually stamped out as the drama progresses. Lady Macbeth calls upon "spirits / That tend on mortal thoughts" (1.5.39–40) to "unsex" her, filling her with "direst cruelty" (1.5.42). In order to fulfil her murderous ambition, she must in effect transform herself into a merciless monster. Shakespeare draws attention to her womanliness in order to emphasise her fierce rejection of her own femininity. Fearing that her husband is "too full o'th' milk of human kindness" (1.5.16), she encourages him to harden his heart and place ambition above consideration for others: "I have given suck, and know / How tender 'tis to love the babe that milks me. / I would, while it was smiling in my face, / Have plucked my nipple from his boneless gums / And dashed the brains out, had I so sworn / As you have done to this." (1.7.54–59).

As the couple settle upon their homicidal plan, their dependency upon one another strengthens, but so, too, does their sense of

Laurence Olivier's *Macbeth* was acclaimed for its "dazzling darkness" in 1955. The glamorous production had Olivier's wife, the film actress Vivien Leigh, as a goading Lady Macbeth.

entrapment and claustrophobia. The couple share a murderous secret that simply cannot be disclosed. The secret ultimately devours them both and serves to put distance between them.

Taunted to murder

Macbeth does not enter blindly into the murder of Duncan, though he does show some unwillingness to commit. Shakespeare complicates our relationship with Macbeth by voicing the character's reluctance to go through with the crime. Having listened to his wife's reaction to the witches' prophecy that he "shalt be king hereafter" (1.3.48), he states firmly that "We will proceed no further in this business" (1.7.31). For a moment it looks as though Macbeth will resist temptation and conquer his "Vaulting ambition" (1.7.27). His wife's stinging taunts, however, make him think again. Lady »

King James I

Macbeth was written during the reign of James I. When James took to the throne in 1603, he became the patron of Shakespeare's acting company, honouring them with the title of the King's Men. Shakespeare wrote plays for audiences in London's playhouses, but he was also writing to entertain his king. In the tale of Macbeth, Shakespeare is playing towards some of the king's interests. James I of England had previously sat on the Scottish throne as James VI of Scotland, so the play's Scottish setting would have had royal appeal. James also believed that he was a direct descendant of Banquo, and Shakespeare's presentation of this figure is duly honourable. He may also have been pandering to one of the king's particular concerns: witchcraft. The king had published a treatise on the subject in 1597 called *Daemonologie*, a fact that would not have gone unnoticed by the playwright. Though *Macbeth*'s dramatic ingredients would have entertained the king, they would of course have appealed to a much broader public as well.

Macbeth launches into a targeted emotional assault that offends, humiliates, and shocks her husband in equal measure: "Was the hope drunk / Wherein you dressed yourself? Hath it slept since? / And wakes it now to look so green and pale / At what it did so freely? From this time / Such I account thy love. Art thou afeard / To be the same in thine own act and valour / As thou art in desire? Wouldst thou have that / Which thou esteem'st the ornament of life, / And live a coward in thine own esteem, / Letting 'I dare not' wait upon 'I would', / Like the poor cat i'th' adage?" (1.7.35–44).

In the space of just 10 lines, Lady Macbeth questions her husband's masculinity, honour, ambition, courage, and love for her.

Macbeth's male pride overpowers his questioning mind, resulting in the defensive riposte "I dare do all that may become a man" (1.7.46). How much did Macbeth actually want the crown for himself, and to what extent does he carry out his part in the murder to confirm and maintain his understanding of his own manhood? Typically, Shakespeare does not settle upon a straightforward answer. The audience's responses to Macbeth's actions are further complicated by the role played by the witches throughout the drama. Did Macbeth have a choice? Was his fate always to murder Duncan and become king himself?

Macbeth's "heat-oppressèd brain" (2.1.39) comes to haunt him as much as the witches' prophecies. Paranoia practically paralyses Macbeth, and his imagination proves a constant torment. As he prepares to murder Duncan, he sees a floating dagger sign-posting his way to the king's bedchamber.

Has this dagger been conjured by the weird sisters? Or is it merely, as Macbeth suspects, a "dagger of the mind" engendered through fear and his reluctance to act upon his ambitions? His imagination will not be suppressed. Having murdered the king, Macbeth imagines that he will never sleep again: "Methought I heard a voice cry 'Sleep no more, / Macbeth does murder sleep' – the innocent sleep, / Sleep that knits up the ravelled sleave of care, / The death of each day's life, sore labour's bath, / Balm

English actress Ellen Terry played Lady Macbeth in London, in 1888. Society portraitist John Singer Sargent was in the audience and painted her in a dress made of iridescent beetle wings.

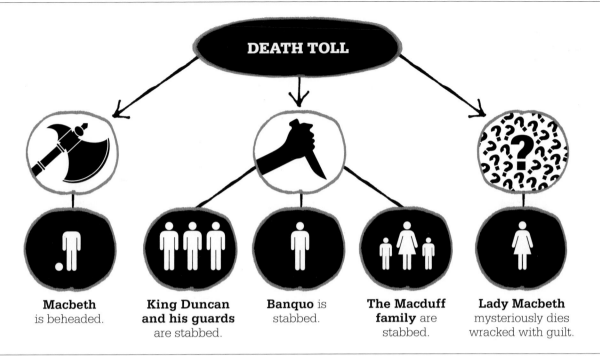

DEATH TOLL

Macbeth is beheaded.

King Duncan and his guards are stabbed.

Banquo is stabbed.

The Macduff family are stabbed.

Lady Macbeth mysteriously dies wracked with guilt.

of hurt minds, great nature's second course, / Chief nourisher in life's feast" (2.2.33–38).

Infected minds

The desire to unburden one's self of problems by telling others is all too human. Shakespeare skilfully depicts the breakdown of a marriage under stress, which leaves Lady Macbeth vulnerable psychologically. Lacking her husband's attention, she ruinously divests herself of her troubles while speaking in her sleep: "Out, damned spot; out, I say. One, two, – why, then 'tis time to do't. Hell is murky. Fie, my lord, fie, a soldier and afeard? What need we fear who knows it when none can call our power to account? Yet who would have thought the old man to have had so much blood in him?" (5.1.33–38).

As the Doctor diagnoses, "infected minds / To their deaf pillows will discharge their secrets" (5.1.69–70). Lady Macbeth's

Is this a dagger which I see before me, The handle toward my hand? Come, let me clutch thee.
Macbeth
Act 2, Scene 1

disclosure puts her own life and her husband's at risk. Shakespeare draws a stark contrast between his initial portrait of Lady Macbeth and her final depiction. While she was once strong and controlling, she becomes a pitiful shadow of her former self. Her deadly secret has drained the life from her, and she is left to obsess about death. Her own will follow soon enough.

At moments of extreme crisis or violence, Shakespeare has Macbeth voice some of the playwright's most poetic reflections upon the nature of existence itself. The murder of Duncan prompts thoughts on the soothing qualities of sleep, while Lady Macbeth's death encourages a meditation upon the transitory nature of life: "Out, out, brief candle. / Life's but a walking shadow, a poor player / That struts and frets his hour upon the stage, / And then is heard no more. It is a tale / Told by an idiot, full of sound and fury, / Signifying nothing." (5.5.22–27).

Banquo's ghost

Having killed the king, Macbeth faces a future of "restless ecstasy" (3.2.24). His mind is "full of scorpions" (3.2.37) and his every thought is about the fact that he has "scorched the snake, not killed it" (3.2.15). While Banquo lives, Macbeth fears exposure. He is also angered by the witches' prophecy » that Banquo's sons will reign after him. Banquo certainly suspects Macbeth of villainy: "Thou hast it now: King, Cawdor, Glamis, all / As the weird women promised; and I fear / Thou played'st most foully for't." (3.1.1–3). Macbeth's decision to have his friend murdered is taken alone; he is keen that his wife "Be innocent of the knowledge" (3.2.46). Banquo's murder creates a rift between husband and wife, and as a result produces one of the play's most thrilling moments: the appearance of Banquo's ghost.

Bloody apparition
As Macbeth attempts to join his guests at the banquet table he cannot see a chair reserved for himself. Though his guests motion towards an empty seat the king recoils in horror and begins to address Banquo's ghostly figure, visible only to himself: "Never shake / Thy gory locks at me" (3.4.49–50). The king's behaviour is sufficiently alarming that it prompts his wife to placate the bewildered and discomfited diners: "The fit is

momentary. Upon a thought / He will again be well. If much you note him / You shall offend him, and extend his passion. / Feed, and regard him not." (3.4.52–57).

In performance this moment can be played to emphasise the black humour. If the king's "fit" is particularly dramatic then it can prove impossible for the diners to "regard him not". As the king's reactions to the ghost grow more extreme, Lady Macbeth's need to take control of the situation becomes pressing. She takes her husband aside and tries to reason with him,

It will have blood, they say. Blood will have blood.
Macbeth
Act 3, Scene 4

The witches become a chorus in Guiseppe Verdi's opera *Macbeth*. Here, the San Francisco Opera company performs a production in modern dress in 2007.

Macbeth's mind is, obsessed with thoughts of blood: "Blood hath been shed ere now, i'th' olden time, / Ere human statute purged the gentle weal; / Ay, and since, too, murders have been performed / Too terrible for the ear. The time has been / That, when the brains were out, the man would die, / And there an end. But now they rise again / With twenty mortal murders on their crowns, / And push us from our stools. This is more strange / Than such a murder is." (3.4.74–82).

Shakespeare is retracing here the dynamic between the Macbeths that he created just after the murder of Duncan. Having killed the king, Macbeth froze with bloody daggers in hand as a wave of nervous thoughts swamped his mind. Fortunately for the Macbeths they were in private, and Lady Macbeth had been able to shake her husband from his terrifying thoughts.

Macbeth's strange behaviour at the banquet is played out in front of the puzzled guests. When the ghost appears before him for a second time, he cannot contain his horror: "It will have blood, they say. Blood will have blood. / Stones have been known to move, and trees to speak, / Augurs and understood relations have / By maggot-pies and choughs and rooks brought forth / The secret'st man of blood." (3.4.121–125).

End of the bloodbath

By the play's close Macbeth's world has come crashing down, and he finds little left in life to delight him:

"I have lived long enough" (5.3.24). The witches' improbable prophecies all come to fruition, and Macbeth leaves the stage fighting despite the odds being against him: "Though Birnam Wood be come to Dunsinane, / And thou opposed being of no woman born, / Yet I will try the last. "(5.10.30–32).

It is only through the deaths of this "dread butcher and his fiend-like queen" (5.11.35) that the blood-letting can be brought to a close. "The time is free" (5.11.21), says Macduff, and he hails the new king Malcolm, who can build a future for Scotland, free from tyranny. ∎

The witches

In Shakespeare's time, witchcraft was a serious matter. King James himself was a judge in the North Berwick witch trials of 1590–92, at which 70 people were tried and many burned at the stake; witch trials would be held in England and Scotland until the 18th century.

Shakespeare's audience would have known of such events. The presence of the witches in *Macbeth* is intended to be unsettling, and their appearance, as described by Banquo, emphasizes their otherworldliness: "What are these, / So withered, and so wild in their attire, / That look not like th'inhabitants o'th'earth / And yet are on't?" (1.3.37–40).

Shakespeare's description encourages spectators to use their imaginations to see more than is before their eyes – to see supernatural and hideous figures. He also creates an image that troubles both the audience's and Macbeth's minds. Modern-day audiences tend to see Macbeth's psychological state as more important than the witches' curses as a driver of the action.

Dagger – Macbeth's murderous intent.

Heart – the intense relationship between Macbeth and his wife.

Crown – Macbeth's determined ambition.

Sword – Macbeth's prowess as a warrior.

Shakespeare dramatically combines a warrior's courage as he wields the sword, "vaulting ambition" in seeking the crown, the bond of hearts with Lady Macbeth, an evil intent in the form of a dagger, and the power of prophecy to bring Macbeth to commit murder, several times over.

AGE CANNOT WITHER
HER, NOR CUSTOM STALE HER
INFINITE VARIETY

ANTONY AND CLEOPATRA (1606)

DRAMATIS PERSONAE

Antony A Roman general who enjoys a passionate love affair with the queen of Egypt, Cleopatra. He is torn between his duty to Rome and his desire for Cleopatra.

Cleopatra Queen of Egypt, and former lover of Julius Caesar. Her passion for Antony provokes displays of jealousy, anger, and compassion.

Enobarbus Antony's most loyal and trusted soldier. He enjoys life in Egypt and understands Antony's love for Cleopatra.

Octavius Caesar Julius Caesar's great-nephew, who governs Rome with Antony and Lepidus. He is disgusted by Antony's life in Egypt.

Octavia Caesar's sister, who marries Antony.

Sextus Pompey A soldier who plans a rebellion against the rulers of Rome, but is persuaded to make peace.

Charmian and Iras Cleopatra's attendants. Iras takes poison to avoid witnessing Cleopatra's own death through suicide.

Lepidus Governs Rome with Antony and Caesar. He proposes the political marriage between Antony and Octavia.

Dolabella Caesar's attendant. He warns Cleopatra that she will be paraded through Rome.

Soothsayer He predicts that Caesar will defeat Antony.

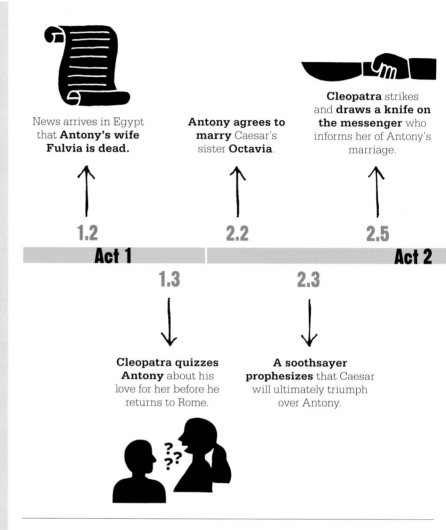

News arrives in Egypt that **Antony's wife Fulvia is dead.**

1.2

Antony agrees to marry Caesar's sister **Octavia**.

2.2

Cleopatra strikes and **draws a knife on the messenger** who informs her of Antony's marriage.

2.5

Act 1

Act 2

1.3

Cleopatra quizzes Antony about his love for her before he returns to Rome.

2.3

A soothsayer prophesizes that Caesar will ultimately triumph over Antony.

Roman soldiers are disgusted with their general, Mark Antony, who has fallen for the charms of the Egyptian queen, Cleopatra. They fear that this love affair has transformed one of the world's most powerful men into a dishonourable fool. When Antony hears that his wife Fulvia has died, he recognizes that he must return to Rome to help Caesar defeat Sextus Pompey. Cleopatra taunts Antony about his love for her; she is jealous of other women, and of Antony's duty to Rome.

Antony returns to Rome while Cleopatra seeks comfort from her companions. Antony meets with Caesar's displeasure on his return. He is criticized for ignoring his responsibilities as a leader, and is encouraged to marry Caesar's sister Octavia, as a sign of his commitment to Rome. Antony agrees to the political marriage. When Cleopatra hears of Antony's marriage she is enraged.

Caesar and Antony meet with the rebellious Sextus Pompey on his boat to prevent civil war. Peace is agreed, although one of Pompey's

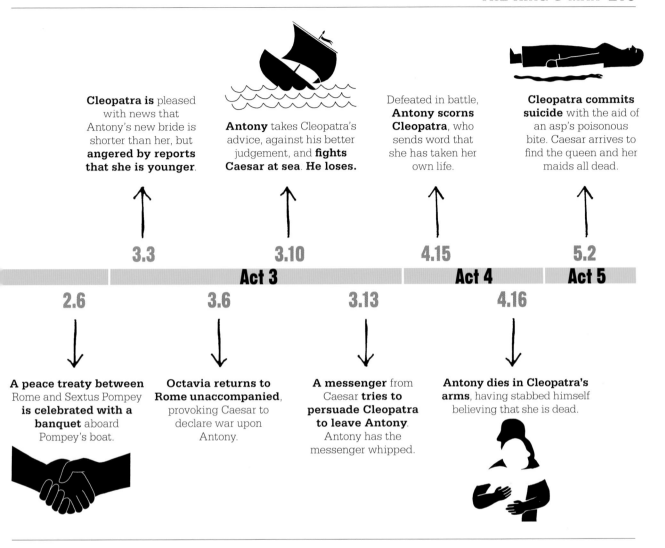

Cleopatra is pleased with news that Antony's new bride is shorter than her, but **angered by reports that she is younger**.

Antony takes Cleopatra's advice, against his better judgement, and **fights Caesar at sea. He loses**.

Defeated in battle, **Antony scorns Cleopatra**, who sends word that she has taken her own life.

Cleopatra commits suicide with the aid of an asp's poisonous bite. Caesar arrives to find the queen and her maids all dead.

3.3

3.10

4.15

5.2

Act 3

Act 4

Act 5

2.6

3.6

3.13

4.16

A peace treaty between Rome and Sextus Pompey **is celebrated with a banquet** aboard Pompey's boat.

Octavia returns to Rome unaccompanied, provoking Caesar to declare war upon Antony.

A messenger from Caesar **tries to persuade Cleopatra to leave Antony**. Antony has the messenger whipped.

Antony dies in Cleopatra's arms, having stabbed himself believing that she is dead.

---

soldiers tries to persuade his master to murder his guests. Pompey ignores this advice, and spends the evening drinking with his former enemies. Enobarbus says that Antony's allegiance to Cleopatra will remain strong, despite his political reunion with Caesar.

Antony returns to Egypt without his new bride. Caesar is angered by Antony's neglect of Octavia and declares war. Antony's soldiers argue that they should fight Caesar on land, but Cleopatra persuades him to fight at sea. She flees the battle, and is

followed closely by Antony, bringing dishonour to his soldiers and his own reputation.

Antony's soldiers begin to lose faith in their general, and his loyal companion Enobarbus defects to Caesar's side. Antony is defeated for a second time and blames Cleopatra for the loss. Fearing for her safety, she sends Antony news that she has died, not anticipating that Antony will respond by seeking to commit suicide himself. He fails to kill himself, and his soldier Eros takes his own life rather than aid his master's death.

News arrives that Cleopatra had feigned her death and is sheltering in a monument. Antony asks to be taken to her and warns her against Caesar before he dies.

Cleopatra discovers Caesar's plan to parade her through Rome. She determines to take her own life, and calls for a poisonous snake to be brought to her. She dresses in her majestic robes before placing the snake to her breast, and dies in the company of one of her maids. Caesar arrives to find Cleopatra dead, and orders that she and Antony be buried together. »

IN CONTEXT

THEMES
Love, power, duty, honour, jealousy, betrayal, death, desire

SETTING
Rome, Alexandria, Athens

SOURCES
1579 Sir Thomas North's translation of Plutarch's *Lives of the Noble Greeks and Romans*. The play compresses events that took place over the space of a decade. Enobarbus speaks words taken directly from the source in his description of Cleopatra sat on her barge.

LEGACY
1765 The critic Samuel Johnson writes that the play's events were "produced without any art of connection or care to disposition".

1890 Actress Lillie Langtry plays Cleopatra at the Princess's Theatre, London.

1922 Poet T S Eliot adapts Shakespeare's description of Cleopatra for *The Waste Land*.

1934 Soviet playwright Alexander Tairov's *Egyptian Nights* draws heavily on Shakespeare's play.

1966 US composer Samuel Barber's operatic version of the play opens in New York.

1972 American star Charlton Heston plays Antony in a heavily adapted film of the play.

1999 Mark Rylance plays Cleopatra at the Globe, London.

Antony and Cleopatra are not young "star-crossed lovers" like Romeo and Juliet. These are mature adults, both past their "salad days" (1.5.72). Antony is married to Fulvia, and yet he is drawn to spending time with his "Egyptian dish" (2.6.126) away from his wife in Rome: "I'th East my pleasure lies" (2.3.38). Though she is unmarried, Cleopatra has also loved before: "She made great Caesar lay his sword to bed. / He ploughed her, and she cropped." (2.2.234–235). The intensity of

The Egyptian court is portrayed in the play as luxurious and exotic, and Antony is drawn inexorably towards it. The court is imagined here by Italian artist Francesco Trevisani.

Antony and Cleopatra's passion for one another can be overwhelming. Shakespeare expresses their hunger, desire, and dependency upon each other in some of the most beautiful and heightened verse to be found anywhere in the Shakespearean canon. "Age cannot wither" either of them, for in one another's eyes, they are like gods. Even in death, Antony will remain like Mars to Cleopatra; following his suicide she declares that "there is nothing left remarkable / Beneath the visiting Moon" (4.16.69–70). However, their relationship is far from idyllic. As a pair, they are heroic, majestic, and superhuman, but they are also mean, monstrous, cowardly, and drunken. Shakespeare presents

Give me some music –
music, moody food
Of us that trade in love.
Cleopatra
Act 2, Scene 5

these characters, individually and
as a pair, in a rich and memorable
manner – audiences are shown the
good, the bad, and the ugly.

Cleopatra the seductress

Cleopatra is one of Shakespeare's
greatest dramatic creations. She
can also prove for some people
one of his most exhausting and
irritating characterizations.
Shakespeare went to great lengths
to impress upon his audience
Cleopatra's charm and vitality. We
hear throughout the play of how
men have fallen for her charms, and
even the priggish Roman, Octavius
Caesar, notes that in death she
looks "As she would catch another
Antony" (5.2.341). Men see her as a
powerful seductress, a witch even,
who holds them under her spell.
She is first described in derogatory
terms; she is, according to two
of Antony's soldiers, a lusty
"strumpet" and "gypsy". Angered
by their general's newfound
domesticity, the soldiers speak of a
woman who can transform a former
"pillar of the world" (1.1.12) into a
"strumpet's fool" (1.1.13). For them,
her allure is intoxicating and
dangerous, destroying Antony's
sense of duty and commitment
to Rome. Other hardened soldiers

Husband and wife Laurence Olivier
and Vivien Leigh took on the title roles
in a 1951 production. Olivier's Antony
was reckless, while Leigh played the
queen as sensuous yet regally aloof.

such as Enobarbus find themselves
reaching for the finest poetic
descriptions to communicate her
appeal to those who have not been
in her presence: "Age cannot wither
her, nor custom stale / Her infinite
variety. Other women cloy / The
appetites they feed, but she makes
hungry / Where most she satisfies.
For vilest things / Become
themselves in her, that the holy
priests / Bless her when she is
riggish." (2.2.241–246).

Enobarbus's words serve
in some respects to justify
Antony's obsession with this
"lass unparalleled" (5.2.310).
How could anyone fail to be
intrigued by a woman who
encompasses such infinite variety
of mood and behaviour? It would
seem that everyone, from priests
to world leaders, finds something
extraordinary about Cleopatra.
She does not need to be in a scene,
or even on the stage to create a
lasting impression. From memory,
Enobarbus conjures her stately
appearance in one of the play's
most richly poetic passages:

I have offended reputation;
A most unnoble swerving.
Antony
Act 3, Scene 11

"The barge she sat in, like a
burnished throne / Burned on the
water. The poop was beaten gold; /
Purple the sails, and so perfuméd
that / The winds were love-sick
with them. The oars were silver, /
Which to the tune of flutes kept
stroke, and made / The water
which they beat to follow faster, /
As amorous of their strokes. For
her own person, / It beggared all
description. She did lie / In her
pavilion – cloth of gold, of tissue –
O'er-picturing that Venus where
we see / The fancy outwork nature.
On each side her / Stood pretty
dimpled boys, like smiling Cupids,
/ With divers-coloured fans whose
wind did seem / To glow the
delicate cheeks which they did
cool, / And what they undid did"
(2.2.198–212).

Enobarbus's speech serves like
a hymn to Cleopatra. The imagery
must have wooed Shakespeare
himself, for this speech owes much
to Shakespeare's source, Thomas »

North's 1579 translation of Plutarch's *Lives of the Noble Grecians and Romans*. Thomas North describes among other things, "the sails of purple", the "pavilion of cloth of gold of tissue", and the "pretty fair boys apparelled as painters do set forth god Cupid, with little fans in their hands, with the which they fanned wind upon her." By adapting his source material, Shakespeare added to the variety of images of Cleopatra, both in print and paint, that have been created since her death in 30 BCE.

In Antony's eyes, Cleopatra is a woman whom "everything becomes" (1.1.51); her magnificence shines through tantrums, laughter, and tears. For Antony she is the personification of the country that she commands; she is an "Egyptian dish" (2.6.126), and a "serpent of old Nile" (1.5.25). She is however also labelled as being a "wrangling queen" (1.1.50), a "triple-turned whore" (4.13.13), and "this false soul of Egypt" (4.13.25). Her temperament is as fluid as the Nile itself: "If you find him sad, / Say I am dancing; if in mirth, report / That I am sudden sick" (1.3.3–5). One moment she wishes to hop around the streets,

"O, whither hast thou led me, Egypt?
Antony
Act 3, Scene 11

and the next she wishes to draw blood from a messenger. Cleopatra is predictable only in her changeability.

Love or duty
In their first interaction, Cleopatra badgers Antony to quantify his love for her. His response plays to her taste for hyperbole: "Let Rome in Tiber melt, and the wide arch / Of the ranged empire fall. Here is my space. / Kingdoms are clay. Our dungy earth alike / Feeds beast as man. The nobleness of life / Is to do thus; when such a mutual pair / And such a twain can do't – in which I bind / On

pain of punishment the world to weet – / We stand up peerless." (1.1.35–42).

Antony's words suggest the extent to which he has fashioned himself as a convert to the Egyptians' way of being. The Roman Antony is a builder of empires, one for whom expansion and growth are key goals and motivations. But in this early speech, which serves to establish Antony's state of mind, his focus is upon contraction and reduction rather than extension. His conquering ambitions have been narrowed to the point at which he can say "Here is my space" (1.1.36) – here being in Egypt, by the side of, or in the arms of Cleopatra. Egypt and its queen have transformed Antony's Roman understanding of honour and nobility, and have changed him from a conquering warrior into a man whose ambition is to be part of a "mutual pair" (1.1.39). Nothing could be more romantic, or more self-centred, depending upon one's point of view.

In order to appreciate Antony's commitment to a life of pleasure, Shakespeare presents its

Parallel Lives

Shakespeare's main source of knowledge about the ancient world was a translation of Plutarch's *Lives of the Noble Greeks and Romans* (also known as *Parallel Lives*). Written in the 1st century CE, the work is a collection of biographies of Greek and Roman figures, arranged in pairs. In each pair, a Roman from the recent past is compared to a Greek figure from the remote past. Plutarch paired Antony with Demetrius, a military leader who ruled Macedon from 294–288 BCE. Demetrius died exactly 200 years before the birth of Antony.

Plutarch says of Demetrius and Antony that both "abandoned themselves to luxury and enjoyment". However, he judges Antony more severely. When preparing for war, Demetrius's "spear was not tipped with ivy, nor did his helmet smell of myrrh". By contrast, Antony was "disarmed by Cleopatra, subdued by her spells, and persuaded to drop from his hands great undertakings and necessary campaigns, only to roam about and play with her on the sea-shores by Canopus and Taphosiris."

> This foul Egyptian hath betrayèd me. My fleet hath yielded to the foe, and yonder They cast their caps up and carouse together Like friends long lost. Triple-turned whore!
> **Antony**
> **Act 4, Scene 13**

antithesis, in his depiction of Octavius Caesar, and life in Rome. In so doing, Shakespeare structured his play around contrasting worlds, filling his drama with a variety of voices and viewpoints. Caesar's rhetoric is cold and clinical; he speaks with the politician's tongue. Lacking the Egyptian's taste for poetic indulgence, Caesar's speeches tend to be purely functional, short, and succinct in expression. Caesar's sense of rigorous discipline leads him to view Antony's behaviour in Egypt as dishonourable; in Caesar's judgement, Antony simply "fishes, drinks, and wastes / The lamps of night in revel; is not more manlike / Than Cleopatra" (1.4.4–6). Caesar is too rash in his judgement of his fellow triumvir: "'tis better playing with a lion's whelp / Than with an old one dying" (3.13.94–95). Like Cleopatra, Antony resists easy labelling; Shakespeare varies his presentation throughout the play, so that audiences see glimpses of the "plated Mars" (1.1.4) as well as the "strumpet's fool" (1.1.13).

Erotic Egypt

Egypt is characterized as a place of excessive appetites, where eight wild roasted boars can be shared between 12 people for breakfast. Caesar's stomach churns at such extravagance: he would "rather fast from all, four days, / Than drink so much in one" (2.7.98–99). The Egyptians' appetite for sexual pleasure is also insatiable, but in Rome covetousness and eroticism are substituted for marriage. Caesar's sister Octavia functions like a pawn in a political game when Antony takes her as his wife. The marriage symbolizes a reunion between Antony and Rome, though many presume that "He will to his Egyptian dish again" (2.6.126).

Did Shakespeare intend his audiences to side with Antony? Is love more important than

Octavius, depicted here in a statue in Rome, stands for Roman martial values in the play. The historical Octavius would go on to be proclaimed emperor of Rome following his defeat of Antony.

duty? As ever, Shakespeare presents a variety of questions, but provides few answers. They are questions for actors to interpret and audiences to decide. Life in Egypt has encouraged Antony to celebrate and feed his appetites, but ultimately his decision to act against his natural "Roman" instinct comes at great personal loss. As his devotion to Cleopatra leads to his defeat in battle, Antony complains: "Authority melts from me of late. When I cried 'Ho!', / Like boys unto a muss kings would start forth, / And cry "Your will?" (3.13.90–92). »

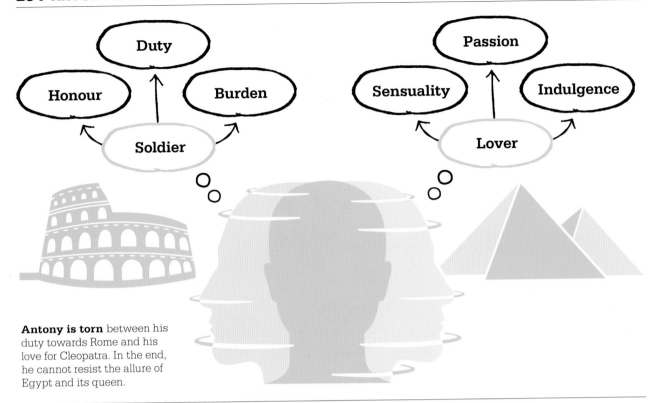

Antony is torn between his duty towards Rome and his love for Cleopatra. In the end, he cannot resist the allure of Egypt and its queen.

Burden of duty
Like King Lear, Antony wishes to be free of his duties, but still desires to hold on to the authority and accolades that such power brings. He battles with his

Give me my robe. Put on my crown. I have Immortal longings in me. Now no more The juice of Egypt's grape shall moist this lip.
Cleopatra
Act 5, Scene 2

conscience, and blames Cleopatra for his own weakness when he deserts a battle in pursuit of her: "Egypt, thou knew'st too well / My heart was to thy rudder tied by th' strings, / And thou shouldst tow me after. O'er my spirit / Thy full supremacy thou knew'st, and that / Thy beck might from the bidding of the gods / Command me." (3.11.56–61).

Although Cleopatra does much to endanger Antony, he remains devoted to her right up to the end. Having experienced her infinite variety of moods to the full, he wards off impending death to lay the "poor last" of "many thousand kisses" (4.16.21) upon her lips.

Tribute to Antony
Cleopatra is one of Shakespeare's most self-absorbed and self-seeking characters, and thus it can come as

something of a surprise to hear her rhapsodize upon someone other than herself. Her emotional tribute to Antony, following his failed suicide, serves to augment her lover's reputation, encouraging a personal rather than political assessment of the man's life.

Through Cleopatra, Shakespeare ensures that our final memory of Antony is not of a strumpet's fool, but of a Herculean god: "His legs bestrid the ocean; his reared arm / Crested the world. His voice was propertied / As all the tunéd spheres, and that to friends; / But when he meant to quail and shake the orb, / He was as rattling thunder. For his bounty, / There was no winter in't; an autumn 'twas, / That grew the more by reaping. His delights / Were dolphin-like; they showed his back above / The element they lived in. In his livery / Walked

> Take up her bed,
> And bear her women from
> the monument.
> She shall be buried by
> her Antony.
> No grave upon the earth
> shall clip in it
> A pair so famous.
> **Caesar**
> Act 5, Scene 2

crowns and crownets. Realms and islands were / As plates dropped from his pocket." (5.2.81–91).

The wonder of Cleopatra's elaborate and rather fanciful tribute should have the effect of wiping all previous remembrances of Antony from one's mind: "The crown o'th, earth doth melt" (4.16.65).

Putting on a show
The Egyptian Queen is a consummate performer, who flows from one mood to another with the ease of an accomplished actress. She wears many faces during the course of the play, expressing a wide range of emotions: love, hate, fear, jealousy, suspicion, and pride. Many of her conversations with Antony are in fact played out in front of an audience of attendants. The most private of conversations

In Shakespeare's time, Cleopatra would have been played by a boy actor. In a 1999 production at the Globe, London, that aimed for authenticity, Mark Rylance took on the role.

are often made public. Having listened to Antony declare his undying love for her, Cleopatra turns to those around her to ask, "Why did he marry Fulvia and not love her?" (1.1.43). Shakespeare perhaps alludes to Antony's distaste for Cleopatra's attention-seeking showiness when he ventures that "Tonight we'll wander through the streets and note / The qualities of people" (1.1.55–56).

There is the slightest of suggestions here that Antony desires Cleopatra's private company, away from the crowds before whom she is constantly performing. Shakespeare also uses this line to make the extraordinary seem familiar. Though Antony and Cleopatra are powerful leaders surrounded by wealth and luxury, they also value love's simple pleasures enjoyed by lovers rich and poor. ∎

Death of Cleopatra
Shakespeare saves Cleopatra's greatest performance until the end of the play. She orchestrates her death scene, which is full of theatricality, ritual, and ceremony. The final Act, in which Cleopatra prepares for death, can often prove one of the play's most powerful passages in performance. Shakespeare shrinks the scope of his play. Audiences are no longer invited to imagine movement between continents, but are asked to feel Cleopatra's grief and loneliness.

Cleopatra calls for Charmian and Iras to fetch her best attire, so that she may dress for death. Shakespeare ensures that our final image of Cleopatra is of the queen in all of her greatness. Her language is sexually charged, and in her final moments she makes an ecstasy of death itself. She talks of "immortal longings", and figures that "the stroke of death" is as a "lover's pinch, / Which hurts and is desired" (5.2.290–291). While Antony's botched suicide attempt is awkward and inelegant, Cleopatra remains in control of herself, her image, and her reputation in death as in life.

THE WEB OF OUR LIFE IS OF A MINGLED YARN, GOOD AND ILL TOGETHER

ALL'S WELL THAT ENDS WELL
(1606–1607)

DRAMATIS PERSONAE

Helen Orphan under the care of the Countess of Roussillon. She is in love with Bertram, son of the countess.

Bertram, Count of Roussillon An ambitious young man, ward of the King.

The Countess of Roussillon Bertram's widowed mother, also guardian to Helen.

The King of France He begins the play suffering from an incurable illness.

Lafeu An elderly lord, who struggles to understand the younger generation.

Paroles Bertram's friend, a renowned soldier, but secretly a coward and a liar, who is revealed to be ready to betray everyone to avoid torture.

Lavatch A gloomy, bad-tempered clown, servant to the Countess of Roussillon.

The Duke of Florence At war with his brother, the Duke of Siena.

Diana A Florentine virgin, pursued by Bertram.

The Widow Diana's mother, who is eager to help Helen.

Reynaldo The Countess's steward, who prepares a letter from the Countess to her son in Paris.

The Dumaine brothers French lords who ambush and interrogate Paroles, making him believe that he has been captured by the enemy.

Bertram leaves his widowed mother **to join the King of France**.

As the lords leave for the wars, **Bertram is angry** at being forced to stay behind. **Helen appears in disguise** before the King and offers to cure him.

The Duke of Florence welcomes the **French lords** who have **volunteered to fight**.

1.1

Act 1

2.1

Act 2

3.1

1.3

The Countess discovers **Helen's love for Bertram**. Helen reveals her **plan to cure the King** using one of her father's drugs.

2.3

The King is cured. **Helen chooses Bertram** as her husband, much to Bertram's disgust. **He decides to run off** to the Florentine wars.

F ollowing the death of his father, Bertram must leave for the court. The Countess and Lafeu discuss the King's illness, and wish that the physician Gérard de Narbonne, were still alive to cure him. Narbonne's daughter, Helen, weeps – but for Bertram's departure not for the death of her father. The Countess learns of Helen's passion for her son.

War has broken out between the dukedoms of Florence and Siena. The King of France refuses to send troops, but gives permission for his young noblemen to fight on either side.

Lafeu introduces a disguised Helen to the court. She promises that if she fails to cure the King, she will willingly be put to death, but if she succeeds, the King must give her a husband of her choice. The King is restored to health, and presents Helen with four lords as potential husbands. She chooses Bertram, who is disgusted at the idea of being married to a physician's daughter. Bertram capitulates, but he refuses to consummate the marriage. He runs off to the Florentine wars with Paroles. In letters to his mother and Helen, he insists that he will only

Helen arrives in Florence **disguised as a pilgrim** and lodges with a Widow. She learns that Bertram has been trying to seduce the Widow's daughter, Diana.

Paroles is captured by the fake enemy soldiers and blindfolded. He immediately **offers to betray** the Florentine side.

The wars are now over, and Bertram is planning to return to France, having been told that Helen is dead.

Bertram agrees to marry Lafeu's daughter, but when he is found to be in possession of Helen's ring, **the King accuses him of murder**. Helen comes back to say that she has met Bertram's conditions. **He asks forgiveness**.

3.5 ↑ **4.1** ↑ **4.3** ↑ **5.3** ↑

Act 3 | **Act 4** | **Act 5**

3.2 ↓ **3.7** ↓ **4.2** ↓ **4.5** ↓

The Countess reads Bertram's letter telling her that he has run away. Helen reads a **letter setting down impossible conditions** for their being man and wife. Helen decides to leave France.

Helen reveals herself as Bertram's wife. She persuades the women to arrange a sexual encounter with Bertram, where she will secretly **take Diana's place**.

Bertram declares his love for Diana. She persuades him to **give up a ring** that has been in his family for generations and arranges a secret liaison.

The Countess grieves for the death of Helen, but she supports Lafeu's plan to marry Bertram to his daughter.

---

acknowledge Helen when she has a ring he never removes, and when she has conceived their child. Helen travels to Florence, where she takes lodgings with a Widow. She discovers that Bertram has won favour for his bravery, and has been trying to seduce the Widow's beautiful daughter, Diana.

The other lords in the Florentine army pretend to be enemy soldiers, take Paroles captive, and blindfold him. Paroles reveals everything he knows about his fellow soldiers. When the blindfold is removed, Paroles's reputation is ruined.

Helen reveals her true identity to the Widow. She offers money for help in satisfying the conditions of Bertram's letter. Diana will arrange a sexual liaison with Bertram, but Helen will take her place. Bertram tries again to seduce Diana. He gives her his ancestral ring, and after their assignation, she gives him another ring in return. Bertram is informed that Helen is dead, and leaves for France to be reconciled to the King.

The King forgives Bertram and supports his proposed marriage to Lafeu's daughter. However, when Bertram offers as a betrothal gift

the ring Diana gave him, the King recognizes it as belonging to Helen. Bertram is arrested on the charge of murdering his wife. Diana arrives, and accuses Bertram of breaking his promise to marry her. She produces the ring Bertram gave her, which the Countess recognizes as the family heirloom. Diana refuses to explain how she got the ring, and is arrested. She sends for someone to stand bail, and Helen enters. She declares that the conditions Bertram set have been met. Bertram asks for her forgiveness, and promises to love her in the future. »

IN CONTEXT

THEMES
**Love, betrayal,
bereavement and death**

SETTING
**Roussillon and Paris,
France, and Florence, Italy**

SOURCES
1353 Italian poet Giovanni
Boccaccio's *Decameron* is the
main source of the play.

1566–67 Shakespeare
probably read Boccaccio's
story in English translator
William Painter's *Palace
of Pleasure*.

LEGACY
1741 The first recorded
performance of the play opens
at Drury Lane, London, with
Peg Woffington as Helen.

1981 US playwright Don Nigro
writes *Loves Labours Wonne*,
a play about Shakespeare's
life. In the play, Anne
Hathaway resembles
Helen, in that she wins
Shakespeare in marriage
by curing his father, John.

2000 In US children's author
Gary Blackwood's novel
Shakespeare's Scribe, an
apprentice, Widge, helps
Shakespeare to write
All's Well.

2012 *All's Well That Ends
Well*, translated into Gujarati,
is performed by the Mumbai-
based company Arpana at
Shakespeare's Globe in
London. The action is
relocated to northwest
India in 1900.

he title of Shakespeare's
comedy *All's Well That
Ends Well* could arguably
end with a question mark. As
American author John Jay Chapman
wrote in 1915: "Melancholy
moulders in the very title of it; for
we feel that all is not well, nor ever
has been nor can be well again."

The play's "mingled yarn" is one
reason for the uncertain reactions
it has provoked. Although it makes
use of a number of fairytale and
folkloric conventions, including
the hero who is set a series of
impossible tasks and the bedtrick
(where one woman substitutes for
another to secure a husband), the
psychological insight with which
the characters are written, and the
realistic setting in which they
are placed make these elements
highly problematic. Indeed, *All's
Well* has often been labelled one of

On learning of Helen's passion
for her son, the countess (Janie Dee,
right, at the Globe, 2011) supports
Helen's (Ellie Piercy) plan to prove
her worthiness by curing the King.

> T'were all one
> That I should love a bright
> particular star
> And think to wed it, he
> is so above me.
> **Helen**
> **Act 1, Scene 1**

Shakespeare's "problem plays",
along with *Measure for Measure*,
Troilus and Cressida, and even
sometimes *Hamlet*. This is not
a term that Shakespeare would
have recognized, as it was
invented in the 19th century to
describe Norwegian playwright
Henrik Ibsen's plays, but it is still
a useful way of thinking about
All's Well. The features of a problem
play include the interweaving
of fantastic plots with realistic

Helen (Joanna Horton, in this 2013 RSC production) cures the king (Greg Hicks) using her father's drugs. As a reward, Helen is offered a choice of husbands. She chooses Bertram.

characters, the struggle to resolve an ethical dilemma, and the experience of emotional suffering including grief. *All's Well* fits all of these criteria. Its mingling of comedy and tragedy is beautifully exemplified by Helen when, having been declared dead, she reappears on stage "quick", which means both alive and pregnant. Yet even this joyful conclusion has often been felt to be overshadowed by the darker undercurrents of the play.

Ambivalent virtue

The first problem is Bertram. If we are to delight in Helen's achieving her ambition to marry him, we have to believe that he is worthy – and this is where audiences have struggled. In general, the play sees human beings as deeply ambivalent: "Our virtues would be proud / if our faults whipped them not, and our crimes would / despair if they were not cherished by our virtues" (4.3.75–77). He demonstrates courage and loyalty as a soldier, but at the same time, he is trying to seduce a young virgin with false promises. In the final scene, he expresses remorse for Helen's loss and even claims to love her, but then shows himself to be incapable of telling the truth, slandering Diana, whom he had also professed to love.

We might defend Bertram on the grounds that he is suffering from the crisis of masculinity that occurs elsewhere in Shakespeare. Like Adonis, who prefers hunting the boar over Venus's seductions in Shakespeare's poem *Venus and*

Adonis, Bertram is still young, and in the process of becoming a man. The desire of a woman like Helen threatens to confine him in the feminine domestic space he has only just succeeded in escaping. Bertram also falls foul of the institution of wardship. This was a system, much criticized in Shakespeare's time, that gave an elder guardian control over the young man's marriage, usually to his/her own advantage. In *All's Well*, we might argue that it is unfair on Bertram that he should be married to pay the King's debt, and especially to a woman whom he declares he cannot love. Equally troubling is the emasculation that is built into this process. The King's wards are paraded in front of Helen so that she may "send forth [her] eye" (2.3.53) and choose one. By this means, Helen adopts the traditionally masculine role of wooer, whilst Bertram is placed in the role of passive female. There is even an echo of Capulet in *Romeo and Juliet* in the King's threats to exile and

revenge himself upon Bertram, which would place Bertram in the role of Juliet.

This all matters less if we can believe that the marriage of Bertram and Helen will prove a good thing for him as well as for her. But the play struggles to reconcile the forceful and manipulative Helen with contemporary ideals of female modesty and submissiveness. »

I think not on my father,
And these great tears grace
his remembrance more
Than those I shed for him.
What was he like?
I have forgot him.
Helen
Act 1, Scene 1

Helen registers what an impossible situation she is in when she has to choose Bertram: "I dare not say I take you, but I give / Me and my service ever whilst I live / Into your guiding power" (2.3.103–105).

If Bertram was not enamoured with Helen before, he certainly will not be now. It is no coincidence that the woman he does actively desire, Diana, is named after the goddess of chastity. She inspires his lust precisely because she seems impervious to love herself. Furthermore, the play implies an unflattering parallel between Helen and Paroles. Both are ambitious, lower-class characters whose designs on Bertram promise to be socially advantageous to them. More specifically, Helen's use of the bedtrick is morally suspect, in that she forces Bertram to have sex with someone against his will, and uses Diana as a public scapegoat for her own desires.

Social mobility

A further ethical debate centres around the meaning and importance of class distinctions. Bertram insists that he will be shamed, and his noble lineage

Wars is no strife
To the dark house and
the detested wife.
Bertram
Act 2, Scene 3

Held up high by his comrades, Bertram (Alex Waldmann in a 2013 RSC production) wins plaudits for his bravery in war. By contrast, the war reveals Paroles to be a coward.

degraded, by uniting with the lower-class Helen. The King argues that all titles were once bestowed for worthy service, and so he can make Helen Bertram's social equal on the basis of her virtue.

Although this sounds very progressive, it is at odds with assumptions elsewhere in the play, and beyond it. One of the few guidelines for wardship was that the ward was not supposed to be married to anyone socially beneath him. Furthermore, the King may argue that everyone's blood is ultimately the same, but he would hardly be in his own position of royal privilege were that the case.

What the play tries to do towards the end is to argue that, rather than jeopardizing Bertram's class status, Helen actually preserves it. He carelessly gives away his ancestral ring, but Helen takes it into her own safe-keeping. Equally, Bertram thinks he is wasting his noble seed in an illicit sexual encounter, but Helen takes possession of this, too, and nurtures it into an heir to honour him.

'Tis only title thou disdain'st
in her, the which
I can build up. Strange is
it that our bloods,
Of colour, weight, and heat,
poured all together,
Would quite confound
distinction, yet stands off
In differences so mighty.
King of France
Act 2, Scene 3

Problematic reconciliation?

The final reconciliation scene can be read and performed in a number of different ways. Bertram may be transfigured by the return of dead Helen, sometimes dressed in white like an avenging angel or the Virgin Mary. He may be filled with gratitude as she releases him from his arrest for murder and exonerates him from any crime against Diana.

Freed from the influence of Paroles and his hyper-masculine ethos, Bertram may give way to an attraction to Helen that he has always secretly felt. Equally, Helen's reaction to Bertram takes on many different hues. A review of the 1992 RSC production, directed by Sir Peter Hall, describes how, "With a pained, dignified 'et cetera' (uttered after a beautifully pointed pause), she spares both of them a full recital, and then determinedly rends the paper in two." We might interpret this action as a fresh start for

the couple, or as a long-awaited expression of Helen's rage against her husband.

Ultimately, the understanding that life is like a "mingled yarn, good and ill together" is reserved for the older generation. When she discovers Helen's love, the Countess reflects on her own past lovesickness, and concludes that it is an essential part of being young: "this thorn / Doth to our rose of youth rightly belong" (1.3.125–126). She also questions the value of young love: "Such were our faults – or then we thought them none" (131).

However, it remains to be seen whether Helen's idolatrous passion for Bertram or his "sick desires" for Diana will be assuaged by marriage, and indeed whether they will be able to put these events behind them. Can we imagine Bertram and Helen a few years on, teasing one another about the fact that Bertram was once accused of hating his wife so much he might have killed her? Or is that part of the weave always likely to bring Helen sorrow because Bertram never fulfils his promise to "love her dearly, ever, ever dearly" (5.3.318)? The difficulties that have to be overcome may be too great for the ending to feel anything other than bittersweet. ∎

A young man married is a
man that's marred.
Paroles
Act 2, Scene 3

The braggart soldier

For Shakespeare's audience, Paroles would have been an instantly recognizable comic type. The braggart soldier, whose much vaunted courage on the battlefield turns out to be a sham, had been a popular figure in classical comedy, and appears elsewhere in Shakespeare's plays in the guise of Pistol in *Henry IV Part 2* and Falstaff in *Henry IV* and *Henry V*. The character's popularity in the 17th century was such that King Charles I wrote "Monsieur Paroles" next to the title in his private copy of *All's Well That Ends Well*, and the play was subsequently adapted to expand his part.

For all his shocking betrayal of his friend Bertram and his fellow soldiers, Paroles gains a certain amount of sympathy from his obvious relief at abandoning the pretence: "Simply the thing I am / Shall make me live" (4.3.334–335). In the 2013 RSC production, as played by Jonathan Slinger, Paroles drops the Sandhurst accent that he had used to ingratiate himself, and finally accepts his homosexuality.

THIS WORLD TO ME IS BUT A CEASELESS STORM WHIRRING ME FROM MY FRIENDS

PERICLES, PRINCE OF TYRE (1607)

DRAMATIS PERSONAE

John Gower The narrator, who also delivers the epilogue.

Pericles, Prince of Tyre Husband of Thaisa, father to Marina.

Thaisa Daughter of King Simonides, wife to Pericles and mother to Marina.

Antiochus King of Antioch, intent on having Pericles killed when Pericles discovers Antiochus's incestuous relationship with his daughter.

Thaliart Villain hired by Antiochus to murder Pericles.

Helicanus Loyal advisor to Pericles.

Simonides King of Pentapolis and father to Thaisa. Allows Pericles to marry his daughter.

Marina Daughter of Pericles and Thaisa, born at sea. Dogged by misfortune, her virtue and chastity ensure her safety.

Cleon Governor of Tarsus. Indebted to Pericles, he pledges to protect and raise Marina.

Dioniza Wife of Cleon, she is jealous of Marina and plots to murder her.

Cerimon A physician in Ephesus who helps restore Thaisa to life when she washes up on the shore.

Lysimachus Governor of Mytilene.

Diana Goddess of chastity.

Gower narrates the story of Pericles, beginning with the incestuous King Antiochus. Pericles works out Antiochus's riddle but **the king secretly orders his murder**.

Still fleeing from Thaliart, **Pericles is shipwrecked**, washing up on the shores of Pentapolis.

Thaisa seemingly dies giving birth en route to Tyre. The superstitious sailors insist that her body be thrown overboard.

↑ 1   ↑ 5   ↑ 11

Scenes 1–5   **Scenes 7–11**

3 ↓   7 & 9 ↓

The hired villain Thaliart arrives in Tyre to poison **Pericles, who manages to escape to Tarsus**.

Disguised for fear of his life, Pericles takes part in a tournament for the suitors of King Simonides' daughter. After **winning the tournament, Pericles marries Thaisa**.

The medieval poet Gower acts as the narrator relating the story of Pericles, Prince of Tyre. His story begins with King Antiochus whose daughter's suitors must answer a riddle in order to win her hand. Pericles solves the riddle, which exposes Antiochus's incestuous lust and forces Pericles to flee back to Tyre for safety. King Antiochus sends the villainous Thaliart to murder Pericles. Pericles hears of Thaliart's murderous plans and escapes on a ship to Tarsus, leaving his trusted counsellor Helicanus to govern Tyre.

Arriving in Tarsus, Pericles relieves the famine-struck city with corn, earning the gratitude of the governor Cleon and his wife Dioniza. After setting sail again in a storm, Pericles is shipwrecked on the shores of Pentapolis, losing all his possessions except his armour. He is rescued by fishermen and incognito taken to the court of King Simonides, who is celebrating his daughter Thaisa's birthday with a tournament. Pericles wins the jousting competition and the king grants him the hand of Princess Thaisa.

Thaisa's body is washed up onto the shores of Ephesus where **a physician revives her** from a death-like sleep and takes her to the Temple of Diana where she serves as a priestess.

Dioniza's plans to murder Marina are thwarted when the girl is kidnapped by pirates and **sold to a brothel at Mytilene**.

The governor of Mytilene, **Lysimachus, frees Marina** from the brothel. When Marina sings for **the prince** he eventually **realizes that she is his daughter**. Pericles agrees to Marina's betrothal to Lysimachus.

Gower explains how **the villainous are punished and the virtuous rewarded**, pointing to the honourable Pericles and his family as good examples.

12   **15 & 16**   **19 & 21**   **22**

Scenes 12–16   **Scenes 19–22**

11   **15**   **18**   **21**

Pericles decides to **take the new-born child, Marina, to Tarsus** to be raised by the governor Cleon and his wife.

Gower narrates the events of Marina's youth. She is now a young woman and, Cleon's jealous wife **Dioniza arranges for her murder**.

Pericles is told that Marina has died. Grief-stricken, he vows to never speak again and to spend the rest of his life in mourning on the seas.

Pericles has a vision of the goddess Diana who tells him to travel to Ephesus where he is **reunited with Thaisa**.

Meanwhile, King Antiochus has died so Pericles is safe to reveal his identity as Prince of Tyre and return home with his now pregnant wife. On the way to Tyre, they encounter a tempest, during which Thaisa appears to die giving birth to a daughter and, at the insistence of the sailors, is buried at sea. Pericles sails to Tarsus where he entrusts his daughter, now named Marina, to the indebted Cleon and Dioniza.

Thaisa's coffin is washed ashore at Ephesus where a physician revives her and sends her to be a priestess at the Temple of Diana.

Gower recounts how 14 years have passed during which time Marina has grown into a virtuous young woman, attracting the envy of Dioniza, who conspires to have her murdered. Marina flees, but is abducted by pirates who sell her to a brothel in Mytilene. Pericles has returned to Tarsus to find Marina but is falsely told that she is dead, causing him to pledge himself to a lifetime of silent mourning sailing the seas.

Marina has steadfastly clung to her chastity, to the annoyance of her bawd (brothel madam), but

while she is there she is able to convince the governor Lysimachus, who has visited the brothel in disguise, to help her. When Pericles' ship arrives by chance at Mytilene, Lysimachus tries to cheer the sorrow-drowned Pericles by sending Marina to sing to him.

Hearing Marina's life's story, Pericles joyfully realizes she is his daughter. The goddess Diana appears to Pericles in a dream telling him to visit her temple at Ephesus. Pericles journeys there with Marina and is miraculously reunited with his wife, Thaisa. »

IN CONTEXT

THEMES
Life's journey, love, fate, family, endurance, reunion

SETTING
Antioch, Tyre, Tarsus, Pentapolis, Ephesus, Mytilene (Mediterranean)

SOURCES
1390s Shakespeare used John Gower's *Apollonius (Pericles) of Tyre* included in *Confessio Amantis*. Gower expanded on the popular Greek story.

1576 Shakespeare also took some details from Laurence Twine's novella *The Pattern of Painful Adventures*.

LEGACY
1623 *Pericles* is not included in the First Folio, leading to persistent doubts surrounding its authorship.

1659 The play is one of the first staged after the reopening of the theatres by Charles II.

1738 George Lillo puts on an adaptation of the play called *Marina* at Covent Garden.

1983 The BBC film the play with Mike Gwilym as Pericles, and Juliet Stevenson as Thaisa.

2003 Yukio Ninagawa's Japanese production creates a fairy-tale world using human puppet shows. It played at the National Theatre, London.

2012 The National Theatre of Greece produces the play as part of the Shakespeare World Festival running alongside the Olympic Games.

Shakespeare shaped his plays to satisfy his audience's expectations. People attending a tragedy would expect to see a tableau of death by the play's close; those attending a romance or comedy anticipated marriages and reunions. *Pericles, Prince of Tyre* is no exception. In this romance, Shakespeare separates his protagonist from his wife and daughter in order to build towards their reunion at the close. Pericles is tossed upon the seas of the Mediterranean from shore to shore and must endure life's "ceaseless storm" (15.71) in order, at the end of the story, to appreciate fully the pleasures of reconciliation.

Believing his wife and daughter to be dead, Pericles slips into a near comatose state. Twenty scenes into the drama Shakespeare asks his audience to imagine that Pericles "for this three months hath not spoken" (21.18). The protagonist

Why, as men do a-land – the great ones eat up the little ones.
Master fisherman
Scene 5

is emotionally exhausted. Grief has transformed the voyager; as Helicanus suggests, when he draws back a curtain to reveal Pericles with an overgrown beard, "This was a goodly person / Till the disaster of one mortal night / Drove him to this" (21.29–30). Separated from his wife and daughter, Pericles all but withdraws from society.

Emotional reunion
Shakespeare's presentation of Pericles's reunion with his daughter Marina is a moving moment. The couple's gradual realization that they are father and daughter is developed across the space of some hundred lines. Marina begins by telling Pericles that she has "endured a grief" (21.76) that may equal his own. By this point in the play, audiences will be acutely aware of the misfortunes that have befallen both characters. They will also be aware that Pericles believes his daughter to be dead. Having listened to Marina's opening words, Pericles shares his private thoughts with the audience in an aside that

John Gower, illustrated in this 14th-century manuscript, was a popular poet and storyteller. Shakespeare drew on his retelling of the Greek tale and made Gower the narrator in the play.

Marina, played here by Ony Uhiaria, defends herself from the bawd, played by Linda Bassett, in this production at Stratford-upon-Avon (2006).

is filled with dramatic irony: "I am great with woe, and shall deliver weeping. / My dearest wife was like this maid, and such / My daughter might have been. My queen's square brows, / Her stature to an inch, as wand-like straight, / As silver-voiced, her eyes as jewel-like, / And cased as richly, in pace another Juno, / Who starves the ears she feeds, and makes them hungry / The more she gives them speech." (21.95–102).

Building tension
Pericles' yearning to see his daughter again is palpable, but Shakespeare delays the revelation, thereby increasing the audience's desire to see this moment. With every speech the pair edge closer to their mutual understanding. When Pericles discovers Marina's name, he fears that the gods are mocking him; when he discovers that her mother died at sea while giving birth, he believes he is experiencing "the rarest dream"

(21.149). When it eventually comes, the revelation also serves as a plot-reminder for the audience: "The King my father did in Tarsus leave me, / Till cruel Cleon, with his wicked wife, / Did seek to murder me, and wooed a villain / To attempt the deed; who having drawn to do't, / A crew of pirates came and rescued me. / To Myteline they brought me. But, good sir, / What will you of me?

O come, be buried
A second time within
these arms.
Pericles
Scene 22

Why do you weep? It may be / You think me an impostor. No, good faith, I am the daughter to King Pericles, / If good King Pericles be." (21.158–167). Pericles' tears begin to fall during Marina's speech, though Marina has yet to realize the import of her story. When she confirms that her mother was called Thaisa, her father shares the knowledge he has determined: "Now blessing on thee! Rise. Thou art my child" (21.200). Marina's thoughts about this are not put into words, but her silence is touchingly truthful.

Closing scenes
There are similarities between *Pericles* and *The Winter's Tale*. Rather than staging the reunion between King Leontes and his daughter Perdita, Shakespeare conveys this information through reported speech. Both plays end with another revelation and a reunion. In *The Winter's Tale*, Shakespeare created a moving scene in which Leontes stares at a life-like statue of his wife; and father and daughter are stunned when it begins to move. There is a similar effect in *Pericles*. Pericles finds himself unwittingly before his wife Thaisa at the Temple of Ephesus. She listens as his story unfolds: "I here confess myself the King of Tyre, / Who, frighted from my country, did espouse / The fair Thaisa at Pentapolis. / At sea in childbed died she, but brought forth / A maid child called Marina, who, O goddess, / Wears yet thy silver liv'ry." (22.22–27). As Pericles reunites mother with child, despair is replaced with hope; the "ceaseless storm" (15.71) of ill fortune has been abated. ■

WHAT IS THE CITY BUT THE PEOPLE?

CORIOLANUS (1608)

DRAMATIS PERSONAE

Caius Martius A fearsome Roman general and proud patrician. He is honoured with the surname "Coriolanus" for acts of bravery in battle.

Menenius A Roman patrician who advises Coriolanus. He also attempts to calm the rioting citizens of Rome.

Volumnia Coriolanus's mother, who raised her son to be a warrior and delights in his prowess on the battlefield.

Virgilia Coriolanus's wife. She accompanies Volumnia and her own son to plead forgiveness when Coriolanus threatens to destroy Rome.

Cominius A Roman general and consul, who proposes the title "Coriolanus" for Caius Martius.

Titus Lartius A Roman patrician and admirer of Coriolanus, who is appointed a general.

Sicinius and Brutus Two tribunes who ensure Coriolanus's unpopularity among the plebeians, and mastermind his banishment from Rome.

Aufidius General of the Volscian army and Coriolanus's great enemy and respected rival. He wins Coriolanus's respect on the battlefield, but ultimately destroys him.

Roman plebeians Rioting citizens angered by the patricians' misgovernment.

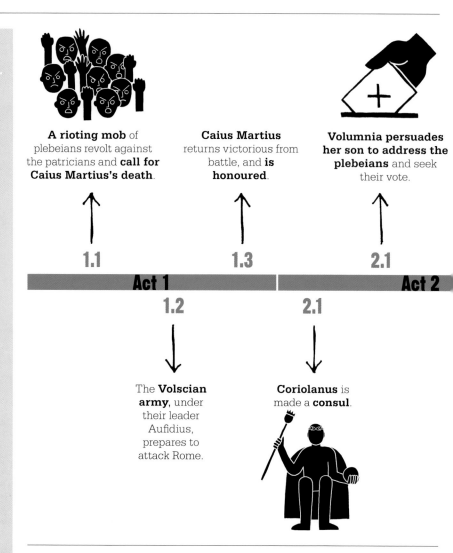

A rioting mob of plebeians revolt against the patricians and **call for Caius Martius's death**.

1.1

Caius Martius returns victorious from battle, and **is honoured**.

1.3

Volumnia persuades her son to address the plebeians and seek their vote.

2.1

Act 1   **Act 2**

1.2

The **Volscian army**, under their leader Aufidius, prepares to attack Rome.

2.1

Coriolanus is made a **consul**.

I n Rome, a mob of plebeians gather to discuss with each other their grievances with the patricians, who they believe are hoarding grain during a time of famine. Having resolved to kill Caius Martius, thought to be the worst of the patricians because of his pride and arrogance, the plebeians are calmed by Menenius, who suggests that they reconsider.

Caius Martius returns covered in blood from a battle with the Volscian army, and his mother, Volumnia, revels in her son's honour and courage. Caius is rewarded with the title "Coriolanus". Two tribunes, Sicinius and Brutus, fear that he will be promoted into a position of political power. As the tribunes feared, the Senate decides to make Coriolanus a consul, but in order to assume this role he must first receive the plebeians' vote. Coriolanus is reluctant to pander to the people and show them the scars they wish to see, but is persuaded to do so by his mother. Although the people give him their voices, the tribunes Sicinius and Brutus persuade them to change their minds.

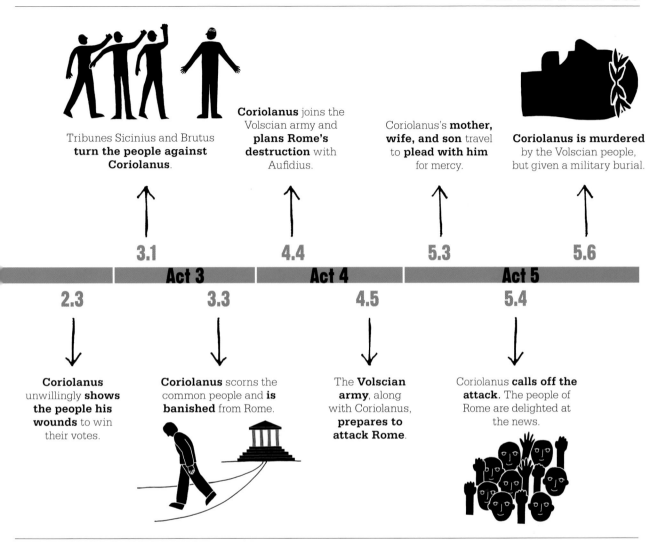

Tribunes Sicinius and Brutus **turn the people against Coriolanus**.

Coriolanus joins the Volscian army and **plans Rome's destruction** with Aufidius.

Coriolanus's **mother, wife, and son** travel to **plead with him** for mercy.

Coriolanus is murdered by the Volscian people, but given a military burial.

3.1

4.4

5.3

5.6

Act 3   **Act 4**   **Act 5**

2.3

3.3

4.5

5.4

Coriolanus unwillingly **shows the people his wounds** to win their votes.

Coriolanus scorns the common people and **is banished** from Rome.

The **Volscian army**, along with Coriolanus, **prepares to attack Rome**.

Coriolanus **calls off the attack**. The people of Rome are delighted at the news.

Coriolanus is outraged that he must appear before the people once more, and cannot contain his disdain. He gladly leaves the city that has shown him ingratitude and joins the enemy Volscian army. Together with Aufidius, his old enemy, he plots Rome's destruction. Aufidius secretly plans Coriolanus's downfall.

When the people of Rome hear about Coriolanus's intention to burn the city, they send Menenius to discourage him, but Coriolanus's mind is resolved. In a final attempt to change his mind, Volumnia and

Coriolanus's wife and son visit the Volscian camp to plead with the soldier to spare them and the city. Coriolanus is steadfast at first, but his resolve melts when his mother pleads on her knees before her son. In sparing Rome, Coriolanus sacrifices his own life by betraying the Volscian army. While the people of Rome rejoice, Coriolanus's mother acknowledges the sacrifice her son has made. He is brutally murdered by the Volscians, but Aufidius states that he should be given a warrior's burial. »

> ❝
> It is held
> That valour is the chiefest virtue, and
> Most dignifies the haver.
> **Cominius**
> **Act 2, Scene 2**
> ❞

THEMES
Class struggle, identity, pride, honour, masculinity, power, politics, family

SETTING
Ancient Rome

SOURCES
1579 Thomas North's English translation of *Plutarch's Lives of the Ancient Greeks and Romans*.

LEGACY
1681 Nahum Tate adapts Shakespeare's *Coriolanus* to create a royalist propaganda piece called *The Ingratitude of a Commonwealth*.

1941 *Coriolanus* is championed in Germany and taught in schools there. The protagonist is identified with Adolf Hitler as a model of charismatic leadership.

1959 Laurence Olivier plays Coriolanus in Stratford-upon-Avon, portraying him as a spoilt, incorrigible boy.

1964 The Berliner Ensemble performs an adaptation by Bertolt Brecht, which emphasizes the plebeians' class struggle.

1990 Michael Bogdanov's production for the English Shakespeare Company sets the play in Eastern Europe during the politically turbulent era of the 1980s.

2011 Ralph Fiennes directs and stars in a British film adaptation of *Coriolanus* set in a modern-day version of Rome.

oriolanus is a play about power, politics, personality, and the fraught relationship between Rome's plebeians and its proud patricians. The play opens with a scene of riotous discontent. The citizens are appalled with a governing class that shows little concern for the people's welfare during a time of famine. Ten lines into the play we hear the first rallying call for the murder of a patrician: "Let us kill him" (1.1.10). The plebeians hate the city's leaders in general for their greed and profligacy, but target Caius Martius as "chief enemy to the people" (1.1.7–8). Of all the patricians who place their own needs above those of the people they govern, Caius Martius (later Coriolanus) is most despicable: "He's a very dog to the commonality" (1.1.27).

Although some of the plebeians recognize that Coriolanus has fought valiantly in battle to protect the city and its people from harm, most resent his "nature", which they perceive to be scornful and self-important. For Coriolanus, the people of Rome represent little more than a stinking, cowardly,

All the contagion of the south light on you,
You shames of Rome!
You herd of – boils
and plagues
Caius Martius
Act 1, Scene 5

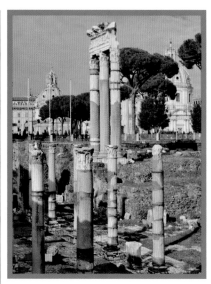

Control of the city of Rome is a central question in *Coriolanus*. Does the city belong to its people, or do the patricians have a right – and duty – to rule as they see fit?

fickle mob worthy only of disdain – a herd of "boils and plagues" (1.5.2) in his words.

Undeserving people
This play pits an individual against society. Coriolanus's greatest battle is not against invading forces, but against his own people, who are fighting for equality and against injustice. The citizens perceive themselves as being the lifeblood of the city itself, but Coriolanus sees them merely as a blot on the landscape. In his mind they are rioting "To curb the will of the nobility" (3.1.41), rather than, as their appointed tribunes would argue, fighting for their liberties and their human rights. The patrician Menenius presents the ruling class as compassionate and paternal: "most charitable care / Have the patricians of you" (1.1.63–64). He argues that the famine should be blamed on the gods, and discourages accusations

of grain-hoarding by the patricians. Coriolanus, however, has no talent as, or desire to be, a political spin-doctor; as Menenius suggests, "His heart's his mouth" (3.1.257). As Coriolanus sees it, the plebeians "Did not deserve corn gratis" (3.1.128) because they performed poorly in battle: "Being i'th' war, / Their mutinies and revolts, wherein they showed / Most valour, spoke not for them" (3.1.128–130).

In other words, Coriolanus champions meritocracy (reserved for patricians) and the status quo, while the "tongues o'th' common mouth" (3.1.23) favour democracy.

Opposing views

Coriolanus is structured around argument and debate. Shakespeare introduces alternative perspectives from the outset. While some citizens respect Coriolanus for his valour, others mock him as a mummy's boy who fought only to please his mother. The divergent opinions voiced by Shakespeare's mob complicates the audience's experience of the play. Should our sympathies lie with this rioting throng intent on violent acts? Is the mob's murderous intent justifiable and based on accurate information?

Over the centuries, readers and audiences have also been inclined to interpret the play in a wide variety of ways, producing a string of alternative and often politically divergent readings. Coriolanus has been interpreted as both the hero and the villain of this drama, and the plebeians have been accused of being dangerously fickle, as well as morally justified in their behaviour. The mob »

His sword, death's stamp,
Where it did mark, it took.
From face to foot
He was a thing of blood,
whose every motion
Was timed with dying cries.
Cominius
Act 2, Scene 2

An 18th-century print depicts Coriolanus with his mother, Volumnia. She is a key influence, first persuading him to run for the Senate, and later to abandon plans to destroy Rome.

also proves a dangerous force, threatening to turn their fury on their own tribunes by the close.

Bad politician

Diplomacy is not a quality for which Coriolanus is renowned. This character makes enemies very easily, and it is perhaps surprising that he avoids assassination for as long as he does. He is at once one of Shakespeare's most unattractive and most compelling characterizations. The patrician soldier is courageous and awe-inspiring on the battlefield, but has little success when he enters the world of politics, for which he requires the citizens' approval.

Coriolanus is larger than life, a killing machine; he would always prove a misfit in public life. "Rather say I play / the man I am." (3.2.13–14) he declares when his mother urges him to play the role of the diplomat in receiving the citizen's voices of election. He

cannot dissemble; he can only speak as he feels. Ultimately, Coriolanus's stinging and unbridled tongue, combined with the machinations of two power-hungry tribunes, will lead to his banishment from Rome. Though the citizens view this as a victory, their safety is no longer assured. In a typical act of arrogant defiance Coriolanus "banishes" Rome, and looks to revenge the people's ingratitude.

Firm voice

Though there are many citizens' voices to be heard in this play, it is Coriolanus's distinctive tone that will remain in the audience's ears. Coriolanus carries with him both the charisma of a celebrity and the terror of a mythological monster. There is crispness and bite in the phrasing of his angry dismissal of the Roman mob: "You common cry of curs, whose breath I hate / As reek o'th' rotten fens, whose loves I prize / As the

Let me have war, say I. It exceeds peace as far as day does night. It's sprightly, walking, audible and full of vent. Peace is a very apoplexy, lethargy; mulled, deaf, sleepy, insensible; a getter of more bastard children than war's a destroyer of men.
First servingman
Act 4, Scene 5

dead carcasses of unburied men / That do corrupt my air: I banish you." (3.3.124–127). Coriolanus's speech is gritty, muscular, and often monosyllabic. Every word he

Do the people of Rome control Rome's freedom and independence, or are such notions in the gift only of a strong and decisive leader whose protection may crush the collective will?

Coriolanus, played here by Toby Stephens in a 1995 RSC production, is covered in blood following the battle at Corioli. He is a man of action, not a man of words.

speaks distances him from the citizens, until he seems to tower above them, delivering his words of condemnation as if they were bolts of lightning: "Despising / For you the city, thus I turn my back. / There is a world elsewhere." (3.3.137–139).

No matter how objectionable Coriolanus's words may be, his magnetism is undeniable. Before leaving for exile, he tells his mother, "I shall be loved when I am lacked" (4.1.16), and these words mirror most people's experience of watching the play in performance; the play loses some of its zest whenever he leaves the stage. While the people of Rome believe themselves to be the city's core, Coriolanus asserts the power of the individual, and it is his character that dominates this play, dwarfing

the role played by the city's people. Coriolanus is alarmingly self-assured and self-reliant, forever acting "Alone" (5.6.117).

A play for all time

In following Thomas North's translation of *Plutarch's Lives of the Noble Greeks and Romans*, Shakespeare presented a fractious and politically explosive period of Roman history. In recent years, historians have questioned whether Coriolanus ever existed, but certainly Plutarch viewed him as a historical character, whose lineage could be traced back to early kings of Rome.

Shakespeare and his contemporaries were living through a similar era of social and political unrest, in which insurrections and corn riots were similarly a feature of their own world. Shakespeare's choice of subject matter was characteristically full of controversy, contemporary relevance, as well as commercial interest: the play exemplifies Ben Jonson's statement, in the Preface to the First Folio in 1623, that Shakespeare's works are "not of an age, but for all time". ∎

O mother, mother!
What have you done?
Behold, the heavens do ope,
The gods look down, and this
unnatural scene
They laugh at.
Coriolanus
Act 5, Scene 3

A German hero?

Shakespeare's Coriolanus is an ambivalent hero, and the audience is never entirely certain whose side to take. This ambivalence has left space over the centuries for *Coriolanus* to be appropriated for political purposes by both right- and left-wing ideologies. This was never more true than in 20th-century Germany, where Shakespeare was the most performed playwright, and all sides sought to claim his legacy.

Under the Nazi regime in the 1930s and 1940s, Coriolanus's position as a powerful leader battling against a failing democratic system was emphasized. Germans were encouraged to see Hitler as a similar figure – with the implication that, to avoid the play's tragedy, it was necessary for the masses to follow him unwaveringly.

In the 1950s, an adaptation by Bertholt Brecht called *Coriolan* stressed the class warfare in the play. It highlighted the attack by the people on their corrupt Roman leaders. Brecht was working in Communist East Germany, and the play was dedicated to the German proletariat.

THOU METST WITH THINGS DYING I WITH THINGS NEW-BORN

THE WINTER'S TALE (1609–1610)

DRAMATIS PERSONAE

Leontes King of Sicily and boyhood friend of Polixenes.

Hermione Wife of Leontes, wrongly accused of adultery.

Mamillius Young son of Leontes and Hermione.

Perdita Daughter of Leontes and Hermione, abandoned as a baby and brought up by the Old Shepherd. Her name means "the lost one".

Camillo Adviser to Leontes, who flees with Polixenes to Bohemia.

Antigonus Sicilian lord, married to Paulina.

Cleomenes and Dion Sicilian lords, sent to the oracle at Delphi.

Paulina Wife to Antigonus, outspoken friend of Hermione.

Emilia Attendant to Hermione.

Polixenes King of Bohemia and boyhood friend of Leontes.

Florizel Son of Polixenes. He is in love with Perdita in the guise of Doricles, a peasant.

Archidamus Bohemian lord.

Autolycus Charming rogue, once in Florizel's service.

Old Shepherd He finds and raises Perdita.

Clown Old Shepherd's son.

Mopsa and Dorcas Shepherdesses who sing at the sheep-shearing fair.

Time A chorus.

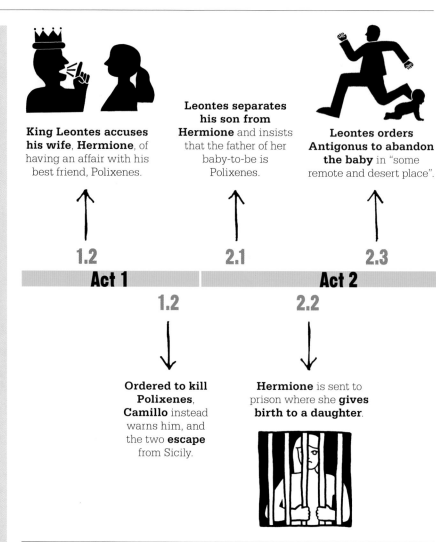

King Leontes accuses his wife, Hermione, of having an affair with his best friend, Polixenes.

Leontes separates his son from Hermione and insists that the father of her baby-to-be is Polixenes.

Leontes orders Antigonus to abandon the baby in "some remote and desert place".

1.2

2.1

2.3

Act 1

Act 2

1.2

2.2

Ordered to kill Polixenes, Camillo instead warns him, and the two **escape** from Sicily.

Hermione is sent to prison where she **gives birth to a daughter**.

Polixenes, King of Bohemia, has been staying with his boyhood friend Leontes, King of Sicily. When his pregnant wife, Hermione, persuades Polixenes to stay longer, Leontes becomes jealous, convinced of an attraction between Polixenes and his wife. Leontes orders his adviser Camillo to kill Polixenes. Camillo, sure of Hermione's innocence, warns Polixenes, and he and Polixenes escape from Sicily.

Leontes's son Mamillius starts to tell his mother a story when Leontes, taking Polixenes's flight as proof of Hermione's guilt, orders Mamillius to be kept from his mother. He asserts that the baby on the way is Polixenes's and sends Hermione to prison. Messengers are sent to the oracle at Delphi to confirm her guilt. Hermione gives birth in prison, and her friend Paulina takes the baby girl to Leontes hoping to soften his attitude. Instead, he turns on her. Paulina defies him, but he accuses her husband Antigonus of egging her on, and tells Antigonus to take the babe far away and abandon it. Messengers return from Delphi.

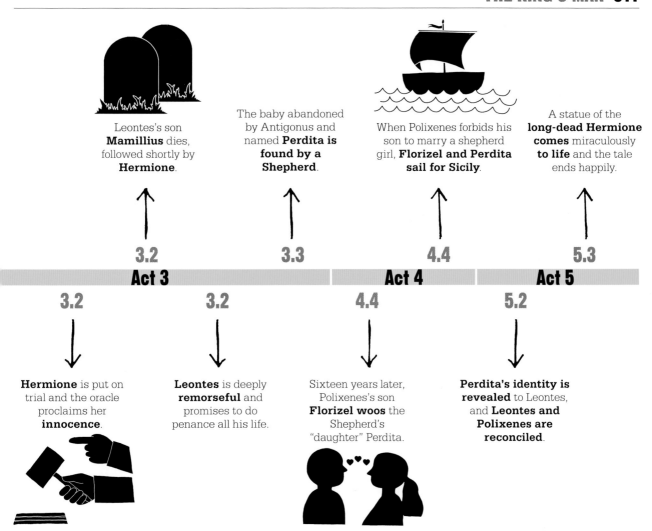

Leontes's son **Mamillius** dies, followed shortly by **Hermione**.

The baby abandoned by Antigonus and named **Perdita is found by a Shepherd**.

When Polixenes forbids his son to marry a shepherd girl, **Florizel and Perdita sail for Sicily**.

A statue of the **long-dead Hermione comes** miraculously **to life** and the tale ends happily.

3.2

3.3

4.4

5.3

Act 3

Act 4

Act 5

3.2

3.2

4.4

5.2

Hermione is put on trial and the oracle proclaims her **innocence**.

Leontes is deeply **remorseful** and promises to do penance all his life.

Sixteen years later, Polixenes's son **Florizel woos** the Shepherd's "daughter" Perdita.

Perdita's identity is revealed to Leontes, and **Leontes and Polixenes are reconciled**.

Leontes puts Hermione on trial. When the oracle's words proclaim Hermione innocent, Leontes declares the oracle false. Then comes news that Mamillius, pining for his mother, has died. Hermione faints and is carried out. Paulina tells Leontes bitterly that Hermione is now also dead from the shock of losing both her children. Leontes, remorseful, sees this as a sign of the gods' wrath. Meanwhile, Antigonus abandons the babe (whom he calls Perdita) on the shores of Bohemia, where she is found by a Shepherd. Antigonus is killed by a bear. Sixteen years later, Polixenes talks with Camillo of his son Florizel's love for a shepherd girl. They decide to go to a festival incognito. On a country road, the clown Autolycus sings of his way of life. Perdita and Florizel (known to Perdita as Doricles) appear dressed in festival costume. At the festival, Polixenes (in disguise) is charmed by Perdita. But when "Doricles" says that he will wed Perdita, Polixenes threatens to disinherit Florizel. Florizel decides to take a ship, and Camillo tells him to go to Sicily to make peace with Leontes. In Sicily, Leontes, still mourning Hermione, vows never to remarry. Florizel and Perdita arrive, bearing Polixenes's message of forgiveness. Leontes is moved, but then comes news that Polixenes has arrived in Sicily. Autolycus reveals how Leontes has found his long-lost daughter. They all go to a chapel in Paulina's house to see a lifelike statue of Hermione. Paulina orders the statue to descend, and Hermione comes alive miraculously. She embraces Leontes, then finds that Perdita is alive. All is forgiven, and Paulina and Camillo are told to wed. »

IN CONTEXT

THEMES
Jealousy, suffering, hope, love, redemption

SETTING
Winter in Sicily, and summer 16 years later in Bohemia and Sicily

SOURCES
1588 Robert Greene's romantic prose tale *Pandosto.*

LEGACY
1611 The first performance is at The Globe in May.

1754 An adaptation, *The Sheep-shearing,* or *Florizel and Perdita,* by McNamara Morgan is staged at Covent Garden.

1802–11 Actor John Philip Kemble stages a series of grand productions in London.

1881 The Duke of Saxe-Meiningen's famous company tours Europe with an acclaimed production.

1912 Director Harley Granville-Barker's psychologically realistic production opens at the Savoy Theatre, London.

1958 Christopher Plummer plays Leontes as a victim in a Canadian production.

2001 Nicholas Hytner's National Theatre production sets the sheep-shearing contest at a rock festival.

2009 Sam Mendes opens his Bridge Project, an Anglo-American theatre partnership, with *The Winter's Tale.* Simon Russell Beale plays Leontes and Ethan Hawke is Autolycus.

The *Winter's Tale* combines the pastoral humour and romance of *As You Like It* with the dark power of *Othello.* Yet the play is something of an enigma. In Shakespeare's day, a winter's tale was something told by old wives at the fireside. It was a fanciful story, typically with a simple salutary lesson. As Leontes's son Mamillius says when he proposes to tell his mother a story, "A sad tale's best for winter" (2.1.27). And in many ways that is what *The Winter's Tale* is: a sad story with a happy ending, a tale of loss and redemption.

Winter and tragedy

The first three acts of the play are not like a fairy tale at all; they are an emotional drama as grim as any classical tragedy. King Leontes of Sicily finds his wife Hermione so successful in persuading his boyhood friend Polixenes to stay longer that he suspects they are having an affair. His mind is eaten up with jealousy, expressed in language so sodden with sexual innuendo that it almost loses sense: "Gone already! / Inch-thick, knee-deep, o'er head and ears a fork'd one!" (1.2.187–188) He is talking about wading deeper into

Too hot, too hot:
To mingle friendship farre
is mingling bloods.
Leontes
Act 1, Scene 2

Sir, spare your treats.
The bug which you would
fright me with, I seek.
Hermione
Act 3, Scene 2

adultery, with the "forked one" the horns of a cuckold, a husband cheated in adultery. But the imagery is phallic and lewd.

As he becomes increasingly obsessed, Leontes behaves erratically, like Othello, but he has no need of an Iago to feed his suspicion; it is all there in his fevered imagination. It is what he memorably calls the spider in the cup – you might swallow it happily in ignorance, but you will throw up if you see it.

His rage escalates, and Leontes proceeds to destroy those closest to him. Separation from his mother kills Mamillius, and the shock of her son's death kills Hermione. Only with the loss of all his family does Leontes come to his senses and realize the horror he has wrought.

The play's first part is almost a full-blown tragedy. And yet the action all takes place in just three short acts, not the conventional five. Leontes's jealousy seems to erupt out of nowhere and takes just a few hundred lines to explode to the point of no return. Some audiences find the abruptness and extremity of his reaction difficult to accept. In barely an hour of stage time, the entire tragedy has been played out. Yet this mini-tragedy's ending is

A production of *The Winter's Tale* at the Deutsches Nationaltheater, Weimar, Germany (2012), presented the Sicilian court as a harsh place reminiscent of an earlier, reactionary Germany.

subtly different from the other tragic plays. In the longer tragedies, the extremity of suffering in the protagonist's self-discovery means that the only way out is death. In *The Winter's Tale*, Leontes is utterly distraught – but he is alive, and will go on living with the knowledge of his mistake for a further 16 years.

As he leaves the stage, not to reappear for an hour, Leontes vows to do penance every day – "…tears shed…" he says, "Shall be my recreation" (3.2.238, 239). He will have no pleasure, but the word "recreation" has another meaning – tears will be his re-creation, his rebuilding and redemption.

The tragedy does not end with Leontes's grief. A brief final scene shows Antigonus laying Leontes's baby daughter on the shores of Bohemia, and naming her Perdita, the "lost one". It is the last disaster made by Leontes's folly – and yet it seems like the beginning of a fairy tale, with an abandoned princess.

In true fairy tale style, the lost babe is discovered by an Old Shepherd – but not before Antigonus meets his end with one of the most famous stage directions of all time, "Exit, pursued by a bear" (Act 3, Scene 3). (In the play's first production, a real bear may have been used – there was a famous bear-pit near the theatre. Now, almost always, however they enact the bear, directors play it for laughs.) With the entry of the Old

Shepherd and his son, with their good-natured rustic quirks, the play suddenly shifts from darkest tragedy to romantic comedy.

A pastoral idyll

When the play recommences in Act 4, it is in a different world. Time has moved on 16 years. The scene is the countryside of Bohemia in early summer. The mood is wholeheartedly comic and romantic, as the baby Perdita, **»**

Geography and the play

In moving the action of *The Winter's Tale* from Sicily to the shores of Bohemia – in reality a landlocked region of central Europe – the modern reader may wonder at the vagueness of some of Shakespeare's geographical settings. There is no evidence that Shakespeare ever left England. He relied on a variety of sources for the locations, mostly around the Mediterranean, where the plots of 31 of his 38 plays are set. His Rome and Egypt in *Julius Caesar* and *Antony and Cleopatra* were gleaned from Plutarch; his Venice in *Othello*

and *The Merchant of Venice* probably derived from travel books and novels such as *The Unfortunate Traveller* by Thomas Nashe, published in 1594. The portrayal of Troy of *Troilus and Cressida* was taken from *The Iliad*.

However, not all the locations in the plays are meant to be taken too literally. Bohemia in *The Winter's Tale*, like Athens in *A Midsummer Night's Dream* and Ardennes in *As You Like It*, represented, to Shakespeare's audience, an exotic idyll and escapism.

now 16 and a shepherdess, is courted by Polixenes's son Florizel at a sheep-shearing festival.

Few plays experience such a dramatic change in genre. Indeed, the shift is so sudden that some critics have labelled *The Winter's Tale* one of Shakespeare's "problem plays". To some extent, it reflects the contemporary vogue for "tragi-comedies" developed by playwrights such as John Marston, but none of the tragi-comedies of the day feature the stark midstream shift of *The Winter's Tale*.

The play is often grouped with *The Tempest*, *Pericles*, and *Cymbeline* as a "late" play. These

A romantic painting (1845) by Augustus Leopold Egg depicts roguish peddler Autolycus singing in Act 4, Scene 4. A British production that year omitted some of the play's "indelicacies".

are sometimes described as "romances" because they have something akin with the poems of the Middle Ages that told stories of courtly love in fantastical settings.

The marked midplay shift in *The Winter's Tale* is quite unique. Even so, the play has the same simple three-part structure as many of Shakespeare plays, including *As You Like It* and *A Midsummer Night's Dream*. These plays begin with a problem in the ordered "real" world of the court. They then move into the fantasy world of nature for the problems to be worked out before returning to the court where everything is resolved. *The Winter's Tale* works in the same way. The key difference is how fully the problem in the real world, the world of Leontes's court, is developed, growing into a full tragedy before the healing journey

into nature begins. Indeed, it is a problem so deep that it cannot be solved by Leontes or Polixenes themselves. It can only be solved by their children.

The shift from Sicily to Bohemia is in some ways a re-generation, a reflection of the fact that nature is always renewing itself. After the harshness of winter, spring brings forth new life, and nature is a continuous cycle of death and rebirth. The Old Shepherd who finds the lost baby Perdita sums up this rebirth when he says: "Thou metst with / things dying, I with things new-born" (3.3.110–111).

Summer and rebirth

The Bohemian section of *The Winter's Tale*, then, symbolizes a rebirth. The structure of the play mirrors, intentionally or not, the story of the European rebirth, the

Winter death
Leontes's jealousy of
Polixenes sets in motion
a series of disasters.
Mamillius and Hermione die.
But the tragedy leaves the
seed of a resolution – in
the form of a banished
baby daughter.

Summer rebirth
The daughter, Perdita,
grows up in a happy land of
festivals and revelry. She falls
in love with Florizel, who is
Polixenes's son. They are a
new generation unmarked
by the sins of the old.

**Renewal,
life continues**
Perdita and Florizel
return to Sicily to heal.
As if through the power of
youth and love, a statue
of Hermione is brought to
life. Leontes is forgiven,
and harmony
is restored.

The play's distinct parts follow nature's
cycle of death, rebirth, and renewal. Winter's
tragedy is replaced by summer's rebirth,
problems are solved, and life continues.

———— **Sicily**   ········ **Bohemia**

Renaissance. The Leontes story is a
dark, Greek-style tragedy set in the
classical Mediterranean. Perdita
and Florizel's story is a romance of
the kind developed in Europe, and
set in Bohemia. Shakespeare is
perhaps showing how the classical
flame has been renewed by a new
European generation.

In *A Midsummer Night's Dream*,
the star-crossed lovers escape into
the woods to fulfil their romance. In
The Winter's Tale, however, when
Polixenes forbids his son Florizel
from marrying the apparently lowly
shepherdess Perdita, the young
lovers flee from the summer fantasy
world of Bohemia to the wintry
Sicilian court. It is this reversal that
enables them to be the bearers of
redemption, bringing warmth and
life back to the chill of Leontes's
Sicily. In fact, their return literally
restores life, because at the
extraordinary climax to the play, a
statue of Hermione comes to life.

Statue of limitations

There has been much debate about
the statue. Is it a statue that comes
miraculously to life, or has

Hermione been in hiding for 16
years, waiting for this moment?
Hints emerge that she has been
hiding, when it is said that Paulina
has been visiting the hidden house
ever since she died. But this whole
moment is unusual in that we, the
audience, don't see it coming. Most
of Shakespeare's plays employ
dramatic irony. We know what
some characters in the play don't,
and the drama comes as they
finally discover the truth. In *Othello*,

Daffodils,
That come before
the swallow dares, and
Take the winds of March
with beauty
Perdita
Act 4, Scene 4

for instance, we know that Othello
has been duped by Iago and we
hang on our seats until the moment
Othello learns what we already
knew. But Hermione's coming to
life is a plot twist out of the blue.
At the end of Act 3 Paulina tells us
that Hermione died, and such is
Paulina's forthrightness that we
have no reason to doubt her word.

Some critics find this twist so
unbelievable that they feel it
weakens the play. Yet the surprise
of the living statue is deliberately
intended by Shakespeare. He
acknowledges through Paulina
that the resurrection is scarcely
believable: "That she is living, /
Were it but told you, should be
hooted at / Like an old tale"
(5.3.117–119). And herein lies an
answer. Are we meant to "hoot" at
it, provoked to laughter, so that we
leave the theatre not lost in gloom
but chuckling at the wonderful
absurdity? Maybe, then, Paulina's
words "You precious winners all"
(5.3.132) are addressed to us.
Shakespeare has given us hope
that even the very worst errors
can be redeemed. ∎

HANG THERE LIKE FRUIT MY SOUL TILL THE TREE DIE

CYMBELINE (1610–1611)

DRAMATIS PERSONAE

Cymbeline King of Britain at the time of Jesus' birth.

Innogen Cymbeline's only daughter and wife to Posthumus, later disguised as the youth Fidele.

Guiderius Known as Polydore, one of Cymbeline's two lost sons.

Arviragus Known as Cadwal, Cymbeline's other lost son.

Queen Cymbeline's second wife, and stepmother to Innogen. A wicked woman.

Cloten The Queen's oafish son by her first husband.

Belarius A banished British lord, living in Wales and calling himself Morgan.

Dr Cornelius A good-hearted physician.

Posthumus Leonatus An orphan adopted and brought up by Cymbeline, husband to Innogen.

Pisanio Posthumus's servant.

Filario Friend to Posthumus.

Giacomo A sly, self-confident Italian friend of Filario.

Caius Lucius Ambassador from Rome, later Roman general.

Helen Lady in waiting to Innogen.

A Frenchman, a Dutchman, and a Spaniard Friends of Filario.

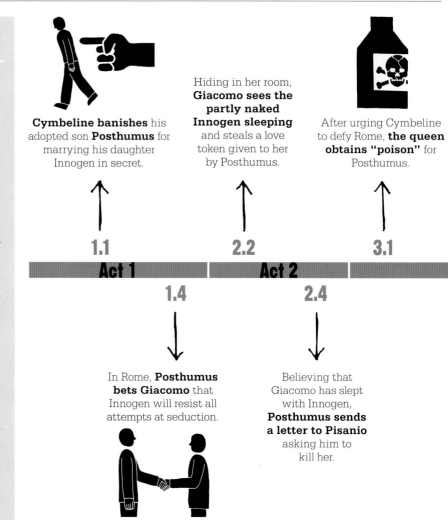

Cymbeline banishes his adopted son **Posthumus** for marrying his daughter Innogen in secret.

1.1

Hiding in her room, **Giacomo sees the partly naked Innogen sleeping** and steals a love token given to her by Posthumus.

2.2

After urging Cymbeline to defy Rome, **the queen obtains "poison"** for Posthumus.

3.1

Act 1 | **Act 2**

1.4

In Rome, **Posthumus bets Giacomo** that Innogen will resist all attempts at seduction.

2.4

Believing that Giacomo has slept with Innogen, **Posthumus sends a letter to Pisanio** asking him to kill her.

King of Britain, Cymbeline banishes Posthumus, his adopted son, who has married his daughter Innogen. Cymbeline's queen wanted her idiot son Cloten to marry Innogen. Posthumus flees to Rome where Giacomo bets him he can seduce Innogen, but when Giacomo arrives in Britain, Innogen resists his efforts. The wicked Queen asks Dr Cornelius for a poison but the doctor gives her a sleeping draft.

Giacomo smuggles himself into Innogen's bedroom in a trunk. He sees her half-naked and steals the bracelet given her by Posthumus. In Rome, Giacomo shows Posthumus the bracelet and describes Innogen's body to prove he has slept with her. Posthumus gives Giacomo Innogen's ring and swears vengeance on her.

Cymbeline refuses the tribute imposed by Rome, so the Roman ambassador Lucius declares that Rome is at war with Britain. In Wales, the exiled Belarius tells tales of the old days to Cymbeline's two sons Guiderius and Arviragus, whom he has stolen. Pisanio receives a letter from Posthumus asking him to kill Innogen, but Pisanio flees

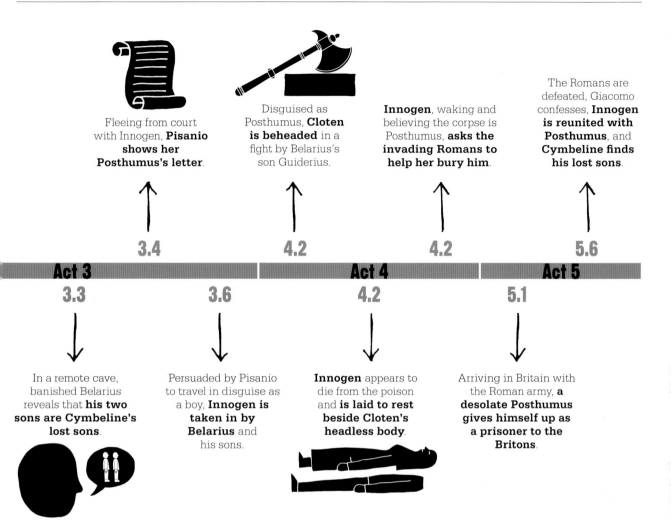

Fleeing from court with Innogen, **Pisanio shows her Posthumus's letter**.

3.4

Disguised as Posthumus, **Cloten is beheaded** in a fight by Belarius's son Guiderius.

4.2

Innogen, waking and believing the corpse is Posthumus, **asks the invading Romans to help her bury him**.

4.2

The Romans are defeated, Giacomo confesses, **Innogen is reunited with Posthumus**, and Cymbeline finds his lost sons.

5.6

Act 3 **Act 4** **Act 5**

3.3

In a remote cave, banished Belarius reveals that **his two sons are Cymbeline's lost sons**.

3.6

Persuaded by Pisanio to travel in disguise as a boy, **Innogen is taken in by Belarius** and his sons.

4.2

Innogen appears to die from the poison and **is laid to rest beside Cloten's headless body**.

5.1

Arriving in Britain with the Roman army, **a desolate Posthumus gives himself up as a prisoner to the Britons**.

with her to Milford Haven, where she hopes to meet Posthumus with the Roman army. The queen has given Pisanio "poison", for Posthumus. In Wales, Pisanio shows Innogen Posthumus's letter. She begs Pisanio to kill her but he persuades her to follow the Roman army in disguise. Cloten pursues Innogen, disguised as Posthumus. Disguised as the youth Fidele, an exhausted Innogen is given shelter by Guiderius and Arviragus.

Innogen takes the "medicine" given her unwittingly by Pisanio. Cloten challenges Guiderius, who

returns with Cloten's head. Arviragus finds Innogen, apparently dead, in the cave. Belarius lays her next to Cloten's headless body. Innogen wakes to see the corpse. She thinks it is Posthumus and that she has been betrayed by Pisanio and Cloten.

Lucius, now general of the Roman army, makes Innogen his servant. Posthumus rues that he urged Pisanio to kill Innogen and joins the British disguised as a poor soldier. Thanks to Belarius and his sons, the British beat the Romans. Posthumus dresses as a Roman and offers himself as a prisoner. He

dreams of his dead family and the god Jupiter urges justice. Belarius and his sons are rewarded. The queen dies and her wickedness is exposed. The Roman captives are brought before Cymbeline. Innogen, still in disguise, sees Giacomo with Posthumus's ring. Giacomo admits he lied to Posthumus. Posthumus confesses his part in Innogen's "death". Innogen shows she is alive, but Posthumus does not recognize her. Pisanio verifies it is Innogen, and she and Posthumus are reunited. Belarius reveals that the two boys are Cymbeline's lost sons.»

IN CONTEXT

THEMES
Jealousy, deception, suffering, hope, love, redemption

SETTING
Cymbeline's court in ancient Britain, Rome, a cave, and later, Milford Haven in Wales

SOURCES
1353 The wager plot in Bocaccio's *Decameron*.

1587 Basic historical background is taken from Holinshed's *Chronicles*.

LEGACY
1610 It is possible that the first performances take place at the indoor Blackfriars Theatre, London.

1611 The first recorded performance takes place.

1634 A performance for Charles I is staged on New Year's Day in Whitehall Palace.

1770 American actress Nancy Hallam makes a famous Innogen.

1837–67 Popular actress Helen Faucit plays Innogen as a paragon of calm virtue.

1896 Ellen Terry's portrayal of Innogen is of a more forthright woman.

1988 Three major productions in the UK, including Peter Hall's at the National Theatre, confirm *Cymbeline*'s place as a great play.

Cymbeline is one of the strangest of Shakespeare's plays. This darkly romantic tale tells the story of the misguided king of ancient Britain, Cymbeline, whose misjudgment loses him two sons and his remarkable daughter Innogen, before, in the end, all is restored. The plot is so convoluted that commentators have ridiculed it as a mess, although now most critics acknowledge that on stage it is a captivating masterpiece.

The play is based, in part, on the historical king Cunobelinus, who ruled over southern England at around the time Jesus was born. Shakespeare found the story of Cunobelinus in Holinshed's famous *Chronicles*, where he is known as Kymbeline. However, the story Shakespeare weaves in his play *Cymbeline* is almost entirely divorced from any historical truth. Indeed, Shakespeare seems completely unconcerned with any historical consistency. When the hero Posthumus is banished from

---

Fear no more the
heat o' th' sun,
Nor the furious winter's rages.
Thou thy worldly task
hast done,
Home art gone, and
ta'en thy wages.
Golden lads and girls all must,
As chimney-sweepers,
come to dust.
Guiderius
Act 4, Scene 2

Pardon's the word to all.
Cymbeline
Act 5, Scene 6

---

ancient Britain, for instance, he ends up in Rome at the time of the Renaissance. There, Posthumus's companions, who have Italian names like Filario and Giacomo, talk anachronistically of France and England. And when the Roman general Lucius lands with his army in Britain, he lands in Milford Haven, the port in west Wales where Henry Tudor landed in 1485 to claim the throne of England as Henry VII. The British court physician is named Doctor Cornelius, which calls to mind the famous 15th-century German magician Cornelius Agrippa, while the Latin name Posthumus is an odd one for an ancient Briton, or for anyone.

Patchwork of influences
This apparent mishmash is surely not carelessness on the part of Shakespeare but a deliberate act of association to create a play that has both contemporary relevance and mythical power. It is part fairy tale – with a wicked stepmother, lost princes living in a cave, and a sleeping beauty – and part tragedy.

Shakespeare brings in a variety of elements from his earlier plays. When Posthumus, fooled by the lies of Giacomo, becomes disastrously jealous of Innogen, it recalls Othello's murderous jealousy of Desdemona fuelled by Iago. And Innogen's

In London-based company Cheek-by-Jowl's emotionally charged 2007 production, Tom Hiddleston took on the dual roles of Posthumus and Cloten. Jodie McNee played Innogen.

in disguise, to try to put matters right. No wonder many critics have heaped scorn on Posthumus as an unworthy husband for the peerless Innogen. Feminist critics have highlighted the male stereotyping that portrays women as either virgins or whores, which the wager seems to play out. But perhaps there is another theme here.

A middle ground

The British court is torn between the decadent corruption and false honour of Rome and the rough innocence of wild Wales, where Cymbeline's lost sons Guiderius and Arviragus are brought up in a cave by Belarius. Even the heroic Posthumus's moral compass is set spinning in the competitive world of Rome, where men trade verbal blows over empty ideas of honour – such as whose country's women are the purest. Away from corrupting influences in the natural world, Guiderius and Arviragus grow up honest and true. "Great men / That had a court no bigger than this cave, / …Could not outpeer these twain" (3.6.79–84), exclaims Innogen when she meets them for the first time. She has no idea, of course, they are her lost brothers.

The opposition of the court and the country is a common theme in several of Shakespeare's plays. In *A Midsummer Night's Dream*, *As You Like It*, and *The Winter's Tale*, characters all journey into the wild to learn to see things afresh before they can return to the court with sense restored. What's different in *Cymbeline* is the third place that lies between civilized Rome and »

discovery of what seems to be her dead husband when she wakes from her deathlike sleep echoes Juliet waking to the dead Romeo.

The complex plot is not easy to follow, but its three main strands – the story of Innogen and Posthumus; the loss of Cymbeline's two sons; and the conflict between Britain and Rome – all echo earlier plays by Shakespeare, brought together in this work by a fast-moving plot.

A matchless heroine

The story of Innogen and Posthumus is the emotional heart of the play. In Innogen, Shakespeare created one of his most admired heroines – steadfast, loyal, brave,

and resourceful. At the beginning of the play, Posthumus is described as a worthy hero, a more than suitable companion for her. Yet as soon as he is away from her in Rome, his nobility drops away and he falls prey, much too easily, to foolish machismo. He not only agrees to Giacomo's bet that he can seduce her, but also readily believes that Giacomo has succeeded. Then, in an act of stomach-churning duplicity and cruelty, he sends two letters, one to Innogen declaring undying love and the other to Pisanio asking him to kill her. Fortunately, Pisanio, perhaps the play's true hero, refuses Posthumus's bidding and helps Innogen escape wild Wales – the British court. It is as if Cymbeline, or Britain, must make a choice between the two.

In the end, Cymbeline doesn't have to make a choice. He makes peace with Rome and welcomes his Welsh-raised sons back into the fold. The queen, who fomented the discord by encouraging him to defy Rome and trying to set up her son Cloten in place of the lost twins, is dead. Reconciliation may be the message of the play. Its relevance would not have been lost on audiences when the king says: "Let / A Roman and a British ensign wave / Friendly together… Never was a war did cease, / Ere bloody hands were washed, with such a peace." (5.6.480–486).

Contemporary resonances

The purpose of the play may become clearer if it is seen in its historical context. The battle for the soul of Britain was still fierce.

The Protestant Reformation had the upper hand, but Catholicism still had an immense presence, and there was a real threat of a Catholic comeback, as the Gunpowder Plot of 1605 had demonstrated. In Rome, Posthumus is played upon by a Frenchman, a Spaniard, and an Italian (Giacomo) – one man from each of the major Catholic countries – and the Dutchman, from the largely Protestant Netherlands then fighting for independence from Catholic Spain, remains silent.

There is every chance that *Cymbeline* would have been performed in front of King James I of England (James VI of Scotland), and the resonances would surely not have passed him by. James, like Cymbeline in the play, was king of all Britain, uniting England, Scotland, Wales, and Ireland for the first time under a single monarch. He also, like Cymbeline, had two sons and a daughter. And James,

Kneel not to me.
The power that I have on you
is to spare you,
The malice towards you to
forgive you. Live,
And deal with others better.
Posthumus
Act 5, Scene 6

at that very moment was, like Cymbeline at the close of the play, entering into negotiations with Rome to find peace.

Contemporary audiences would not have missed the point that the crucial intervention in Cymbeline

The court of Cymbeline

- Cymbeline — Married to → Queen (His second wife)
- Cymbeline — Father to → Innogen (Disguises herself as Fidele), Arviragus (Disguises himself as Cadwal), Guiderius (Also known as Polydore)
- Queen — Mother to → Lord Cloten
- Guiderius — Kills → Lord Cloten
- Innogen — Married to → Posthumus Leonartus
- Posthumus Leonartus — Friends → Filario
- Posthumus Leonartus ← Servant to — Pisanio
- Pisanio — Friends → Giacomo
- Giacomo — Friends → Filario
- Giacomo — Friends → Posthumus Leonartus
- Belarius (Banished Lord, calling himself Morgan) — Takes in → Arviragus, Guiderius

In a Japanese production of *Cymbeline* at the Barbican, London, in 2012, director Yukio Ninagawa brought an epic grandeur to the tale. The production was a big, bold, and brash telling of the story.

comes from Wales, the home of the Tudor dynasty that had ruled England until James's accession on the death of Elizabeth I in 1603. The focal point of the action is Milford Haven in west Wales. This town had nothing whatsoever to do with ancient Roman or ancient British history, but as the place where Henry Tudor landed to start the Tudor dynasty, finally ending the Wars of the Roses, it was a name that still resonated strongly in Shakespeare's England.

History and myths

Of course, Rome is not just the contemporary city that Posthumus finds, but it also signifies ancient, classical Rome, the Rome of Augustus when much of Europe, including Britain, was united in the comparative peace of the Roman Empire, the *Pax Romana*. It was also the time of the classical gods – and it is the Roman god Jupiter who appears to Posthumus and promises justice and the return of Innogen. In fact, Innogen's deliverance comes from a Wales steeped in Celtic myth. At the end, Cymbeline promises to march through Lud's town – London, named after the Celtic king of Britain and mythical god Lud – to the temple of the classical god Jupiter.

The final scene, in which all the convoluted knots of the plot untangle, was once scorned for its improbability, though now critics agree that it works dazzlingly well on stage. It is almost impossible not to be moved by Giacomo's confession and Posthumus's howls of anguish as he lashes out at Innogen – before all is revealed, the lovers are reunited, Cymbeline finds his lost sons, and everyone is reconciled, but for the wicked queen who, conveniently, is dead. The message seems to be that, however improbable it seems, peace and forgiveness is possible if it is looked for. ∎

Giacomo and Innogen

Giacomo's soliloquy as he creeps about Innogen's chamber has a tenderness that seduces the ear – and, some critics argue, makes the audience complicit in the act.

Having emerged from a trunk in her room, he describes the sleeping Innogen in memorably exquisite poetic language: "Tis her breathing that / Perfumes the chamber thus: the flame o' the taper / Bows toward her, and would under-peep her lids, / To see the enclosed lights, now canopied / Under these windows, white and azure laced / With blue of heaven's own tinct." (2.2.18–23).

The distinguishing mark on her breast, the evidence for his claim to have seduced her, "the crimson drops / I' the bottom of a cowslip" – is an image of such natural purity that it is easy to forget the intrusion he is making.

Giacomo, with his seductive language, tries to twist even rape into something beautiful. He likens his deed to the ancient Roman king Tarquin's brutal rape of the noblewoman Lucrece in such a way that it sounds like an act of tenderness. This poetic pornography makes for a deeply disturbing speech.

WE ARE SUCH STUFF AS DREAMS ARE MADE ON

THE TEMPEST (1610–1611)

DRAMATIS PERSONAE

Prospero Exiled Duke of Milan, living on a magical island where he was shipwrecked with his daughter, having been put to sea by his brother, Antonio.

Miranda Prospero's 15-year-old daughter, driven into exile with him.

Antonio Prospero's brother, the usurping Duke of Milan.

Alonso King of Naples.

Sebastian Alonso's scheming brother.

Ferdinand Alonso's son, who falls in love with Miranda.

Gonzalo An honest Neapolitan courtier, who allowed Prospero to take his books with him into exile.

Adrian and Francisco Neapolitan lords

Trinculo Alonso's jester.

Stefano Alonso's drunken butler.

Master and Boatswain Sailors aboard the storm-tossed ship.

Ariel A magical spirit of air, trapped by the dead witch Sycorax, but freed by Prospero to serve him.

Caliban Sycorax's monstrous son, enslaved by Prospero. He finds a new master in Stefano.

Iris, Ceres, and Juno Spirits appearing in the masques as nymphs.

Antonio, Alonso, and his son **Ferdinand** are cast ashore on an apparently **deserted island**.

Prospero tells how the **spirit Ariel** and the **beast Caliban** became **his servants**.

Antonio and Sebastian plot to kill Alonso while he sleeps, but Ariel wakes him.

1.1 **1.2** **2.1**

Act 1 **Act 2**

1.2 **1.2**

Prospero reveals **to** his daughter **Miranda** how his brother **Antonio** acquired a taste for power and **exiled them**.

Ferdinand, enticed from the others by Prospero's magic, **meets Miranda and they fall in love**.

The ship carrying Alonso and Antonio is caught in a storm and wrecked on a strange island. From the shore, the wizard Prospero assures his worried daughter Miranda that the storm was conjured by his own magic and that all aboard are safe. Prospero then tells her how he was once Duke of Milan, until his usurping brother Antonio drove him to sea in a storm 12 years ago, when Miranda was an infant. Washed up on the island, Prospero used his knowledge to make servants of the island's magical spirit Ariel and the monster Caliban, son of the witch Sycorax, who is being punished for trying to rape Miranda.

Alonso's son Ferdinand meets Miranda and they fall in love, despite Prospero's feigned disapproval. Fearing that Ferdinand drowned, Alonso and most of his company are lulled to sleep by Ariel. Antonio and Sebastian plot to murder Alonso and the good courtier Gonzalo, who dreams of a commonwealth where all might be happy. But Ariel wakes up the company before Antonio

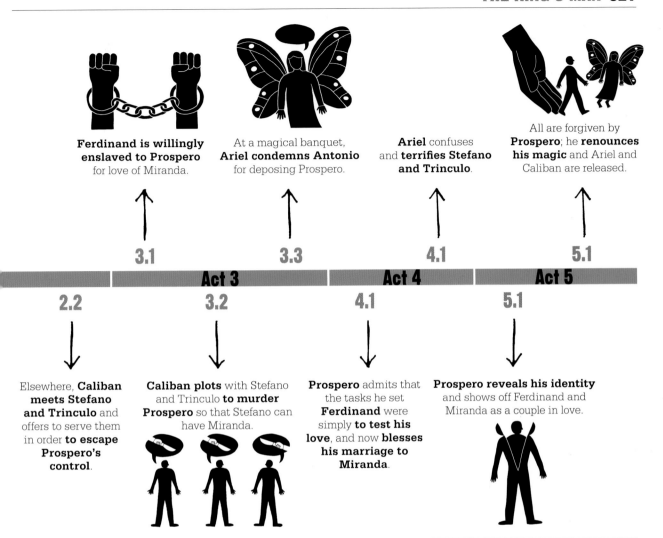

Ferdinand is willingly enslaved to Prospero for love of Miranda.

3.1

At a magical banquet, **Ariel condemns Antonio** for deposing Prospero.

3.3

Ariel confuses and **terrifies Stefano and Trinculo**.

4.1

All are forgiven by **Prospero**; he **renounces his magic** and Ariel and Caliban are released.

5.1

Act 3 **Act 4** **Act 5**

2.2

Elsewhere, **Caliban meets Stefano and Trinculo** and offers to serve them in order **to escape Prospero's control**.

3.2

Caliban plots with Stefano and Trinculo **to murder Prospero** so that Stefano can have Miranda.

4.1

Prospero admits that the tasks he set **Ferdinand** were simply **to test his love**, and now **blesses his marriage to Miranda**.

5.1

Prospero reveals his identity and shows off Ferdinand and Miranda as a couple in love.

and Sebastian can do any harm. Elsewhere, Caliban meets the drunken Stefano and Trinculo and believes they are gods.

Prospero enslaves Ferdinand and makes him carry logs, which he does willingly out of love for Miranda. Ferdinand and Miranda pledge to marry. Caliban tells Stefano and Trinculo how he is Prospero's slave, but will be theirs, and Stefano may have Miranda, if they help him kill Prospero. Ariel sets them all arguing by impersonating each. He conjures up a magical banquet for Alonso and

company to the sound of music, but before they can eat, he condemns Antonio for usurping his brother.

Prospero admits he was merely testing Ferdinand, and gives his blessing to the marriage. He conjures a magical masque to celebrate with song and dancing nymphs. Suddenly remembering that Stefano, Trinculo, and Caliban are plotting to kill him, Prospero halts the masque and orders Ferdinand and Miranda to hide. Stefano and Trinculo are lured by Prospero's magical robes, then chased off in terror by spirits

transformed into dogs. As Prospero dons his magic regalia, Ariel tells him that Alonso and his court are full of remorse. Moved by Ariel's gentleness, Prospero decides to forgive. He traps them all in a magic circle, explains his true identity, and then reveals, to their amazement, Miranda and Ferdinand playing chess. Stefano, Trinculo, and Caliban are forgiven, too. As they all take ship to Naples for the wedding, Prospero frees Ariel and renounces his magic, and then asks the audience to set him free by clapping their hands. »

IN CONTEXT

THEMES
Loyalty, servitude, freedom, love, magic

SETTING
A magic island, probably in the Mediterranean

SOURCES
8 CE The play is original, but draws inspiration from Ovid's *Metamorphoses*.

1603 Michel de Montaigne's essay "Of the Cannibals".

1610 News of the shipwreck of the *Sea Venture*.

LEGACY
1610 First performance is possibly at the Blackfriars Theatre, London.

1611 The play is performed before King James I in Whitehall Palace.

1667 John Dryden and William Davenant stage a spectacular called *The Tempest, or the Enchanted Island*.

1857 Charles Kean's staging at London's Princess Theatre has a storm sequence that wows Hans Christian Andersen

1930 John Gielgud plays Caliban at London's Old Vic. Gielgud goes on to become a highly acclaimed Prospero, too.

1945 Canada Lee is the first black Caliban, in New York, as audiences begin to see parallels with slave history.

2004 A major opera of the play by British composer Thomas Adès opens in London.

Set on an enchanted island ruled by the wizard-like Prospero, *The Tempest* is a play of magic and wonder, beautiful poetry and fantastical imagery. It has the most spectacular opening of any of Shakespeare's plays – in the form of the mighty storm of the play's title. Yet it is one of the hardest plays to fathom, a mystery that has absorbed countless hours of debate, and inspired radically different interpretations. It is perhaps this very mystery that is key to the play's power.

The Tempest was probably the last play Shakespeare wrote by himself, and some interpretations have hung on this biographical detail. Critics a century ago began to describe it as a "late" play, arguing that it was the culmination of the Bard's work, his swansong to the theatre. Prospero, they believed, was a portrait of Shakespeare himself, creating the storm and the island's magic out of the air just as Shakespeare creates his magic on the stage. Prospero's evocative speech, which ends the magical wedding masque, was read as Shakespeare's own rueful farewell:

"Our revels now are ended. These our actors, / As I foretold you, were all spirits, and / Are melted into air, into thin air; / And like the baseless fabric of this vision, / The cloud-capped towers, the gorgeous palaces, / The solemn temples, the great globe itself, / Yea, all which it inherit, shall dissolve; / And, like this insubstantial pageant faded, / Leave not a rack behind." (4.1.148–156).

This does indeed sound like a poetic goodbye for a great magician of the theatre. But this is not actually the end of the play. Prospero's words here are a conjuring trick to lull Ferdinand and Miranda into sleep while he deals with another plot against him. Neither Prospero nor Shakespeare are quite yet done. And if Prospero really is Shakespeare, then he has painted an unflattering portrait of himself. It is not until his magic spirit Ariel shows Prospero the

A 19th-century etching by Robert Dudley shows the alarmed Alonso, Antonio, Sebastian, and Gonzalo as they stumble upon banqueting spirits. Invisible to them, Prospero watches on.

Tempestuous relationships

```
Trinculo          Plot together    Caliban       Plot together    Stefano
Alonso's jester  <------------->  Prospero's slave <------------->  Alonso's butler

                  Seeks to                                Seeks to
                  murder          Hates                   murder

Alonso           Respects        Prospero        Hates and        Antonio
King of Naples   ------------>   Exiled Duke of Milan  envies       Prospero's brother

Seeks to
murder                                            Enslaved to

Sebastian                                          Ariel
His brother                                        Spirit of the air     ──── Live on
                                                                               the island

         Father to        Father to
                                                                       ──── Shipwrecked
                                                                            by the storm
Ferdinand         Loves         Miranda
              <----------->
```

value of kindness at the end of the play that he learns the wisdom of forgiveness. Up until then he is proud, vengeful, and something of a tyrant. When Prospero conjures the tempest to trap Alonso and Antonio on the island, he is bent on revenge, not reconciliation, and uses his magic to enslave Ariel and Caliban, not to liberate them.

Art or nature?

Few critics today would argue that Prospero is a direct portrayal of Shakespeare, or that *The Tempest* is autobiographical. Nonetheless, there are parallels between Prospero's role and the work of a dramatist. The key word is "art". Just as it is Prospero's "art" to control Ariel and Caliban through magic and bring his abusers to the island, so it is the dramatist's "art" to create an enchanted island on a simple wooden stage.

The play asks what it means to be human – and art, according to the humanist philosophers of the age, was the highest expression of humanity. Art is what lifts humanity above "base" nature – what separates Prospero from the raw, unprocessed beast Caliban.

Shakespeare puns on the two meanings of "art" – art as a noun meaning skill, and art as a verb meaning "be". "Thee," Prospero tells Miranda, "…who / Art ignorant of what thou art." (1.2.18–19). Then a few lines later he says, "Lie there, my art" (1.2.25) to his magic robe as she helps him remove it. The question of which forms the essence of humanity – the magic arts of a master scholar like Prospero, or art as simply "being" – is at the heart of the play.

Liberal and occult arts

Since classical times, students had learned the liberal arts, the skills needed to play an active role in civic life, and Prospero was, as Duke of Milan before his exile, "for the liberal arts / Without a parallel." But he became so absorbed in study that he delved into deeper arts, and neglected the real world. This is, in some ways, an echo of Doctor Faustus in the famous play of that name by Christopher Marlowe, written in the 1590s. Faustus, whose name, like Prospero's means "fortunate", »

Full fathom five thy father lies.
Of his bones are coral made;
Those are pearls that
were his eyes;
Nothing of him that doth fade
But doth suffer a sea-change
Into something rich and strange.
Ariel
Act 1, Scene 2

A 2009 production by the Baxter Theatre Centre of Cape Town, with Antony Sher as Prospero and Atandwa Kani as Ariel, mixed racial politics with playful African mythology.

is also a brilliant scholar who, becoming bored with the liberal arts, plunges into hidden, secret methods, until finally selling his soul to the devil in exchange for ultimate knowledge and power.

Even the most serious philosophers of the age believed that there was another realm beyond Nature, an occult realm of the spirit, and that its discovery was the goal of philosophy. The word "Magic" was used to describe the knowledge and mastery of this hidden dimension. Shakespeare's contemporary Francis Bacon was the great pioneer of modern scientific method based on physical evidence, yet even he believed that magic was "sublime wisdom", while the brilliant 16th-century mathematician and alchemist John Dee, perhaps another inspiration for Prospero, spent much of his life trying to communicate with angels.

The loss of human feeling

Yet the problems with Prospero's absorption in this other world are apparent from the start. As the ship founders in the storm he has conjured, and the sailors cry in terror, only Miranda has the humanity to empathize: "I have sufferèd / With those that I saw suffer!" (1.2.5–6). Prospero's blithe reassurance that there's "No harm" (1.2.16) done seems barely adequate in the face of such anguish, and brings Miranda's all-too-human response: "O, woe the day!" (1.2.15). It is with a shock that Prospero at last learns human feeling and

sympathy from the inhuman Ariel: "Hast thou, which art but air, a touch, a feeling / Of their afflictions, and shall not myself, / One of their kind, that relish all as sharply / Passion as they, be kindlier moved than thou art?" (5.1.21–24).

Prospero's treatment of Ariel and Caliban is even more dubious. He tells the story of how he freed Ariel from the tree in which he was trapped by the witch Sycorax, but he keeps Ariel in servitude. His treatment of Caliban is worse. Caliban, the product of his mother Sycorax's night with the devil, is enslaved by Prospero, and turned from an innocent child of Nature, who willingly showed his visitors the wonders of the island, into a resentful beast. As Caliban retorts, schooling has brought him no benefits: "You taught me language, and my profit on't / Is I know how to curse." (1.2.365–366).

One of Shakespeare's sources for *The Tempest* was Michel de Montaigne's essay "Of the

We are such stuff
As dreams are made on;
and our little life
Is rounded with a sleep.
Prospero
Act 4, Scene 1

Cannibals", which is quoted almost word for word in Gonzalo's plea for a commonwealth based on humanity. In the essay, Montaigne describes the "noble savage" of the New World, untouched by the corruption of the old, and Caliban, it seems, was once such a creature. Caliban retains traces of a sensitivity to the island's natural spirit that he expresses more poetically than Prospero; it is Prospero whose schooling turns Caliban to a "piece of filth".

For all Prospero's knowledge, he has learned only mastery. He is, then, not so different from Antonio who usurps his rule, or Sebastian who plots with Antonio to kill Alonso. More tellingly, mastery is the lesson he teaches Caliban, who plots to kill Prospero.

Prospero the colonial

Over the last half century, more and more critics have focused on Prospero as a forerunner of a European colonist and have seen in his enslavement of the island's original inhabitants, Ariel and Caliban, an exploitation of native people by European masters. This resonance in the play may be no accident. Explorer Sir Walter Raleigh had tried to establish a colony at Roanoke, Virginia, in the 1590s, and Shakespeare was in contact with the Virginia Company that founded the first successful English settlement at Jamestown in 1607.

Letting go

In the end, though, Prospero learns the folly of his attempts to control everything. He breaks his staff to end his magic power, "drowns" his books, forgives his foes, and at last sets Caliban and Ariel free.

As Prospero admits in the Epilogue, with all his magic gone, he has only his own faint human strength to rely on. But he, like Shakespeare the playwright, acknowledges that the real power lies not with him but with the audience, who can either approve or disapprove of the play. Their applause will set him free from the bondage of expectation. ∎

A 2010 US fantasy film, *The Tempest*, based on the play, cast Helen Mirren as "Prospera", and Djimon Hounsou as a powerfully physical Caliban.

An American play?

In September 1610, a sensational story reached London of a storm that had engulfed the *Sea Venture*, a ship carrying settlers to Jamestown, Virginia. All 150 aboard were washed onto a reef off Bermuda, and there found an exotic island, seas teeming with fish, and skies filled with gorgeous birds. Helped by the natives, the survivors lived on the island while they built a new ship. That Shakespeare was partly inspired by this story is clear, and *The Tempest* has been called the "American" play, even though Prospero's island was in the Mediterranean.

In the Americas at the time there was a Spanish empire that, in the 15th century, had enslaved the indigenous people with the godlike power of its technology. Whether Shakespeare intended it or not, the play has found such a resonance with the colonial past that this has become a key thread in many interpretations. Caliban, not Prospero, is often the focus. Black actors have been cast to emphasize the way European colonials enslaved native populations.

FAREWELL, A LONG FAREWELL TO ALL MY GREATNESS!

HENRY VIII (1613)

DRAMATIS PERSONAE

Henry VIII King of England.

Katherine of Aragon Queen of England, later Princess Dowager.

Cardinal Wolsey Archbishop of York and Lord Chancellor.

Thomas Cromwell Wolsey's secretary.

Duke of Buckingham A noble fiercely opposed to Wolsey.

Duke of Norfolk A noble more moderately opposed to Wolsey.

Duke of Suffolk, Lord Sands, Sir Thomas Lovell, Sir Anthony Denny, Sir Henry Guildford, Sir Nicholas Vaux, the Lord Chamberlain, and the Lord Chancellor Nobles, officials, and gentlemen of the royal court.

Cardinal Campeius Ambassador of the Pope.

Thomas Cranmer A Protestant cleric, later Archbishop of Canterbury.

Bishop of Lincoln Cranmer's colleague.

Stephen Gardiner Henry's new secretary, later Bishop of Winchester.

Anne Boleyn Queen Katherine's maid of honour, later Henry's queen.

Griffith Katherine's usher.

Old Lady Anne's confidante.

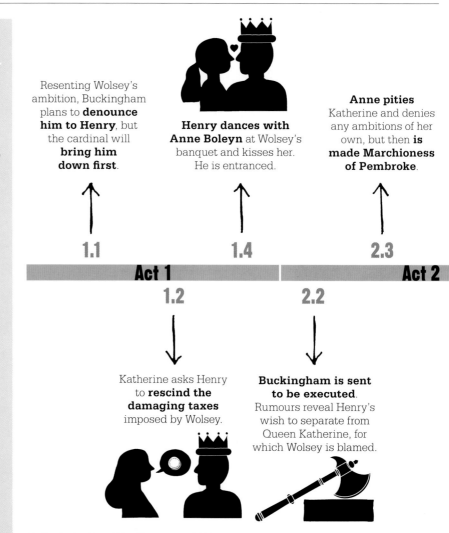

Resenting Wolsey's ambition, Buckingham plans to **denounce him to Henry**, but the cardinal will **bring him down first**.

1.1

Henry dances with **Anne Boleyn** at Wolsey's banquet and kisses her. He is entranced.

1.4

Anne pities Katherine and denies any ambitions of her own, but then **is made Marchioness of Pembroke**.

2.3

Act 1

1.2

Katherine asks Henry to **rescind the damaging taxes** imposed by Wolsey.

2.2

Buckingham is sent to be executed. Rumours reveal Henry's wish to separate from Queen Katherine, for which Wolsey is blamed.

Act 2

Buckingham vents his anger at Cardinal Wolsey's pride and ambition, displayed in his extravagant celebration of a hollow peace treaty with France. But before he can denounce Wolsey to the king, the cardinal lays false accusations against him. The duke is arrested. At the same time we hear of the impending fall of queen Katherine who, a few scenes earlier, had successfully intervened with the king against harsh taxes secretly imposed by Wolsey. The crafty cardinal gives out that he is responsible for this reprieve.

Katherine loses status when Henry falls in love with Anne Boleyn. Brought before a court whose judges, especially Wolsey, she denounces as biased, the queen defends her marriage. In a private meeting with Wolsey, she continues her spirited defence, but finally accepts defeat. Katherine's hostility towards Wolsey, however, persists until her final hour, in exile at Kimbolton. Having been told of the cardinal's death she gives a scathing verdict of his character, yet allows her gentleman usher to enumerate his virtues.

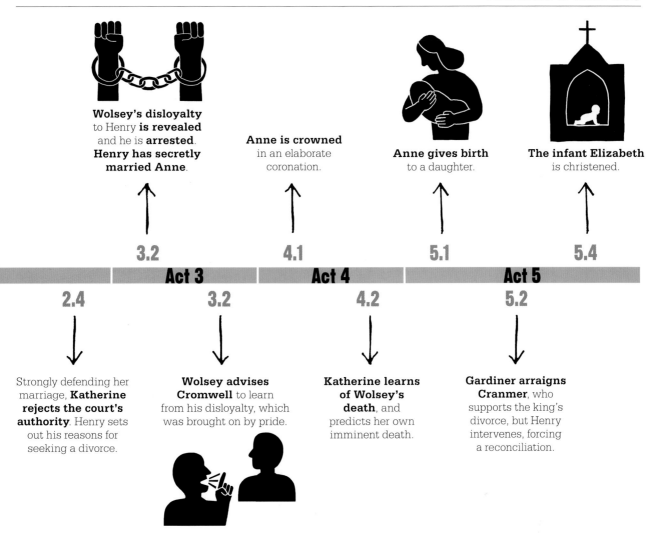

Wolsey's disloyalty to Henry **is revealed** and he is **arrested**. **Henry has secretly married Anne.**

3.2

Anne is crowned in an elaborate coronation.

4.1

Anne gives birth to a daughter.

5.1

The infant Elizabeth is christened.

5.4

2.4

Act 3

3.2

Act 4

4.2

Act 5

5.2

Strongly defending her marriage, **Katherine rejects the court's authority.** Henry sets out his reasons for seeking a divorce.

Wolsey advises Cromwell to learn from his disloyalty, which was brought on by pride.

Katherine learns of Wolsey's death, and predicts her own imminent death.

Gardiner arraigns Cranmer, who supports the king's divorce, but Henry intervenes, forcing a reconciliation.

As Katherine falls, Anne rises. Soon after meeting the king at Wolsey's banquet, she is awarded the title Marchioness of Pembroke. The cardinal, however, favours a marriage with the French king's sister and fears Anne's Lutheran faith. Publicly he pretends to advance the divorce, thus securing the king's favour. Secretly, he asks the pope to delay the proceedings as long as possible. When Henry learns of this double-dealing, Wolsey loses power, and shortly after dies. The dukes of Norfolk and Suffolk, who supported Katherine over the unfair taxes, quickly adapt to the new power balance, welcome Henry's secret marriage to Anne, and appear newly raised to the titles of Earl Marshal and High Steward at Anne's subsequent coronation.

Henry becomes his own man with Wolsey's fall. He replaces the cardinal's men with councillors of his own choice. The christening of Henry and Anne's daughter Elizabeth closes the play, with the archbishop predicting that her golden reign will justify Henry's dubious dynastic dealings. »

Yet I am richer than my base accusers, That never knew what truth meant.
Buckingham
Act 2, Scene 1

IN CONTEXT

THEMES
Integrity, royal marriage, political ambition

SETTING
Court of King Henry VIII; York Place, Cardinal Wolsey's London home; Westminster Abbey; Kimbolton Castle

SOURCES
1548 Edward Halle's *The Union of the Two Noble and Illustre Families of Lancaster and York.*

1563 John Foxe's *Acts and Monuments.*

1587 Holinshed's *Chronicles of England, Scotland, and Ireland.*

LEGACY
1613 On 29 June, a stage cannon accidentally sets the roof thatch alight and burns down the Globe Theatre during a performance of *Henry VIII.*

1742–68 Garrick's production plays to the enthusiasm for pageantry with 140 actors on stage for Anne's coronation.

18th–19th centuries Textual cuts make room for added spectacle and end the play when Wolsey leaves the stage.

1969 Trevor Nunn's RSC production focuses on Henry's maturation as father and man.

1983 Also for the RSC, Howard Davies explores the accretion of power to Wolsey.

2010 The play is revived at the Globe Theatre, London, with ceremonial cannon fired as in the 1613 production.

C o-written by Shakespeare with John Fletcher, *Henry VIII*, or *All is True*, explores a decisive period of the king's long and famous reign: his divorce from Katherine of Aragon, his marriage to Anne Boleyn, and the birth of the future Elizabeth I. Against a background of ceremony and spectacle, the action maps the rise and fall of some of Henry's closest courtiers and, as the play's alternative title suggests, casts an ironic light on the motivation of all concerned.

Wolsey's power
Henry is presented as the source of greatness. Like the sun, his royal beams gild life by granting status and power to those he favours. When this light is withheld for whatever reason, the individual withers and declines. For the first part of the play, the king's favour is strongly influenced by Wolsey. By carefully controlling access to the king, he is able to mediate what Henry sees and hears, and so selectively shape what he believes to be the truth. It is a privileged position that allows Wolsey to replace courtiers he distrusts with those who will do his bidding. He even acts on the king's behalf

This imperious man
will work us all
From princes into pages.
Norfolk
Act 2, Scene 2

Herbert Beerbohm Tree played Wolsey in a lavish 1910 London production that boasted a huge cast. The play went on to have a long and successful run on Broadway, New York.

without his knowledge, as when he initiates the harsh taxes against which Katherine appeals. As custodian of the king's great seal (the stamp of royal authority), Wolsey thinks he has Henry in his pocket. These gatekeeping powers make him a dangerous enemy, as the Lord Chamberlain points out: "If you cannot / Bar his access to th' king, never attempt / Anything on him" (3.2.16–18).

Fall from favour
Buckingham is the first to fall from grace. Furious at Wolsey's abuse of power, he wants to denounce him to Henry. But Wolsey blocks his move with lies, priming the duke's surveyor to give false testimony so that, before Buckingham can speak out, he is arrested as a traitor and executed. Katherine seems secure in Henry's favour when, kneeling, she petitions him against Wolsey's

taxes, and he raises her to sit beside him as he rescinds that law. But when she next appears, Henry fails to repeat the gesture, leaving her on her knees before the court of the divorce hearing. It seems that Wolsey's carefully sown doubts about Henry's divorce now trouble the royal conscience.

Wolsey has risen from a humble butcher's son to become Lord Chancellor of England; and his fall from greatness, when it comes, is just as far. Proud and arrogant, he is detested by those who know of his double-dealing. But as long as he has the king's ear, his position is secure. It is ironically appropriate that, unwittingly, Wolsey himself betrays his deception to Henry. An incriminating letter asking the pope to delay the divorce as long as possible, along with an inventory of his personal wealth, get mixed up in some state papers sent by the cardinal to the king. Wolsey's own hand undoes him. With Anne rising in the king's favour, Wolsey had feared that her Lutheran faith would work against his ambition to become pope. He needed more time to persuade the king away from her and towards a possible French marriage. It is a satisfying twist that such a concealer of truths and manipulator of events should be brought low by this momentary failure to control either. Only when his glories are gone does Wolsey recognize that Henry has outwitted him: "The King has gone beyond me" (3.2.409). This is a turning point in the play, for after Wolsey's fall Henry exerts his will with far greater authority.

Variable truths

Henry VIII presents historical truth as relative, and dependent on more than a single point of view. This is evident in the way the audience is positioned to read the drama's state ceremonies. It is made clear that each one conveys a message that

> Love thyself last. Cherish those hearts that hate thee. Corruption wins not more than honesty.
> **Wolsey**
> Act 3, Scene 2

only partly fits the truth. Wolsey's Field of the Cloth of Gold (a lavish peace conference near Calais), we learn, celebrates a short-lived treaty. The trial of Katherine can't afford her the "right and justice" (2.4.11) its ceremony promises because, as is evident from her position on her knees before the court, Henry intends a specific outcome. And her refusal to continue the charade makes this plain. Even in the elaborate closing ceremony celebrating the christening of Elizabeth, a noticeable, ominous absence is that of the new Queen Anne.

Shakespeare and Fletcher convey these shifting perspectives by altering historical chronology to create a moral pattern of rise and fall, which they set alongside a secular pattern of political stratagem masked by theatrical show. Thus, as the Prologue admits, their play is as much a "chosen truth" (Prologue: 18) as the history it portrays. ∎

A 2009 production in Ashland, Oregon, USA, stayed true to the play's original stage directions, with elaborate, crowd-pleasing ceremonies and pageants.

IS THERE RECORD OF ANY TWO
THAT LOVED
BETTER
THAN WE DO, ARCITE?
THE TWO NOBLE KINSMEN (1613)

DRAMATIS PERSONAE

Palamon Best friend and cousin to Arcite, nephew of King Creon. His friendship with his cousin turns to hatred when they both fall for Emilia.

Arcite Best friend and cousin to Palamon, nephew of King Creon. He enters and wins the Athenian games for which he is made "master of the horse".

Theseus Duke of Athens. He arranges a tournament between Palamon and Arcite in which the winner will marry Emilia and the loser will be executed.

Hippolyta Queen of the Amazons, and wife to Theseus. She encourages him to postpone their wedding until after he defeats Creon of Thebes.

Emilia Sister of Hippolyta. The object of desire for both Palamon and Arcite. Palamon ultimately wins her hand after Arcite's death.

A jailer Duke Theseus's prison keeper.

The jailer's daughter She is driven mad by her unrequited love for Palamon.

Three queens Widows of kings killed in the siege of Thebes.

A wooer He is in love with the jailer's daughter.

A doctor He is summoned to cure the jailer's daughter.

The wedding of King Theseus and Hippolyta is disrupted by grieving queens, whose husbands have been denied burial rights by their enemy, King Creon of Thebes.

Creon loses to Theseus, and **Palamon and Arcite are captured** and imprisoned in Athens.

Arcite leaves prison and **disguises himself in order to be near Emilia**.

 1.1

 1.4

 2.3

Act 1	Act 2

1.2

2.2

Debating whether to flee Thebes, **the two kinsmen** (Arcite and Palamon) stay to **fight when Theseus attacks the city**.

Palamon and Arcite spy Emilia gathering flowers through their prison window and immediately **begin to argue over who saw her first**.

The wedding of Theseus, Duke of Athens, and Hippolyta, Queen of the Amazons, is disrupted by three grieving queens who plead with Theseus to attack Thebes and its evil ruler Creon, who has killed their husbands in battle and denied them burial. In Thebes, cousins Arcite and Palamon are disgusted by their corrupt uncle Creon and contemplate fleeing the city when news comes of Theseus's imminent attack. Despite their anxieties, they remain and fight, but are captured, taken to Athens, and imprisoned.

While in jail, Palamon and Arcite surprise their captors by consoling one another with their close friendship. However, their relationship is tested when Palamon looks out of the prison window and sees the Amazonian princess Emilia gathering flowers. He proclaims instant love for her, as does Arcite, and the two friends argue over a woman they do not know, nor seemingly have any hope of attaining.

Arcite is suddenly released from prison and banished to Thebes, but disguises himself, determined

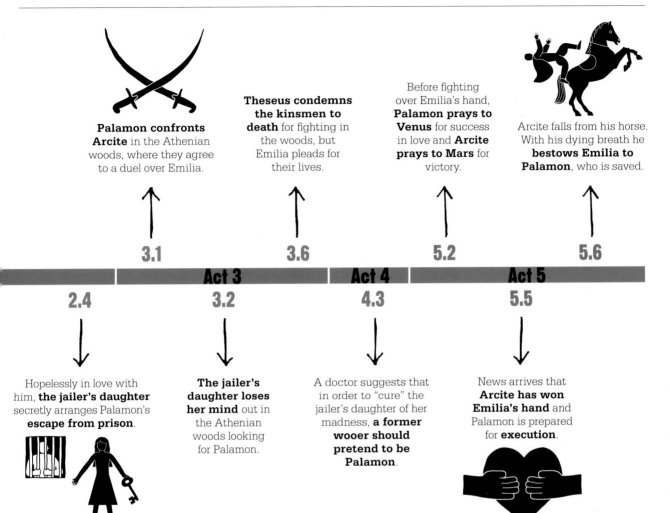

Palamon confronts Arcite in the Athenian woods, where they agree to a duel over Emilia.

Theseus condemns the kinsmen to death for fighting in the woods, but Emilia pleads for their lives.

Before fighting over Emilia's hand, **Palamon prays to Venus** for success in love and **Arcite prays to Mars** for victory.

Arcite falls from his horse. With his dying breath he **bestows Emilia to Palamon**, who is saved.

3.1

3.6

5.2

5.6

2.4

Act 3

3.2

Act 4

4.3

Act 5

5.5

Hopelessly in love with him, **the jailer's daughter** secretly arranges Palamon's **escape from prison**.

The jailer's daughter loses her mind out in the Athenian woods looking for Palamon.

A doctor suggests that in order to "cure" the jailer's daughter of her madness, **a former wooer should pretend to be Palamon**.

News arrives that **Arcite has won Emilia's hand** and Palamon is prepared for **execution**.

to get close to Emilia. Palamon becomes the object of affection for the jailer's daughter, who plans and executes his escape in hope of winning his love.

Arcite enters a sporting contest hosted by Theseus in which he wins a wrestling match and is rewarded by being made Emilia's servant and "master of the horse". On a May Day outing in the Athenian woods, Arcite encounters Palamon; an argument ensues over Emilia, and the kinsmen decide to duel for her. Their duel is interrupted by Theseus who

condemns them both to death. Pleading for their banishment rather than death, Emilia is forced by Theseus to choose one of the cousins as her suitor. When Emilia is unable to choose, Theseus agrees to organize one final fight between the cousins – the winner will receive Emilia's hand, the loser will be executed.

Meanwhile, the jailer's daughter goes mad searching for Palamon in the woods and is treated by a doctor, whose cure is to have a would-be-suitor pretend to be Palamon and bed her. Emilia

cannot bring herself to attend the contest between Palamon and Arcite and the progress of the fight is reported back to her. She prays to the Goddess Diana that whoever loves her best should win. Arcite is the winner and claims Emilia for his own, regretful that his friend must die.

News arrives, just as Palamon is about to be executed, that Arcite has fallen from his horse and is fatally wounded. The kinsmen are momentarily reunited in friendship, and with his last breath Arcite bestows Emilia to Palamon. »

IN CONTEXT

THEMES
Love, loss, friendship, madness, war, death, identity

SETTING
Athens and Thebes

SOURCES
14th century The "Knight's Tale" from Geoffrey Chaucer's *The Canterbury Tales* is the main source for the play.

c.1340 It is possible that Shakespeare and Fletcher were familiar with Chaucer's source, Boccacio's *Teseida*. The jailer's daughter does not appear in this source and may be an original creation of the authors.

LEGACY
1634 The play is published for the first time.

1664 William Davenant creates an adaptation of the play called *The Rivals*.

1795 F G Waldron calls his musical adaptation *Love and Madness; or, The Two Noble Kinsmen*.

1986 Barry Kyle's production of *The Two Noble Kinsmen* opens the new RSC Swan Theatre in Stratford-upon-Avon.

2000 *The Two Noble Kinsmen* is performed at the Globe Theatre in London, directed by Tim Carroll. Jasper Britton plays a hot-headed Palamon, while Will Kean's Arcite is more worldly wise.

The Two Noble Kinsmen is a collaborative work by William Shakespeare and John Fletcher, who also collaborated on *Henry VIII* and *Cardenio* (now lost). Shakespeare is believed to have written the following scenes: Act 1 / 2.1 / 3.1 / 3.2 / 5.1 / 5.3 / 5.4, although he may not have been responsible for all the writing in some of these scenes. Scholars believe that Fletcher was entirely responsible for the character of the jailer's daughter, who in her madness echoes Shakespeare's Ophelia. *The Two Noble Kinsmen* was not among the plays included in the First Folio of 1623, and was unpublished until 1634. The play is notable for its use of theatrical effects and spectacle, common features in plays written for indoor theatres such as Blackfriars.

A highly physical production by the iconoclastic Cherub Company at the Young Vic, London, in 1979, had an all-male cast. Anthony Rothe and Daniel Foley played the duelling kinsmen.

Friendship tested
Trials of friendship feature throughout Shakespeare's works. In charting the deterioration of the relationship between friends, Shakespeare dramatized a rich range of emotional responses: resentment, disappointment, frustration, and anger. From a dramatic perspective, it is far more interesting (and entertaining) to present conflict between friends than contentment. Major obstacles must be overcome if feuding friends are to be reconciled. Little wonder then that Shakespeare's career opened and closed with tales in which friends momentarily transform into rivals.

Though 20 or more years passed between his writing of *The Two Gentlemen of Verona* and *The Two Noble Kinsmen*, Shakespeare's belief that tests of friendship made for good drama remained firm. He and Fletcher went to some lengths to emphasize the bond of friendship between Palamon and Arcite, a bond that would be broken

In Chaucer's *The Knight's Tale*, Arcite and Palamon joust in chivalric fashion to win the hand of Emelye. Arcite wins but then is fatally injured. Before he dies he tells Emelye to marry Palamon.

with the entry of Emilia into their lives. When imprisoned, the two men take comfort from the fact that they will be locked up together, shut away from the world, "enjoying of our griefs together" (2.2.60). Rather than revolting against their captivity, the cousins embrace the opportunity to enjoy one another's company; the jailer's daughter is surprised to see that "they eat well, look merrily, discourse of many things, but nothing of their own restraint and disasters" (2.1.37–39). The chivalrous men look upon their prison as a "holy sanctuary" (2.2.71) that will help preserve them from worldly vice and corruption: "We are young, and yet desire the ways of honour / That liberty and common conversation, / The poison of pure spirits, might, like women, / Woo us to wander from." (2.2.73–76).

Friendship broken

Given occasion to reflect upon his relationship with Arcite, Palamon is moved to utter "I do not think it possible our friendship / Shall ever leave us" (2.2.114–115). Palamon's

Dear Palamon, dearer in love than blood
Arcite
Act 1, Scene 2

confident assertion is filled with dramatic irony. The heightened language of devotion will soon turn into exclamations of contempt: "Why should a friend be treacherous? If that / Get him a wife so noble and so fair, / Let honest man ne'er love again." (2.2.233–235). Having established the bond between the men, the dramatists overturn their courtly gentility within a few lines: "**Palamon**: You love her then?
Arcite: Who would not?
Palamon: And desire her?
Arcite: Before my liberty.
Palamon: I saw her first."
(2.2.159–163)

Palamon's closing line, "I saw her first", which can be amusing in performance, marks the beginning of the rift between the two men. Before the cousins part, Arcite reprimands his rival for dealing "so cunningly, / So strangely, so unlike a noble kinsman" (2.2.193–194).

Though they become rivals for Emilia's affections, the men's respect for one another remains. Their conflict is enacted in a courtly fashion throughout, providing great comic potential on stage. As the cousins arm one another for combat, their conversation befits their gallant refinement: "**Arcite**: Will you fight bare-armed?

Palamon: We shall be the nimbler.
Arcite: But use your gauntlets, though – those are o'th' least. Prithee take mine, good cousin." (3.6.63–65).

Arcite's dying words express his love for Palamon, which rivals, if not supersedes his love for Emilia: "Take Emilia, / And with her all the world's joy." (5.6.90–91).

Bonds between maids

While Palamon and Arcite doubt that there is a record of "any two that loved" (2.2.113) more than they, audiences may disagree. Emilia's love for her childhood friend Flavina rivals the intimate bond enjoyed between the two noble kinsmen. Remembering her dead friend, Emilia speaks with a passion and tenderness that she cannot muster to describe her feelings for Palamon or Arcite: "That the true love 'tween maid and maid may be / More than sex in sex dividual." (1.3.81–82).

At the close of the play, Emilia and Palamon are bonded by the fact that they have both endured the "loss of dear love" (5.6.112). The couple are thrown together leaving Theseus to ruminate upon this surprising turn of events: "O you heavenly charmers, / What things you make of us!" (5.6.131–132). ∎

Is this winning? O all you heavenly powers, where is your mercy?
Emilia
Act 5, Scene 5

INDEX

Numbers in **bold** indicate main entries.

A

Aaron 50–51, **53**, 244
Aberg, Maria 182
Abraham, F Murray 130
Achilles 208–13
Ackroyd, Peter 225
Adam 180, 187
Adès, Thomas 328
Admiral's Men 22
Adonis 74–77
Adriana 70–73
Aeneas 212
Agamemnon 208–09, 212
Agincourt, Battle of 18, 149, 153, 166, **167**, 168, 169
Agrippa, Cornelius 320
Aguecheek, Sir Andrew 200–01, 203–04
Ajax 208–10, 212
Alagna, Roberto 248
Albany, Duke of 252–53, 258
Alcibiades 262, 263, 265
Aldridge, Ira 52, 244, **245**
Alexander, Bill 144
All is True see Henry VIII
Allam, Roger 138
All's Well That Ends Well 17, 19, 230, **286–93**
Alonso, King of Naples 326–29, 331
Amiens 180, 184
Amin, Idi 175
Andersen, Hans Christian 328
Andromache 208, 212
Angelo 234–39
Anne, Lady 56–57, 59–61
Anne of Denmark, Queen 22
Antenor 209, 212
Antigonus 310–11, 313
Antioch 296–99
Antiochus, King of Antioch 296–97
Antipholus of Ephesus 70–73
Antipholus of Syracuse 70–73
Antonio
    The Merchant of Venice 126–31
    Much Ado About Nothing 156, 161
    The Tempest 326–39, 331
    Twelfth Night 200–21, 205

Antony, Mark
    Antony and Cleopatra 278–85
    Julius Caesar 18, 172–77
Antony and Cleopatra 18, 230, **276–85**, 313
Apemantus 262–65
Apollonius of Tyre (Gower) 72
The Arabian Nights 34
Aragon, Prince of 126–27
Aravind, Ramesh 72
Arcite 340–43
Arden, forest of 115, 182, 183, 184, 185
Arden, Mary 12, 184
Ardennes 182, 184, 185, 313
Ariel 326–31
Ariosto, Ludovico, *Orlando Furioso* 158
Aristophanes 264
Armado, Don Adriano de 88–91
Armagnac, Earl of 45
Arthur, Duke of Brittany 120–23
Artois, Robert, Comte de 64
Arviragus (Cadwal) 318–19, 321–3
As You Like It 12, 17, 91, **178–87**, 259, 312, 314, 321
Ashcroft, Peggy 39, 247
Athens *see* Greece, ancient
Auden, W H 219, 223
Audrey 180, 186
Aufidius 302–03
Augustus, Emperor *see* Octavius Caesar
Aumerle, Duke of 94–95, 98
Austria, Duke of 120
Autolycus 310–12, 314
Auvergne, Countess of 47

B

Bacon, Francis 330
Bagot 94–96
Balthasar 126–27
Bandello, Matteo, *Novelle* 158
Banquo 268–69, 271, 273–75
Baptista Minola 32
Barber, Samuel 280
Bardolph
    Henry IV Part 2 148, 152
    Henry V 164–66, 168
    The Merry Wives of Windsor 142
Barnet, Battle of 43

Barry, Spranger 104
Bartlett, Keith 46
Barton, John 38, 39, 58, 236
Bassett, Linda 299
Bassanio 126–27, 130–31
Bassianus 50–51, 52
Beale, Simon Russell 150, 161, 254, 265, 312
Beatrice 19, **156–61**
Beaufort, Cardinal 36–37
Beckett, Samuel 254
Beckinsale, Kate 159
Bedford, Duke of 44
Belarius 318–19, 321, 322
Belch, Sir Toby 200–01, 203–05
Belleforest, François de, *Histoires Tragiques* 192
Benedick 16, 19, **156–61**
Benjamin, Christopher 145
Benson, Frank 46, 166
Benson, John 222
Benvolio 102, 106
Bergner, Elisabeth 187
Berlin Wall 39
Berlioz, Hector 158
Bernstein, Leonard 104, 109
Bertram, Count of Roussillon 288–93
Betterton, Thomas 114, 150
Bhardwaj, Vishal 270
Bianca
    Othello 242–43, 248
    The Taming of the Shrew 32–35
Bieito, Calixto 43
Bigot 121, 123
Biron 88–91
Bishop's Ban 85
Blackfriars Theatre 231, 342
Blackwood, Gary 290
Blanche of Spain, Lady 120
Blanchett, Cate 96, 99
Boas, Frederick 213
Boccaccio, Giovanni
    De Casibus Virorum Illustrum 98–99
    Decameron 28, 290, 320
    Teseida 342
Bogdanov, Michael 38, 46, 166, 304
Bohemia 310–15
Bokassa, Jean-Bédel 175
Boleyn, Anne 226–27, 334–37
Bolingbroke, Henry *see* Henry IV, King
Bona, Lady 40–41
Booth, Edwin 246

Borachio 156–60
Bosworth, Battle of 57, 59
Bottom 18, 19, 112–13, 114, 116, 117
Bourchier, Arthur 270
Bowdler, Revd Thomas 137
Boyd, Michael 158
Boyet, Lord 88–89
The Boys from Syracuse (musical) 72
Brabanzio 242, 244, 245, 246
Bradley, A C 247
Branagh, Kenneth 90, 158, 159, 166, 168, 182, 187, 192
Brando, Marlon 175
Brecht, Bertolt 304, 307
Britten, Benjamin 78, 81, 114, 116, 216, 223, 254
Britton, Jasper 342
Brook, Peter 88, 114, 116, 192, 236, 255, 264
Brooke, Arthur, *The Tragical History of Romeus and Juliet* 104, 105–06
Browning, Robert 223
Brutus (tribune) 302–03
Brutus, Marcus 172–77
Bu Wancang 28
Buckingham, Duke of
    Henry VIII 334, 336–37
    Richard III 56–57, 59, 60
Burbage, James 22
Burbage, Richard 14, 84, 230
Burgundy, Duke of 44–45
Burton, Richard 34, 122, 136, 137
Bushy 94–96

C

Cade, Jack 36–39
Caesar, Julius 172–77
Caius, Doctor 142–43
Caius Martius (Coriolanus) 19, **302–07**
Calchas 208–09, 212
Caliban 326–31
Calpurnia 16, 172, 176
Camillo 310–11
Canterna, Adrienne 109
Capulets **102–09**, 116
Cardenio 18, 231, 342
Carlisle, Bishop of 94–95, 98
Carroll, Tim 342
Casca 172–73, 177
Cassandra 208, 212
Cassio 242–43, 245–49
Cassius, Caius 172–77
Catesby, Robert 230
Catherine, Princess of France 164, 169

Catherine the Great 144
Catholicism 22, 23, 85, 105, 223, 225, 226, 230–31, 322
Cecil, Robert 105
Celia 180–81, 183–85, 187
censorship 85, 137, 216, 226–27
Cervantes, Miguel de, *Don Quixote* 231
Chapman, George 210
Chapman, John Jay 290
Charles I, King 293, 320
Charles II, King 298
Charles VI, King of France 164–65
Charles, Dauphin of France 44–45
Charles (wrestler) 180
Chaucer, Geoffrey
    The Knight's Tale 342, 343
    Troilus and Criseyde 210
Chester, Robert, *Love's Martyr; or Rosalind's Complaint* 225
Chettle 226
Chimes at Midnight (film) 136, 150
Chiron 50–53
Chorus, *Henry V* 15, 164, 167, 169
Churchill, Winston 166
Cibber, Colley 58
Cicero 177
Cinna 172–73, 175, 177
Cinthio, Giraldi 244, 236
Clarence, George, Duke of 40–41, 43, 56–58, 60
Clarence, Thomas, Duke of 148
Claudio
    Measure for Measure 234–35, 237–39
    Much Ado About Nothing 156–61
Claudius, King of Denmark 190–97
Cleon 296–97, 299
Cleopatra, Queen of Egypt 19, **278–85**
Clifford, Lord 36–37, 40–41, 43
Cloten 318–19, 322
Cobbe Portrait 222
Coleridge, Samuel Taylor, *Biographia Literaria* 46, 74, 77, 78, 81, 236
Collatine 78–80
Collions, Lynn 128
The Comedy of Errors 17, **68–73**, 84
Complete Oxford Shakespeare 19
Condell, Henry 14
Conrad 156, 160–61
Constance, Lady 120–21, 123
Cooke, Nigel 226
Cordelia 18, 252–59
Corin 180–81, 184
Coriolanus 18, 19, 231, **300–07**
Cornelius, Dr 318–20
Cornwall, Duke of 252–53, 255, 258
Costard 88–89, 91
Cottrell, Richard 96
Cox, Brian 52

Cranko, John 254
Cranmer, Thomas 334–35
Crécy, Battle of 64–66
Creon, King of Thebes 340
Cressida 208–13
Cromwell, Oliver 131
Cromwell, Thomas 334–35
Crowne, Thomas 42
Cunobelinus, King 320
Curio 200, 203
Curtain Theatre 22, 85
Cushman, Charlotte and Susan 104
Cymbeline 16, 18, 77, 231, 314, **316–23**
Cymbeline, King of Britain 318–23
Cyprus 242–49

D

da Porto, Luigi, *Giulietta e Romeo* 105
Danes, Clare 109
Daniel, Samuel 96, 136, 150
Dankworth, Johnny 216, 223
Dante, *Purgatorio* 105
Dark Lady sonnets 220
Davenant, William 158, 270, 328, 342
David II, King of Scotland 64, 66, 67
Davies, Howard 336
Davies, John 224
de Vere, Elizabeth 115
Decius Brutus 172–73
Decker, Thomas 226
Dee, Janie 290
Dee, John 330
Deiphobus 212
Demetrius
    A Midsummer Night's Dream 112–13, 117
    ruler of Macedon 282
    Titus Andronicus 50–53
Dench, Judi 270
Derby, Earl of 115
Desdemona **242–49**, 320
Deverell, Walter Howell 202
di Caprio, Leonardo 109
Diana
    All's Well That Ends Well 288–89, 291–93
    Pericles 296–97
Diomedes 208–10, 212–13
Dioniza 296–97
Dogberry 156–57, 160–61
Doit, John 152
Don John 53, 123, **156–61**
Don Pedro, Prince of Aragon 156–61
Donalbain 268–69

Donne, John 217
Doran, Gregory 175
Dorset, Earl of 56, 58
Dougall, John 195
Drake, Sir Francis 84
Dromio of Ephesus 70–73
Dromio of Syracuse 70–73
Dryden, John 210, 222, 328
Dudley, Robert 328
Dull 88–90
Dumaine 88–89, 91
Dumas, Alexandre 194
Duncan, King of Scotland 81, 268–75
Dyce, William 256

E

Edgar 252–53, 257, 258
Edmond 18, 123, 252–53, 255–58
Edward III 19, 23, **62–67**
Edward III, King 64–67
Edward IV, King 40–43, 56–58, 60
Edward V, King 41, 43, 56–57, 60
Edward VII, King 144
Edward, the Black Prince 64–67
Edward, Prince 40–41, 43
Edwardes, Richard 28
Edzard, Christine 187
Egeon 70–73
Egeus 112, 115, 117
Egg, Augustus Leopold 314
Eglamour 26–27
Egypt 278–85, 313
Eleanor, Queen (Eleanor of Aquitaine) 120, 123
Eliot, T S 192, 280
Elizabeth I, Queen 14, 17, 23, 42, 84, 85, 88, 96–97, 98, 105, 114, 144, 174, 225, 226, 230, 335
Elizabeth, Queen of Bohemia 158, 231
Elizabeth of York, Queen 56–61
Ellington, Duke 264
Elliot, Michael 182
Elsinore castle 190–97
Elyot, Sir Thomas, *The Governor* 28
Emeruwa, Ladi 195
Emilia
    Comedy of Errors 70–71, 73
    Othello 242–45, 248, 249
    The Two Noble Kinsmen 340–43
Enobarbus 278–79, 280, 281–82
Ephesus 70–73, 296–99
Equivoci, Gli (opera) 72
Escalus (aide to Duke of Vienna) 234, 236
Escalus, Prince of Verona 102–03, 109

Essex, Earl of 23, 85, 96, 98, 225
Evans, Edith 187
Evans, Sir Hugh 142–43, 145
Exton, Sir Piers 94–95, 98, 99
Eyre, Richard 58

F

Fabyan, Robert 46
Fairbanks, Douglas 34
Falconbridge, Robert 120
Falstaff, Sir John 17, 19, 84, 164, 169, 293
    Henry IV Parts 1 and 2 **134–93**, 144, **148–53**
    Henry V 144
    The Merry Wives of Windsor **142–45**
The Famous Victories of Henry V 136, 150
Faucit, Helen 320
Fawkes, Guy 231, 265
Fearon, Ray 175
Feeble 152
Feinstein, Elaine, *Lear's Daughters* 254
Fenton, Master 142–43, 145
Ferdinand 326–9
Ferdinand, King of Navarre 88–91
Feste 200, 202–04
Field, Richard 76, 80
Field of the Cloth of Gold 337
Fiennes, Ralph 304
Filario 318, 320, 322
Fiorentino, Giovanni, *Il Pecorone* 128
First Folio 14, 38, 66, 144, 219, 298, 342
Fitzwater, Lord 94, 98
Flavius 262–65
Fleance 268–69
Fletcher, John 18, 34, 144, 231, 336, 337, 342
Florence 288–89
Florizel 310–11, 314–15
Fluellen 164–65, 169
Foley, Daniel 342
Fool, *King Lear* 252–53, 254, 256, 258, 259
Ford, Master Frank 142–43
Ford, Mistress Alice 142–43, 145
Fortinbras, Prince 190–91, 192, 197
Foxe, John, *Acts and Monuments* 336
France, King of 288–89, 291–93
France, Princess of 88–91
Francis, Friar 156–57
Frederick V, King of Bohemia 231
Frederick, Duke 180–83, 187
Frederick, Naomi 239
Freshwater, Geoffrey 257
Froissart, Jean, *Chronicles* 66
Fry, Stephen 204

G

Ganymede 180–81, 185–86
Garai, Romola 187
Gardiner, Stephen 334–35
Garrick, David 104, 192, 336
Gascoigne, George 34
Geoffrey II, Duke of Brittany 123
Geoffrey of Monmouth 254
George IV, King 150
Gertrude, Queen of Denmark 16, 190–92, 194–96
Gesta Romanorum (anon.) 52
ghetto, Venice 128
Giacomo 318–22, 323
Gielgud, John 96, 104, 175, 202, 328
Globe Theatre 15, 17, 18, 85, 98, 231, 336
Gloucester, Earl of 252–53, 255–59
Gloucester, Eleanor Cobham, Duchess of 36–37, 39
Gloucester, Humphrey, Duke of
    Henry IV Part 2 148
    Henry VI Parts 2 and 3 36–37, 39, 44–47
Gloucester, Richard, Duke of *see* Richard III, King
Glyndwr, Owain 134–35, 137
Goetz, Hermann 34
Golding, Arthur 74, 77
Goneril 252–59
Gonzalo 326, 328, 331
Gounod, Charles, *Roméo et Juliette* 109
Gower, John 72, 296–97, 298
Grammaticus, Saxo, "Amleth" 192
Granville-Barker, Harley 114, 202, 312
Gray, Lady 40–41
Graziano 126–27
Greece, ancient
    A Midsummer Night's Dream 112–17, 313
    Pericles 296–99
    Timon of Athens 262–65
    Troilus and Cressida 208–13
    The Two Noble Kinsmen 340–43
    Venus and Adonis 74–77
Greene, Robert 15, 22, 42, 52, 312
Gremio 32–34
Grey, Earl 56, 58
Grosart, A B 225
Gross, John 128
Guare, John 28
Guiderius (Polydore) 318–23
Guildenstern 190–91, 195, 196
Gunpowder Plot 230, 230–31, 265, 322
Guthrie, Tyrone 128
Gwilym, Mike 298

H

Hal/Harry, Prince see Henry V, King
Hall, Elizabeth 14
Hall, John 14
Hall, Peter 38, 39, 58, 129, 153, 293, 320
Hallam, Nancy 320
Halle, Edward 38, 42, 46, 166, 336
Hamlet 12, 16, 17, 18, 19, 77, 84, 85, 177, **188–97**, 290
Hamlet, Prince of Denmark 19, 99, **190–97**, 255, 256
Harpsfield, Nicholas 226
Harry Potter and the Prisoner of Azkaban (film) 270
Hart, Lorenz 72
Harvey, Gabriel 77
Hastings, Lord 56–58, 60
Hathaway, Anne (actress) 290
Hathaway, Anne (wife) 13, 219
Hawke, Ethan 192, 312
Haydon, Benjamin Robert 222
Hazlitt, William 90, 259
Hector 208–13
Helen
    All's Well That Ends Well 288–92
    Troilus and Cressida 208, 210–13
Helena 112–13, 117
Helenus 212
Helicanus 296, 298
Heminges, John 18
Henriad 17, 23, 169
Henry III 120–21, 123
Henry III, King of France 22
Henry IV
    Part 1 17, 19, 84, **132–39**, 150, 169, 293
    Part 2 17, 19, 84, 144, **146–53**, 169, 293
Henry IV, King 45, 122
    Henry IV Part 1 134–39
    Henry IV Part 2 148–53
    Richard II 94–99
Henry IV, King of France 22, 23
Henry V 15, 17, 18, 84, 85, **162–69**, 293
Henry V, King 18, 19, 44, 45, 46, 66, 67, **134–39**, **148–53**, **164–69**
Henry VI
    Part 1 22, 23, 38, **44–47**, 66, 99, 169
    Part 2 22, 23, **36–39**, 66, 99, 169
    Part 3 22, 23, **40–43**, 66, 99, 169
Henry VI, King 17, **36–47**, 58, 60, 61, 165
Henry VII, King 42, 56–57, 60–61, 320, 323
Henry VIII 18, 231, **332–37**, 342
Henry VIII, King 23, 42, 85, 105, 226–27, **334–37**
Henryson, Robert 210

Henslowe, Philip 22
Hepburn, Katharine 182, 187
Hermia 112–13, 115, 116–17
Hermione 310–12, 315
Hero 156–61
Hesiod 184
Heston, Charlton 280
Heywood, Thomas 226
Hicks, Greg 257, 291
Hiddleston, Tom 321
Hippolyta, Queen of the Amazons
    A Midsummer Night's Dream 112–15, 117
    The Two Noble Kinsmen 340–41
Hitler, Adolf 304, 307
Hodge, Douglas 52
Hoelck, Kristin 254
Hoffman, Dustin 129
Hoffman, Michael 116
Holbein, Hans 227
Holinshed, Raphael 38, 39, 42, 46, 66, 96, 122, 136, 138, 150, 166, 226, 254, 270, 320, 336
Hollow Crown (TV series) 150
Holm, Ian 58
Holofernes 88–91
Homer, *The Iliad* 210, 313
Hopkins, Anthony 52
Horatio 190–91, 192, 197
Hortensio 32–34
Horton, Joanna 291
Host of the Garter Inn 142–43
Hotspur see Percy, Henry
Hounsou, Djimon 331
Howell, Anthony 176
Howell, Jane 39
Hubert 120–22
Hughes, Margaret 244
Hughes, Willie 216
Huguenots 22, 230
Hundred Years War 66, 167
Hunsdon, Henry Carey 14, 84
Huntly, Marquess of 23
Hussey, Olivia 105, 109
Hytner, Nicholas 166, 265, 312

IJ

Iago 53, 123, **242–49**, 320
iambic pentameters 77, 81, 216
Ibsen, Henrik 290
Illyria 200–05
Gl'ingannati (Italian play) 202
Innogen 318–23
Irons, Jeremy 128

Irving, George 176
Irving, Henry 246
Isabel, Queen 94–95, 97, 98
Isabella 234–39
Israel, Manasseh ben 131
Iwuji, Chuck 39
Jack Cade's Rebellion 37, 38–39
Jailer's daughter 340–43
James I, King 85, 128, 158, 182, 230, 255, **271**, 275, 322, 328
Jamestown, Virginia 331
Jaquenetta 88–89
Jaques de Boys 12, 180, 183–87
jazz 216, 223, 264
Jessica 126–27, 129–31
Jews, demonization of 131
Joan la Pucelle (Joan of Arc) 44–47
John, King 120–23
John II de Valois, King of France 64–65, 67
John of Gaunt 94–95, **97**, 98
John of Lancaster, Prince 148–49, 152–53
Johnson, Charles, *Love in a Forest* 182
Johnson, Samuel 222, 258, 280
Jonson, Ben 17, 47, 144, 231, 307
    Every Man in His Humour 85
    The Isle of Dogs 84
    Volpone 230
Joseph, Patterson 175
Julia 26–29
Juliet **102–09**, 116, 218, 280, 321
Julius Caesar 16, 17, 18, 19, 85, **170–77**, 313
Jupiter 323

K

Kani, Atandwa 330
Katherine
    Love's Labour's Lost 88–89
    The Taming of the Shrew 32–35
Katherine of Aragon, Queen 226–27, 334
Kean, Charles 328
Kean, Edmund 96
Kean, Will 342
Keats, John 216, 222–23
Kemble, John Philip 312
Kemp, William 14, 84
Kennedy, John F 39
Kent, Earl of 252–53, 258
Kermode, Frank 183
Kerrigan, John, *Motives of Woe* 224
Kholer, Estelle 236
King Lear 12, 17, 19, 177, 230, 245, **250–59**
King's Men 14, 17, 230, 231, 271

Kinnear, Rory 246
Kiss Me Kate (musical) 34
Kissoon, Jeffery 175
Knolles, Richard 244
Komisarjevski, Theodore 72
Kozintsev, Grigori 192
Kurosawa, Akira 254, 270
Kyd, Thomas 15, 196
Kyle, Barry 342
Kyogen of Errors 72, **73**

L

Laertes 190–94, 196, 197
Lafeu 288–89
Laine, Cleo 216
Lambarde, William 96
Lancaster, John, Duke of 148
Lance 18, 26
Langham, Michael 264
Langtry, Lillie 280
Laurence, Friar 102–03, 106, 107
Lavinia 50–51, 52
Lean, David 97
Lear 18, 19, **252–59**, 265, 284
Leavis, F R 247
Lechtenbrink, Volker 254
Lee, Canada 328
Leicester, Earl of 96
Leigh, Vivien 202, 271, 281
Leonato, Governor of Messina 156–61
Leontes, King of Sicily 18, 299, 310–15
Lepidus 172–73
Lester, Adrian 187, 246
The Life and Death of King John 17, 84, **118–23**
Lillo, George 298
Livy, *History of Rome* 78, 81
Lloyd, Phyllida 174
Lodge, Thomas 52, 182, 184, 185
Lodovico 242, 249
Lodowick 64, 66
Longueville 88–89, 91
Longworth, Clara 225
Lopez, Rodrigo 131
Lord Chamberlain's Men 14, 17, 84, 85, 98
Lord Chief Justice of England 148, 152
Lord of Misrule 202
Lorenzo 126–27, 131
Lorraine, Duc de 64
Louis XII, King of France 40–41
Louis, Dauphin of France 120–21, 164
"A Lover's Complaint" 19, 218, **224**
Love's Labour's Lost 17, 84, **86–91**, 218
Lucentio 32–34

Lucetta 26
Lucian 264
Luciana 70–73
Lucio 234–35, 237–38
Lucius 50–51
Lucius, Caius 318–19
Lucrece 78–81, 323
Lud 323
Luhrmann, Baz 109
Luther, Martin 223
Lyly, John 15
Lysander 112–13, 116–17
Lysimachus 296–97

M

Macbeth 16, 19, 81, 186, 255, **268–75**
Macbeth 12, 16, 17, 18, 19, 81, 177, 186, 230, **266–75**
Macbeth, Lady 19, **268–75**
McBurney, Simon 239
McCarthy, Lillah 202
MacDonald, David 97
Macduff 268–69, 273, 275
McKellen, Ian 58, 96, 226, 270
Macklin, Charles 187
Maclise, Daniel 244
McNee, Jodie 321
Macowan, Michael 210
Magna Carta 122
Malcolm 268–69, 275
Malone, Edmond 224
Malvolio 130, 200–04, **205**
Mamillius 310–12, 315
Mandela, Nelson 174
Mankiewicz, Joseph 175
Maori wars 213
Maqbool (film) 270
Marcus Andronicus 50–51
Margaret 156–57, 159, 160
Margaret, Queen (Margaret of Anjou) 36–47, 56–60
Maria
    Love's Labour's Lost 88–89
    Twelfth Night 200–01, 203, 205
Mariana 234–36, 238
Marina 296–99
Marling, Laura 182
Marlowe, Christopher 23, 107
    Doctor Faustus 15, 329
    Edward II 15, 96, 97
    The Jew of Malta 15, 22, 128, 129, 131
    The Passionate Shepherd to His Love 184
    Tamburlaine 15, 22

Marston, John 314
Martius 50–51, 52
Marx, Karl 264, 265
Mary I, Queen 23
Mary, Queen of Scots 23, 230
Master of the Revels 85
Maurice, Clemence 109
Measure for Measure 17, 158, 230, **232–39**, 290
Melville, Herman 254
Mendelssohn, Felix 116
Mendes, Sam 61, 312
Menelaus, King of Greece 208, 210–12
Menenius 302–05
The Merchant of Venice 17, 18, 19, 84, **124–31**
Mercutio 102–03, 106–08, 217
Meres, Francis 84, 218
The Merry Wives of Windsor 13, 17, 84, **140–45**, 217
Meskin, Aharon 128
Meyrick, Sir Gelly 85
Michelangelo 97
Middleton, Thomas 17, 231, 264
A Midsummer Night's Dream 12, 17, 18, 19, 84, 105, **110–17**, 313, 314, 315, 321
Milan, Duke of 26–27
Milford Haven 319, 320, 323
Millais, John Everett 197
Miranda 18, **326–31**
Mirren, Helen 42, 331
The Mirror for Magistrates 99
Modi, Sohrab 122
moneylenders 128–29, 131
Montagues **102–09**, 116
Montaigne, Michel de 328, 330–31
Montemayor, Jorge de, *Diana* 28
Monteverdi, Claudio, *L'Orfeo* 230
morality plays 58, 60
More, Thomas
    History of King Richard III 42, 58, 61
    Sir Thomas More **226–27**
Morgan, McNamara 312
Morocco, Prince of 126–27
Mortimer, Lord Edmund 134–35
Mote 88, 91
Mountjoy, Christopher 230
Mowbray, Lord 148
Mowbray, Thomas, Duke of Norfolk 94, 96, 98
Much Ado About Nothing 16, 17, 19, 53, 85, **154–61**
Mugabe, Robert 175
Mula, Inva 248
Munday, Anthony 226
Murray, John 226
Mutius 50, 53

N

Nashe, Thomas 46, 84, 313
Nathaniel, Sir 88–89, 91
Navarre 88–91
Nazi Germany 129, 304, 307
Nerissa 126–27, 130–31
Nestor 208, 212
New Place (Stratford) 84
Newark Castle (Nottinghamshire) 122
Nigro, Don 290
Nim
    Henry V 164, 168
    The Merry Wives of Windsor 142–43, 164, 168
Ninagawa, Yukio 298, 323
Noh theatre 73
Norfolk, Duke of
    Henry VIII 334–36
    Richard II 94, 96, 98
North, Sir Thomas 174, 280, 281–82, 304, 307
Northumberland, Percy, Earl of
    Henry IV Parts 1 and 2 134, 136–37, 148
    Richard II 94, 98
Nunn, Trevor 72, 136, 202, 336
Nurse, Juliet's 19, 102, 106, 107
Nuttall, A D 210
Nyewood House (East Sussex) 91

O

Oberon 18, 112–13, 115, 117
Obey, André, *Le Viol de Lucrèce* 78, 81
Octavia 278–79, 283
Octavius Caesar
    Antony and Cleopatra 278–81, 283, 285
    Julius Caesar 172–74, 177
O'Donnell, Hugh 23
Oldcastle, Sir John 137
Oliver 180–81, 186
Olivia, Countess 200–01, 203, 205
Olivier, Laurence 58, 59, 104, 128, 150, 166, 192, 202, 271, 281, 304
O'Neill, Hugh 23
Ophelia **190–97**, 342
Orlando 180–87
Orsino, Duke of Illyria 200–05
O'Sullivan, Camille 79

Othello 17, 53, 129, 137, 230, **240–49**, 312, 315
Othello **242–49**, 312, 315, 320
Otway, Thomas 104
Ovid
    Amores 76
    The Book of Days 78, 81
    Metamorphoses 51, 52, 74, 76–77, 105, 114, 328

PQ

Pacino, Al 128
Padua 32–35
Page, Anne 142–43, 145, 217
Page, Master George 142–43
Page, Mistress Margaret 142–43, 145
Page, William 142, 146
Painter, William 66, 264, 290
Palamon 340–43
Palma Giovane 80
Pandarus 208–09, 211
Pandolf, Cardinal 120–22
Paris
    Romeo and Juliet 102–03
    Troilus and Cressida 208–13
Paris, Siege of 47
Parker, Jamie 138
Paroles 19, 288–89, 292, **293**
The Passionate Pilgrim 218
Patroclus 208, 212
Paul, St 73
Paulina 310–11, 315
Peasant's Revolt 39
Peele, George 15, 52
Pembroke, Earl of 120–21, 123
Pembroke, William Herbert, Earl of 219
Pepys, Samuel 114
Percy, Henry (Hotspur) 148, 152
    Henry IV Part 1 134–39
    Richard II 94, 98
Percy, Lady 148
Perdita 299, 310–15
Pericles, Prince of Tyre 18, 230, 231, **294–99**, 314
Pericles 296–99
Perkes o'th'Hill, Clement 152
Petrarch, Francesco 108, 216, 217
Petruccio 32–35
Phaethon 96, 97, 98
Philip II, King of France 120, 122
Philip II, King of Spain 23
Philip the Bastard 120–22, **123**
Philippa, Queen 64–65, 67

Philippe VI, King of France 67
Philippi, Battle of 173, 176, 177
Phoebe 180–81, 185–86
"The Phoenix and Turtle" 19, **225**
Pickford, Mary 34
Piercy, Ellie 290
Pisanio 318–19, 321–22
Pistol, Ensign
    Henry IV Part 2 148–50, 152, 293
    Henry V 164–65, 168–69
    The Merry Wives of Windsor 142–44
Plantagenet, George *see* Clarence, George, Duke of
Plantagenet, Richard *see* Philip the Bastard; Richard III; York, Richard, 3rd Duke of
Plato 264
Platter, Thomas (the Younger) 174
Plautus 72
Plummer, Christopher 312
Plutarch 174, 264, 280, **282**, 304, 307, 313
Poel, William 202
Poins, Ned
    Henry IV Part 1 134
    Henry IV Part 2 148, 151–52
Poitiers, Battle of 66
Polixenes 310–12, 314–15
Polonius 190–91, 195, 196
Pompey, Sextus 278–79
Pope, Alexander 222
Porter, Cole 34
Portia
    Julius Caesar 16, 172, 176–77
    The Merchant of Venice 126–31
Posthumus Leonatus 318–21
Pralipe 104
Presgurvic, Gérard 109
Priam, King of Troy 208–13
Primaudaye, Pierre de la 90
The Prince of the Pagodas (ballet) 254
Pritchard, Hannah 187, 202
Prokofiev, Sergei 104, 109
Prospero 18, **326–31**
Protestantism 22, 23, 105, 223, 226, 230–31, 322, 335, 337
Proteus 26–29
Puck 112–13, 116, 117
Purcell, Henry 114, 116
puritanism 136, 137, 203, 205
Pyper, Laura 210
quatrains 216
Queen (wife of Cymbeline) 318–19, 322
Quickly, Mistress Nell
    Henry IV Parts 1 and 2 134, 148–49
    Henry V 164–65, 169
    The Merry Wives of Windsor 142–45
Quintus 50–51, 52

R

Radford, Michael 128
Raleigh, Sir Walter 331
Ran (film) 254
The Rape of Lucrece 14, 19, 23, 76, 77, **78–81**, 218, 222, 224
Redgrave, Vanessa 182, 187
Reformation 22, 23, 42, 105, 223, 226, 322, 335, 337
Regan 252–54, 256–58
Reinhardt, Max 114, 116
religious verse 217, 223
Renaissance 136, 139, 315
Rialto Bridge (Venice) 23
Rich, Barnabe 202
Richard I, King 120, 123
Richard II 17, 84, 85, **92–99**, 122, 169
Richard II, King 45, **94–99**, 122, 134, 136, 139, 152, 153
Richard III 23, 38, 39, 43, **54–61**, 84, 99, 169, 245
Richard III, King 17, 40–43, **56–61**, 270
Richmond, Henry, Earl of *see* Henry VII
Rivers, Earl 56, 58
Roanoke, Virginia 331
Robeson, Paul 244, 247
Robson, Flora 236
Roderigo 242–46
Rodgers, Richard 72
Rome
    Antony and Cleopatra 278–85
    Coriolanus 302–07
    Cymbeline 318–23
    Julius Caesar 172–77, 313
    The Rape of Lucrece 78–81
    Titus Andronicus 50–53
Romeo 17, **102–09**, 116, 195, 217, 218, 280, 321
Romeo and Juliet 17, 18, 19, 77, 84, 91, **100–09**, 217, 218, 291
Rosalind 180–87
Rosaline 88–89, 91
Rose Theatre 22, 46
Rosencrantz 190–91, 195, 196
Ross, Lord 94, 98
Rossini, Gioachino, *Otello* 244
Rothe, Anthony 342
Rous, John 61
Roussillon, Countess of 288–90
Roxburgh Castle, Siege of 64, 66
Rumour 148, 152
Rutland, Earl of 40–43
Rylance, Mark 204, 280, 285
Rymer, Thomas 249

S

Saed-e-Havas (film) 122
St Albans, Battle of 39, 40
Salieri, Antonio 144
Salisbury, Countess of 64–67
Salisbury, Earl of
    Edward III 64–67
    Henry VI Part 1 44
    Henry VI Part 2 36–37, 39
    The Life and Death of King John 120–21, 123
    Richard II 94, 98
Salvini, Tommaso 247
Sargent, John Singer 272
Saturnalia 202
Saturnius, Emperor of Rome 50–51
Saxe-Meiningen, Duke of 312
Scofield, Paul 255
Scrope, Richard le 148, 150
Sea Venture (ship) 328, 331
Sebastian
    The Tempest 326–29, 331
    Twelfth Night 200–21, 203, 205
Seneca 52, 58
Senior, Duke 180–81
seven ages of man 186
sexuality, notions of 205
Shadwell, Thomas 264
Shakespeare, Edmund 12–13
Shakespeare, Hamnet 13, 22
Shakespeare, John 12, 13
Shakespeare, Judith 13, 14, 22
Shakespeare, Mary *see* Arden, Mary
Shakespeare, Susanna 13, 14
Shakespeare World Festival 298
Shakespeare's Globe 15, 16
Shakespeare's Sonnets (1609) 218, 222, 224, 231
Shallow, Justice Robert
    Henry IV Part 2 148–49
    The Merry Wives of Windsor 142
Shapiro, Mel 28
Shaw, Fiona 96, 99, 187
Shaw, George Bernard 182, 213
Shelton, Thomas 231
Sher, Antony 58, 330
She's the One (film) 205
Shrewsbury, Battle of 135, 137, 139, 148
Shrewsbury, Earl of 227
Shylock 19, 126–31
Sicily 156–61, 310–15
Sicinius 302–03
Siddons, Sarah 270
Sidney, Sir Philip 217, 184, 258

Silence 148–49
Silvia 26–29
Silvius 180–81, 186
Simonides, King of Pentapolis 296
Sinden, Donald 39
Sir Thomas More 19, 85, **226–27**
Sivadier, Jean-François 259
Slender, Master Abraham 142–43, 217
Slinger, Jonathan 293
Sluys, Battle of 64–67
Sly, Christopher 32, 34
Smiley, Jane 254, 259
Smith, Maggie 187
Smithson, Harriet 192
Snout 112, 117
Solinus, Duke of Ephesus 70
Somerset, Duke of 36–37, 44–46
Sondheim, Stephen 104, 109
Songs and Sonnets 217
sonnets 12, 107–08, **214–23**, 231
Soothsayer 172, 177
Southampton, Henry Wriothesley, 3rd Earl of 76, 80, 219, 220, 222
Spacey, Kevin 61
Spanish Armada 23
Speed 26, 28
Spenser, Edmund 85, 114, 184, 224
Squeal, Will 152
Stafford, Sir Humphrey 36–37
Stanley, Lord 56, 58, 60
Star Trek (TV series) 270
Stein, Peter 182, 211
Stephano 326–27, 329
Stephens, Katy 46
Stephens, Toby 307
Stevenson, Juliet 298
Stewart, Patrick 193, 247
Strange, Lord 225
Stratford-upon-Avon 12–13, 84, 230
Stubbs, Imogen 202
Suchet, David 264
Suffolk, Duke of 334–35
Suffolk, William de la Pole, Duke of 36–37, 39, 44–45, 47
Supple, Tim 114
Surrey, Earl of 217, 227
Sycorax 326, 330
Syracuse 70–73

T

Tairov, Alexander 280
Talbot, Lord 44–47
The Taming of the Shrew 17, 22, 23, **30–35**, 161

Tamora, Queen of the Goths 50–53
Tarquin 78–81, 323
Tarsus 296–99
Tate, Nahum 254, 258, 304
Taylor, Elizabeth 34
Taylor, Gary 19
Taylor, Sam 34
Taymor, Julie 52
Tearsheet, Doll 148–49, 152
The Tempest 16, 18, 19, 231, 314, **324–31**
10 Things I Hate About You (film) 34
Tennant, David 193
Terry, Ellen 272, 320
Tewkesbury, Battle of 43
Thaisa 296–99
Thaliart 296
the Theatre (Shoreditch) 15, 22, 85
Thersites 208–10, 212–13
Theseus, Duke of Athens
    A Midsummer Night's Dream 112–13, 115–17
    The Two Noble Kinsmen 340–41
This England (film) 97
This Happy Breed (film) 97
Thomas, Ambroise 194
Thomas, Rasta 109
Thompson, Emma 159
Thomson, Hugh 183
Thorpe, Thomas 218, 219, 231
threnody 225
Throne of Blood (film) 270
Thurio 26–27
Tilney, Edmund 226
Timon of Athens 17, 230, 231, **260–65**
Titania 18, 112–14, 116, 117
Titian 74
Titus Andronicus 14, 15, 17, 22, 23, **48–53**, 77, 84
Tottel's Miscellany 217
Touchstone 180–81, 186–87
Towton, Battle of 41, 42, 43
Tranio 32–33
Trebonius 172
Tree, Herbert Beerbohm 122, 174, 336
Tresnjak, Darko 130
Trevisani, Francesco 280
Trinculo 326–27, 329
Troilus 208–13
Troilus and Cressida 17, 85, **206–13**, 290, 313
The Troublesome Reign of King John 122
Troy 194, 208–13, 313
Tudor dynasty 67, 136, 320, 323, 335
Twelfth Night 12, 17, 84, 85, 130, **198–205**
Twine, Laurence 298

The Two Gentlemen of Verona 17, 18, 22–23, **24–29**, 84, 342
The Two Noble Kinsmen 18, 231, **338–43**
Tybalt 102–03, 106
Tyler, Wat 39
Tynan, Kenneth 255
Tyre 296–99
Tyrrel 56, 59

UV

Uhiaria, Ony 299
Ulta Palta (film) 72
Ulysses 208–10, 212–13
Urban VI, Pope 22
Ursula 156–57, 159, 160
Vale, Michael 175
Valentine
    Twelfth Night 200, 203
    The Two Gentlemen of Verona 26–29
Venice 126–31, 242–49, 313
Venice, Duke of 126, 131
Venus and Adonis 14, 19, 23, **74–77**, 80, 81, 84, 218, 222, 291
Verdi, Giuseppe 144, 244, 248, 270, 274
Verona 26–29, 102–09, 116
Vice, figure of 58, 60
Vickers, Brian 224
Vienna 234–39
Villiers 64–65, 67
Vincentio 32–33
Vincentio, Duke 234–39
Viola 130, **200–05**
Virgil, Eclogues 184
Virginia Company 331
Volumnia 302–03, 305

W

Wagner, Richard 236
Wainwright, Rufus 216, 221, 223
Wakefield, Battle of 40, 43
Waldmann, Alex 292
Waldron, F G 342
Wales, Edward, Prince of
    see Edward V, king
Wanamaker, Sam 16
Wanamaker, Zoe 161
Warner, Deborah 52, 96
Wars of the Roses 23, 38, 39, 42, 43, 44–47, 54–61, 99, 323
The Wars of the Roses 38, 39

Warwick, Earl of
    Edward III 64
    Henry IV Part 2 148
    Henry VI Parts 1, 2, and 3 36–37, 40–43, 44
Watteau, Jean-Antoine 90
Watts, James Thomas 187
Welles, Orson 136, 150, 174, 247
West, Samuel 150
West Side Story (musical) 104, 109
West, Timothy 150
W.H., Mr 218–20
Whetstone, George 236
Wilde, Oscar 216
Wilkins, George 18, 231
William
    As You Like It 180–81
    The Merry Wives of Windsor 13
Willoughby, Lord 94, 98
Wills, Garry 174
Wilson Knight, G 194
Wilson, Robert 221
Winchester, Bishop of 334–37
Windsor 142–45
The Winter's Tale 18, 231, 299, **308–15**, 321
witchcraft 271, 275
Witches
    Henry VI Part 2 36
    Macbeth 268–75
    The Tempest 326, 330
Woffington, Peg 182, 290
Wolsey, Cardinal 334–37
Worcester, Earl of 134, 136
Wordsworth, William 216, 222, 223
World War II 97, 166
Wriothesley, Henry *see* Southampton, Earl of
Wyatt, Sir Thomas 217

XYZ

Xenophon of Ephesus 105
Yelland, David 153
Yorick 191, 194, 196
York, Duchess of
    Richard II 94–95, 98
    Richard III 56, 59, 60
York, Duke of, *Richard II* 94–95, 98
York, Richard, 3rd Duke of, *Henry VI Parts 1, 2 and 3* 36–47
York, Richard of Shrewsbury, Duke of, *Richard III* 56–57, 60
Your Own Thing (musical) 202
Zeffirelli, Franco 34, 105, 109

ACKNOWLEDGMENTS

Dorling Kindersley and Tall Tree would like to thank Helen Peters for the index. Special thanks also to Dr Romana Beyenburg-Restori for her help with the text.

PICTURE CREDITS

The publisher would like to thank the following for their kind permission to reproduce their photographs:

(Key: a-above; b-below/bottom; c-centre; f-far; l-left; r-right; t-top)

29 Alamy Images: epa european pressphoto agency b.v. (bl). **34 Alamy Images:** AF archive (br). **35 Getty Images:** Universal History Archive / UIG via Getty Images (tr). **38 Alamy Images:** ark 2013 (tr). **39 Getty Images** (tr). **43 Alamy Images:** Geraint Lewis (tl). **Getty Images:** E+ (bl). **46 Alamy Images:** Lebrecht Music and Arts Photo Library (tr). **47 Corbis:** Leemage (br). **52 Alamy Images:** Lebrecht Music and Arts Photo Library (br). **53 Corbis:** Bettmann (tr). **59 Alamy Images:** AF archive (t). **61 Alamy Images:** Geraint Lewis (tr). **Dreamstime.com:** Georgios Kollidas (bl). **66 Corbis:** Angelo Hornak (bc). **67 Getty Images:** UniversalImagesGroup (tr). **73 Photostage** (tr). **75 Corbis** (t). **75 Corbis** (t). **76 Corbis:** Ken Welsh / Design Pics (tc). **77 Alamy Images:** Peter Coombs (br). **79 Corbis:** Robbie Jack (t). **80 Alamy Images:** Heritage Image Partnership Ltd (b). **81 Getty Images:** Alinari Archives, Florence (tr). **90 Alamy Images:** AF archive (bc). **91 Corbis:** Clive Nichols / Arcaid (tr). **97 Getty Images:** Time Life Pictures / Mansell / The LIFE Picture Collection (bl). **99 Corbis:** Historical Picture Archive (br). **105 Corbis:** Hulton-Deutsch Collection (tr); Leemage (bl). **107 Alamy Images:** Mary Evans Picture Library (br). **108 Dreamstime.com:** Raffaele Orefice (tl). **109 Alamy Images:** AF archive (tr). Corbis: Reynaldo Paganelli / NurPhoto (bl). **114 Alamy Images** (br). **115 Dreamstime.com:** Honourableandbold (tr). **116 Alamy Images:** United Archives GmbH (bl).

122 Dreamstime.com: Barnschop (br). **123 Corbis:** Robbie Jack (tr). **128 Alamy Images:** Lebrecht Music and Arts Photo Library (br). **129 Alamy Images:** Alastair Muir (tr). **130 Alamy Images** (bl). **131 Alamy Images:** The Print Collector (bl). **137 Corbis:** Hulton-Deutsch Collection (bl); Robbie Jack (tr). **138 Corbis:** Robbie Jack (tr). **145 Alamy Images:** Geraint Lewis (t). **150 Corbis:** Robbie Jack (bc). **152 Dreamstime.com:** Jorge Salcedo (bl). **153 Alamy Images:** Geraint Lewis (tl). **159 Alamy Images:** AF archive (bl). **161 Alamy Images:** Geraint Lewis (tr). **166 Corbis:** Michael Nicholson (br). **167 Corbis:** Lebrecht Music & Arts (tr). **168 Alamy Images:** Moviestore collection Ltd (br). **175 Corbis:** Metro-Goldwyn-Mayer Pictures / Sunset Boulevard (tr); Sharifulin Valery / ITAR-TASS Photo (bl). **176 Alamy Images:** Geraint Lewis (bl). **182 Corbis:** (bc). **183 Alamy Images:** Lebrecht Music and Arts Photo Library (tr). **184 Getty Images:** Daniel Zuchnik / FilmMagic (tl); Leemage / UIG (bl). **185 Dreamstime.com:** Dirk De Keyser (br). **187 Corbis:** Fine Art Photographic Library (bl); Hulton-Deutsch Collection (tr). **192 Alamy Images:** (bc). **193 Corbis:** Robbie Jack (tr). **Dreamstime.com:** Zaretskaya (tl). **194 Corbis:** Bettmann (bl); Swim Ink 2, LLC (tc). **195 Corbis:** Facundo Arrizabalaga / epa (br). **197 Getty Images:** Leemage (t). **202 Corbis:** Christie's Images (br). **204 Corbis:** Christie's Images (tl). **205 Alamy Images:** AF archive (bc). **Corbis:** Historical Picture Archive (tr). **210 Corbis:** Robbie Jack (tr). **211 Alamy Images:** Geraint Lewis (br). **213 Corbis:** epa / Facundo Arrizabalaga (t). **217 Corbis:** Michael Nicholson (tr). **219 Corbis:** Neil Farrin / Robert Harding World Imagery (t). **220 Alamy Images:** Paul Springett 02 (tl). **221 Corbis:** Tim Brakemeier / epa (b). **222 Corbis** (bl). **223 Dreamstime.com:** Georgios Kollidas (tr). **227 Corbis:** (tr). **236 Corbis:** Hulton-Deutsch Collection (tr). **237 Alamy Images:** Prisma Archivo (b). **238 Getty Images:** Hulton Archive / Culture Club (tl). **239 Alamy Images:** Geraint Lewis (tr, bl). **244 Corbis:** Christie's Images (br). **245 Corbis:** Smithsonian Institution

(tr). **246 Corbis:** Robbie Jack (tl). **247 Corbis:** Hulton-Deutsch Collection (tr); John Springer Collection (bl). **248 Getty Images:** AFP / Boris Horvat (br). **254 Corbis:** dpa / Uwe Zucchi (br). **255 Alamy Images:** Moviestore collection Ltd (tr). **256 Getty Images:** National Galleries Of Scotland (tl). **257 Corbis:** Robbie Jack (bl). **259 Corbis:** Reuters / Heinz-Peter Bader (bl). **Getty Images:** AFP / Anne-Christine Poujoulat (tr). **265 Alamy Images:** Geraint Lewis (tr). **271 Corbis:** Bettmann (tr); Leemage (bl). **272 Corbis:** The Print Collector (bl). **274 Corbis:** San Francisco Chronicle / Katy Raddatz (tr). **275 Getty Images:** he LIFE Picture Collection / William Sumits (tr). **280 Corbis:** Summerfield Press (br). **281 Corbis:** Bettmann (tr). **282 Corbis:** Bettmann (bl). **283 Dreamstime.com:** Csaba Peterdi (tr). **285 Corbis:** Christie's Images (tr); Robbie Jack (bc). **290 Alamy Images:** Geraint Lewis (br). **291 Alamy Images:** Geraint Lewis (tr). **292 Alamy Images:** Geraint Lewis (tr). **293 Getty Images:** Universal History Archive / UIG via Getty Images (tr). **298 Alamy Images:** The Art Archive (bc). **299 Alamy Images:** Geraint Lewis (tl). **304 Dreamstime.com:** Dennis Dolkens (tr). **305 Corbis:** Stapleton Collection (b). **307 Alamy Images:** INTERFOTO (tr). **Corbis:** Robbie Jack (tl). **313 Alamy Images:** dpa picture alliance archive (tr). **Getty Images:** DEA / M. SEEMULLER (bl). **314 Getty Images:** Heritage Images (b). **321 Alamy Images:** RIA Novosti (tl). **323 Corbis:** Robbie Jack (tr). **Getty Images:** Universal History Archive / UIG via Getty Images (bl). **328 Getty Images:** Universal History Archive / UIG via Getty Images (br). **330 Alamy Images:** Geraint Lewis (tl). **331 Alamy Images:** AF archive (bl). **Dreamstime.com:** Yakov Stavchansky (tr). **336 Corbis:** Lebrecht Music & Arts (tr). **337 Corbis:** Nik Wheeler (bl). **342 Corbis** (br). **343 Alamy Images:** Mary Evans Picture Library (tc)

All other images © Dorling Kindersley. For more information see: **www.dkimages.com**